THE AMERICAN DIRECTORY
OF HORSESHOE PITCHING

THE AMERICAN DIRECTORY
OF HORSESHOE PITCHING

Edited by
OTTIE W. RENO, SR.

New York • London • Toronto
Cornwall Books

Cornwall Books
440 Forsgate Drive
Cranbury, N. J. 08512

Cornwall Books
25 Sicilian Avenue
London WC1A 2QH, England

Cornwall Books
2133 Royal Windsor Drive, Unit 1
Mississauga, Ont., Canada L5J 1K5

Library of Congress Cataloging in Publication Data
Main entry under title:

The American directory of horseshoe pitching.

   1. Horseshoe pitching—United States—Directories.
I. Reno, Ottie W.
GV1095.A28   1984   796.2'4'0922 [B]   83-23951
ISBN 0-8453-4744-6

Printed in the United States of America

THE AMERICAN DIRECTORY
OF HORSESHOE PITCHING

A

ABBOTT, JOSEPH P., b. May 26, 1925. W. Delores, (dec.); child—Irene. Electrical Engineer. S. Imperial; t. one and a quarter, right handed. Vice-President of the National Horseshoe Pitchers Association, 1967, 1968. Secretary Pennsylvania State Horseshoe Pitchers Association for 8 years. Secretary Erie Horseshoe Club for 14 years. Erie Club Champion 1966, 1970; Class C State Champion 1968, 1969; 1970 won both Northwest and Van Port Open. Hit 28 consecutive ringers in tournament play. Responsible for bringing 1969 World Tournament to Erie and acted as Tournament director. Enjoys square dancing. Home: 580 Peck Road, Erie, PA 16510.

ABELL, VIRGINIA, Maryland Women's State Champion, 1978. Home: P.O. Box 133, Hollywood, MD 20636.

ABERCROMBIE, T.V., President Baldwin County Horseshoe Pitchers Association; S. Allen; t. three quarter, left-handed. Played in second state tournament in Robertsdale 1965; President Alabama Horseshoe Pitchers Association one year. Home: P.O. Box 3348, Robertsdale, AL 36567.

ABRAMS, ALICE, b. August 8, 1917. Women's Texas State Champion, 1972, 1973, 1974, 1980 with 8-0-44.2%. H. George; children—Roy, Tommy, Roscoe, David. Housewife. S. Ohio; t. flip, right handed. Tournament competition 11 years; 80 tournaments, several world tournaments; Highest average 44.2%, highest game, 68.5%. Enjoys swimming and bowling. Home: 5475 Reed Court, Arvada, CO 80002.

ACOCK, JAMES E., b. July 10, 1917. Missouri State Secretary, 12 years; W. Thelma; child—William Jay. Postal employee. S. Allen; t. one and three quarters, right handed. World tournament, Murray City, UT, 1966.

Finished 9th in Class C, average 56.9%. Home: 16315 East Pacific, Independence, MO 64050.

ADAMS, ARTHUR E., b. February 5, 1894. 1975 Member Saskatchewan Hall of Fame. 1981 member NHPA Hall of Fame. W. Katherine Annie, (dec.); children—Jack, Joan, Donald, Bruce. Masonry contractor. S. Diamond; t. one and three quarters, right handed. Competed in Canadian Nationals in 1938; in several tournaments hit more than 80% ringers; Saskatoon City Champion 1931–1944; Saskatchewan Provincial Champion 1933–1944. For many years pitched exhibitions and trick shows. In area of promotion,—served as contact for President Harry T. Woodfield of the NHPA. He formed the first indoor league in Saskatoon and Western Canada on a four court layout in 1930. Three streets have been named in his honor. Home: 319 108th Street, Saskatoon, Saskatchewan, Canada 5N7 1P7.

ADAMS, JACK, b. October 18, 1921. Secretary of Canadian Chapter of the NHPA and Regional Director. W. Olive, Mechnical Engineer. S. Allen, Imperial; t. one and three quarters, right handed. Son of Arthur E. Adams. Has been a member of the Canadian Chapter of the NHPA for 35 years, serving as Regional Director since 1960; member of the Canadian Association Executive Council since 1945; co-ordinator or President of the Canadian Association from 1975 to date; executive member of British Columbia Horseshoe Pitchers Association 1974–75; Secretary-Treasurer of Saskatoon Horseshoe Club, 1977–78; Vice-President of Saskatchewan Horseshoe Players Association 1978–79. Won junior boys championship of the Province of Saskatchewan, 1938 and men's singles in Maritime Provinces, 1945; qualified for Class B in World Tournament, 1971, 1973, 1978. Home: 35 O'Neil Crescent, Saskatoon, Saskatchewan, Canada S7N 1P7.

ADAMS, JIM, b. June 12, 1918. NHPA Regional Director. W. Helen; children—Robert, James, Jr. Hardware warehouseman. S. Ohio; t. one and a quarter, right handed. Has played for 50 years, 20 years in tournament competition, during that time as President of Turlock Club; served as Vice-President or Secretary-Treasurer at Sunnyvale; Class D champion in Northern California Horseshoe Pitchers Association, 1979, with a record of 7-0-42%. Home: 601 Georgetown Ave., Turlock, CA 95380.

ADAMS, MARION, 1955, 1956 Maine State Women's Champion.

AKERS, LEE, 1930, 1931 Kentucky State Champion.

ALECKSON, JIM, b. December 7, 1937. Vice-President, Minnesota Gopher State Horseshoe Pitchers Association. W. Muriel; child—Danny. Painter-Paperhanger. S. Imperial; t. three quarters, right handed. Assistant Regional Director for Central Minnesota; won the 1979 St. Patrick's Open at Preimesberger Arena in Genola with an average of 73.4%; hit highest single game of 88% to defeat Minnesota state champion Jack O'Connor; fifth in Minnesota state tournament; in 1979 defeated Ralph Simon in Deluth; in the top 100 averages in the country. Enjoys bowling. Home: Route 1, Box 148A Princeton, MI 55371.

ALLBAUGH, ALDEN, b. January 21, 1917. 1975 Kansas State Champion. W. Ruby; children—Thomas, Karen Snyder. High School Teacher. S. Allen; t. one and a quarter, right handed. Class A pitcher with an average of 11-0-65% when he won the Kansas State Champion in 1975; has a tournament high of 67.4%, and a game high of 83.3%; president of the Kansas Horseshoe Pitchers Association from 1972 to 1974, and Vice-President from 1971 to 1972; in 1970 was President of Mid-Kansas Horseshoe League; in 1974 served as Chairman of committee to rewrite Constitution and By-Laws of Kansas HPA; in 1980 Chairman of nominating committee. Home: 619 Park Road, Newton, KA 67114.

ALLEN, IRA, 1923, 1926 Colorado State Champion. W. Elsie. Heavy log hauler. Brother of Ted Allen. Won the Northwest Open in Gresham, Oregon in 1932; in 1939 won the World Exposition Tournament in San Francisco; won Fresno tournament and others in California; won the 1962 Pleasanton Open with 5-0-76% ringer; finished twentieth in 1963 World Tournament with record of 16-19-73.6%; in the 1964 California State tournament he finished second with a record of 12-3-74.3%; won about fifty major Class A tournament championships. Plays tennis and enjoys bowling.

ALLEN, L.B. Minnesota State Singles Champion, 1919 and 1920. Lived in Hopkins, Minnesota and teamed with F. Gardner to win the 1919 state doubles championship.

ALLEN, RICHARD, Colorado State Champion, 1952, 1954. Record of 10-2-65.7% in 1952; and 9-1-65.7% in 1954.

ALLEN, TED, b. March 29, 1908. Horseshoe manufacturer. Shoe, Allen; turn, one and a quarter; right handed. Ted Allen is a living legend, called by many the greatest horseshoe pitcher of all time. Between 1933 and 1959 Allen won the World Championship ten times, a record. Playing in 31 world tournaments between 1933 and 1973 Allen amassed a record 771 victories, established world records for 72 consecutive ringers against Oregon's Cletus Chapelle in 1951; qualifying with 187 ringers out of 200 shoes and 570 points in 1955; 12 consecutive four-deads with Stan DeLeary of Arizona in 1947; a 174 shoe game with Indiana's Curt Day in 1957 in which each pitcher hit 155 ringers, 55 four-deads, 69 doubles and an 89% ringer average; total ringers and doubles in a world tournament in 1961; 67 consecutive victories ending in 1956. His world championships came in 1933, 1934, 1935, 1940, 1946, 1953, 1955, 1956, 1957 and 1959. Ted Allen manufactures the Allen pitching shoe. State championships included, Colorado 1922, 1924, 1925, 1927, 1928, 1929, 1930, 1931, 1943 and 1968; California 1934 and 1935; and Oregon 1932. Won dozens of open tournaments; barnstorming tours for 24 years in the United States, Canada and Cuba; pitching exhibitions with Barnum & Bailey Circus from country crossroad towns to Madison Square Garden. In 20 world tournaments he averaged above 80% ringers and in three of them was undefeated, 1934 with 23-0, 1955 with 35-0 and 1959 with 35-0, his best percentage being the 86.3% for 35 games in 1935. Home Address: 1045 Linden Avenue, Boulder, Colorado, 80302.

ALLISON, WALTER B., b. December 9, 1905. W. Goldie Brown; children—Vivian E., Roger B. Meat cutter. S. Allen; t. one and three quarters, right handed. Has pitched competitive horseshoes for 60 years, and is a Class A competitor in state and local tournaments. Has won several Gallia County and Jackson County tournaments; won the 1962 Southeastern Ohio District championship. Has hit ten consecutive doubles and averages in the mid-sixties. He is also an expert checker player. Home: 133 Portsmouth Road, Gallipolis, OH 45631.

ALLONES, RUDY 1974 Member of Washington HPA Hall of Fame.

ALSUP, BARBARA WILLIAMS, b. August 4, 1957. 1974 California Girls State Champion. H. Daniel; child—Michael. Housewife. S. Allen; t. one and a quarter, left handed. Won the Girls Class B World Championship, 1973, 1974. Home: Sheppard Air Force Base, TX.

AMBROSE LARYE, b. March 3, 1921. President, Minnesota Gopher State Horseshoe Pitchers Association; 1977 Minnesota State Champion, with record of 10-1-75.9%. W. Mae; children—Wendy, Nancy. Farmer. S. Allen and Deadeye; t. three quarter reverse, left handed. Started in a league 1967, finished year with 48% ringers; in 1975 made championship division of world tournament in Lafayette, Indiana, won 18 and lost 17; highest tournament in 1976 Duluth Open, averaged 81% ringers; highest single game 94% (47 ringers out of 50); fourth best ringer percentage 70.3% in 1979 NHPA sanctioned league play; averaged 71.76% ringers for fifteen weeks play during 1977 travelling league, southwest Minnesota. Home: Route 2, Jackson, MI 56143.

AMOS, J.L., Tennessee State Championship, 1926, 1927, 1928. Averaged 49.5% in 1928; tied for title 1926 at 8-1 with Jack McElroy. Amos 56.0%—McElroy 47.4% to win three game playoff.

AMTHOR, JEFFREY M., b. June 16, 1959. 1976 Kansas Boys State Champion, with record of 6-1-44.6%. W. Carol Lynn. Carpenter. S. Imperial; t. one and a quarter, right handed. Pitched horseshoes ten years, has been an active NHPA member for five. First tournament win 1973 Atchison Open with record of 6-0-16.4%; won St. Joseph 5-2-45.9%, Mound City 7-0-44.4%, and St. Joseph Open 7-0-62.2%; best tournament average 62.2%, highest single game 78.5%. Home: 1223 Mound Drive, Atchison, KA 66002.

ANDELIN, WILFORD, Member, Utah Horseshoe Pitchers Association Hall of Fame.

ANDERSON BETTY, AHPA Indiana State Women's Champion 1973, 1974, 1977. H. Richard; children—Keith, Paula. Housewife. S. Allen; t. flip, right handed. Runnerup 1978, 1979 in AHPA Indiana State Women's championship. Has played eight years, competed in county ladies league and played about five tournaments a year. Averaged 65% ringers in 1974 through state tournament and was given AHPA Mrs. Horseshoes Award; has hit an average 101 points per 50 shoe game, with a high of 109 in best performance. Shares hobby with son Keith, who has won several trophies in local and state AHPA tournaments. Home: 459 South Colfax Street, Martinsville, IN 46151.

ANDERSON, CHARLES (PECK), Indiana AHPA State Champion, 1979. b. November 19, 1929. W. Phyllis Jean; child—Lisa Jean Battin. Police Officer. S. Allen; t. one and a quarter, right handed. Serves as President of his local league and on the American Horseshoe Pitchers Association Board of Directors; former Director of Morgan County Board; former Vice-President of AHPA; nine years Secretary-Treasurer of AHPA Travel League. Has pitched 30 years and played in leagues and tournaments for 20 years; AHPA member for 15 years. Indiana State Championship runnerup 1975, 1976; won the following: Ed Jeffers Classic, 500 Festival, Frank Casner Open Doubles, Pre-Fourth of July Tourny, Fourth of July Tourny, Henry LaFollette Tourney, Tom Flemming Mid-West, Paragon Homecoming, Orville Harris Classic, Fall Foliage Festival; won the only NHPA tournament he entered with 5-0-70%. Best tournament average was 126 points per 50 shoe game in count-all with high game of 144 points and 94% ringers; named Mr. Horseshoes in 1971; won a Pitch for Heart special award; appeared on WTTV—Bloomington and WISH-TV Indianapolis. He and his wife have won the state mixed doubles championship for the last six years in a row. Home: 952 Cloverleaf Court, Martinsville, IN 46151.

ANDERSON, CHESTER C. b. February 16, 1910. NHPA Regional Director. W. Verla A.; children—Roger, Craig, Carol. Farmer. S. Allen; t. reverse one and a quarter, right handed. Has played for 25 years, playing a tournament schedule for 15 years, and has been a member of NHPA for 10. Has been President of local club several times; is a state regional director at present. Best tournament average 53% and best game 70%. Won 35 trophies and many ribbons. Home: Route 1 Storm Lake, Iowa 50588.

ANDERSON, DICK, Former President of Morgan County Horseshoe Pitchers Association. W. Betty. S. Allen; t. one and a quarter. Won with his wife the handicap mixed doubles state championship, and have placed second in several tournaments. He averages 90–100 in 50 shoe count-all. Home: 459 South Colfax Street, Martinsville, IN 46151.

ANDERSON, GLEN, 1956 World tournament qualified with score of 519, finished with record of 27 wins, 8 losses and a ringer percentage of 73.7%; 1957 World tournament, finished 7th in the preliminaries with a 10-7-74.4% record, in the finals of the 14 man group he had 3-10-75.2%; Illinois State tournament, 1957 finished 3rd with 9-2-75%.3%; 1958 World tournament record of 7-6-73.5%; runner-up in Illinois State tournament, 1958 with a 8-3-75.0% record. In top class of world tournament play he won 161 games, lost 97, averaged 72.3% ringers and 502 points qualifying. Died October 18, 1958. Home: Moline, IL.

ANDERSON, GROVER F., b. November 15, 1892. Eight time West Virginia State Champion. W. Erma; child—Mary Glenn. Retired. S. Ohio, Gordon or Allen; t. one and a quarter, right handed. Started pitching 1922 and pitched for 56 years. Played against Guy Zimmerman at Iowa State Fair 1924 and 1925; lost to Zimmerman by one point 216–215 in a 100 shoe count-all game; best game in sanctioned play was 93% against John Fulton in 1951 Eastern National at Clearfield, PA. Former President of West Virginia State Horseshoe Pitchers Association.

Grover Anderson's Eight State Titles

Year	Won	Lost	Shoes	Ringers	Ringer Percentage
1936	9	0	446	264	59.0
1937	9	0	494	297	60.0
1938	9	0	466	304	65.0
1939	9	0	518	342	66.0
1940	9	0	538	367	68.0
1941	8	1	376	204	54.0
1946	9	0	508	300	59.5
1947	9	1	562	367	65.5

Home: 605 Jamesson Street, Parkersburg, West VI 26101.

ANDERSON, L. ANN, b. February 20, 1940. Maryland Women's State Champion, 1975, 1976, 1977, 1979, 1980. H. Arthur M.; children—Arthur M., Andrew M., Amy L. Bookkeeper, Secretary. S. Diamond; t. flip, right handed. Has pitched for 25 years. Won the Raymond Frye Memorial, 1978 at Winchester, Virginia with 48.4%; in the Maryland State Tournament, 1980 she hit 5-0-49.6%. Home: 23 Sam Will Ave., Timonium, MD 21093.

ANDERSON, LEONA ZIMMERMAN, b. December 21, 1917. California State Champion, 1971, 1972, 1973. H. Guy (dec.); children—Eugene (dec.), Bob, Joyce Smith, Rosalie Linch, (dec.); H. (2) Anderson. Retired. S. Allen; t. one and a quarter, right handed. First husband Guy Zimmerman was 1954 World Champion; played exhibition games with Guy in 1930's. Undefeated in California State Championships with 5-0-50% in 1971; 3-0-61.4% in 1972; 11-0-54.9% in 1973; qualified for championship division of World Tournament, 1973 in Eureka, California, and finished fifth; won Western States Open, 1971; won Northern California and Nevada Open, 1971. Home: 2790 Oro Bangor Highway, Oroville, CA 95965.

ANDERSON, NORMA, Indiana Women's State Champion, 1960.

ANDERSON, O. W., First President of Grand League American Horseshoe Pitchers. Manufacturer of horseshoes. The Grand League was the first National horseshoe pitchers association in America, it began May 6, 1914 with Judge Walter W. Lacy, Henry Meade and O. W. Anderson as the founders; the League conducted the first national tournaments. Home: 1211 Orville Avenue, Kansas City, KA.

ANDERSON, PHYLLIS, b. September 24, 1933. Indiana AHPA State Champion, 1971, 1972. H. Charles (Peck); child—Lisa Jean Battin. Manager, Heather Heights Apartments. S. Allen; t. one and a quarter, right handed. Five time runnerup for Indiana AHPA State Champion; Flemming Midwest, 1975, had a tournament average of 65%; in 1975 Ladies League averaged 107 points per 50 shoe game; first women to receive "Mrs. Horseshoes" award; appeared twice on the Bob Braun TV show in Cincinnati, and once on WTTV—Bloomington. Tournament championships as follows: Indianapolis 500 Festival, Vincennes Open, Flemming Midwest, Paragon Homecoming, Ed Jeffers Classic, Martinsville Fall Festival, Morgan County and others. In NHPA tournament won four of five games and lost her only game to Indiana NHPA Champion Bonnie Seibold by one ringer who was runnerup for 1980 World Championship. Secretary for AHPA Board of Directors of Morgan County League; Secretary-Treasurer of AHPA for 3 years; former President of Morgan County Ladies League and organizational director. Organized with her husband the Morgan County Mixed Doubles League; won with her husband the state mixed doubles league, 6 times. Played basketball, also enjoys bowling. Home: 952 Cloverleaf Court, Martinsville, IN 46151.

ANDERSON, TERRY, Wyoming Boys State Champion, 1962 (with a record of 4-2-23.3%) and defended his title in 1963.

ANDERSON, WILLARD R., Utah State Champion, 1934. Hit 75.1% for a five game tournament. Served as Secretary of Salt Lake City Horseshoe Club.

ANTHONY, DALE, President of the Darke County, Ohio Horseshoe Club. Helped to maintain the indoor league at Darke County Fairgrounds; hosted the Greenville Annual Snowball Tournament. Home: 4435 North Range Line Road, Covington, OH 44318.

ANTHONY, DOUGLAS R., b. September 3, 1956. Ohio Junior Boys State Champion, 1972 (with a record of 5-0-56.9%), 1973 (with 3-0-58.1%). W. Lynda; children—Jeremy, Benjamin, Kevin. Lawn specialist for Chemlawn Corporation. S. Diamond and Allen; t. one and a quarter, right handed. Has pitched for 10 years, played in leagues and tournaments for 9 years and NHPA events for 8. Received a plaque from the Piqua Horseshoe Club for being Ohio Junior Boys State Champion, 1972, 1973. Highest tournament 60% and highest game 86%. Home: 3211 Chelsea Court, Kokomo, IN 46901.

ANTHONY, HAROLD, b. February 26, 1915. Class B World Champion, 1970. W. Marjorie; children—James, Judy Miller,

Jerry. Retired, Fram Corporation. S. Imperial; t. one and a quarter, right handed. Class A championships include: Michigan Water Wonderland, Toledo Open, Ohio-Pennsylvania Open, Ostrander Open, Wellesley Ontario Open, Day-Bel Open, Snowball Open, Darke County Fair, 6 Darke County Club titles, Piqua Open, 2 Southwest Ohio District, Darke County, Bremen Open, Pike County Indoor, National Threshers Open and many more. Finished second 7 times to 4 different champions in the Ohio State Championship. Averaging in the high seventies, with a high tournament average of 80% and a sanctioned tournament single game high of 91%. Was 49 years old when entering first tournament competition, has since pitched in 12 world tournaments, 9 times in Championship Division and 3 times in Class B. Received the Most Improved Player Award in 1966. 3 times was involved in the longest game, 166 shoes at Keene, New Hampshire, 144 at Middlesex, New Jersey and 150 at Greenville, Ohio. Has defeated every top contender in the United States and finished near top in a number of tournaments. Had 151 career wins, 148 defeats, averaged 75.3% ringers and 511 points qualifying. Home: 9085 State Route 571, Arcanum, OH 45304.

ANTHONY, JERRY, b. February 3, 1957. Ohio Junior Boys State Champion, 1970. S. Imperial; t. three quarters reverse, right handed. Pitched for 10 years and has been a NHPA member for 9 years. At age of 8 played his first World Tournament at Keene, New Hampshire, 1965, the youngest boy to play in it. Had a 67.5% ringer average, and a 5-0 record in the Ohio Junior Boys State Championship in 1970; two 7th place finishes in world tournament, finished 4th in 1970; Won Greenville Ringer Classic Championship, 1968 along with several other junior titles. Highest single game 76%. Enjoys baseball and other sports. Graduated

Bowling Green State University. Home: 9085 State Route 571, Arcanum, OH 45304.

ANZALDI, JOSEPH A., b. December 6, 1930. Member Minnesota Hall of Fame, 1976. W. Eileen; children—Mary, Diane, Joan. Water Department, Laborer. S. Ohio Pro; t. one and a quarter, right handed. Has pitched horseshoes for 28 years, an NHPA member for 25 years; has played 27 years in the Minnesota State Tournament. Highest tournament average 73.8% in 1970 Kindred, North Dakota meet, highest game, 88% league game in which he hit 44 ringers out of 50 shoes. Minnesota State Tournament, 1974, averaged 84.8% with 56 out of 66. Was the St. Paul and Ramsey County Champion for 15 consecutive years; played in 6 world tournaments and pitched exhibitions with Ted Allen and Dan Kuchcinski. State Secretary, Regional Director for four-state area of Minnesota, North Dakota, South Dakota, Wisconsin, 1963, 1964, 1965. Delegate to National Convention, 1967, 1969, 1970; as delegate made the motion to induct Vicki Chapelle Winston (the first woman honored) into the National Hall of Fame, 1970. Served as Vice-President of St. Paul and Ramsey County Club, 1956, 1973, 1974, and league secretary in 1960; served as team captain for 20 years. Was ranked number 1 by Fargo Forum who rated the top 10 players in area. Has won 117 trophies, 2 medals, 2 certificates and 3 plaques. Started the Minnesota State Hall of Fame in 1969, served as first chairman for 2 years, designing the first plaques and the Minnesota state patch. His tournament titles include: Detroit Lake Open, 1976, 6-0-61.5%; Northwest Water Carnival; Hibbing Open, 1971, 11-0-65.3%; Minneapolis Open, 1974, 7-0-66.8%; Sioux Falls Open, 1965, 11-0-65%; Wadena Open, 1972, 7-0-72.4%; 3 Kindred Opens, 1965, 8-1-64.1%, 1966, 7-2-66.9%, 1970, 9-0-73.8%; Fargo Open, 1967, 9-0-60.5%; Northwest Open, 1974, 6-1-70%; Eau Claire Open, 1970, 11-1-71.6%. Ranked fourth in Minnesota in 1976 with 70% and in 1975, 79th nationally with 70.7%. Was Minnesota State V.F.W. Champion in 1978 with 5-0-66.12%, and in 1979 with 6-1-65.7%. 1948 through 1952 in Army Engineers; spent time in France and Germany, coming out as Sergeant; life member of V.F.W. and National Home for Children of Deceased Veterans. Won the Minnesota State V.F.W. Championship, 1980 in Coon Rapids with a record of 7-0-66%. Home: 1034 North Chatsworth Avenue, St. Paul, MN 55103.

APGAR, ALAN, New Jersey Boys State Champion, 1972, 1973, 1974, 1975, 1976. Home: 436 Giles Avenue, Middlesex, NJ 08846.

ARCHER, MARY, Women's Canadian National Champion, 1977. In regular round robin play she and defending champion Myrna Kissick tied at 4-1 with respective percentages of 59.4% and 56.6%. Archer won the play-off 55–47 hitting 60.6%.

ARMSTRONG, CHARLES, Alabama Doubles State Champion, 1965 (teamed with J. Gill). S. Ohio Pro; t. double flip.

ARMSTRONG, SUE, Ohio Girls State Champion, 1963 (record of 3-0-11.1%) and in 1964.

ARNOLD, BOB, Indiana Boys State Champion, 1956.

ASHCRAFT, RAY, Washington State Champion 1929, 1930. In 1929, won 18, lost 2 with 54% record; 1930 won 15 lost none with 56.2% record.

ASHER, FRANCIS, b. March 2, 1921, Secretary-Treasurer, Ohio Buckeye Horseshoe Pitchers Association. Assistant Superintendent. S. Allen and Deadeye; t. one a a quarter, right handed. Secretary-Treasurer, Piqua Club, 1970, also President since 1971; in 1972 started a NHPA tournament in Piqua for 7 consecutive years; started club in Lakeview, 1974, and helped construct 6 courts; in 1972 started a Troy Fairgrounds tournament which has been held every year since; organized Troy Horseshoe Club, 1978, now has 50 members and 6 lighted courts, travelled the United States pitching and promoting horseshoes; received Achievement Award from NHPA at World Tournament, 1975 in Lafayette, Indiana. Officer in Darke County Horseshoe Club, Greenville, Ohio. Ringer percentage, 52%. Home: 9500 Camp Creek Road, Lucasville, OH 45648.

ASTOR, AMANDA, Nevada Girls State Champion, 1974, 1975. Daughter of Lance and Jessie Astor. Home: 73 Reservation Road, Reno, NV 89502.

ASTOR, JESSIE, Nevada Women's State Champion, 1974, 1978. b. June 10, 1940. Nevada Women's State Champion, 1974, 1978. H. Lance; children—Eddie, Amanda, Lancia. Teacher in Head Start Program. S. American; t. flip, right handed. Averages 42% ringers. Entire family enjoys the sport and all have won trophies in league and tournament competition.

ASTOR, LANCE, b. September 10, 1936. Former President, Nevada Horseshoe Pitchers Association. W. Jessie; children—Eddie, Amanda, Lancia. Director of legal department, Reno-Sparks Indian College. S. American; t. flip, right handed. Vice-President, Nevada Horseshoe Pitchers Association, 1980. Won Class A Championship Reno Open, 1977. Has pitched since 1968 and helped build several playing courts in Reno-Sparks area. Home: 73 Reservation Road, Reno, NV 89502.

ASTOR, LANCIA, Nevada Girls State Champion, 1971, with a 3-1 record. Daughter of Lance and Jessie Astor. Home: 73 Reservation Road, Reno, NV 89502.

ASTRAB, DONALD, New York Boys State Champion, 1972 with a 3-0-53% record. Home: Old Crompond Road, Peekskill, NY 10566

ASTRAB, ROBERT, New York Boys State Champion, 1971 with a 38.7%. Home: Old Crompond Road, Peekskill, NY 10566.

ATKINSON, GEORGE, Indiana State Champion, 1922.

ATNIP, ASA G., Tennessee State Champion, 1925.

ATWELL, JIM, Indiana Boys State Champion, 1959. Also competed in Junior Division of World Tournament.

AUSTIN, ABE L., b. October 7, 1906. Intermediate World Champion, 1972. W. Virginia; children—Delano F., Carolyn D. Carpenter—contractor. S. Gordon; t. one and three quarters, right handed. Has been active in NHPA for 20 years. Pitched 70% ringers in a game lost to Curt Day in Cayuga, Indiana; Memorial day 1979, in Peoria hit 61 of 76 for 80.3%; won World Class C Championship, 1968 in Keene, New Hampshire; played with Paul Focht in World Tournament, 1977, hit 76.7% and lost, set several Senior Division World Records for a 7 game tournament. Focht hit 73 ringers to 69 for Austin, 29 doubles to 26, combined ringer percentage 78.8%. They had 15 four deads. President of the Freedom Through Truth Foundation and author of a newspaper column called "Bits and Tips about Money" for Senior Citizen Journal of Midlothian, Illinois and Economist-Record of Oak Park, Illinois. Home: 801 South Home Avenue, Oak Park, IL 60304.

B

BABB, JERRY, b. December 28, 1938. Texas Women's State Champion, 1977, 1978, 1979, 1980. H. C. C. (Jack); children—Jackie, Kathy, Bonnie Blount, Bill. Housewife. S. Ohio O or Diamond Tournament; t. flip, right handed. Played tournament horseshoes for 4 years, averaging about 35% ringers with high game of 60%. Tournaments won: Class A Championships include Matt Bowers Open, 1978, 1979, Del Rio Open, 1979, 1980, Shamrock Open, 1980, Stephenville Open, 1980. Stephenville, 1980 competition finished first, Margie Viles was second, game televised by NBC for show "Games People Play".

BABINSKI, WILLIAM, Massachusetts State Champion, 1960, winning record was 7-0-64.8%. Home: 17 Curtis Street, Westfield, MA 01085

BACKER, REINHARD, b. May 3, 1913. Member Utah Horseshoe Pitchers Association Hall of Fame, 1980. W. Ruby; children—Gary, William, Richard, Pat. Owner of bakery. As a non-pitcher served as President of Utah State Horseshoe Pitchers Association for 9 years; President of National Horseshoe Pitchers Association, 1960, 1961; NHPA Regional Director, 1962; Arch Stokes Memorial Award, 1966. Home: 1644 Wasatch Drive, Salt Lake City, UT 84108. Died 1978.

BACKER, RICHARD, B. August 12, 1944. Class C World Champion, 1966 Child—Tara. Real Estate Agent. S. Allen; t. one and a quarter, right handed. Has pitched horseshoes since 1956; was second in Junior World Championship, 1958; second to Harold Wolfe in Class C World Tournament, 1961. Home: 1644 Wasatch Drive, Salt Lake City, UT 84108.

BACKER, WILLIAM B. (BILLY), b. March 29, 1943. Junior Boys World Champion, 1958. W. Carol; children Deborah, Darin. Engineer. S. Allen; t. one and a quarter, right handed. Has played for 25 years, 10 years in tournament competition; finished second in Junior Boys World Championship, 1956, 1957, 1959; best finish in men's division, world tournament was 12th place in Class B, 1965; highest single game 85%. Enjoys bowling, plays golf and softball. Home: 5015 Halison Street, Torrance, CA 90503.

BAGI, JOHN, b. 1921. President Lakewood Horseshoe Club. White Motors. S. Gordon; t. one and a quarter, right handed. Lakewood Horseshoe Club has been active since 1920's and grew out of Greater Cleveland Team League; is also Secretary of Club. Bagi and team has won annual Tri-city Tournament from Lakewood-Independence-Seven Hills 3 times; highest game 129 points for 50 shoes. Home: 2060 Revely, Lakewood, OH 44101.

BAGLEY, WALTER, B. May 4, 1917. Connecticut State Champion, 1952, 1953. Security guard. S. American; t. three quarters, 1933-1942, one and three quarters since, right handed. Started pitching in 1933; spent 8 years in Navy as Petty Officer. Attended World Tournament in Murray City, Utah, 1953 where he missed Championship Class by four ringers and finished 8th in Class B. Highlights of career include meeting World Champion Charlie Davis as a boy of 11; qualifying for New England Tournament on first try, 1938; qualifying at 450 in World Tournament, 1953, and averaging 66% ringers for 13 games to get a four-way tie for 1954 New England Championship, finishing 3rd in play-off. Highest single game, 81.2% in 1954; pitched state tournaments in New York, Rhode Island and 10 times in Connecticut; qualified in Class D World Tournament 1979 with 58% and 418 points. Home: 100 East Elm Street, Greenwich, CT 06830.

BAILEY, RUTH, b. September 19, 1913. Iowa Women's State Champion, 1968, record of 3-1-42.6%, 1973, record of 3-0-28.3%, won a third time in 1974. H. Leonard. Colonial Manors Nursing Home employee. S. Diamond; t. three quarters, right handed. Was second several times and won several other open tournaments. Home: Anita, IO 50020.

BAIR, P. W., World Tournament, 1922 finished 15th with a 3-12 record in finals. Home: Kansas City, KA.

BAIRD, WASH, Missouri State Champion, 1922, 1923.

BAKER, CARL H., b. November 1, 1942. Organizer and Tournament Director of New Hope Horseshoe Club. W. Judy; children—Brian, Brent. Machine operator, Baker Sand and Gravel Company. S. Allen; t. one and a quarter, right handed. Has pitched horseshoes for 20 years, started playing in NHPA and tournament games in 1976; helped plan and build courts for New Hope Horseshoe Club; Assistant Tournament Director for Alabama State Association. Has a tournament high of 51.5% and game high of 66.6%; has won 2 of the New Hope Opens and Icebreaker at Huntsville, 1977; finished second and third in several other tournaments. Home: 2778 Hobbs Island Road, Huntsville, AL 35803.

BAKER, DAVID, b. August 4, 1939. Missouri State Champion 14 times. W. Virginia; children—Judith, Janice. Greenhouse owner and operator. S. Allen; t. one and a quarter, right handed. Won 1966 Class B World Championship; tied for 5th place in World Championship play, 1958; placed in top fifteen in World Tournament play 7 times; highest single game 96.6% in Springfield, Missouri tournament; highest tournament average, 83.3% in 1978 Neosho Open; hit 6-1-71.1% to win 1980 Missouri title; in world tournament competition has won 122, lost 118 and averaged 73.2% in championship division. Home: Route 1, Wentworth, MO 64873.

BAKER, FRANK, Vermont State Champion, 1940, with 11-0-49%.

BAKER, VIRGINIA, b. April 1, 1944. H. Dave; children—Judy, Janice, Daniel. Mathmatics teacher, Sarroxie High School. S. Allen; t. one and a quarter, right handed. Started to play when she married Dave, who is Missouri State Champion. Pitched in Class B World Tournament, 1966, Murray City, Utah. Home: Route 1, Wentworth, MO 64873.

BALES, ROBERT C., by June 1, 1909 in Oklahoma. Missouri State Champion, 1940, 1942, 1961. W. Dora; children—Robert, Roland, Ronald, Rosemary. Retired, Armco Steel. S. Ohio; t. one and a quarter, right handed. Started pitching as a boy, has pitched for 58 years. First league play, Kansas City in 1932; World Tournament in Des Moines, averaged 77%, finished tied for 5th; Missouri tournament, 1940, hit 76.6% ringers in going 15-0 which was a state record at that time; state tournament in 1941, pitched a perfect game with 100% ringers, the game started with 2 consecutive four-deads. His opponent never hit another ringer, and Bales hit 18 more. On 4 different occasions hit 38 consecutive ringers. Big wins include beating Casey Jones and Guy Zimmerman in tournament play and over Ted Allen 50-47 in exhibition game at Klamm Park in Kansas City while Ted Allen was World Champion, Bales hit 81% and Allen 80%; won Moline Dispatch Tournament, Kansas Open, and the Four-State Open and many others. Played in Kansas State Horseshoe Tournament several times, finished second one time; won Kansas City Championship several times; in Kansas title had a chance to win with 47 on the board and a chance to win with a double. The second one missed, and Alvin Gandy won it; suffered bitter loss to World Champion Charles C. Davis in a city tournament sponsored by Union Wire Rope Corporation with the score 47-47, Bales and Davis had nine consecutive four-deads. On last pitch, he hit one and Davis two and ended it at 122

Top, left, Arthur Adams. *Right,* Jack Adams. *Center,* Greenville Courts, site of several national and world championships. *Bottom, left,* Reinhard, Richard, and Billy Backer. *Right,* Richard and Billy Backer with Chapelle, Hall of Fame member.

Top, Ruth Bennett with the 1966 Women's World finalist group. *Center*, Italian playing courts. *Bottom, left*, Harold Barr. *Center*, Giuseppe Bavassano, Italian president. *Right*, Elmer Beller and Ralph Dykes.

shoes and with both players over 80%. He also plays baseball, and as a pitcher he had one no-hit game. In golf, he carded a hole-in-one on a 318 yard par four hole and won one tournament. Has bowled in 32 ABC bowling tournaments and still carries a 182 average; biggest bowling purse, $3,000.00; with son Roland won the Missouri State Doubles Titles, both have sanctioned 300 games. Home 1237 Oakley, Kansas City, MO

BALLINGHAM, ART, b. May 1, 1921, Grouse Creek, Utah. Vice-President, Utah HPA, 1974–1979. W. Mary; 8 children. Southern Pacific Railroad as track laborer, signal operator and signal maintainer. Served in armed forces, 1944–1946. S. American or Diamond; t. one and a quarter, right handed. Pitched horseshoes most of his life; started pitching NHPA tournaments 14 years ago; averages about 33% ringers; won Class D in state tournament, 1974; his best finish was second place in Class C in 1970. Now holds office of Vice-President of UHPA. Home: 4574 South 300 West, Ogden, UT 84403.

BARB, JERRY, Missouri Boys State Champion, 1975.

BARLOW, ROBERT C., b. May 5, 1955. New Hampshire Boys State Champion, 1971, with record of 5-1-48.3%. S. American; t. Barrell Flip, right handed and uses right foot lead. Electrician. Started pitching 13 years ago; has been competing in tournaments for 11 years; was fifth in Boys Division, 1971 New England Tournament; competing in men's class, has finished second and third; high game as junior player was 75% and high tournament 60%; in men's competition his highest game was 65%, and his highest tournament 51%; in New England tournament, 1971 against Mark Pepin he hit 22 consecutive ringers and the two had eight four-deads; served as Tournament Director for Keene Horseshoe Club in 1979. Hobbies

include softball, hockey, photography, ten-pin bowling, skiing, fly fishing and fly tying. Home: 56 Page Street, Keene, NH 03431.

BARNETT, HOWARD R., b. May 17, 1940. Tournament Director, West Vierginia Horseshoe Pitchers Association, W. Brenda Jo; children—Van, Kathy. Lab Technician, DuPont Corp. S. Imperial; t. one and a quarter or one and three quarters, with either hand, competes mostly right handed. Has played for 30 years, 20 in tournament play; at age 13 pitched in men's division in West Virginia State Tournament, 1953, finishing second in Class B. has been Class A contender in most years since; was runnerup in state championship, 1980, tying and losing a playoff; won Washington County Open in Marietta, Ohio with 69.9% ringers; best ever ringer spree was 94 out of a consecutive 100 shoes. Currently is serving as an Evangelist and in past has pastored 2 Pentecostal Churches. Is President of ACE Union and President of a Bowhunting Club. Home: Route 4, Box 123F, Charleston, W. Va. 25312.

BARNETTE, TIM, b. August 23, 1967. Student. S. Allen; t. one and a quarter, right handed. In third year of tournament competition; was runnerup to Ross Perry in Virginia Juniors tournament and has won 18 trophies; won Class D in World Tournament, 1979; in 1980 qualified at 73% for championship division and pitched his way to seventh place in twelve man class; highest tournament average is 72% at Frye Memorial, Winchester, Virginia, 1980; best game is 81.8% in World Tournament, 1980; in game with Peter Clark he hit 10 consecutive doubles which resulted in ten consecutive four-deads. Home: 159 Riner Street, Dublin, VA 24084.

BARNES, J. B., Virginia State Champion, 1957.

BARNES, MERRILL B. (dec.) Carpenter.

Maine State Champion 7 times, hitting 8-1-52% in 1939, 9-0-59.1% in 1940, 10-1-57.8% in 1941, 7-0-70.2% in 1942, 64.3% in 1946, 13-1 in 1947, 9-1-55% in 1954; the 70.2% average in 1942 is a state record. He pitched a low three quarter turn. Home: Bangor, ME.

BARR, HAROLD H., b. December 8, 1909. Former Chairman of Metropolitan Association AAU in New York City for 12 years. W. Hazel M; children Charles, Bette. Assistant High School Principal. Started playing at the age of 12; played 15 years in local competition but never played NHPA horseshoes. Home: 80-75 208th Street, Queens Village, NY 11427.

BARRON, KATHY, b. May 17, 1955. Idaho State Champion, 1980 with a record of 5-0-35.3%. H. (dec.); child—Ty. Housewife. S. Diamond Tournament; t. single flip, right handed. Has pitched tournament horseshoes for 6 seasons; won mixed doubles, Camas County Annual Tournament; won Class A Championship at Coors Open in Fairfield. Enjoys bowling and hunting arrowheads. Home: Box 324 Fairfield, ID 83327.

BARSCHY, MIKE, Wisconsin State Champion, 1947.

BARTEL, LEONARD, Past Secretary-Treasurer, Oregon Horseshoe Pitchers Association. Divorced; children—David, Laurie, James, Sandra. Instrument Technician. S. Allen; t. one and a quarter, right handed. Has played since he was a boy, and has played NHPA tournaments since 1972; record tournament high 40.9% and high game 53.2%; organized the Oregon City Horseshoe Club and helped build the Oregon City courts; held offices of Secretary-Treasurer and Vice-President of Oregon City Horseshoe Club. Home: 14220 South Livesay Road, Oregon City, OR 97045.

BARTEL, SANDY, b. January 24, 1961. Oregon State Women's Champion 1979 with a 7-0-59% and in 1980 with 7-1-62.2%. Oregon State Girls Champion 1975 with 7-1-57.76% and in 1976 with 8-0-61.9%. Legal Secretary—Receptionist. S. Gordon; t. flip, right handed. As a junior girl found little competition and was placed with junior boys, and other times in class with women. First tournament in 1972 in Portland Sandy averaged only 5%; in 1973 climbed to 20.9% and won her first trophy in LaGrande; won Fathers Day tournament, 1974 in Junior Boys Division with 5-0-28.3%; won Tri-City Junior Boys Championship with 6-0 record; won Hermiston Open Junior Boys, 1975 with a 5-0-46.08%; won Sagebrush Open Junior Boys with 5-1-50.79%; won Sagebrush Open in 1976 with 8-0-41.22% and the Tri-City Championships with 4-1-50%; won Pacific Northwest Women's Championship with 6-1-60.2%; won the Rose Festival in 1979 with 6-0-46.7% and the Territorial Days Open 5-0-58.87%; she qualified for Championship Division in World Tournament at Statesville, North Carolina and finished 10th with a record of 3-8-61.1%; highest tournament average 72.4% in 1979 and highest game of 83.3% in same tournament; has appeared on television in show called "Evening"; served as Secretary-Treasurer in 1979 for Oregon City Club. Home: 4532 South East Roethe Road, No. 73, Milwaukie, OR 97222.

BARTLEN, VINCENT "TOMMY", b. February 1, 1917, Tarpon Springs, Florida. Wisconsin State Champion, 1949, 1953, 1957, 1959, 1965, 1967; Member WHPA Hall of Fame, 1979. W. Jane. Chemist Assistant, Evinrude Motors. S. Gordon and Ohio; t. one and a quarter, right handed. Started playing 47 years ago and has been involved in local league or tournament competition and 24 years in NHPA competition; President of Washington Park Club in Milwaukee; in 1951 he and Casey Jones tied for high Qualifying score in world tournament with 524 points; Bartlen finished in 15th place averaging 70.9%; in 1952 he was 14th with 68.7% and in 1950, his only other world tournament, he was 24th with 69.4%; from 1934 through 1973 Bartlen played 1278 tournament games winning 956 and losing 322; he put on an exhibition at Milwaukee Athletic Club in 1950; appeared on "Pitching Horseshoes" on WTMJTV in 1955; was Milwaukee city champion, 1949, 1950, 1951; highest game was 96.4% in Wisconsin State Tournament, 1953; highest tournament average was 75% in Wisconsin State Tournament, 1948; Bartlen picked up name of "Tommy" for his tommygun ringer pitching at Exposition Park in Los Angeles, 1938; won the Los Angeles City Tournament in 1934 hitting 78.4%; was involved in four-handed game played at Exposition Park, 1938 and scored by Earl Collins which produced these results: Eddie Packham, 174 ringers with 66 doubles, Henry Harper, 162 ringers with 66 doubles, Dean Brown, 166 ringers with 68 doubles, Vincent Bartlen 162 ringers with 62 doubles. There were 664 ringers, 258 doubles and 81 four-deads in this game. Home 1964 South 97th Street, West Allis, WI 53227.

BARTLETT, BOB, b. May 21, 1961. Washington Boys State Champion, 1977, 1978, 1979, when he hit 5-0-83.3%. Cook. S. Ohio Pro; t. three quarters, right handed. Has pitched for 14 years with 11 years in tournament and league competition; won fifty Class A events including 1977 Northwest, Seattle Open, Billingham Open, and 3 state championships; won the Class C Junior World championship in 1977 and placed 4th in Class A in 1978 averaging 75.7% ahd hitting a 90% game; set several state records for junior boys, averaging 84.21% in 1978 with 128 ringers out of 152 shoes at Bremerton; hit 14 consecutive doubles at Yakima in

1978; and combined with Peter Clark in 1978 game to set records for both players with 80 doubles, 194 ringers, 6 consecutive four-deads, 30 total four-deads, most shoes 240 and highest combined average 80.83%; also set shortest game with 17 of 18 against Ross Morgan in Bremerton. Enjoys bowling and football. Home: 18 Intercity Avenue, Everett, WA 98204.

BARTLETT, JOE, b. November 20, 1959. Washington Boys State Champion, 1975, with 7-0-59% average. Cook. S. Ohio; t. one and a quarter, right handed. Has played for 14 years and pitched tournament shoes for 12; in 1976 was second with 5-2-58%; won the Class B world championship with 5-0-61%; best tournament average 65% and highest game 89%. HOme: 18 Inter City Avenue, Everett, WA 98201.

BARTLEY, FLOYD, b. June 18, 1924. Secretary of Lake Orion Horseshoe Club. W. Marian V.; children—Robert, Karen. Pontiac Motors Division of General Motors, Retired. S. Allen; t. one and three quarters, right handed. Has been pitching for 26 years, 12 years in league play and 8 in tournament action; won Pontiac City Championships in 1954, 1957, 1959, 1961; won 20 Michigan tournaments and 4 Florida tournaments; in 1977 was Class B runnerup in world tournament; in 1979 hit his all time high game of 86% at Lapeer, Michigan; in 1980 Lake Orion handicap league his ringer percentage for 52 games was 69.2%. Enjoys golf, table tennis, biking and bowling. Home: 25 East Longfellow Avenue, Pontiac, MI 48055.

BARTNIK, KIRK, b. June 21, 1966. S. Ohio Pro; t. one and one quarter, right handed. Wisconsin Boys State Champion, 1980, with 6-1-72.3%. Student. Has played for 5 years, winning 12 trophies; 7 trophies have been for Class A Championships, 1978 at Eau Claire, Preimesberger Arena Halloween Opens, 1978, 1979, 1980; Crossroads

Inn Mall Exhibition, 1980; in the Preimesberger Halloween, 1979 he hit the magic circle with his highest ever tournament average of 81.7%; against Slim Bowman he hit his career high game of 95%; hit 88% against Bret Pritzlaff; has had 9 consecutive doubles; Preimesberger Halloween Open, 1980, won 10 straight games averaging 87.8% ringers and hit perfect game of 50 ringers out of 50 shoes; won the Class C World Championship in 1980. Home: Route 1, Box 8, Mountain, WI 54149.

BARTRAM, SAMUEL, First President Connecticut HPA. Introduced the game and promoted its growth in Connecticut. Home: 3911 Main Street, Stratford, CT 06497.

BASSETT, MARK, Massachusetts Boys State Champion, 1979, with 5-0-58.9%. Home: Box 288, Brattleboro Road, Bernardston, MA

BATCHELLER, GARY, Washington Boys State Champion, 1963 with a record of 4-0-30.2%.

BAUGHN, REECE, b. September 22, 1914. W. Martha; 2 children. Tool Process Engineer. S. Gordon—Imperial—Allen; t. one and a quarter, right handed. Started pitching when he was 46 years old, entered his first tournament at 51; pitched an 80% tournament; hit a single game high of 93%, and ran 55 consecutive ringers, 27 doubles in a row in tournament competition; won many Class A championships on the local, state and national level; won the Richmond Rose Festival and Anderson Club Championships. At present is State Secretary for District 25 Indiana for Lions Clubs International; was the organizer and first president of the 8 court layout and club at Newcastle. Home 1516 Riley Road, Newcastle, IN 47362.

BAUMAN, MARK, b. Octobert 22, 1956. Farmer. S. Allen; t. one and a quarter, left handed. In 3 of the last 4 years won league

championship; his tournament average is 65%; in 1979 he averaged 68.2%; best tournament was 76%; bets game was 82% in 1977; hit 24 ringers in a row with 78% average in 1979. Home: Route 2, Olivia, MI 56277.

BAVASSANO, GIUSEPPE MARIA, b. 1929. President and founder, National Horseshoe Pitchers Association of Italy. Has adopted in Italy the Constitution and By-Laws of the National Horseshoe Pitchers Association of America; is perfecting a shoe for manufacture and is interesting in promoting the game in Italy and other European countries; has supervised the construction of 6 regulation courts in Milan where tournaments both local and international are played. Founded for the first time in Italy the Bowmen Association which has become an important association with 26 regional teams, each made up of 30 bowmen; the Italian bowmen took 4th place in the Olympic games; has organized tournaments for paraplegic people in bow competition; has taught handicapped children horseback riding. Home: 20090 Lucino Di Rodano, Milan, Italy 20060.

BAXTER, RALPH, Michigan State Champion, 1924, 1933 with a record of 10-1-59.5%.

BEACH, DR. C.E., Became the First Secretary of the National Horseshoe Pitchers Association; worked closely with Arthur Headlough who acted as Tournament Director in 1919 and 1920 in winter tournaments in Florida. Home: Hinsdale, Michigan.

BEAIRD, CHRISTINE, (dec.) Member South Dakota Hall of Fame, 1978. H. John; children—Maryan Mahoney, John, Buddy, Ronald, Roy. Home: Route 3, Box 123 Rapid City, S.D. 57701.

BEAIRD, JOHN O., b. September 18, 1906. Member South Dakota Hall of Fame,

1978; Past President of SDHPA. W. Christine (dec); children—Maryan Mahoney, John, Buddy, Ronald, Ray. Contractor. S. Allen; t. three quarter, right handed. Has been pitching tournament horseshoes for 31 years; in addition to being President of SDHPA he also served as Secretary; twice won the Class C State championship; his high tournament game was 84%. Enjoys bowling in the winter. Home: Route 3, Box 123, Rapid City SD 57701.

BEARDSLEY, ED, Utah State Champion, 1944.

BECHTEL, RAYMOND L., b. January 30, 1932. Vice-President, Eastern Pennsylvania NHPA Chapter. W. Julene; children—Stephanie, Tim. Owner and operator, Bechtel Roofing. S. Imperial; t. one and a quarter, right handed. Has pitched over 20 years, 15 in the NPHA: won 7 local tournaments; participated in 1976 World Tournament; has achieved a single game high of 85.7%. Home: 2210 Sycamore Road, York, PA 17404.

BECKMAN, EDWARD, Kentucky State Champion 1926, 1928, with 48.9% ringers. Home: Route 2, Box 405, Louisville, KY.

BEEM, RON S., b. January 18, 1922. North Dakota State Champion, 1974, with a 63.3% average. W. Armenonhie; children—Glenn, Tonia, Valeria, Grant, Julie; 9 grandchildren. Farmer and trapper. S. Ohio; t. one and three quarters, right handed. Has played for 20 years, 11 in NHPA; was president for 10 years of Sheldon Horseshoe Club; hit a high game of 78.8% ringers and one string of 20 consecutive ringers; won the American Legion Championship in Moorhead, Minnesota, 1977. Home: Route 2, Lisbon, ND 58054.

BEER, PAUL, Former President and held several positions with the Erie Horseshoe Club. The Erie Club hosted several Eastern National, the Northwest Open, a World Tournament and many others. Beer has been involved in all of these events. Home: 2051 West 51st Street, Erie, PA 16509.

BELL, CLARACY, b. June 30, 1938. Kentucky State Champion, 1975, with 50% ringers; and in 1977 with a 47% average. H. Russell; children—Clyde, Vicki, Connie, Ricky. Security Officer. S. Ohio Pro; t. flip, right handed. Won the Avon and James Gaine Tournaments in 1977; presently is vice-president of local club. Home: 124 Paris Avenue, Lexington, KY 40505.

BELL, CLYDE, b. March 16, 1958. Kentucky State Boys Champion, 1973, 1974, 1975. W. Denise; child—Clyde Thomas. Electrician. S. Allen; t. one and three quarters, left handed. Has been playing for 7 years; after moving to men's division he won 2 state Class B titles and finished 4th in Class A in 1978; in 1978 state tournament hit best tournament with 64.9%; in same tournament hit highest game of 80%, against Tony Wash; finished 2nd in several Class A tournaments. Home 124 Paris Avenue, Lexington, KY 40505.

BELL, RICKY, b. April 6, 1963. Kentucky State Boys Champion, 1976, 1977, 1978, 1979, 1980. Cook at McDonalds Restaurant. S. Allen; t. one and a quarter, right handed. Has been competing for 6 years; highest tournament is 72%, and highest game 78%; won every local junior tournament he entered; finished 9th place in World Tournament Junior Boys Division in 1979; ready to enter the men's division and is averaging about 62% ringers. Home 124 Paris Avenue, Lexington, KY 40505.

BELLER, ELMER, b. in Nebraska in 1890 (dec.) Member of NHPA Hall of Fame, 1967. Operated a garage in Mojave, California until retirement. Served 20 years as Vice-President and the office of Secretary-Treasurer; spent much of his life as an officer in the California HPA; served as President of Long Beach Horseshoe Club for 10 years; President of Southern California Horseshoe Pitcher Association for 10 years; received the Arch Stokes Memorial Award in 1958, was the first recipient of this award; following his death an Annual Tournament, The Elmer Beller Open has been held in his memory each year in California.

BELLMAN, CLARENCE, b. June 12, 1921. Indiana State Champion, 1975, 1976. W. Evelyn Ruth, children—Caren Jean Miller, Diann Nannette Starr, Bonnie Lou Hawkins, Schona Kay, Stuart Allen. Feed Delivery man. S. Allen; t. one and a quarter, right handed. Has played for 50 years, for 24 years has played NHPA tournamens; won the American Associations's State Championship and the NHPA Indiana State Championship in 1976; won the New Castle Tournament averaging above 80.0%; and averaged over 80.0% through the World Tournament; won the Northern Indiana Title 5 years in a row in the 1960's; has had several games above 90.0%; has won over 100 trophies; averaged 82.5% ringers and defeated Stan Manker in a play-off in Newcastle Open; in World Tournament, 1977 was 10th with an 80.7%, with 2063 ringers; in game with Walter Ray Williams hit 51 ringers out of 52 after Williams reached 47 points; in the championship division of the world tournament he has a composite record of 114-83-75.4%. Home: 4241 East Shore Drive, Bremen, IN.

BENEDICT, CLAUDE A. "RED", b. April 20, 1895. (dec.) W. Lola; child—Shirley Cavendish; (2) Lois. Insurance salesman, photographer, writer and a Johnstown, Ohio postmaster. Served in United States Army in France during World War I. Pitched horseshoes for 40 years; served as President of Ohio Buckeye Horseshoe Pitchers Association for 15 years; operated the Ohio State Fair horseshoe pitching program

for 10 years; owned and operated the Ohio Horseshoe Company, makers of drop-forged pitching shoes for 5 years; a member of the National Horseshoe Pitchers Association for 40 years; member of American League of Horseshoe Pitchers; formed the World League of Horseshoe Pitchers; publisher of *The Horseshoe World,* a national magazine promoting the game; made the championship division of World Tournament one time and played several times in Class A of the Ohio State tournament.

BENNETT, CHERRY, Utah State Champion, 1945.

BENNETT, JOE, Illinois State Champion, 1932. Was second to Gaylord Peterson in the 1928 tournament; in World Tournament in Moline, 1935 was 8th with record of 14-9-69.1%. Home: Moline, IL.

BENNETT, LEE, b. January 19, 1918. Horseshoe Manufacturer. W. Ruth; children—David, Ruth Ann, Connie. Owner and operator of Bennett's Mower Service. S. Steel Lee; t. one and a quarter, right handed. The Lee shoe was made in both steel and bronze and was used by many champions and is still in demand; in year he started he was pitching over 50% and in 2 years he was in championship division of the world tournament hitting 4-31-62.7%; record in world tournament in 1963 was 11-24-65.2%; in 1964 it was 13-22-72.2%, and in 1965 it was 3-32-61%; had a tournament high of 76% and hit 15 consecutive doubles in tournament play; had 2 88% games, defeating Ralph Maddox in world tournament play with one of them and James "Pop" Johnson with the other in the Ohio State Tournament; highest finish in Ohio was 8th; built indoor courts at his home; conducted league play for years. Home: 4920 Eck Road, West Middletown, OH 45042.

BENNETT, RUTH, b. October 1, 1920. Ohio Women's State Champion as follows:

1963 won 5 lost 0 with record of 62.9%, 1964 won 5 lost 0 with a 65.0%, 1965 retained title, no meet, 1966 won 3 lost 0 with a record of 53.5%, 1967 won 5 lost 0 with a 66.1%, 1968 won 3 lost 0 with a 62.3% record. H. Lee; children—David, Ruth Ann, Connie. Bookkeeper. S. Bronze Lee; t. three quarter, right handed. Pitched in men's league at husband's indoor courts because of scarcity of women to pitch against; had a 66.1% state tournament record in 1967 until broken by Opal Reno in 1973; pitched in 5 world tournaments in championship division; combined record is 17-17-58.6%. Home: 4920 Eck Road, West Middletown, OH 45042.

BENTZ, HOWARD B., President, New Mexico Horseshoe Pitchers Association. b. July 23, 1916. Retired military—General Contractor in home construction. W. Catharina; children—Sandra, Ann Marie. S. Imperial, Ohio "O" and Allen; t. one and a quarter, right handed. Has pitched horseshoe for 50 years, 12 of them in tournaments; was runnerup for New Mexico State title in 1979 with high game of 72%; Albuquerque Class B champion in 1978; was President of Albuquerque Horseshoe Club for one year and League Director for 4. Has a BBA Degree from University of New Mexico and enjoys electronic and woodworking. Home: 8613 Guierrez NE, Albuquerque, NM 87111.

BERG, NORMAN, Alaskan Regional Director, W. Dorothea. Home: P.O. Box 635, Clear, Alaska 99701.

BERMAN, DR. SOL, b. September 21, 1912. Chairman, National Promotion Committee; New Jersey State Champion, 1955, 1957, 1965, 1969, 1970, 1973, 1975, 1978. W. Rita Ganz, M.D.; children—Miles J., Mrs. Leslie Weiner. Doctor of Medicine. S. Imperial; t. one and three quarters, right handed. Has played for 60 years; current ringer percentage, mid 60's; won National AAU in 1976 Doubles Championship teaming with Al Cherry; 12 New Jersey state doubles championships; U.S. Army Championship in 1943 at Papua, New Guinea; was selected New Jersey Hall of Fame, 1976; received NHPA Recognition and Achievement Award, 1976; highest tournament average 70.3%, New Jersey State Qualifying Tournament, 1959; highest single game 91.7%, Union County Experimental Tournament, 1979; has served as Chairman National Change for Progress Committee, Chairman National Qualifying Format Committee, President and Secretary-Treasurer of New Jersey Association. Home 351 Rahway Avenue, Elizabeth, NJ 07202.

BERNIER, SHAWN., North Dakota Junior Champion, 1980 with record 4-1-30.9%.

BERTRAND, SHERMAN EDWARD, JR., b. March 24, 1939. President, West Virginia Horseshoe Pitchers Association. W. Betty Lou; children—David, Charles, Katherine, Tammie. S. Allen; t. Reverse three quarter. right handed. Has pitched for 25 years, in tournaments since 1969; is Secretary of the Moundsville Club; in state tournament play has been runnerup 4 times; holds West Virginia state record for most shoes pitched, and most ringers pitched in one tournament; has been top qualifier 5 times, best round being 45 out of 50 for 90%; in World Tournament play has made championship division 6 times averaging 75% ringers; highest finish was 21st place; highest game in tournament play was 94.1% against Joe Carter in Mingo Open; Class A titles include Worthington Open, 1972 Moundsville City Championship, Western Open, Hebron Open 2, Wood County Open 3, Marietta Open and Washington County Open 6 years in a row. Home: 1204 Thompson Avenue, Moundsville, W VA 26041.

BERTSCHY, ALLEN, Former State Secretary of Maryland Horseshoe Pitchers Association. Devoted time to court construction and tournament promotion. Home: 8016 Carey Branch Drive, Oxon Hill, MD 20022.

BERUBE, CONNIE, Main State Womens Champion, 1979 with record of 39.3%.

BESHORE, DAN, b. September 26, 1922. State Secretary-Treasurer Eastern Pennsylvania NHPA Chapter. m. five children. Plantman, Gulf Oil Corporation. S. Allen; t. one and three quarters, right handed. Has pitched 15 years, 10 as NHPA member and tournament player; won York County championship 1977 with 75.3%, 1978 with 75.1% and 1979 with 77.5%; 1979 tournament hit 85.1% ringers in 62 shoes; won Class B title Winchester with 79 of 92 for 85.8%; first member of York County Hall of Fame, 1975; last 4 Pennsylvania state tournament as follows: 1976, finished 4th, won 10, lost 5, with 71.5%; 1977, finished 3rd, won 12, lost 3, with 74.7%; 1978, finished 4th, won 11, lost 4, with 75.7%; 1979, finished 5th, won 10, lost 5, with 73.2%. Home: Route 1, New Cumberland, PA 17070.

BESSEY, JAMES, JR., Connecticut State Champion, 1949 with record 9-2-59.2%.

BESTUL, CURT, b. August 14, 1924. Assistant NHPA Regional Director; member Wisconsin Hall of Fame Committee. W. Beaty; children—Dottie, Donald, David, Debby. Line crew foreman. S. Allen; t. one and a quarter, right handed. 18 years of league and tournament horseshoes; served as NHPA Regional Director; Vice-President Wisconsin Horseshoe Pitchers Association; President Eau Claire Club, and Secretary and Tournament Chairman; highest tournament average is 70.2%; 1970, 1971 hit 45 ringers out of 50 shoes in league play for 90%; 1970 world tournament hit qualifying score of 511 to place 17th in Championship Division, making him 1st Wisconsin pitcher since

Casey Jones to get in the top class; won Eau Claire City Championships, 1967–1975 and 1977, 1978; won Orlando Florida Open, 1974; won Minneapolis Open, 1972 and defeated Frank Stinson in play-off; in play-off game hit 61 ringers out of 70 shoes for 87.1%; with Frank Stinson had 9 consecutive four-deads; formed Eau Claire Club, 1965, was 1st President; helped organize and charter Wisconsin Chapter NHPA; influenced city of Eau Claire to build 12 lighted clay courts, site of the 1967 state tournaments. Home: 1412 Sherwin Avenue, Eau Claire, WI 54701.

BESTFUL, HAROLD G., b. February 24, 1916. Second Vice-President Wisconsin HPA. W. Martha; childred—Greg, David, Terry, Steve, Fran, Chris, Randy, Fairie, Tom, Mike. Retired. S. Ohio Pro; t. one and three quarters, right handed. Has played for 59 years, in league and tournament competition for 44 years; in Wisconsin state tournaments and other major open tournaments has finished, 2nd, 3rd and 4th many times; Home: 105 Wigwam Road, Rosholt, WI 54473.

BETTERTON, FRED, b. March 10, 1926. W. Ima; children—Freda Simms, Wayne, Joe, grandchildren—Jimmy, John, Heather, Preston, Holly. Loom Fixer, Huntsville Manufacturing Company. S. Deadeye; t. three quarter, right handed. Started playing as a boy but was not exposed to organized games until 1976, when 10 coursts were built in Brahan Springs Park, Hunstville; has played Huntsville League and in tournaments all over Alabama; won Rocket City Tournament, 1976; Dogwood, 1977; William A. Nelson Hall of Fame tournament, 1979; New Hope Open, 1980; several 2nd place finishes including Alabama State 1977 where he tied for state title and lost two out of three play-offs; won Madison County in 1989; won Anniston and New Hope championships and played in Class C of World

Tournament with record 4-1-58.2% missing finals on percentage only. Home: 3802 Eight Avenue S.W., Huntsville, Alabama 35805.

BETTISWORTH, CASEY, (dec.), Played state, world and open tournaments all over country; played in Class B in world tournament and Class A in state and open tournaments; played with Henry Franke at Peoria in 1971 in top game of state tournament, Franke hit 60 of 68 for 88.2% and Bettisworth had 49 of 68 for 72% in the 52-9 game. Home: Galesburg, IL.

BICKERTON, DONALD, New York State Champion, 1934. Home: Buffalo, New York.

BIGHAM, GERRI, Canadian Women's Champion, 1975, averaging 38.3%. Home: Langley, B.C., Canada.

BILLINGS, FLOYD, Wisconsin State Champion, 1925.

BILLS, ALFRED, SR., b. March 5, 1936. President, Indiana State Horseshoe Pitchers Association. W. Lorna; children—Alfred, Jr., Lorna. Upholsterer. S. Allen; t. one and a quarter, right handed. Has played for 30 years, last 7 in NHPA Competition; President of Connersville Horseshoe Club; owned and operated 8 court Rush Indoor Courts since 1975; with brother, Larry constructed 8 court outdoor layout in Rushville; has held various offices in Rushville Club; served as vice-president of state association 1976, 1977. Home: 211 West Fourth Street, Rushville, IN 46173.

BILLS, DOROTHY, b. September 8, 1945. President of Rushville local, 1978. H. Larry; children—Susan, Gregory. Factory Worker. S. Ohio; t. flip, right handed. Has played for 8 years; highest game was 60%, highest tournament 43%; won Class C Indiana State Tournament; 2nd place in 1978 in Class B, Lafayette; won Whitewater Canal Days Class A in 1979; won Class A Rush Indoor

New Years Open in 1980; received Rush Indoor League Sportsmanship Award in 1974–75. Home 322 West 4th Street, Rushville, IN 46173.

BINDSCHADLER, GOLDIE, Secretary, Treasurer Wyoming HPA. b. May, 1908. H. Harold; children—Darryl, Lela Jean Pexton. Housewife. Member of NHPA but does not pitch; she is Secretary-Treasurer of Laramie Club and served as Secretary-Treasurer of Wyoming Horseshoe Pitchers Association; since 1966 has kept records in tournaments held in state; has kept score and ordered trophies and supplies for many years. Home: 520 South 12th Street, Laramie, WY 82070.

BINDSCHADLER, HAROLD, b. November 4, 1908, President of Wyoming Horseshoe Pitchers Association, and Assistant NHPA Regional Director. W. Goldie; children—Darryl, Lela Jean Pexton. Soil Scientist USDA. S. American or Allen; t. one and a half. Has pitched for 20 years, 18 in NHPA; highest game 70.1% and best tournament 49.3%; former NHPA Regional Director; 4th Vice-President of Wyoming HPA for 1 year; Secretary-Treasurer Wyoming HPA for 5 years; President of Wyoming HPA for 10 years. Home: 520 South 12th Street, Laramie, WY 82070.

BISHE, ROBERT J., b. November 5, 1921. W. Grace C.; children—Pat, Ken, Terri, Carol, Steve. Inspector, New Jersey Bell Telephone Company. S. Gordon; t. one and a quarter, right handed. Started playing as a small boy; started competing in state and local games and became member of NHPA, 1967; served as Vice-President of New Jersey HPA; highest tournament average 67.4%, and highest game 77.6%; 1969 upset Doc Berman who had won the Union County Championship 21 consecutive years hitting 5-0-55%; teamed with Vince Yannetti in 1968 to win New Jersey doubles state championship; won 1971 Class B National AAU, 1968 tournament with 7-0-51%; averaged 62% for 5th place in Class C world tournament; other champsionships won, New Jersey AAU junior title with 52%, Essex County 1970 with 54%, Aunterdon County with 51% in 1970 and 55% in 1971, New Jersey AAU Open, 1971 with 58%. Home: 23 Cayuga Road, Cranford, NJ 07016.

BJORLIN, JUDY, Minnesota State Girls Champion, 1980 with 5-0-59.6%. Home: Donnelly, MI 56235.

BLACK, JERRY LEE, b. February 12, 1955. North Dakota State Champion 4 times. S. Imperial; t. one and three quarters, right handed. Semi Truck driver. Has played for 14 years; won 68 open tournaments; highest tournament average 75.6% in 1973 Greenville Classic; 6 tournament games have been 90% or higher, with the highest one 94%; qualified 5 times for Championship division of the world tournament; won over Mark Siebold with a 50-28 in 1973 Greenville Classic hitting 86.2%; serves as State Secretary for North Dakota's chapter and Regional Director; in 1980 state championship hit 10-1-65.2% ringers. Pitched a one and a quarter until 21 when he was in an automobile accident breaking his shoulder blades, which took 3 years for recovery; he then had to switch to one and three quarters turn. Home: 3102 North 9th Street, Fargo, N DA 58102.

BLACKETER, OMAR E., b. November 21, 1912. President Louisville Metro Club. W. Mallie; children—Betty Sue Lowe, Robert. Machinist. S. Allen; t. one and a quarter, right handed. Has played for 40 years; played NHPA horseshoes for 6 years; won 116 trophies for 1st, 2nd and 3rd place; won Kentucky State Class B 3 times; won World Senior Class B Title in 1979; highest tournament 64%; best game 76.4% for 118 shoes. Has played baseball for 28 years, and

softball for 37. Home: 7912 Third Street Road, Louisville, KY 40214.

BLACKMAN, HAROLD E., b. August 11, 1916 (dec.); Player and Promoter, 50 years. W. Isabel; children—Mary Lynn, Douglas Harold. S. Allen; t. one and a quarter, right handed. Served as Regional Director for Province of Ontario; won Provincial Legion Championship.

BLACKWELL, DONES "SONNY", Georgia State Champion, 1970, 1975, 1976. Home: Route 3, Henderson Road, Alpharetta, GA 30201.

BLAKELY, JOHN, Indiana State Champion, 1919.

BLAKEMAN, DONNA, Kentucky Girls State Champion, 1970, won 5, lost 0 with 4.5% and 1971, won 4, lost 1 with 18.6%

BLEXRUDE, WILLIAM E., b. August 2, 1901 (dec.), California State Champion, 1963 with 12-1-72.7%, and in 1965 with 10-3-67.5%. W. Loretta; child—Richard, 3 grandchildren. Welder for American Tractor Equipment Corp. S. Gordon; t. one and a quarter, ambidextrous. Pitched for 42 years, always competing in tournaments and winning many; Alameda County Champion from 1956 through 1964; member of Northern California Horseshoe Pitchers Association Hall of Fame; served as Secretary of Mosswood Horseshoe Club; in World Tournament, 1963 made Championship Division with record of 8-27-67.7%. Enjoyed bowling. Home: 2936 Florida Street, Oakland, CA 94602.

BLINKHORN, ROBERT, Nova Scotia Provincial Champion, 1978. Was the youngest provincial champion in Canada with record of 7-0-47.1% ringers. Home: Sydney Mines.

BLUM, EDWARD, b. October 26, 1918. Beaver County Champion from 1970 through 1977. W. Mary; children—Nancy Morris, James. Steel worker, Babcock & Wilcox. S. Allen; t. one and a quarter, right handed. Has played for 45 years, 25 in NHPA events; won 50 trophies for all tournaments, one for 1976 Class E of world tournament with 58.6%; highest tournament average 64% and highest single game 88%; twice hit 23 of 24 during a tournament game, once in Eastern National and one in world tournament in Greenville, Ohio. Enjoyed playing baseball. Home: Box 101 Darlington, PA 16115.

BLUNT, JO ANN, May 25, 1946. Virginia Women's State Champion, 1975. H. Howard Temple; children—Howard Temple, Jr., Pam. Housewife. S. Gordon; t. flip, right handed. In first tournament, 1974 averaged 17% ringers and in last tournament, 1975 averaged 59.2% ringers; won Frye Memorial, Winchester in 1974; won Regional Award for most tournaments won in 1975; highest single game 71%, Winchester Ladies Open; won state doubles championship with Norma Hottinger; won Hill City Open at Lynchburg; won Twin-Valley at Waynesboro; also won Hill City Ladies Invitational, the Apple Capitol Open and the Frye Memorial. Her career ended in fall of 1975 when she develoepd muscle problems in neck and shoulders. Home: Route 1, Box 223-A, Ashland VA 23005.

BLUTT, HELEN, b. August 25, 1921, Montana State Champion, 1978 with 72.2% and 1979 with 73.7%. H. Joe; children— Josie, Myrna, Kenny, Denney, Larry. Housewife. S. Allen; t. flip, right handed. Has played for 15 years and NHPA for 8 years; for 6 years pitched from men's distance of 40 feet and competed against men because of scarcity of women pitchers in area; high tournament average 58%; high game 68%; won Class B Championship 1978 with record 5-0 and 70.1% ringers; in World Tournament 1979 made championship divi-

sion and posted 5 wins against 6 losses, averaging 62% ringers; won Eastern Montana plaque 1979 for outstanding contribution and dedication to horseshoes; feels her greatest accomplishment was pitching against men from 40 feet; in 5 years worked from Class E to Class A; only 2 Class A men in Eastern Montana's Chapter she has not beaten. Home: Box 242 Ekalaka, MT 59324.

BOBBITT, CHARLES, b. 1896 (dec.), World Champion 1921 in St. Petersburg, Florida with 20-1 record. Shoe worker. Hit 439 ringers in 21 games; pitched one and quarter turn; was runnerup in 1920 with record 35-2 and 799 ringers; after winning title in 1921 had a combined record of 55-3.

BOBBITT, EVERETT, b. 1897 (dec.), W. Lola Loyd; children—Royce, James, Kenneth, Donald, Marlena, Twila, Alma, Dorothy, Juanita, Marquietta. Shoe worker. t. one and a quarter. Was runnerup for Ohio State Championship; was Class A contestant in World Tournament 1921. Home: Lancaster, OH.

BOERMA, KATHY, Girls Michigan State Champion 1974. Home: Route 1, Diamondale, MI 48821.

BOESCH, JEROME "JERRY", b. January 22, 1914. W. Agnes; children Mike, Tom, Jim. Supervisor, Stokely-Van Camp. S. Ohio; t. one and a quarter, right handed. Has played horseshoes for 20 years; for 10 years President of Whetstone Horseshoe Club; President New Rome Club for 2 years; was Intermediate Class B World Champion, 1974; best tournament average 64%; best game 82%; feels the NHPA sanctioned league play should be further developed and have national league play as part of world tournament competiton instead of lower classes. Home: 4464 Blythe Road, Columbus, OH 43224.

BOGGESS, FRANK, b. June 13, 1952.

West Virginia State Champion 1973. W. Karen; child—Melissa. S. Ohio Pro; t. one and three quarters, right handed. Social Worker for Erie Pennsylvania Veterans Administration Medical Center; B.A. Degree in Sociology from West Virginia State College and M.S.W. from West Virginia University. Spent 2 years in U.S. Military Police Corps as First Lieutenant. Has pitched since he was 13; pitched competively for 15 years, 12 in NHPA; hit 65% ringers in Pennsylvania Title Division. Home 3908 Briggs Avenue, Apt. No. 7, Erie, PA 16504.

BOGGESS, JAMES FRANKIN, Has been active tournament player in West Virginia for many years; served as officer in state association and has helped to promote the game; was a Class A contender for West Virginia title. Home 5004 Morgan Drive, Charleston, W. VA 25312.

BOLDUC, ROGER W., b. August 29, 1920. Chairman, Maine Hall of Fame Committee. W. Juliette; children—Gerard, Murielle, Doris. Furniture and machinery mover. S. Ohio O; t. one and a quarter, left handed. Tournament Director for Auburn Club; former President of State Association; member of Executive Committee; organized New England Association Hall of Fame and Annual Mr. Horseshoe Honor Plaque; developed 3 horseshoe court layouts in Maine; played for 45 years, competing in NHPA events for 20 years; highest tournament average 55% and highest game 67.5%; as tournament director runs the Spring Roundup, Maine state tournament and every other year the New England Championships; planned and financed the First Annual Fall Classic with $1,000.00 in cash prizes for top 12 pitchers in New England area; won Class B Main state title, 1964 with 49.2% and 1965 with 48%; won Class B Vermont Open 1965 as well as class titles in 1968 Massachusetts Open and Vermont Open, 1971. Home: 120 Gill Street, Auburn, ME 04210.

BOMKE, EARL A., b. February 16, 1913. Illinois State Champion 1946, 1947, 1951; Member Illinois Hall of Fame, 1980. W. Irma; children—Karen, Marjorie, Ronald. Farmer. S. Ohio; t. one and three quarters, right handed. Has played for 56 years; tournament high 77.5%; single game high 92.5%. Enjoys bowling and golf. Home: Route 6, Springfield, IL 62707.

BOMSTAD, HAROLD, North Dakota State Champion 1937 with 11-2, in 1938 with 11-0 and 1942 with 9-0. Home North 2227 Cedar, Spokane, WA 99200.

BONEWIT, JOHN, b. July 1, 1910. Indiana Senior State Championship 1980 with 5-0-43.1%. W. Ona Mae; children—Barbara Mattsen, Mary Donaldson, John Jr., Sue Schallow, Linda O'Hara. Paper maker, CC-A. S. Gordon or Ohio Pro; t. one and three quarters, right handed. Has played for 8 years, playing tournament for 3; best game was 66.6%; 20 out of 30 in the Paul Cunningham Memorial, 1980; won 8 trophies in 1980 with tournament high of 45.4%. Enjoys hunting and fishing. Home: 363 Indiana Street, Wabash, IN 46992.

BONNEVIE, ALICE, Maine Women State Champion, 1973 with 4-2-37.6%. Was Class A runnerup 1974 and competed in Class B in 1971, 1972.

BOOE, ROBERT G., b. August 23, 1937. NHPA Regional Director for Missouri and Kansas. W. Alexine; children—Julie Ann, James Robert, Susan Lynn. Controller. S. Allen; t. one and a quarter, right handed. Has played for 20 years, 14 as NHPA member; President Atchison Horseshoe Club and Tri-City Horseshoe League; former President Kansas State NHPA; high tournament average of 67.4% and high game of 78%; won the following Class A tournament championships: Atchison Open, Leavenworth Open, St. Joseph Open, Topeka Sunflower Open and Ericks Open; ranked

3rd place in Kansas State tournament. Home 1211 Guthrie Circle, Atchison, KA 66002.

BORN, HENRY, b. Atlantic City, New Jersey. Played in world tournaments in the 20's, winning 86 games while losing 71 averaging 31.1% ringers.

BOSER, CURTIS, b. August 5, 1964. Minnesota Boys State Champion, 1980, with 5-0-77.2%. Student. S. Ohio; t. flip, right handed. Started playing 3 years ago, 2 years of NHPA competition; won Class A title Duluth with 5-0-66%; won Class A Championship Genola's Thanksgiving Open with 7-0-70%; high game of 78%; received high tournament percentage trophy; participated in 1980 World Tournament. Home: Route 2, Lot no. 22, Pierz Fish Lake, Pierz, MI 56364.

BOSS, DALE, b. March 28, 1938. Colorado State Secretary since 1978. Married with three children. AMF Head Ski. S. Allen; t. three quarters and one and a quarter, right handed. Has played for 25 years, 8 in NHPA. Secretary of Boulder Horseshoe Club since 1976. Home 4224 Greenbriar, Boulder, CO 80303.

BOTTS, HAZEL. Minnesota Womens State Champion, 1922. Played in one World Tournament winning 17 out of 20 games.

BOURGEOIS, HENRY AL, b. June 1, 1918. Rhode Island State Champion, 1956, 1959, 1960, 1961, 1962, 1964, 1967, 1970, 1972, 1973, 1974, 1975. Best was 1967 average of 74.1%. W. Juliette; children—Raymond, Janice, David, Robert, Laurel. S. Imperial; t. one and a quarter, right handed. Has played for 53 years, 48 in tournament play. former President, Secretary and Treasurer of Rhode Island State Horseshoe Pitchers Association; high record of 31 out of 32 games with 96.9%; twice runnerup in New England Championship; was first New England player in 35 years to make champion-ship division in 1968 with 3-32-64.5%; in New England Hall of Fame, 1979. Home: 125 Metropolitan Park Drive, Barrington, RI 02806.

BOWEN, DAVE, Former State Secretary of Delaware Horseshoe Pitchers Association, Home: 125 Roosevelt Avenue, Dover, DE 19901.

BOWER, CAS, b. February 10, 1918. Nevada State Champion, 1978. W. Marge. Warehouse Manager. S. Gordon; t. three quarter, right handed. Has played for 13 years, 11 in NHPA; finished 2nd in state meet 5 times; won local league championship and other local tournaments; has been awarded plaques for service to game by local league and Nevada State Association; served 4 years as National Vice-President and 2 years as League President, and worked with Reno Indian Colony; highest game 72%, highest tournament 62%; elected President of Nevada Horseshoe Pitchers Association, 1980. Home: 2880 Kietzke No. 31, Reno, NE 89502.

BOWER, MARGE E., b. September 6, 1916. Secretary-Treasurer Nevada Horseshoe Pitchers Association, 7 years. H. Cas. Housewife. S. Imperial; t. flip, right handed. Has played in NHPA tournaments for 12 years, including World Tournament, 1973 in Eureka, California; tournament wins include Nevada State Open Championship, 1975, 7 league tournament titles and about 15 other trophies; highest tournament game 56% and best complete tournament 50%. Home: 2880 Kietzke No. 31, Reno, NE 89502.

BOWERS, MATT, (dec.). Texas State Champion, 1960 with 9-1-45.6%.

BOWKER, COQUELLE (COKE) GENE, b. April 15, 1944. W. R.G.; children—Coquelle Gene, Jr., Arleigh Burke. United States Postal Service. S. Deadeye; t. one and a quarter, right handed. Has played for 6 years, 3 in tournament competition; First Vice-President, 1979 of local horseshoe club, including public relations and liaison work; was Most Improved Pitcher in Texas Association, 1978, 1979; runnerup for Texas state championship, 1979; world tournament 1979 posted a high game of 82.3% and finished 4th in Class D. Enjoys basketball, jogs, collects bottles, writes songs and poetry. Home: 1005 Stewart Court, Azle, TX 76020.

BOWMAN, BRYON, Boys World Champion, 1954, 1955. In 1954, record percentage was 54.0, and in 1955 record was 54.1%. Home: 270 South 100 West, Bountiful, UT 84010.

BOWMAN, MILDRED, Womens Maine State Champion, 1954 with 16% ringers. Home: Oxford, ME.

BOWMAN, ROBERT, Colorado State Champion, 1946, 1948 with 10-1-62.6%, 1957 with 9-2-60.2%.

BOWMAN, SWEN, b. July 30, 1912, (dec.) November 25, 1980. Wisconsin Hall of Fame, 1979. W. Clara Slatkey; children— Jim, Marlene. Worked for Wisconsin State Commission until retirement. Past President Wisconsin State Horseshoe Pitchers Association; orgininated annual tournament in Green Bay called Swen's Open.

BOYER, HERMAN, b. May 24, 1916. Pennsylvania HPA Hall of Fame, 1979. W. Delores; children—Mary, James, Frank. Assemblyman. S. Allen; t. one and a quarter, right handed. Has played for 45 years and won dozens of tournaments and class titles. Received the Penn Achievement Award, 1962; plaque from Beaver County Horseshoe Pitchers Association, 1977. Best tournament game in Pennsylvania State meet, 1964 with 72 ringers out of 94 shoes for 76.5% but was beaten by Buck Engle with 77 out of 94 for 81.9%. Home: 6195 Tusculum Road, Beaver, PA 15009.

BOZICH, OSCAR S., b. January 23, 1916. Missouri State Champion, 1939 with record of 15-0-72.2%. W. Therese; children— David, Dona Jacobs. Electrician. S. Gordon and Allen; t. one and three quarters, right handed. Has played for 48 years, 20 years in tournaments. Won city championship of Kansas City for 5 years; had 28 consecutive ringers in one game, and he and Ira Allen hit 8 consecutive four deads; played against Dean Brown, C. C. Davis, Bob Bales, Fernando Isais and other great players at different times and places; in World Tournament, 1935 played at Moline, Illinois and finished 13th. He is an expert pool player and expert fisherman. Home: 11846 South Acocia Avenue, Hawthorne, CA 90250.

BRACEY, THOMAS L., b. June 30, 1924. State Secretary, Michigan Wolverine State Horseshoe Pitchers Association. W. Delores; children—Janet Michael, Mary, Laura. Accountant. S. Ohio Pro; t. one and three quarters, right handed. Two years President and one year Treasurer of Jackson County Horseshoe Club; played in tournaments for 6 years. Home: 1035 South Bowen Street, Jackson, Michigan 49203.

BRACKEN, JOHN EDWARD, b. December 26, 1919. Nevada State Champion, 1980 with record of 5-2-41.7%. W. Elsie; children—Patsy, Eileen, Gregory, Rulon, Clarissa. Mining Foreman. S. Diamond; t. three quarters, right handed. Has played organized horseshoes for 25 years, in tournaments for 8 years; won Washington County, Utah title while a 7th grader; while in army during World War II won Europen Theater Championship; runnerup for Nevada state championship, 1950; during 1980 pitched in 6 tournaments and won them all; highest tournament game 87%. Enjoys raising and racing horses. Home: 5 Oak Court, Box 61, Gabbs, NE 89409.

BRADFIELD, W. R., California State Champion, 1921.

BRAININE, ED, Kansas State Champion, 1923.

BRANDT, GUS A. b. December 19, 1889, Silton, Saskatchewan. Member Saskatchewan Hall of Fame, 1979. Played and promoted the sport most of his adult life.

BRANT, BRITT, Missouri Boys State Champion, 1976. Home: 4701 Valley Lane, St. Joseph, MO 64503.

BREWER, CHARLES M., b. November 28, 1922. Oklahoma State Champion, 1971, 1976, 1978, 1980. W. Iris; children—David, Linda Hughes. United States Postal Clerk. S. Allen or Deadeye; t. three quarters, right handed. Has pitched for 50 years, in tournaments for 13 years; has served as President for Oklahoma Association and the Yukon Club; hit a high game of 74% in Yukon Czeck Tournament, 1980; State Tournament, 1980 record was 5-2-52.8%. Enjoys oil painting. Home: P.O. Box 414, Yukon, OK 73099.

BRICKLER, JOE, Tournament photographer. W. Phyllis; child—Rene. S. no preference of brand; t. one and a quarter, right handed. Has pitched horseshoes since childhood, began to play in organized competition in 1975; has been "official" tournament photographer at world tournaments, the Midwest Ringer Roundup, Greenville Classic and others. is compiling a library of pictures of pitchers in action along with his wife. Home: 2304 Central Street, Lafayette, IN.

BRINKLEY, WILLIAM A., Won Utah State Championship, 1941 at Liberty Park defeating Bruce Walters.; was a member of Salt Lake City Team and won Salt Lake County Championship several times.

BRINKMAN, GILBERT, Member of New England Hall of Fame, 1976. Has played since 1930, and ventured into organized games in 1935 when he helped start an indoor 4 team league at YMCA in Springfield, the league lasted until 1939 with Brinkman serving as Secretary; from 1939 to 1970 served as secretary continuously for many leagues, including Triple A League, Cafe League, Industrial League and indoor club league; helped to reorganize Forest Park Club (name was changed to Westside Club in 1965) and held office as secretary-treasurer until 1970; was responsible in 1965 for obtaining the use of Park property which was used to build 20 clay courts with lights which the West Side Club uses; helped to run 1961 and 1964 New England meets; was Massachusetts State Association President in 1961 and Vice-President for 2 years; was club tournament director in 1969 and 1973 running the Western Massachusetts, Massachusetts Open and Massachusetts State meets; in recent years has concentrated on trying to promote Junior horseshoe pitching in West Springfield area. Home: 52 Worthan Street, West Springfield, MA 01089.

BROCHU, MICHELLE L., b. September 29, 1961. New Hampshire Girls State Champion 1978, Single. U.S. Navy, Great Lakes, Illinois. S. American; t. flip, left handed. Has played tournament horseshoes for 3 years before joining the Navy. Enjoys tap dancing and gymnastics. Home: 64 Elm Street, Penacook, NH 03301.

BROCHU, SHERRY. New Hampshire Girls Champion, 1977 with 9.8% ringers.

BROOKS. JAMES E., JR., b. April 10. Georgia State Champion, 1973 with record of 6-0-56.5%. W. Celia; children—Edwin, Teresa. Plumber. S. Ohio; t. one and a quarter, right handed. Has played for 20 years, 16 years in tournaments. Home: 2100 Birmingham Road, Alpharetta, GE 30201.

BROOKS, CELIA MAE, b. December 24, 1942. Georgia Women's State Champion, 1972 with a 3-0 record. H. James; children—Edwin, Teresa. Housewife. S. Ohio; t. flip, right handed. Has played in tournaments in Statesville, North Carolina and won several trophies. Home: 2100 Birmingham Road, Alpharetta, GE 30201.

BROTHERTON, R.O. (RAY), Author of ALL YOU HAVE TO DO IS COME CLOSE, a publication about horseshoe pitching. Has been a free lance writer for 30 years, writing short stories, articles and several books. His book on horseshoe pitching includes his own experiences and many tips, action photos and records of U.S. and Canadian champions. A member of the National Horseshoe Pitchers Association and has worked with Dr. Sol Berman on the NHPA Promotional Committee; is an enthusiastic promoter of the sport. Home: P.O. Box 72, Marcell, MI 56657.

BROUGHTON, MARVIN E. "MICKEY", Has been pitching horseshoes in tournaments and leagues for 30 years, averaging around 60% ringers; won many events in Florida, Ohio and elsewhere. Enjoys bowling and loves all sports. Home: 2909 Knights Avenue, Tampa, FL 33611.

BROUILETTE, MILDRED, Women's World Champion, 1926, 1927.

Year	Finish	Won	Lost	Record %
1922	7th	2	6	48.4
1923	4th	4	3	18.5
1924	4th	3	3	28.0
1924	2nd	10	1	36.0
Play off	2nd	0	2	25.0
1925	3rd	5	3	33.4
1925	3rd	6	6	37.6
1926	1st	5	0	44.1
1926	1st	9	0	43.2
1927	3rd	2	2	33.5
1927	1st	8	1	47.0
1927	2nd	6	1	48.5
1927	2nd	7	2	56.1
1928	1st	4	0	45.1
1928	2nd	6	3	54.9
1928	5th	4	3	38.9
1929	3rd	1	1	
1933	4th	1	4	51.3
1934	6th	2	5	52.2

Mildred Brouilette's World tournament record shows 82-46-40.8% in 13 tournaments; had 82 victories in championship division, placing her 3rd on the all-time victory list of 1980; won Minnesota Women's State Championship, 1924.

Home: Minneapolis, MI.

BROWN, AVANELLE, b. October 26, 1927. Owns an indoor court in her home, along with her husband. H. Ellis. Retired Deputy Court Clerk. S. Allen; t. one and a quarter, right handed. Has been pitching horseshoes since 1961; has pitched in Ohio State Tournament, missing only one year since; shares record for longest game pitched

Top, Gaylord Peterson with the Illinois State Tournament Team of 1908. *Center,* Southgate Courts, site of several world tournaments. *Bottom, left,* Dr. Sol Berman. *Center,* Charles Bobbitt, world champion. *Right,* Coke Bowker.

Top, left, Joe Brickler, official NHPA photographer. *Right,* Hal Brown, World Champion. *Center,* 1978 World Invitational Tournament *(Bottom row)* Jerry Schneider, Amos Hodson, Eston E. Brown. *(Center)* Jesse Gonzales. *(Top row)* Glen Henton, Walter Ray Williams, Jr., Bob West, Carl Steinfeldt, Mark Siebold. *Bottom,* Bob Brown with the New York State Championship team of the early 30s.

at 144 shoes; high game 62%, and highest tournament 43%; won games from many top players including Sue Gillespie Kuchcinski, Bonnie Siebold, Gary Roberts and Lester Rose; won about 150 trophies, including Pike County Women's League; member of team league champions and several class championships; played in tournaments in many states, including 7 world tournaments; presently is Vice-President of Pike County Horseshoe Club. Home 22531 State Route 335, Waverly, OH 45690.

BROWN, DAN, b. January 20, 1966. Student. S. Allen; t. one and a quarter, right handed. Started playing 8 years ago; won 2 Class A championships, the Diamondale Open 5-0-62% and Burr Oak 5-1-56%; was 11th in Class A of the world tournament in 1979 hitting 60%; in 1980 moved up to 9th with 64%; won Class B of the Greenville Ringer Classic with his highest percentage ever 67.2%; highest single game was in Ringer Classic with 78% in 1979. Home: Route 7, Fruit Ridge Drive, Defiance, OH 43512.

BROWN, DEAN, California State Championship, 1926, 1928, 1938, 1939. S. Gordon; t. one and three quarters. Started pitching horseshoes in 1922 and for many years was regarded as one of California's best players; in world tournament competition ranks 23rd on all time victory list in the championship division, having won 259, lost 143, averaged 74.5% ringers and averaged 489 points qualifying; a 1930 report indicated that he pitched 201 ringers in a 50 point game against Guy Zimmerman in unofficial match and lost to Guy who hit 205. The account did not relate the number of shoes thrown, but the official record is 194, far less than their game. Home: Long Beach, CA.

BROWN, DWIGHT, attended Ohio State University for 3 years, receiving B.S. and M.S. degrees in music from Miami University; directed Greenville Band for 52 years, conducting regular concerts at City Park and County Fair; was president of local unit of Musician's Union for 26 years; taught in Greenville school system 37 years; several years held position of Superintendent of Greenville City Park and devoted full time to this after retirement from school system in 1964; through his efforts and those of Levi Brumbaugh and Cricket Coppock of Darke County Horseshoe Club, the Ohio State Horseshoe Pitching Tournament was held in Greenville for the first time in 1957, and has returned to Greenville each year since; he continued to work closely with the Darke County Horseshoe Club in his capacity as Park Superintendent, until his death in 1974; the Greenville Open, a spring warmup tournament was held annually from 1959 through 1970; the prestigious Greenville Ringer Classic was first held in 1963 and has been held annually since that time; his efforts contributed heavily to the success of all the tournaments and in identifying Greenville to many as the horseshoe pitching capital of the world; in 1963 he was honored by receiving the VFW "Outstanding Citizen" award; the Darke County Horseshoe Club dedicated the 1977 World Tournament to Dwight Brown and E. J. "Cricket" Coppock, the two men were the moving force in Greenville's success in hosting world tournaments in 1962, 1964, 1972, 1977; was awarded the NHPA 1972 Achievement Award.

BROWN, ELLIS, b. September 19, 1926. Member—Ohio League Team Champions, 1961. W. Avanelle. Builder, School bus driver and Lumber Store clerk. S. Gordon; t. one and a quarter, right handed. Built a 50 × 16 court in his home in 1974; past President of the Pike County Club and has pitched since 1957; as a member of Pike County Team, 1961 won the Ohio Team League; is a 45% pitcher whose highest tournament was 52%; highest game was 71.7% against Ralph Jennings. Home: 22531 State Route 335, Waverly, OH 45690.

BROWN, ESTON E., b. October 11, 1920. Single. Sales—Automotive Parts. S. Gordon or Allen; t. one and a quarter, right handed. Has played horseshoes for 45 years, for 25 years played league and tournament competition and for 20 years has been an NHPA member and contestant; served 8 years as President of Orange City Horseshoe Club, Vice-President of the Southern California Horseshoe Pitchers Association and Secretary of World Invitational Committee; pitched in local tournaments until 1933 winning 1933, 1934 Oregon State Boy's Championship; qualified and competed with men in both years averaging above 50% ringers; pitched from 40 feet, and recalls that stakes were shorter than the present 14 inches; originated and formed the City of Orange horseshoe Club and established many beginners leagues and tournaments; along with Amos Hodson organized the World Invitational Horseshoe Tournament at Los Angeles County Fair, an annual event beginning in 1978; high tournament record of 75% and a high single game of 96.6%; among Class A Championships are 1969 Clark Bell Open and 1978 Elmer Beller Open. Home: 1142 Fay Lane, Anaheim, CA 92805.

BROWN, FRED, b. March 25, 1938. W. Helen; children—Marv, Dan, Amy. Maintenance Clerk for General Motors. S. Allen; t. reverse three quarters, right handed. Has played over 30 years, 10 in NHPA competition; pitched in Class A World Tournament, 1976 hitting his highest average of 67.2%, and a high game of 82.5%; has won many class titles. Home: Route 7, Fruit Ridge Drive, Defiance, OH 43512.

BROWN, GAROLD, Kansas State Champion 1937, winning 20, lost 3 with record of 65%; and in 1943, won 7, lost 0, with a record of 63%.

BROWN, GLENN R., b. June 10, 1935, Vice-President, Eastern Pennsylvania Association. Wife and 3 children. Tool Grinder. S. Gordon; t. one and a quarter, current ringer percentage, 63%. Has been playing most of his life, 21 years in organized play; runs tournaments in New Freedom and York County; tournament titles are York County Champion, 1962, 1963; highest tournament average, 66.4%, in Pennsylvania State Tournament, 1968; highest single game 83% at York County Tournament, 1962. Home: Route 3, Box 100, Felton, PA 17322.

BROWN, HAL, b. June 21, 1947. Boys World Champion, 1960 with 7-0-55.9%. W. Sue; children—Ty, Heather, Anissa. Farmer; graduated from Purdue University college of Agriculture, 1969. S. Allen; t. one and a quarter, right handed. Tied for 2nd place in world tournament, 1961; won Indiana Boys State Championship, 1960, 1961; for 4 years was undefeated at Purdue University in SCA intramural horseshoes from 1966 through 1969. Home: Rural Route 1, Box 169A, Mulberry, IN 46058.

BROWN, JESSE E., b. July 14, 1937. First Vice-President Texas Horseshoe Pitchers Association. W. Mary Margaret; children—Jesse Jr., Mindy, Jennifer. Major U.S. Army, Retired; truck owner and operator. S. Ohio Pro; t. one and a quarter, right handed. Has played for 35 years, played in tournaments 3 years; was third Vice-President of Texas HPA and League Director of Lakeside Horseshoe Club in San Antonio in 1980; President of Lakeside Club, 1978; believes future of horseshoes lies in promotion of league play, handicap in particular. Home: 4806 El Presidio, San Antonio, TX 78233.

BROWN, JOHN L., b. November 1, 1930. W. Carol; children—Jon, Eric. S. Ohio "O"; t. one and three quarters, right handed. Has played for 42 years, averages about 58% ringers and plays everywhere he can find a tournament; Vice-President of local club; helps with local events and travels to all parts of country for world tournaments, Valley of the Sun Mesa Arizona, Carolina Dogwood Festival in Statesville, North Carolina and elsewhere; won many class titles and has beaten many Class A contenders. Home: 1536 Graf Street, Lancaster, OH 43130.

BROWN, LYLE, Iowa State Champion, 1938. Started pitching in 1919; in world tournament in Des Moines, 1922, finished third behind Frank Lundin and Frank Jackson with an 11-4 record; defeated world champion Lundin 50-48 for Lundin's only loss; won the Nebraska interstate title defeating John Paxton of Fairfield in the playoff in 1926. Pitched the Ohio shoe.

BROWN, MARV, b. August 10, 1963. Ohio Boys State Champion, 1978, set state record for highest tournament average of 84%. Son of Fred and Helen Brown. Student S. Allen; t. reverse three quarters, right handed. Dethroned defending champion Randy Hymer 50-25 with a game of 82.7% in 1978; won Class B World Championship, 1979 with 5-0-69%; won Greenville Ringer Classic, 1980 with 5-0-77.7%; made World Tournament Championship Division with qualifying score of 249 and 79% ringers; in round robin play record was 6-5-67% with a

6th place finish; has games of 86.5% and 89.5%. Home: Route 7, Fruit Ridge Drive, Defiance, OH 43512.

BROWN, MAYNARD P., b. Sept. 3, 1917. Vermont State Champion 13 times. W. Estelle; children—Roger L., David H. Pharmacist. S. Ohio; t. one and three quarters, right handed. Has pitched horseshoes all his life; has not played in tournament competition since 1971 after having a heart attack; in 1951 state tournament he set a state record with a high game of 83.3%; in 1965 his 70.6% for a tournament was a state record; Brown and Fred Butler set a state record with 9 four-deads in one game; career highs were 71.5% for a tournament and 85.7% for a game; longest string of consecutive doubles in tournament play was 12; won the Brattleboro title 8 times, the Southern Vermont title 12 times and finished 2nd in New England tournament, 1954; played in New England 5 times; served as President of Vermont Horseshoe Pitchers Association as well as President of Brattleboro Horseshoe Club; in 1965 world tournament at Keene, New Hampshire he qualified with 65.3% and finished 6th in Class B with 60.2%. Vermont State Championship record:

Year	Won	Lost	R%
1939	11	0	56.0
1947	10	1	54.0
1948	10	1	58.0
1950	11	0	62.0
1951	11	0	67.5
1952	11	0	62.0
1953	10	1	67.8
1954	11	0	69.3
1956	9	0	62.2
1965	7	0	70.6
1966	6	1	66.5
1969	7	0	59.7
1970	6	1	55.9

Home: 43 Fairview Street, Brattleboro, VT 05301.

BROWN, RHONDA, Georgia Women's State Champion, 1978.

BROWN, ROBERT, b. January 3, 1907. New York State Champion, 1931, 1932, 1935. W. Vera M.; children—Lawrence, Carol Metcalf. t. one and a quarter, right handed. Pitched for 12 years; President of New York Horseshoe Pitchers Association, also held office of State Secretary; member of New York Hall of Fame; highest tournament average was 73.8%; in state tournament, 1935 he won 34 and lost 6 hitting 69.7% with 1,761 ringers and 610 doubles out of 2,524 shoes pitched; had 4 games over 80%; Brown and Vito Filiccia went 120 shoes in the final game with Brown hitting 93 ringers and Filiccia 91; Brown's 36 doubles in that game was called the world record at that time for one game; set a state qualifying record in 1935 with 483 points for 200 shoes; high game of 86.5% was a state record. Brown's 8 year record in state tournament play:

Year	Won	Lost	Shoes	Ringers	Ringer%	Finish
1926	19	10	1842	604	32.7	5th
1927	23	11	2070	782	37.7	7th
1928	15	18	2194	866	39.4	10th
1930	28	16	2800	1322	47.2	2nd
1931	38	8	2736	1289	47.1	1st
1932	28	2	1606	879	54.3	1st
1933	32	4	2068	1327	63.4	2nd
1935	34	6	2524	1761	69.7	1st
	217	75	17,840	8,824	49.4	

Brown lost the title to Vito Filiccia in 1936; in title game Vito hit 79.6% to Brown's 77.2%, the best game in state history and one which saw 26 four-deads going 118 shoes. Brown quit playing in 1939. (d). September 10, 1973. Home: 4456 West Scioto Street, R.D. 2, Scio, NY 15880.

BROWN, ROGER, b. August 8, 1912. W. Flora; child—Charles. Retired. S. Ohio; t. one and three quarters, right handed. Has been involved in horseshoe pitching for 55 years; is a superb and sought after score keeper; member of Washington County Club. Home: Penn Street, Box 26, Pennsville, OH 43770.

BROWNELL, THOMAS R., b. April 22, 1923 (deceased). New York State Champion Six times; Member—New York HPA Hall of Fame. W. Shirley M. Palmieri; child Thomas. Manager of Drafting and Documentation, General Electric Co. Fast Breeder Reactor Department; U.S. Army, 1943-1946, European theatre. Started a string of 4 consecutive titles in 1948 averaging 75% ringers; in 1954 averaged 79.1%, in 1955 78.3% and in 1956 76.1%; established 2 state records with Carl Steinfeldt with 146 shoes in one game and 38 four-deads in one game; tournament average in 1954 was 79.1% was a state record at the time although broken since; finished 3rd in world tournament play in 1955 averaging 78.2% ringers; in all world tournament play he won 140 games, lost 149, averaged 75.9% ringers and 503 points qualifying; elected Secretary-Treasurer of New York State Horseshoe Pitchers Association in 1954; some personal highs include 44 consecutive ringers, 49 ringers out of 50 shoes, 96 ringers out of 100 shoes, 50 four-deads in a world tournament game of 96.9% with 31 out of 32 and a New York State qualifying score of 270; other tournament wins include Fulton County in 1937, with 54.9% and 75.8% in 1939, New York State Fair Open with 75.5%; in World Tournament, 1948 averaged 80.9% for 31 games and finished in 5th place; one of a group of Americans who went to South Africa in 1974 and pitched as part of a sports exchange. Home: 2244 Bello Avenue, San Jose, CA 95125.

BROWNING, CARL, Maine State Champion, 1948.

BRUCE, CLAIR H., b. January 14, 1932. W. Ruth; children—Dennis, Carol. Right of Way Representative. S. Imperial; t. one and three quarters, right handed. Has been pitching for 30 years, in tournaments for 17 years; served as Tournament Director for New Castle Horseshoe Club for 10 years; in World Tournament, 1969 placed 8th in the world with record 23-12-78.9%; hit a high game of 90% in world tournament play in 1972; composite world tournament record in championship division is 84 wins, 126 lost, 73% ringers and average qualifying score of 505; finished 3rd place 3 times in Pennsylvania State Tournament; hitting in the 70% plus area he has won many tournaments; won the Brady's Run title in 1980 with 6-1-70.6%; serves as officer and promoter on local and state level in Pennsylvania; helped to build the Scottland Meadows Park Courts at Newcastle, which are the scene of annual tournaments. Home: 119 Glen Moore Boulevard, New Castle, PA 16105.

BRUMBAUGH, LEVI, (dec.) January 8, 1966. Employed Greenville Post Office for 34 years. Close friend of Ted Allen, 10 time World Horseshoe Pitching Champion during years 1933 through 1959; together with Cricket Coppock, Chick Coppess, Wayne and Floyd Coblentz, Walter Fender and others organized the Darke County Horseshoe Club in 1956, and was elected the first club President and served for several years;

through his influence Greenville, Ohio became a leading center of horseshoe interest; the Ohio State Tournament was held in Greenville in 1957, and has returned each year since, the Greenville Open was added in 1958, and continued annually until 1970; the Greenville Ringer Classic was added in 1963 and became one of top tournaments in the country; through the efforts of Brumbaugh, Coppock and Brown the 1962 World Tournament was held in Greenville for the first time, returning in 1964, 1972 and 1977.

BRUMFIELD, GENE R., b. September 17, 1928. Indiana State Champion, 1956 with 12-1-76.8%. W. Joan; children—Bill, Gary. Skilled tradesman—Delco-Remy, Division of General Motors of Anderson. S. Gordon; t. one and a quarter, right handed. Has played for about 30 years, and has promoted and advertised the game; built courts for factory and union parks, conducted clinics, pitched on television and appeared on sports shows; came in 2nd in first NHPA tournament in which he played; qualified 13 and finished 11th in his first world tournament in 1957 in Salt Lake City; has pitched in championship division 5 times; averaged 80.4% for 35 games in 1961; best percentage for 35 games was 81.3% and highest finish in world tournament was 3rd; hit a high game of 95% in Indiana State tournament; has played world champions, Allen, Isais, Titcomb, Reno, Focht, Day, Hohl and Steinfeldt; played Titcomb in 1956 while he was California champ, and led Titcomb 40-20 and threw 34 consecutive ringers after he had 40 points—Titcomb won game 50-48 overcoming the 34 straight and coming from 20 points. Enjoys sports and cars; has had success in track, baseball, basketball, boxing, racing and shooting. Home: Route 1, Box 330, Markleville, IN 46056.

BRUNDIGE, C. C., lived in Columbus, Ohio. Played in championship division of world tournament play several times, with a career record of 95 wins, 110 losses and 46.2% ringers.

BRUNDIGE, FRED, lived in Lake Worth, Florida. Played in the 1920's in championship division of world tournaments, with a record of 118 wins, lost 116 games and averaged 43.9% ringers.

BRUNEY, JAYNE, Texas Women's State Champion, 1976.

BRUST, FRED M. lived in Columbus, Ohio. Member, NHPA Hall of Fame, 1971; World Champion, 1919., winning 53 games and losing only one, scoring 367 ringers; won at least 128 games in 6 world tournaments and lost at least 54; available ringer percentage is 28.7%. World tournament record:

Year	Finish	Won	Lost	R%
1919	1st	53	1	367R
1920	3rd	21	3	412R
1921	9th	12	9	355R
1922	3rd	18	3	457R
1923W	23rd	10	19	29.1%
1023S	36th	1	10	28.2%

FRED M. BRUST continued

Was considered one of the founding fathers of the NHPA, and served as Vice-President in 1919; founded the Ohio Horseshoe Company, where he designed and manufactured the Ohio Pitching shoe, the company is still producing 2 popular models of pitching shoes.

BRYANT, HOWARD, Dayton Power & Light. S. Ohio; t, reverse three quarters, right handed. Has played in Class A division of Ohio state tournaments; has hit a 90% game and averages 70% plus in tournament playing; made championship division of the world tournament in 1961 where he won 7, lost 28, and averaged 64.5% ringers for 33rd place finish. Home: 634 McArthur Way, Washington Court House, OH 43160.

BRYANT, MARSHALL, 1970 South Carolina State Champion with record of 8-1-60.2%.

BUCHERT, CINDY, Washington Girls State Champion, 1974 with 26.9% record, 1976 26.4% and 1977 33.3%. Home: 7248 27th Avenue Northeast, Seattle, WA 98115.

BUCKERT, JOSEPH, One of the founders of the National League of Horseshoe and Quoit Pitchers of the United States in 1919, and was a Vice-president in its original slate of officers. Home: Binford, North Dakota.

BUCKMAN, A. J., Was active in World Tournament play in the 1920's and compiled a world tournament record of 80 wins, 37 losses and a ringer percentage of 44.4%.

BUELL, C. LEO, b. December 20, 1930. World Class D Champion, 1978, with 58.8%, winning 10 straight games. W. Joan; children—Christina, Lauretta, Catherine, Mark. Production Manager for Builders Components, Inc. S. Allen; t. three quarters, right handed. Has played for 30 years, 15 in tournaments; was 2nd in Class B in Iowa State Tournament, 1980; in Preimesberger Arena tournament hit highest game with 78% including 17 ringers out of the last 20 shoes; is among the top 200 NHPA averages. Enjoys fishing, bow hunting and cabinet making. Home: 1234 Arthur Street, Iowa City, IO 55240.

BUHLER, MARGE, Women's State Champion in Michigan, 4 times: 1965, 1967 4-1-44.0%; 1969, 1970 9-1-37.2%.

BULLION, JAMES, a Class A contender in Virginia tournaments; averages in the 60%, can hit a 70% tournament and an 80% game; has won many tournament and class titles. Home: Route 2, Box 470, Evington, VA 24550.

BUNGE, TRUDI, Indiana Girls State Championship, 1976.

BUNNER, CHARLES MELVIN, b. February 26, 1935. President, West Virginia Horseshoe Pitchers Association. W. Betty; children—Terry, Mona, Linda, Mel. S. Ohio; t. one and a quarter, right handed. U.S. Postal Clerk—MSG e8 U.S. Army Retired. Has played horseshoes for 30 years, a NHPA member and tournament player for 3 years; is a member of West Virginia HPA publicity committee and First Vice-President of the Monongahela Valley HPA; during 20 years in the Army he played in tournaments in Alaska, South Korea, South Vietnam, West Germany; won singles championship in Fort Lee, Virginia, 1964 and the doubles title in Indiantown Gap, Pennsylvania; in West Germany won singles championship in Pirmasens and runnerup spot at Kaiserslautern in 1968; won a doubles tournament in South Vietnam, 1969; single high game is 76.3% in 1980 NHPA sanctioned league; in 1980 his 65% qualifying score put him in Class A of West Virginia State Tournament; received from President Carter an Outstanding Community Achievement Award for his involvement in community affairs, more specifically his activity in horseshoes in 1979; with 15 other players, helped form Monongahela Valley HPA and build 12 permanent courts in East Marion Recreational Facility; author of song "Shoes of Steel". Enjoys bowling. Home: 508 Ohio Avenue, Fairmont, W VA 26554.

BURCH, ARTHUR H., b. May 8, 1939. Vice-President, Indiana Horseshoe Pitchers Association. W. Patti; children—Lisa Pulliam, Mellani. Disabled test mechanic—Cummins Engine Company, for 18½ years. S. No preference; t. one and a quarter, right handed. Has played for 25 years, started playing in tournaments 1969; qualified in 20th place in World Tournament, 1973; had high tournament of 68% and 2 NHPA sanctioned games above 80%; President of Scottsburg Club; fondest memories are of the 1973 World Tournament at Eureka, California when he won games from Glen Henton and Jim Knisley, scored 31 against Elmer Hohl and extended Art Tyson 104 shoes before losing 48-50, Home: Route 3, Box 172, Scottsburg, IN 47170.

BURGE, WILLIS L., b. November 6, 1929. Vice-President, Steelmark Horseshoe Club, Mingo Junction, Ohio. W. Evelyn; children—Richard, Barbara, Daniel. Steelworker. S. Allen; t. one and a quarter, right handed. Has played for 40 years, has played in NHPA tournaments for 6 years; won Class A championship in Petersburg, West Virginia Open, 1974; won Smithfield Open Class A title in 1975; won class titles in Washington County Open and Steelmark Open as well as several trophies for runnerup spots; played in World Tournaments, 1976–1980. Home: 3043 Orchard Street, Weirton, W VA 26062.

BURGESS, REV. MARVIN E., b. December 16, 1907. Chaplain of the NHPA; Texas State Champion 9 times; Member, Texas HPA Hall of Fame. W. Eleanor; children—Linda Lenore, Brian Robert, Johnathan Paul. Pastor-Chaplain. S. Hohl; t. two full turns, right handed. Has played for 50 years, 30 in organized play of all kinds and 22 in NHPA events; his Texas State Champion record is as follows: 1959 with 8-1 record, 1961 with 5-1-45.6%, 1963 with 3-0, 1964 with 3-1, 1965 with 6-0-62.5%, 1966 with 6-0-54%, 1967 with 5-1-58.1%, 1969 with 8-1-54.5%, 1970 with 9-1-47.8%; in 1965 state tournament average of 62.5% is his best for an entire tournament and his highest single game is 80%; in Southgate tournament in 1966 he qualified at 72%; in Texas chapter held office of President from 1961 through 1965, and is now Patriarch; conducts morning worship services on Sundays during the World Tournament. Home: 900 14th—Route 2 Ballinger, TX 76921.

BURGESS, RONNIE L., b. May 28, 1952. Junior Boys State Champion, 1964, 1966. W. Katie; children—Jeff, Jeanne, Kari, Norm, Onna, Austin. Owner of Retail Stores ReMemories. S. Allen; t. one and a quarter, right handed. Is a solid 70% performer with tournaments ranging from 65% through 75%; placed 3rd in Iowa Men's state championship tournament, 1976; Has a country band made up of his father, his wife and brother. Home: 218½ Main Cedar Falls, IO 50613.

BURKE, JAMES, Oregon State Champion, 1973 with 11-0-75.7%. Made championship division of world tournament in 1973, finishing 31st with 8-27-66.6%. Home: 3735 Knox Butte Road, Albany, OR 97321.

BURKE, RANDY, Oregon Boys State Champion, 1972 with 59.9% ringers. Is son of James Burke, a former state men's champion. Home: 3735 Knox Butte Road, Albany, OR 97321.

BURKETT, MELVIN E., b. August 23, 1926. Won Elk County Fair Competition, 6-0-70%, best game of 85%. W. Helen; children—Peggy Jean Swope, Susan Jane. Track man. S. Imperial; t. one and a quarter, right handed. Hit 32 consecutive ringers before scoring a point, Brookville-Western Pennsylvania Laurel Festival. Home: 21 Rock Street—Box 24, Falls Creek, Pennsylvania 15840.

BURKHARD, J. W., 1927 North Dakota State Champion.

BURNS, AGNES M., b. November 17, 1897. 1970 Tri-State Women's Title Champion at age 73 for Wyoming—Nebraska—Colorado. H. Robert, deceased; children—Margaret, Agnes, Robert, Eleanor. Housewife. S. All brands; t. has pitched them all, right handed. Set Wyoming state records for women with 952 shoes in one tournament, 110 shoes in one game, 1970. Member, International Bell Collectors. Home: 1317 Garfield, Laramie, Wyoming 82070.

BURNS, JAMES LUTHER, d. December 31, 1974. Tennessee State Champion 1969–71. W.; children—Connie, Randy, Gail. Machinist for combustion engineering. S. Imperial or Gordon; t. one and three quarters, left handed. Won 1969–70 championships with 76.6%; set state record, 90% game, 1972 Tennessee State Tournament; won Southeastern Classic, Winston-Salem, N. C., Hill City Open, Lynchburg, Va., Carolina Dogwood Festival, Statesville, N.C.; hit high game of 90.7% against Maryland State Champion Dale Carson (Hill City Open).

BURNS, ROBERT H., d. 1973, auto accident. Pitched horseshoes sixty years, won honors in Wyoming, California, Afghanistan, Iran. W. Agnes; children—Margaret, Agnes, Robert, Eleanor. Was instrumental in founding Laramie Horseshoe Club with Harold Bindschadler. Member, International Bell Collectors. Home: 1317 Garfield Street, Laramie, Wyoming 82070.

BURNS, STUART, b. October 17, 1932. N.H.P.A. Special Achievement Award (joint recipient with wife) for 1978 World Tournament, Des Moines, Iowa. W. Sue; children—Sheila, Becky Jo, T. J. Professor of literature, Drake University. S. Gordon; t. one and a quarter, ambidextrous. 1977 president, Greater Des Moines Horseshoe League. Home: 5804 Ingersoll Avenue, Des Moines, Iowa 50312.

BURNS, SUE, 1980 Iowa Women's State Champion. H. Stuart; children—Sheila, Becky Jo, T. J. Iowa State Secretary, Horseshoe Pitchers Association. N.H.P.A. Special Achievement Award (joint recipient with husband) for 1978 World Tournament, Des Moines, Iowa; won Iowa Women's Championship, 1978, 5-0-47%; 1980 championship record, 5-0-58.9%; honored by Iowa Hawkeye State Horseshoe Pitchers Association for secretarial services. Home: 5804 Ingersoll Avenue, Des Moines, Iowa 50312.

BURROW, JONES, b. April 15, 1934. Won 1980 Class A Title at Winston-Salem's Southeastern Classic, 7-1-62%. W. Jo Ann; child—Robin. Head Fixer on knitting machines, Burlington Mills. S. Ohio; t. one and a quarter, right handed. Enjoys raccoon-hunting, bowling. Home: 5624 Kerwin Circle, Kernersville, North Carolina 27284.

BUSH, MILTON, 1927 Maine State Champion. Home: Auburn, Maine.

BUSKEY, GEORGE E., b. August 25, 1909. New Hampshire State Champion, 1961–63. W. Francise; child—Diane M. Lerandeau. Retired. S. Ohio or Deadeye; t. one and three quarters, right handed. Serves as statistician, Florida State Horseshoe Pitchers Association. Enjoys golf. Home: 603 South Gate Park, Clearwater, Florida 33516.

BUSSARD, A. G., 1924 Montana State Champion.

BUSSARD, TAMMY, 1969 Indiana Girls State Champion.

BUSSEY, DICK, 1961–62 Minnesota Boys State Champion from thirty feet. 1962 record, 9-0. Home: Hibbing, Minnesota.

BUTLER, FRED T., b. February 6, 1906. Vermont State Champion fourteen times between 1941 and 1964. W. Gladys; child—Gerald. Contractor. S. Gordon or Ohio; t. one and a quarter, right handed. 1960 New England Champion; won Vermont Open, 1959–61; past president, Vermont Horseshoe Pitchers Association; high tournament, 68.8%; high game, 82%; served as commissioner of horseshoes, secretary, V.H.P.A.; helped start Bennington Club, 1965; won 98 out of 101 games, between 1958 and 1962, Brattleboro courts. Home: 307 North Street, Bennington, Vermont 05201.

BUXBAUM, DENNIS, b. October 27, 1946. Secretary, Eastern Montana Horseshoe Pitchers Association. W. Debbie; four children. Hardware store owner. S. Diamond; t. flip, left handed. Won twenty-seven trophies, averages 31% ringers. Home: Box 423, Sidney, Montana 59270.

BUYS, ROLAND LYNN, d. December 10, 1977. Past State Secretary, Utah Horseshoe Pitchers Association. W. Geneve R.; children—Marlene Pulsipher, Joe, D'Ann Tonn, Jim, Rhonda Lee. School teacher and clerk of Tooele County School Board. Right handed. Home: 408 Pioneer Avenue, Tooele, Utah 84074.

BYERS, L. J., Vice President, National Horseshoe Pitchers Association, 1919, member of first group of elected officers. Home: Coldwater, Michigan.

BYERS, SARA, 1951–52 World Champion, 7-0-44.3%, 7-0-53.5%, respectively. Played only twice in World Tournament, retired undefeated. Home: Portland, Oregon.

BYRAM, TOMMY LEE, b. August 27, 1940. 1976 Cullman County Champion. W. Donna Joyce Webb; child—Carla Joyce. Car dealer and car salvage owner. S. Deadeye or Diamond; t. one turn, right handed. Second vice-president, Alabama Horseshoe Pitchers Association; founder and president, Cullman Horseshoe Pitchers Club. Home:

Route 5—Box 440, Cullman, Alabama 35055.

BYRD, BORDEN, 1970–71 Alabama Boys State Champion, 7-0-24%, 5-0-27%. Home: Boys Ranch, Alabama.

C

CAHILL, SHIRLEY, b. September 30, 1936. New Mexico State Secretary. H. Michael; child—Edward. Engineering specialist. S. Imperial; t. flip, left handed but pitches right handed. High game, 55%, Raton, New Mexico, 1980. Home: 1324 Canyon Tr. SW, Albuquerque, New Mexico 87105.

CAIN, GINGER, Oklahoma State Secretary. H. Homer; child—Tina. Home: Route 1, Maryland, Oklahoma 74644.

CAIN, HOMER, President, Oklahoma Horseshoe Pitchers Association. Qualified in Class C, World Tournament, 1980. Home: Route 1, Maryland, Oklahoma 74644.

CAIN, TINA, 1980 Oklahoma Women's State Champion, 5-0-37.2% (first women's division competition). Won girls state championship, 14%, 1977. Home: Route 1, Maryland, Oklahoma 74644.

CALHOUN, W. J. "BILL," b. August 26, 1920. President, Alabama Horseshoe Pitchers Association. W.; three children. Director of Parks and Recreation, Opelika, Alabama. Worked to promote 1980 World Tournament, Huntsville, Alabama; pitched forty-five years, averages 40%; high game, 54.4%.

CALLAS, GEORGE, d. 1969. Was secretary-treasurer, Golden Gate Club, San Francisco. Averaged 55% with one and a quarter turn.

CAMPBELL, DON, 1974 Nevada Boys State Champion.

CAMPBELL, ZACK, b. September 5, 1915.

Secretary-treasurer, Warren County Horseshoe Club. W. Gladys; children—Lois, William, Reva, Brenda, Rose, Jack. Forge operator. S. Imperial; t. one and three quarters, right handed. Won Warren County title six times, the Xenia Club title, 1979, Ohio Class B State title, 1961, 1980, and Warren County League eight times; hit 66.8%, high game 77.8%, in state tournament, 1980; attended barber college, 1937; was precision blacksmith twenty-eight years. Home: 3129 Crestview Avenue, Lebanon, Ohio 45036.

CAMPION, CHRIS, 1975, 1978 Alberta Provincial Champion. Home: Edmonton, Alberta, Canada.

CANTRELL, RALPH D., b. July 5, 1932. Secretary, Alabama State Horseshoe Pitchers Association. W. Nancy; children—Ralph D., Jr., David L., Darrell W., Pamela E. Retired from Army. S. Gordon and Deadeye; t. single flip and one and a quarter, right handed. Finished first or second in six of the Huntsville Spring League Tournaments; high tournament, 42% (Madison County Tournament); high game, 54%. Home: 14014 Maebeth Drive, Huntsville, Alabama 35803.

CARL, BUD, 1969–70 Colorado Boys State Champion.

CARLBERG, IRWIN, deceased. 1956 Michigan State Champion. Won District of Columbia championship 1938–42, 14-1-72.3%, 602 ringers out of 832 shoes; high game, 84%, 1942; recipient of Stokes Memorial Trophy, 1965; elected vice-president, N.H.P.A., 1948. Home: Grand Rapids, Michigan.

CARLSON, CLARENCE, 1932–35 Wyoming State Champion. Record in 1935, 12-0-60.4%.

CARLSON, DENNIS, b. June 14, 1936. Tournament director, 1980 Minnesota State Tournament. Children—Denise, Dale,

Dean, Danette. Highway engineer. S. Deadeye, Clydesdale, or Ohio O; t. one and a quarter, right handed. Organized Tri-County Horseshoe Pitchers Association, 1977, one of largest clubs in U.S.; served as president, vice-president, local club. Enjoys bowling, dancing, golf. Home: 2009 Prospect Drive, St. Cloud, Minnesota 56301.

CARLSON, GLENISS, 1975 Saskatchewan Women's Provincial Champion. Home: Sturgis.

CARLSON, KAY, 1976 South Dakota Women's State Champion. Home: 4500 19th—No. 372, Boulder, Colorado 80302.

CARMACK, JOSEPH "ABE," Won 1962 Ozark Open, 9-0-71.8%. Record for championship division play in world tournament: 1964, 11-24-74.1%, 1965, 18-17-76.5%, 1967, 7-28-65.3%, 1969, 8-27-71.9%. Home: Lecoma, Missouri 65540.

CARNAHAN, WINFIELD E. "DICK," b. April 3, 1924. 1980 Class D World Champion. W. Frances; children—Jeffrey, Delbert, Daniel, Beverly. Retired. S. Imperial; t. three quarters, right handed. Won Class A Gennessee Open, the Class B Lockport Open, Class B Queen City Open, and New York State Class E, all 1973; won Class C, Eastern National, 1976; Queen City B champion, 1974; won Gennessee Open Class A, and Neoso Open Class B, 1975; set club record for doubles for three games; 92 ringers out of 120 shoes; served as president, Leroy Horseshoe Club, New York. Enjoys bowling, golf, hunting, fishing, reading, cards. Home: Route 2, Pine Terrace, Shippenville, Pennsylvania 16254.

CARNAHAN, FRANCES E., b. December 29, 1932. 1979 New York State Champion, 1980 Pennsylvania State Champion, 7-0-64.6%, 1981 and 1982. H. Winfield "Dick"; children—Jeffrey, Delbert, Daniel, Beverly. Housewife. S. Reno; t. flip, left handed. Won Class B championship of NEOSO, 1976; won Class A title, Northern Open, Canton, New York, 1977–79; won Class A championships, Queen City Open, Dave McKernon Open, 1978; won Genessee Open, 1979; won Class A title, NEOSO Open, and North Pine Grove Open, 1980; qualified for Class A, 1980 World Tournament; high game, 79.2% (Pennsylvania State Tournament). Enjoys sewing, reading, bowling, hunting, fishing, golf. Home: Route 2, Pine Terrace, Shippenville, Pennsylvania 16254.

CARR, RALPH, Colorado State Champion four times: 1940, 14-1-62%, 1944, 12-2-67%, 1945, 14-1-60.3%, 1947, 12-2-59%.

CARSON DALE, b. July 23, 1904. Maryland State Champion twenty-four times. W. Arlene; children—Ray, Donald. Retired—Revere Copper and Brass. S. Imperial; t. one and three quarters, right handed. Won Pennsylvania State Championship, 1936; Maryland State Championship, 1950–65, 1967–76; pitched against Ted Allen, Jimmy Risk, Blair Nunamaker; pitched exhibitions for President Harry Truman; won Eastern National twice; won Lakeside Open; awarded trophy as Most Improved Player, 1969 World Tournament; qualified at 538, Erie World Tournament, 1969; qualified at 550, Greenville World Tournament, 1977; hit fifty-four consecutive ringers. Enjoys gardening. Home: 2828 Herkimer Street, Baltimore, Maryland 21230.

CARTER, CATHY, Iowa Girls State Champion three times: 1977, 3-0-35%, 1978, 3-0-38%, 1979, 4-0-41.7%. Pitched in championship division, Girls World Tournament, Des Moines, Iowa, 1978. Home: 1907 Westside Drive, Council Bluffs, Iowa 51501.

CARTER, JOSEPH S., b. October 30, 1915. Listed in top 200 in U.S. in N.H.P.A. averages. W. Maxine; children—Kenneth, Jack, Jane, Tommy. Railroader. S. Allen; t.

one and a quarter, right handed. Won 1980 Beaver County Open; won Class B, Moundsville, hitting two games above 80% with 68% tournament average, 1979. Home: Route 1, Mingo Junction, Ohio 43938.

CARTER, ROSEMARY GIBSON, b. 1959. 1973 Girls World Champion, Illinois Women's State Champion, 1974–76. H. S. Allen; t. one and three quarters, right handed. Pitched in Junior Girls division, World Tournament, 1971–76; averages 55%–65%. Home: Florida.

CASH, JACKIE, 1975 Alabama Women's State Champion, 3-0-18.8%. Home: Boys Ranch, Alabama.

CASH, J. W., 1962 Texas State Champion, 6-1-43.2%. S. Allen; t. one and a quarter, right handed. Played in pro-celebrity tournament, San Antonio, Texas, shown on Channel 9-TV, teamed with Col. Harlan Sanders against state champion Ottie Reno and John Davidson: Reno-Davidson won by one point, 1974; won several Class A titles.

CASH, ROBERT, 1947 Ohio State Champion, 13-2-73.3%. Posted record of 9-22-66%, championship division, World Tournament, 1948; was member, Cleveland Horseshoe Club.

CASTOR, GARY, 1970 New Hampshire Boys State Champion, 5-0-44.5%. Home: 221 Cheshire Homes, Keene, New Hampshire 03431.

CAVE, LUELLA, b. October 20, 1942. Elected Most Improved Player, three times, local league. H. Leslie; children—Carolyn, Cindy, Kevin, Corine, Carmella, Christy. Housewife/egg picker. S. Gordon; t. flip, right handed. Finished fourth in class of twelve, championship flight, 1980 Minnesota State Tournament; high game, 80%. Enjoys sewing, playing guitar anad organ. Home: Route 2, Rice, Minnesota 56367.

CAVIN, RAY, b. January 7, 1912. Won Missouri State Title, Senior Division, 1978. W. Bonnie; children—Danny, Karen Sue. Retired. S. Allen or Deadeye; t. one and a quarter, right handed. Runnerup, Missouri State Tournament, five times, hit 72% and tied for title losing playoff, 1966; won 80 championship trophies, tournament career spans thirty years; served twenty-seven years as tournament director, and is past president, St. Joseph Pony Express Horseshoe Club. Home: 1824 Holman Street, St. Joseph, Missouri 64501.

CESSNA, RANDY, b. March 8, 1963. 1978 Illinois Boys State Champion. Student. S. Allen; t. three quarters, right handed. Started pitching in 1974; championship record: (out of class of ten) 41 ringers, 131 points in 50-shoe count-all game, high game, 82%. Enjoys coin collecting, basketball. Home: 101 West Street—Box 145, Potomac, Illinois 61865.

CHABOYER, JEAN, b. June 4, 1936. Won Manitoba Singles Championship and doubles title, 8-0-50%, 1979. W. Margaret; children—Clement, Muriel, Russell, Junior, Derek. Skilled laborer. S. Deadeye or Imperial; t. three quarter, right handed. Vice-president, Manitoba Horseshoe Players Association; president, St. Laurent Horseshoe Club; finished second, Provincial singles, 1975, 1977, and third, 1978; high tournament, 65%; high game, 80%; won singles titles, Eddystone, Brandon Fair, Stonewall, Morris, Bourkevale tournaments, 1979; won several doubles tournaments with Bill Morin. Home: P.O. Box 35, St. Laurent, Manitoba, Canada ROC 250.

CHADWICK, HARRY E., b. July 13, 1936. State Police Olympic Champion (Ohio), 1979–80. W. Betty; children—Sandy, Darlene, Harry, Beverly, Michael, Marjorie. Police officer. S. Allen; t. one and three quarters, right handed. Played in Lancaster Pre-World Warmup against Elmer Hohl, Curt Day, Wilbur Kabel, Glen Riffle, missed playoff by one point, 1972; won three Class A titles, London Open, Greenfield Open, Columbus Open; averaged 100 points per game in 50-shoe count-all league play thirteen consecutive years; member, N.H.P.A.; was all-league football player, all-Ohio baseball player, and member of swimming and basketball teams in high school; holds degree in law enforcement—police administration; served in Army two years; is seven-gallon donor in American Red Cross Blood Program. Enjoys bowling, softball, ping pong, golf. Home: 2298 Forest Creek, Columbus, Ohio 43223.

CHAMBERS, RALPH B., 1972–73 South Carolina State Champion. Home: Route 2, Box 45, Rock Hill, South Carolina 29730.

CHAMBERS, TOM, JR., 1980 Iowa Boys State Champion, 6-1-65.2%. Home: Carlson, Iowa.

CHAPELLE, BARRY, b. May 21, 1942. N.H.P.A. Regional Director for Oregon, Washington, Idaho. W. Barbara; children—Connie, Kristen. High school math teacher and coach. S. Allen; t. one and three quarters, right handed. Serves as secretary-treasurer. Oregon Horseshoe Pitchers Association, president, Pacific Northwest Horseshoe Pitchers Association; pitched in Junior Division, World Tournament, in 1950s; won Class C World Championship (Men's), World Tournament, 1973; finished third, Oregon State Tournament, 1973, 1978; administered the only loss to Walter Ray "Deadeye" Williams, Hermiston, Oregon Tournament, hit over 70% for eight consecutive tournaments, 1978; high tournament, 75%. Home: 2716 S. E. 61st Street, Portland, Oregon 97206.

CHAPELLE, CLETUS C., b. August 3, 1912. Member NHPA Hall of Fame. Oregon State Champion, 1941, 1943, 1947, 1950. W. Daisy; children—Vicki Chapelle Winston, Barry. Retired mail carrier. S. Allen or Deadeye; t. one and a quarter, first forty years, now one and three quarters. Pitched fifty-four years, thirty years in N.H.P.A. play, in state play since 1928; member of Portland Club since 1940; past president, past vice-president, N.H.P.A.; served as president, secretary-treasurer, Oregon State H.P.A. and Portland Club, and vice-president, Northwest H.P.A.; member, National Hall of Fame Committee; finished eighth, World Tournament, Murray City, Utah, 1954; hit 82.6% and tied 9-9 with Ted Allen at end of 20 shoes, killed 58 of Allen's world record seventy-two consecutive ringers, 1955; high game, 96.8%; played in championship division, World Tournament, 84-96-69.5%, qualifying average 491 points. Home: 7018 North Greenwich Avenue, Portland, Oregon 97217.

CHAPELLE, DAISY, Statistician, Oregon State Horseshoe Pitchers Association. H. Cletus; children—Vicki Winston, Barry. Housewife. Home: 7018 North Greenwich Avenue, Portland, Oregon 97217.

CHAPMAN, GEORGE H., Montana State Champion, 1975–77, 1979 (1979, 10-1-59.1%, 80% high game). Home: P.O. Box 31, Laurel, Montana 59044.

CHAPMAN, R. R., 1923 Oregon State Champion (first recognized state champion).

CHAPMAN, ROBERT W., b. August 18, 1933. 1971 Vermont State Champion. W. Suzanne; children—Laura Lynn, John Robert. School teacher and coach. S. Gordon; t. three quarters, right handed. Championship record, 7-1-54.3%; won Northern Vermont championship; coaches cross country and track for high school; I.A.A.B.O. basketball official; sports film photographer covering football. Home: 83 Puritan Road, Buzzard's Bay, Massachusetts 02532 and

Tabor's Point, West Swanton, Vermont 05488.

CHAPPEL, BOBBY, 1969 Ohio Boys State Champion, 3-0-67.3%. Home: Route 1, Camden, Ohio 45311.

CHASE, TED, 1965 Wyoming State Championg, 7-0-53.4%.

CHERRIER, RON, d. August 1971. Minnesota State Champion ten times. Baker. S. Gordon; t. one and a quarter, right handed. Championship record: 1946, 9-2-63%, 1949, 15-0-71.3%, 1959, 13-0-73.5%, 1951, 11-1-66.4%, 1953, 14-0-69.9%, 1954, 15-0-67%, 1955, 6-1-67.6%, 1956, 11-0-67.8%, 1957, 11-0-70.4%, 1959, 9-2-61%; played in championship division, World Tournaments, 159-257-67.3%, averaged 482 points in qualifying rounds, 1947–61.

CHERRIX, CHARLES, 1976–77 Maryland Boys State Champion, 5-0-28.3% (1977).

CHERRY, ALVIN B., b. January 19, 1934. President, Middlesex Horseshoe Club, New Jersey. W. Roberta; child—Randy. Director of Knickerbocker Toy Company. S. Imperial; t. one and a quarter, right handed. Won Class D World Championship, Bristol, Pennsylvania, 1976; won Middlesex Club championship four times; elected to Middlesex Club's Hall of Fame, 1979; past president of New Jersey H.P.A., past vice-president and tournament director, N.J.H.P.A. Home: 320 Lee Place, Plainfield, New Jersey 07063.

CHESTER, WILLIAM "BILL," b. February 6, 1925. Kansas State Secretary. W. Lois; children—David, Terrie, Mark, Bettymae, John. Professional educator. S. Ohio O; t. one and a half, right handed. Served as secretary-treasurer, Leavenworth City Club, ten years; received first K.H.P.A. award for leadership, 1979; high tournament, 52.5%; high game, 72.8%; won Leavenworth City Championship, 1970; pitched for fifty years.

Home: 805 Middle, Leavenworth, Kansas 66048.

CHILDRESS, FRED, Member, Virginia HPA Fall of Fame. W. Shirley. Sales engineer, Lynchburg Foundry Company. S. Allen; t. one and a quarter, right handed. Won Tri-County Tournament championship, Lynchburg, 1961, qualified with 96%, 48 out of 50; played Southeastern Classic against Harold Reno, lost 50-47, 1965; served as president, vice-president, Hill City Horseshoe Club, vice-president, Virginia State H.P.A.; director, Southeastern States Regional, N.H.P.A. Enjoys golf (six handicap). Home: 1527 Fairway Place, Lynchburg, Virginia 24503.

CHIPMAN, HAROLD, Member, Utah Hall of Fame.

CHRISTENSEN, H. M., 1933 South Dakota State Champion.

CHRISTENSEN, RUBY, 1967 Iowa Women's State Champion. H. Allen; children—Richard, Robert, Rodney, Janet. Postal clerk; s. Gordon; t. flip, right handed. Home: 104 Truman Road, Anita, Iowa 50020.

CHRISTIANSEN, ARNOLD, South Dakota State Champion, 1941, 23-0-59.1%, 1964, 7-1-63.8%, 1965, 9-2-61.8%, 1966, 11-0-62.9%.

CHRISTIANSEN, TED, b. November 5, 1901, d. April 17, 1975. Helped organize Hillsboro Horseshoe Club, served as first president. W. Gertrude; children—Rozella, Rodney. Public health sanitarian, thirty years, educator, ten years. S. Allen; t. one and a quarter, right handed. Home: 470 Birchwood Drive, Hillsboro, Oregon 97123.

CHRISTLIEB, I. C. Helped organize Minnesota Horseshoe Pitchers Association, 1919. Pharmacist. Home: Hutchinson, Minnesota.

CHURCH, FRED, b. July 16, 1924. 1978, 1980 North Carolina State Champion, 6-1-59.2%. W. Nancy; children—Renee, Mark. Electronic technician. S. Allen; t. one and a quarter, right handed. Won Winston-Salem championship, 1953, 1976–78; played in Class A, 1980 World Tournament, Huntsville, Alabama, 6-25-60%; tied for state title, lost playoff to J. B. Fuller, 1979; played organized shoes since 1938. Home: 4401 Fernbook Drive, Winston-Salem, North Carolina.

CLARK, ALEX, b. June 30, 1910. 1960 Michigan State Champion. W. Alma. Electrician, Ford Motor Company, 43 years. S. Gordon and Lee; t. one and three quarters, right handed. Championship record, 8-0-70%, runnerup for state title five times; member, Michigan Wolverine Horseshoe Pitchers Association Hall of Fame; averaged 75%, many games in 85–90% bracket. Enjoys golf. Home: 29565 Hennepin, Garden City, Michigan 48135.

CLARK, BONNIE JO, b. June 24, 1964. 1979, 1980 Washington Girls State Champion. Student, South Kitsap High School. S. Gordon; t. flip, right handed. Championship record, 27.9%, high game, 36.3%; awarded sportsmanship trophy, Port Orchard Club, 1979; serves as secretary-treasurer, Port Orchard Horseshoe Club. Home: 4842 Dana Drive SE, Port Orchard, Washington 98366.

CLARK, CHARLES, b. April 12, 1914. President, West Virginia HPA. W. Jean; child—Charlotte Bonar. Retired mail carrier. S. Gordon; t. one and a quarter, right handed. President, Moundsville Club; high tournament, 7-0-42%, West Virginia State Tournament, 1971; high game, 62%; won Moundsville City League, 1972; helps promote Annual Moundsville Open Tournament; inducted into West Virginia Horseshoe Pitchers Hall of Fame. Home: 1202 Ninth Street, Moundsville, West Virginia 26041.

CLARK, NAT B., b. May 24, 1922. Member, Western Montana HPA Hall of Fame. W. Joy; child—Mike. Cattle rancher. S. Imperial; t. one and a quarter, right handed. Secretary-treasurer, Western Montana Horseshoe Pitchers Association; fifth member to be inducted into Hall of Fame. Home: McLeod, Montana 59052.

CLARK, PETER ALAN, b. September 28, 1966. Son of Mr. and Mrs. Robert L. Clark. Student, Marcus Whitman Junior High School. S. Deadeye; t. reverse one and a quarter, right handed. Winner, Washington Boys State Championship, 1979, 1980. Winner, 3 times, Pacific Northwest Junior Boys Championship. Runnerup, 1980 World Tournament. Highest Ringer Percentage, 83.33% for tournament, 96.2% for game. In a 1978 game with Bob Bartlett these state records were set: Most doubles, 80; most ringers, 100; most four-deads, 30; most consecutive four-deads, 6; most shoes, 240. Home: 4842 Dana Drive SE, Port Orchard, WA 98366.

CLARK, PORTER, Winner 6 times, Maine State Championship: 1955 15-1-59.7%, 1956 6-1-64%, 1959 11-9-63.5%, 1961 7-2-50%, 1963 12-1-61.8%, 1971 4-1-57.1%. Winner, Turble Memorial Championship, 1965. Highest ringer percentage: 67.2. Home: 9 Oak Street, Auburn, ME 04210.

CLARK, SANDRA WOHLGEMUTH, b. March 27, 1948. Children—Michelle, Cary. Secretary, Shar Products. S. Gordon; t. flip, right handed. Winner, Michigan Women's State Championship, 1975, 1976, 1977, 1978, 1979. Tournament average: 60.3%. Plays major league women's softball; golfs, bowls, plays tennis: Home: 2234 Dexter Road, Ann Arbor, MI 48104.

CLAVES, JACK, Served as Vice-President, National Horseshoe Pitchers Association, 1939.

CLAYBERG, MARVIN, Was Colorado

State Champion, 1935, 1937; 1937 Record: 14-1-65.1%.

CLEAR, HARVEY, National Secretary, National Horseshoe Pitchers Association, 1947–1951. Resident, Santa Cruz, CA.

CLECKLER, JIMMIE, Winner, Alabama Boys State Championship, 1972, 1973. Ringer percentage: 1972, 15.1; 1973, 22.

CLINE, ROY, b. February 2, 1930. W. Hazel Fae; children—Sheena, Roy Aaron, Anthony. Hemodialysis Technician. S. Imperial, Ohio Pro; t. one and three quarters, right-handed. Past President, West Virginia Horseshoe Players Association. Member, West Virginia Horseshoe Players Association Hall of Fame. Organizer and Past President, local Tri-County Horseshoe Club. Director, Beckley Coal Festival, Mountaineer Classic tournaments. Winner, Beckley City Championship, singles and doubles. Highest tournament percentage: 61; Highest game percentage: 88. Home: Route 2, Box 114, Beckley, WV 25801.

CLINGAN, JOHN M. "Popeye," b. January 15, 1896. W. Mary: 12 children. S. Ohio Pro; t. one and three quarters, right handed. Has pitched horseshoes for 80 years. Won Pennsylvania State Championship, 1950; Won Florida State Championship, 1962, 1967. Became member, Florida State Hall of Fame, 1976. Won Sportsmanship Award in the Eastern National, 1963. Highest tournament average, 76%; best game, 85%. Has horseshoe court in his back yard. Home: 1521 South Floral Way, Apopka, FL 32703.

CLINTON, ORLEAN EARL, b. April 17, 1945. Student/Teacher. S. Diamond Super Ringers; t. single flip, has also used three-quarters and one and a quarter; right handed. Winner, Western Washington Fair, 1975, 1977, 1978. Teamed up with Art Sperber to win Washington State Doubles Champion-

ship, 1977. Winner, Class A Championship, 1977. Winner, Class K World Championship, World Tournament, 1977. Best tournament percentage: 62.2%. Highest single game percentage: 86.36. An avid bowler. Home: 1818 South 132nd, Seattle, WA 98168.

CLIPPINGER, HAROLD, First Vice-President, Eastern Pennsylvania Chapter, NHPA. A pitcher and administrator in horseshoe pitching activities. Home: 209 Hill Street, Mt. Holly Springs, PE 17065.

COBB, F. ELLIS, b. September 19, 1909. W. Virginia; children—Norma Jean Holdiman, Teri Lynn. Printing Company Supervisor. S. Ohio, t. one and a quarter, right handed. Has pitched horseshoes for 52 years. For 23 years Editor, The Horseshoe Pitchers' News Digest. For past 30 years, State Secretary, Illinois HPA. Vice-President, Illinois HPA, 1947, 1948, 1949. Winner, Northern Illinois Championship, 1966. Winner, Aurora City Championship, 1966. Averaged 76.5% through Cornbelt Open, 1970. Recipient, Stokes Award, 1962. Inducted into National Hall of Fame, 1970. Inducted into Illinois Hall of Fame, 1977. Posed as model for figure used on horseshoe trophies. Instrumental in getting Championship Horseshoe series on NBC television, 1956. Home: 1307 Solfisburg Avenue, P.O. Box 1606, Aurora, IL 60507.

COBB, VIRGINIA, b. June 16, 1906. H. Ellis; children—Norma Jean Holdiman, Terri Lynn. Secretary to Purchasing Agent, City of Aurora, IL. Non-player but active for more than 40 years in horseshoe pitching sport activities on local, state, and national levels. Assistant to the Editor (Her Husband, F. Ellis Cobb) of The Horseshoe Pitchers' News Digest for 23 years. Elected to Illinois State Hall of Fame, 1979. Home: 1307 Solfisburg Avenue, P.O. Box 1606, Aurora, IL 60507.

Top, **Homer Cain with the 1980 Class C World Tournament team.** *Center, left,*
Robert Brown. *Center,* **Marvin Burgess.** *Right,* **Rosemary Gibson Carter, World**
Champion. *Bottom,* **Irwin Carlberg, 1956 Michigan State Champion, with the**
world tournament team in Murray City, Utah, 1959.

Top, Tina Cain with the 1978 Girls World Championship team in Des Moines, Iowa. *Center, left*, Fred T. Butler. *Center*, Sandra Clark. *Right*, F. Ellis Cobb, Editor of National Magazine and Hall of Fame member. *Bottom*, Earl Winston and Cletus Chapelle.

COCHRAN, JOSEPH M., b. November 1, 1925. W. Almeda, children—Joyce, Mike, Gary. Supervisor, Bendix Corporation, and Farmer, S. Imperial; t. one and a quarter or one and three quarters, right handed. President, West Virginia Horseshoe Pitchers Association. Has pitched horseshoes for 35 years, played in tournaments for 20 years, Pitched games in the 80% bracket. Winner of many trophies. Is also an avid coon hunter. Home: Route 2, Box 85, Ronceverte, WV 24970.

COCHRAN, MICHAEL JOSEPH, b. March 7, 1950. W. Diana; child—Michael. World in Retail Sales. S. Imperial; t. one and a quarter, right handed. Won the Greenbriar Open five times. Won the Tri-County tournament four times. With his father, Joseph M. Cochran, won the doubles championship in the Raleigh Register Horseshoe Tournament five consecutive years. Finished second and third in the State Championship Tournament. In the 1980 Frye Memorial with Cecil Monday had 16 consecutive four-deads, one more than the World Tournament record. In the Mountaineer League, averaged 80% ringers; with high scratch game of 95%. Home: Route 2, Box 26V, Lewisburg, WV 24901.

CODY, MIKE, Won the Indiana Boys State Championship, 1957. Record was 6-1-30.2%.

COLE, DORIS M., Played in the Women's Division of eight World Tournaments. Compiled career record of 28 wins, 43 losses, and a ringer percentage of 30.3%. Resident of Ann Arbor, MI.

COLES, HOLLY R., b. October 11, 1948. H. Collin; children—Gordon, Jamie. Escrow Officer. S. Diamonds and Gordons; t. flip, right handed. Won Idaho Women's State Championship with record of 4-0-45.5%, 1979. In 1980 hit her highest tournament average of 52.8%, her highest game of 62%. Home: P.O. Box 1875, Coeur d'Alene, ID 83814.

COLLARD, GEORGE, Won the Rhode Island State Championship two times. Records were 7-0-68%, 1963; 7-0-73.8%, 1965. Resident of Albion, RI.

COLLIER, HOWARD, Won the Illinois State Championship, 1936.

COLLINS, HARRY, Won the Ohio State Championship, 1929.

COLLINS, JAMES M., b. September 29, 1931. Children—James, Jr., William Gary, Steve. Brick mason. S. Imperial; t. one and three quarters, right handed. Won the South Carolina State Championship, 1979. Won Class A Championship at Bulls Gap and Cleveland, Tennessee. Won five tournaments. Highest game, 95.3%, 42 ringers of 44 shoes. Has played ball, owned coon dogs, raised game foul. Home: Rt. 5, Box 412A, Simpsonville, SC 29681.

COMEAU, JOSEPH, Started pitching in 1933. Won Greater Lynn, Massachusetts, title, 1935, 1937, 1938. Won Greater Boston Championship, 1938. Won Massachusetts State Championship, 1951, 1954, 1955, 1963. Won New England Championship two times. Won two Massachusetts Open Titles and one Keene Open Title. In one year, 1963, won the Massachusetts State, New England, Massachusetts Open, and Keene Open contests, averaging 72%, with a record of 36 wins and 4 losses. State Record in 1963 was 8-1-72.1%. In 1974 was inducted into the New England Hall of Fame.

CONE, KEVIN, b. May 24, 1962. Student, University of Northern Iowa. S. Imperial; t. one and a quarter, right handed. Began pitching at age of six, played in first state tournament at seven Winner, Class B, 1978 World Championship in Des Moines, Iowa. Winner, Junior Championship in the Buena Vista Open, 1978, with record of 6-1-59.7%

Winner, Men's Championship in the Buena Vista Open, 1979. Best percentage, 74.5. Registered a perfect game, with 18 ringers of 18 shoes.

CONRAD, TERRY RAE, b. January 2, 1962. Maintenance Worker in Public Service of Indiana. S. Allen; t. one and a quarter, right handed. Won Indiana Boys State Championships three consecutive years, 1977, 1978, 1979. Runner-up, Boys World Championship, 1979. Inducted into Junior Hall of Fame in Indiana, 1979. High tournament, 78%; High game, 88%; has scored 64 consecutive ringers, 32 doubles in a row. Plays tennis and works on cars. Home: 31 Maple Drive, Rockville, IN 47872.

COOK, HAROLD F. "SARG," b. July 26, 1921. W. Lucille, child—Cheryl L. Martin. U.S. Army, Retired. S. Imperial; t. one and three quarters, left handed. Has pitched horseshoes for 47 years. Joined CCC's during the depression and promoted horsehoe pitching in the camps. While in army, pitched horseshoes in Panama, Philippines, Hawaii, Gaudacanal and other Pacific Islands. Won Pacific Area Championship, 1941. Elected President, Florida NPA, 1967. Became Editor, Florida Horseshoe News, 1967. Held both positions for many years. Received Charles Stevens Sportsmanship Award, 1973; Won 1967 NHPA Stokes Memorial Award. Is secretary of the Seminole Horseshoe Club. Highest tournament play, 85.4%; highest game, 94%. Has built horseshoe pitching clubs throughout state of Florida. Home: 10926 87th Avenue North, Seminole, FL 33542.

COOK, HENRY "SLIM," (dec.) b. 1882, d. 1980. T. one and a quarter, right handed. Pitched horseshoes actively for 68 years. Helped organize the Oregon Horseshoe Pitchers' Association; directed its first tournament. First Winner, Oregon State Championship. Founded Eugene Horseshoe Pitch-

ing Club, 1918; President of club for 30 years. A Henry Cook Invitational staged in his honor, 1977; inducted into the Oregon Horseshoe Pitchers Hall of Fame, 1973, as one of its charter members. Pitched 80% games; once pitched 34 consecutive ringers.

COOK, KATHY, Winner, Georgia Women's State Championship, 1974.

COOK, MAURINE STOKES, b. September 29, 1918. H. Clifton Lewis. Assisted father, Arch Stokes, a member of the Horseshoe Committee of the Centennial Committee of Utah, 1947–1959. Secretary, NHPA for 16 years. Served as Third Vice-President, NHPA. Member, Utah Horseshoe Pitchers Hall of Fame.

COOL, CONNIE F., b. October 23, 1955. Insurance Agent. S. Imperial; t. three quarters, right handed. Winner, Greenville Ringer Classic, two times. Runnerup, World Championship at Middlesex, NJ, 1971. Winner, Ohio Girls State Championship, 1969, 1970, 1972. Her 48.1% in 1972 tournament, state record at the time. First woman to win Darke County Club Championship, 1979. Trustee of Darke County Horseshoe Pitching Association. Highest game, 77.6%; best tournament, 68%. Home: 768 Martin Street, Greenville, OH 45331.

COOPER, ELWYN D., b. August 10, 1933. W. Katie, children—Vicky, Terresa, Janet, Nancy. Manager of Routing-Motor Carrier. S. Allen; t. one and a quarter, right handed. Has played horseshoes for 30 years. President, local horseshoe club. Winner, Warrensburg, MO, tournament, with a 7-1-72% record. Highest tournament average, 75%; highest game, 90%. Home: 6920 NW 78th Street, Kansas City, MO 64152.

COOPER, FRAN, b. December 30, 1929. H. Stanley; children—Linda, Loretta, Shirley. S. Allen; t. three quarter flip, right handed. Winner, Oregon State Championship, 1973, 1974, 1975. Record of 6-1-46.3% in 1973 contest. Highest single game, 75%. Hobbies: Hunting, Fishing, Making Candy. Home: Route 3—Box 3080, Hermiston, OR 97838.

COOPER, FRANK (II), b. April 18, 1963. Son of Frank and Naomi Cooper. Student. S. Imperial; t. one and three quarters, left handed. Winner, Virginia Boys State Championship, 1976, with a record of 7-0-64.4%. Member Junior Doubles State Championship team, 1978, 1979. Holds Boo Henson Open title, 1976, and Berkley County Club title, 1977. Hobbies: Weight Lifting, Hunting, Bowling. Home: Route 5, Box 825, Winchester, VA 22601.

COOPER, JOE S., b. March 21, 1952. W. Barbara; Child—Erik. Production Supervisor, American Woodmark, Inc. S. Allen; t. one and three quarters, left handed. Winner, Virginia Boys State Championship, 1968, with a record of 3-0-25%. Winner, Winchester Recreation Park Boys Title, 1965. Won several of the lower classes of the men's division in the Raymond Frye Memorial, Boo Henson Open, and Lynchburg tournaments. Is an avid bowler. Home: P.O. Box 96, Rippen WV 25441.

COPELAND, ANSIL, b. November 4, 1914. W. Wavelyn; child—Ronald. Machinst. S. Allen; t. one and three quarters, right handed. Has played horseshoes for 30 years. Winner, Class B. World Championship. 1975. Winner, Phoenix City Open Class A title, 1957. Has won 54 tournament trophies. Highest sanctioned tournament average, 79.07%; highest game, 94%. World Tournament career record won 125, lost 174 averaging 71.5%. Home: 3065 Hayne Road, Akron, OH 44312.

COPPOCK, E. J. "Cricket," (dec.) An active horseshoe pitcher in his younger years. Instrumental in organizing the Darke County, OH, Horseshoe Club, 1956. In-strumental in organizing the Greenville, OH, World tournament, 1962, 1964. Served as Social Chairman of that tournament, 1972.

CORBETT, OPAL MC KEE, b. June 20, 1915. H. Theodore; children—Lauretta Corbett Klein, Sandra Geiger. S. Allen; t. double flips, right handed. Has won 38 tournament championships, including 5 Pennsylvania Championships and 5 Florida State Championships. Won Eastern National in Erie, PA, 1971. Won in Class D category. World Tournament, 1979. Highest tournament percentage: 63. Served as Secretary-Treasurer and Tournament Director, New Castle, PA, for many years. Secretary, Youngstown, O, horseshoe club for two years. Served as Secretary-Treasurer of horseshoe club and Tournament Director, Orlando, FL. Editor, Florida Newsletter, 1978–1979. Inducted into Lawrence County All Sports Hall of Fame, 1976; Pennsylvania Horseshoe Pitchers Association Hall of Fame, 1979; Florida Horseshoe Pitchers Hall of Fame, 1980. Home: 810 East Mount Vernon Street, Orlando, FL 32803.

CORK, WILLIAM H., b. November 17, 1925. W. Judy; children—Byron, Rae Marie, Leroy. Electrician. S. Hohl; t. one and three quarters, right handed. Has pitched horseshoes for 32 years. Member NHPA, 27 years. Has played in tournaments in 9 states. High tournament average 64.9%; high game 85%. Home: Box 124, Shoshone, CA 92384.

CORK, BYRON, Son of William and Judy Cork. Winner, Nevada Boys State Championship, 1969.

CORK, JUDY, H. William. Winner, Nevada Women's State Championship, 1969.

CORNS, TERESA DOUGLAS, b. September 6, 1964. H. Charles; child—Jessica Dawn. S. Imperial; t. flip, right handed.

Won West Virginia Women's State Championship with a record of 8-1-34.8%. Second place, Parkersburg, WV, tournament, two times. Home: Route 1, Box 58. Elizabeth, WV 26143.

COTHERN, JOHN, b. January 15, 1930. W. Barbara; children—Lynn, Leah, Mike, Pat, Bill. Farmer. S. Imperial; t. one and a quarter, right handed. Has pitched horseshoes for 35 years. Winner, Idaho State Championship, 1976; runner-up, three times. Has served as President, Idaho Horseshoe Pitchers Association, two times. Highest tournament, 58%; highest game, 70%. Has hit 18 consecutive ringers and 4 consecutive four-deads. Is an instructor pilot. Home: Route 1, Buhl, ID 83316.

COTTON, FRANK M. Retired. Worked in car shops of Wabash Railroad for 43 years. T. one and quarter. Started pitching horseshoes at the age of 15. Has played in many tournaments, including World Tournament at Murray City, Utah, 1955. Runs horseshoe league in Phoenix Manor, AZ. Winner, Class A, Mattoon Opens. Staged open tournament at Macon County Fair, 1958. Has traveled widely throughout the United States. Takes pride in his great collection of horseshoe publications. Hobby: Bowling. Home: 4010 North 20th Street, Phoenix, AZ 85016.

COTTRELL, DAVID D., (dec.) Owner of magazine distribution agency. Secretary-Treasurer, NHPA, 1923–1933. In 1928, compiled and published book for NHPA, *Horseshoe Pitching—How to Play the Game.* Designed some of the first score sheets for horseshoe pitching contests. Promoter, organizer, and director of horseshoe tournaments. Charter member, NHPA Hall of Fame.

COURNOYER, SERGE, Resident of Sorel, Quebec. Winner, Quebec Provincial Championship, 1979.

COURSEN, FRANKLIN M., b. January 22, 1920. W. Velma; children—Robert, Janet, Patricia, Joann. Employer, Westinghouse Electric Company. S. Ohio O; t, one and a quarter, right handed. Has pitched horseshoes for 40 years; 23 years in tournament play. First class championship—Class E in Lakeside Open, 1960. Has won many other championships since. Home: Route 1, Clever Road. Bellville, OH 44813.

COURTWRIGHT, WILLIAM A., b. February 22, 1924. W. Janet; children—Tom, Tim, Susan, Nancy. Owner, Hi Temp Refractories Co.; manufactures the Deadeye pitching shoe. Has played horseshoes for 42 years, including tournament play. Has averaged 72% ringers for a full season; has hit 38 consecutive ringers. A former PBA bowler. Home: 10360 Badgley Drive, St. Louis, MO 63126.

COWLES, W. J., Winner, Connecticut State Championship, 1928.

COX, CHARLES ROY, Winner, First Ohio State Championship, 1915.

COX, DARREL, Winner, Oregon Boys State Championship, 1977. Hit 31.9% to win this championship.

COX, JIM, Winner, Indiana State Championship, 1938.

COY, DONALD J, b. September 7, 1912. W. Fern; Children—Robert, Shiela, James, Cindy. Track Foreman, CN & W Railroad. S. Deadeye; t. one and a quarter, right handed. Has pitched horseshoes for 52 years. Played tournaments 21 years. Winner, South Dakota Class A Crown, 1979. Runnerup, South Dakota State Championship, 1970, 1971. Highest percentage; 71.7. Most four-deads in one game: 11. Member, South Dakota HPA Hall of Fame Selection Committee; also, a State Director. Entire Coy Family inducted as a unit into South Dakota HPA Hall of Fame, 1974. Fern has pitched in tournaments and leagues; has kept tournament records. Robert has pitched in many state and open tournaments, averaging about 40% ringers; has acted as scoring judge. Shiela has posted ringer percentages in tournaments, kept scores and books. James has pitched in state and open tournaments, averaged about 45% ringers; high game: 70%. Has acted as court judge and assistant to tournament director. Cindy has calculated ringer percentages; has kept and posted scores. Home: P.O. Box 382, Parker, SD 57053.

CRABTREE, ALBIN WATSON, b. August 18, 1910. W. Bernice; children—Bob, Bill, Cathy, Grain Farmer. S, Allen; t. one and a quarter, right handed. Has pitched horseshoes for over 30 years. Winner, Class B, California State Tournament, 1973. Has won many other tournaments. Highest tournament average: 69%; highest game, 84%. Home: 301 Crabtree Road, Waterford CA 95386.

CRAIG, GARY, b. January 11, 1948. W. Darlene; children—Donn Alan, Kerris Duane. Draftsman. S. Ohio; t. one and a quarter, right handed. Winner, Indiana Boys State Championship, 1961, 1963. Winner, Indiana—Ohio Open Junion Championship, 1963. Highest tournament, 49%; highest game, 66%. Member, Lafayette Horseshoe Club. Home: 283 Conjunction Street, Box 586, Dayton, IN 47941.

CRAIG, HAROLD, W. Mary. President, NHPA, 1961–1967. Wife served as Vice-President, NHPA. They were co-recipients of the Stokes Memorial Trophy, 1960. They played a major role in World Tournaments in Muncie, IN, 1960, 1961. Harold's average as a pitcher: 50% ringers. Home: 1217 West Carson Drive, Muncie, IN 47303.

CRAIG, MARVIN D., b. August 23, 1920. W. Lorado; children—Karen, Gary, Ronnie, Dean, Theresa. Foreman, Outdoor Advertising Company. S. Ohio O; t. one and three quarters, right handed. Has pitched competitive horseshoes for 50 years; has played in NHPA tournaments for 23 years. President, Parker City, IN, horseshoe club. Vice-President, Muncie, IN, horseshoe club. State Director, Eastern Indiana. Highest tournament averages: local, 83%, state, 78.6%; world, 76.4%. Highest game averages: local, 100%; state, 91.1%; world, 89.3%. With Paul Lattray, scored 12 consecutive four-deads in world tournament. With Paul Focht, hit a ringer percentage of 91.15 in world tournament. Home: Route 1, Box 335, Parker City, IN 47363.

CRANDALL, RICK, Set record, winning New York Boys State Championship five times, 1965 through 1969. Averaged over 50% ringers for the 5 years. Runnerup, Junior Boys World Championship. Home: 385 Fairview Avenue, Hornell, NY 14843.

CRANDALL, STEVE, b. January 30, 1963. Student. S. Allen, Ohio Pro; t. one and a quarter, one and three quarters, right handed. Winner, New York Boys State Championship, 1976, 1977, 1978, 1979. Winner, Eastern National Boys Championship, 1978. Highest tournament percentage, 72%; highest game percentage, 86.3. Home: 385 Fairview Avenue, Box 402, Hornell, NY 14843.

CRANK, E. M. Resident, Wilburn, IL. Placed 14th in World Tournament in Des Moines, IA, with a 3-12 record in the finals, 1922.

CRANK, VICKI BELL, b. June 27, 1960. H. Jeff. Employee, Proof Department, Bank of Lexington. S. Gordon or Ohio; t. flip, right handed. Winner, Kentucky State Championship, Avon Warmup, 1977. Third place in World Tournament, 1977. Winner, Bluegrass Tournament Title, 1978. A 60% pitcher. Home: 527 Laketower Drive, Apt. 16, Lexington, KY 40502.

CRICK, BILLY, SR. From Los Angeles, CA. First recognized winner, California State Championship, 1920. Placed 6th with a 10-5 record in the finals of World Tournament, Des Moines, Iowa, 1922.

CRISS, HERBERT R., b. April 14, 1924. W. Audrey; children—Peggy, Rocky, Mike. Retired Fireman. S. Ohio Pro; t. one and a quarter, right handed. Has played horseshoe for 25 years. Has won many tournaments, including Bellingham International with 7-0-75.2%, 1979; Allones Open with 75.3%, 1979; Gilbo Open with 7-0-72.2%, 1979; Seattle Memorial with 13-1-74.9%, 1979; Tacoma Daffodil with 9-0-76.8%, 1980. City Champion of Bremerton, WA, for past 12 years. Highest tournament average, 76.8%; highest single game, 93.3%—hit 41 ringers of 44 shoes. Home: 3648 Seabeck Highway, N. W., Bremerton, WA 98310.

CROFUT, WILLIAM, Winner, Connecticut State Championship five times, from 1936 through 1941. Highest ringer percentage: 64.4. Played in New England Championship contests twice, averaging 61% ringers.

CROTEAU, LAWRENCE J., b. January 16, 1927. W. Phyllis; children—William, James, Kenneth, Steven, Diane. Tool Crib Manager, MPB Corp. S. Imperial; t. one and a quarter, right handed. Has been playing horseshoes for 35 years. Winner, New Hampshire Men's State Championship, 1968. Vice-President, New Hampshire State Horseshoe Pitchers Association. Tournament Director, Keene Horseshoe Club. Past President, Keene Horseshoe Club. Bowls in Candlepin Bowling League. Home: 25 Prescott Street, Keene, NH 03431.

CRUMM, FRANK, President, Grand League of American Horseshoe Pitchers, 1914. League first recorded move to standardize playing rules and equipment.

CUMMING, ALEX, From Minneapolis, MN. First Vice-President, NHPA, 1923. President, NHPA, 1933.

CUMMING, MRS. ALEX, Wife of Alex Cumming. Assisted him when he served as President and Vice-President, NHPA. Played in 7 world tournaments, winning 12 games. Averaged 12.1% ringers. Best finish: 5th in 1922 with 4-4 record.

CUMMINGS, ADRIAN, From Norway, ME. Winner, Maine State Championship, 1926. In 1927 tournament, described as "tall right hander who can pitch 50% ringers with a deadly three quarter turn."

CUMMINGS, ARTHUR J., (dec.) From Minneapolis, MN. t. one and a quarter. Winner, Minnesota State Championship, 1926. In World Tournament championship play, won 144 games and averaged 52.2 ringers. Was softball pitcher and bowler. Member, Minnesota Bowlers Hall of Fame.

CUMMINS, CLARENCE, b. June 16, 1911. W. Nita. Government Employee. S. Gordon or Diamond; t. three quarters, right handed. Has played horseshoes for fifty years, 32 years in tournament competition. Winner, Idaho State Championship, 1973, 1974, 1975, 1977, 1979. Has pitched an 83.3% game; has hit 13 doubles in a row; has hit 48 ringers of the last 52 shoes in a game. Home: Route 4, Box 49, St. Maries, ID 83861.

CUNNINGHAM, FREDERICK "Paul" (dec.) b., March 8, 1917. W. Barbara; children—Fred, Vic, Mary, Becky, Bob, Shirley, Nancy, Cathy, Terrie, Michael, Tammi. Employee, American Bank and VA Hospital. S. Allen; t. one and a quarter, right handed. Active as a tournament player for 20 years. President, Indiana State Horseshoe Pitchers Association, 1975, 1976. Vice-President, Indiana State Horseshoe Pitchers Association, 1973, 1974. President, Marion,

IN, Horseshoe Club, 1970, 1971, 1972, 1973. Inducted into Indiana Horseshoe Pitchers Association Hall of Fame, 1977. Family Residence: 2716 West 38 Street, Marion, IN 46952.

CUNNINGHAM, TAMMI KAY, b. April 29, 1962, Student, Indiana Business College. Winner, Indiana State Championship in NHPA sanctioned tournament, 1974, 1975, 1977, 1978. Winner, AHPA Title, 1976. Winner, NHPA Indoor Title, 1977. Home: 2303 South Meridian Street, Marion, In 46952.

CURRAN, CHARLES, Formerly operated poultry business. Winner, First New Mexico State Championship, 1939. First President, New Mexico HPA, 1939. Home: 321 Rencher, Clovis, NM.

CURRAN, EDWARD ROBERTS, b. January 22, 1931. W. Ella Mae; children—Jim, Wayne, Larry, Ricky, Crystal. Farmer. S. Allen; t. three quarters, one and three quarters, right handed. Winner, Scott County Fair, 1970; Avon SRS, 1970; Milville Open, 1971, 1972; Avon Depot Open, 1971; Scott County Fair, 1971; Blue Grass Fair, 1971; Avon National, 1972. Winner, Greenville, OH, Class D. World Tournament, 1972, with 77.8% ringers, a Class D world record. Home: Route 5, Paris, KY 40361.

CURRAN, RICKY LEE, W. Diana. T. Flip, left handed. Winner, Kentucky Boys State Championship, 1969, 1970. Placed second in Class B, World Tournament, 1972. Won a number of junior tournaments from 1969 through 1972. Home: 558 Walnut Street, Georgetown, KY 40324.

CURRY, DEAN, b. April 10, 1924. Father of four children. Transportation Employee. S. Allen; t. one and a quarter, right handed. Has played horseshoes for 20 years. Winner, Idaho State Championship, six times—1964, 1969, 1971, 1978, 1980. Served three terms as President of Idaho State Horseshoe Pitchers Association and President of local club. Is an avid pool player. Home: 1705 First Street, Lewiston, ID 83501.

CURRY, GEORGE, Winner, Pennsylvania State Championship, 1931, 1937. Record for 1937 was 10-1-68.3%. Pitched in tournaments in several states; pitched in exhibitions.

CURTIS, ALBERT, Secretary, Eastern Pennsylvania Chapter, NHPA. Has spent many years working with and encouraging local clubs. Home: 1005 West Godfrey Avenue, Philadelphia, PA 19141.

CURTS, WILLIAM, Winner, South Dakota State Championship, 1929.

CYPHER, EVA, Winner, Nevada Women's State Championship, 1975. Home: 81 Colony Road, Reno, NV 89502.

D

DAHL, PHYLLIS, b. April 15, 1914. H. Stanley; children—Stan, Ken, Linda. Bookbinder. S. Allen; t. three quarters, right handed. Provincial Secretary, British Columbia Horseshoe Association. Has won several local tournament championships and two silver medals in the British Columbia Summer Games. Active in handicrafts. Home: 101-6664 Dow Avenue, Bunaby, British Columbia, Canada V5H 3C9.

DAHL, STANLEY, b. October 19, 1910. W. Phyllis; children—Stan, Ken, Linda. Lithographer. T. one and a quarter, right handed. Has played horseshoes for 55 years. Has won the British Columbia Championship 16 times. Runnerup, Senior World Championship, 1973. Has been President of British Columbia Horseshoe Pitchers Association and Provincial Advisor for the British Columbia Summer Games. Home: 101-6664

Dow Avenue, Burnaby, British Columbia, Canada V5H 3C9.

DAHLENE, ALVIN (dec.) 1905–1979. Played horseshoes for 60 years. Winner, Kansas State Championship, 1941, 1942. Played in 42 Kansas State Championship contests. Played in 7 World Tournaments. Placed fifth in World Tournament, Des Moines, IA, 1941. Hit 41 of 42 for 96.6% in 1938 Kansas State Championship meet and scored 76.9% ringers in the 1942 meet, both records at the time. Longest consecutive ringer streak: 54. Elected Vice-President, NHPA, 1939. Served many times as President and Secretary of local clubs.

DALY, HENRY, Winner, Kansas State Championship, 1920, 1921.

DAMARIN, ELDEN, b. December 6, 1920. Welder. S. Allen; t. one and a quarter, right handed. Has been a tournament pitcher for 25 years. Winner, Illinois State Championship, 1971, with 10-1-71.1%. Runnerup for title two times. Has won many tournament titles, including Galesburg National Open, Heart of Illinois, Monmouth Open, and Wyoming Open. In Sterling-Rock Falls tournament, averaged 79%. Highest game: 87%. Home: 1536 West Kettelle Street, Peoria, IL 61605.

DANIELSON, ERNIE (ERNEST) EUGENE, JR., b. October 13, 1942. W. Donna; child—Eric. Fertilizer Plant Maintenance Worker. S. Ohio; t. one and a quarter, right handed. At fourteen, won Iowa Boys State Championship, 1957, with a high game of 76% pitching from 40 feet. At Des Moines, IA, State Fair, hit 8 consecutive doubles and 4 consecutive four-deads. Pitched horseshoes while serving with U.S. Army in Viet Nam. Has also played golf. Home: 710 South Central Avenue, Burlington, IA 52601.

DANIELSON, ERNEST, SR., b. November 1, 1902. W. Viola; children—Violet Knouse, Ernie, Beverly. House Painter. S. Ohio; t. one and three quarters, right handed. Has pitched horseshoes for 65 years. Has pitched 701,000 horseshoes in tournament play. Has played in 239 Class A tournaments. Won Rock Falls Labor Day meet, 1969, and the Clay County Fair meet, 1971. Highest tournament average, 78%; highest game, 92.2%. Vice-President, Burlington, IA, Horseshoe Club. Has served as Vice-President and as Publicity Director, Iowa Horseshoe Pitchers Association. Became a member of the Iowa State Hall of Fame, 1980. Home: 221 South Tenth Street, Burlington, IA 52601.

DANNER, CLARENCE A., JR., b. June 4, 1918. W. Helen; child—Freddie. Railroad Trainman, P. and L. E. S. Imperial and Allen; t. one and three quarters, left handed. Winner, Pennsylvania Class B. State Championship, 1977. Placed fourth in Class C of World Tournament, 1976; placed fifth in Class C of World Tournament, 1977. Recording Secretary, Mt. Pleasant Indoor Club. Member, Pennsylvania NPA Hall of Fame Committee. Home: Box 288, Newell, PA 15466.

DARNOLD, HAROLD, b. 1925. Child—Jerry. Machinist, Burlington Northern Railroad. S. Deadeye; t. one and a quarter, right handed. Has been playing horseshoes for 39 years. Has played tournaments in 20 states. Has been promoter and tournament manager for the Corn Belt Open, Burlington, IA, for 27 years. Winner: Four consecutive Quincy, IL, Opens; Red Oak, IA, Open; Peoria, IL, Memorial Day Open; Tremont, Il, Turkey Festival. Won the Class C World Championship, 1974. Highest percentage tournament 79.8%; highest percentage game, 95%. Home: 1503 Mt. Pleasant, Burlington, Iowa 52601.

DARNOLD, JERRY, b. February 21, 1963.

Student. S. Allen; t. one and a quarter, right handed. A third generation horseshoe pitcher. Winner, three Class A championships. Finished third in State Tournament, 1977, 1978. Has made Championship Division of World Tournament two times, finishing seventh in 1977; fourth, in 1979. Best tournament percentage: 72.5; highest game percentage: 95.5. Home: 1826 Mt. Pleasant Street, Burlington, IA 52601.

DARR, CHARLES C., Winner, Virginia State Championship, 1931. Win and loss record: 11-0.

DAVIDSON, HAROLD ALLEN, b. December 17, 1912. W. Audrey Elenore; children—Lelia Mickle, Eugene, Linda McGee. U.S.D.A. Employee. S. Gordon; t. one and a quarter, right handed. Has played horseshoes for 54 years. Has won 15 trophies, including 2 first-place trophies in 1980. Has played in two World Tournaments, 1975, 1978. Instrumental in installing courts in Boone, IA, and in getting radio publicity for horseshoe games. Hosts two annual tournaments. Tournament Director for Senior Championship Tournament. Regional Director, Iowa Hawkeye Horseshoe Pitchers Association. Iowa delegate to the 1978 National Convention. Member, 1978 World Tournament Committee. Home: 515 Third Street, Boone, IA 50036.

DAVIS, BERNARD, Winner, Class D World Championship, 1974, with 55.8% ringer average. Winner, Franklin, NH, Warmup Championship, with a record of 7-0-60.7%.

DAVIS, CHARLES C., Turn, one and three quarters, with a Mossman shoe. Winner of five World Championships, the first in 1922, with 21-0 score. Played his last World Tournament in 1935. Winner, Missouri State Championship, 1934, 1935. First pitcher to average 70% ringers. His average of 70.2% in 1928 world record at the time. Ranks sixth in all-time list of World Tournament winners, with 411 wins, 56 losses, a ringer percentage of 64.2 and an average qualifying score of 522 points. Highest ringer percentage: 73.6. Did exhibition horseshoe pitching and trick pitching all over the United States. Became member of NHPA Hall of Fame, 1969.

DAVIS, CARL (dec.) Was high-ranking Class A player. Member, Utah Horseshoe Pitchers Association Hall of Fame.

DAVIS, ETHEL M., b. February 20, 1926. H. Lowell; children—Darrel, Daniel. Former Bookkeeper. S. Allen; t. one and a quarter, right handed. Winner, Corvallis Open, with 5-0-47.3%, 1980. Winner, Lane County Women's Championship. Winner, Class B, Pacific Northwest Tournament, 1979. Best single game, 62.5%. Secretary, Emerald Horseshoe Pitchers Association of Eugene, OR. Home: 82884 North Pacific Highway, Creswell, OR 97426.

DAVIS, HARRY D., Winner, West Virginia State Championship, 1980. with a record of 11-2-56.7%. Home: 215 Church Street, Bridgeport, WV 26330.

DAVIS, JEFFREY, b. October 31, 1965. Son of Albert Davis. Student. S. Allen; t. one and a quarter, right handed. Winner, Ohio Boys State Championship, 1980, with 80% ringers. Has won Southwestern District four times. Has won Rose Festival two times. Plays violin and participates in karate and basketball. Home: 1240 Western Avenue, Hamilton, OH 45013.

DAVIS, JIMMIE, Co-Winner (with Eino Tulikainen) of Colorado State Championship, 1949. Only known instance of state co-champions.

DAVIS, JOSEPH JAMES, b. August 10, 1920. W. Edna Mae; children—Nancy Gillis, Stephen, and Cathy Tuttle. Shoe Cutter, Sabago Moc Inc. S. Gordon; t. one and three quarters, right handed. Has played horseshoes for 62 years. Winner, Maine State Championship, 1958, with a record of 8-1-62%; Runnerup three times. Has won several city and county championships. Played in 27 consecutive tournaments in which he placed third or higher. Finished 10th in Class B of World Tournament. Has hit 92 ringers of consecutive 100 shoes. Inducted into Maine Horseshoe Pitchers Association Hall of Fame, 1978. Home: Route 5, Box 140, Groveville Road (Buxton) Gorham, ME 04038.

DAVIS, JOHN CARLYLE, (dec.) W. Lola; children—Mrs. H. W. Reed, John C. Native of Oakmont, PA. Winner, Florida State Championship, 1961, with a record of 5-2-60.4%.

DAVIS, LEE R., b. April 19, 1907. W. Peggy; children—Carol Joy, Donna Lee. Worked for Bethlehem Steel; retired. S. Allen; t. one and three quarters, right handed. Has played horseshoes for 60 years. Has won over 100 trophies. Winner, New Jersey State Championship, 1960. Organized the Englewood, NJ, Horseshoe Club, 1935. Has served as President and Secretary, New Jersey Association, NHPA; Regional Director, Eastern States; Chairman, Florida Hall of Fame. Designed Florida Hall of Fame Plaque. Has attended 18 world tournaments. Has promoted handicap leagues. Inducted into the National Horseshoe Pitchers Hall of Fame at Statesville, NC, 1979. Home: P.O. Box 3426, Seminole, FL 33542.

DAVIS, LOWELL C., b. April 4, 1922. W. Ethel; children—Darrell, Dan, Toni. Logger. S. Allen; t. one and a quarter, right handed. Has played horseshoes for 23 years. Winner, Oregon State Championship, 1965, 1978, 1980. Hit 78.2% in 1978 contest. Winner, Pacific Northwest Championship, 1978. Highest single game, 93.2%. Finished first in the 1980 Oregon Horseshoe Pitchers League, with 80 wins and 25 losses. Member, Oregon Hall of Fame. Also enjoys deer hunting. Home: 82884 North Pacific Highway, Creswell, OR 97426.

DAVISSON, HELEN SCHULTZ, Former Bakery Operator. With her sisters, Caroline and Charlotte, enjoyed a horseshoe pitching career as The Schultz Sisters. The Schultz Sisters staged horseshoe pitching exhibitions all over the country. Act one of the side attractions of the Barnum and Bailey Circus. Home: 3387 Erie Avenue, Apt. 120, Cincinnati, OH 45208.

DAWES, KENNY, (dec.) 1916–1980. W. Josephine. Worked for Dayton, OH, Power and Light. S. Allen and Ohio; t. one and a quarter, right handed. Pitched horseshoes for 21 years. Won over 200 trophies, many for Class A Championships. Averaged in the high sixties, with many games above 80%. Home: 4128 Main Street, Washington Court House, OH 43160.

DAWSEY, JOSEPH, Winner, Arizona State Championship, 1976. Home: 1417 East Polk, Phoenix, AZ 85006.

DAY, CURT, b. July 6, 1917. W. Mary; children—James, Robert, Joyce Houseer, Richard, Margie Roberts, Paul. General Stores Attendant. S. Allen; t. three quarters reverse from cross-fire position, right handed. Has played horseshoes for over 50 years; 33 years in NHPA. Winner, World Championship, 1966, 1971, 1974. Highest tournament average, 88.79%; highest game, 97.2%. Secretary-Treasurer, Indiana State Horseshoe Pitchers Association, 1950, 1951. Third Vice-President, NHPA, 1958. Has served as President, Vice-President, Secretary, and Treasurer of local clubs. Became member, National Hall of Fame, 1969. Became charter member, Indiana Hall of Fame, 1975. Won Indiana State championship 18 times, Midwest Ringer Roundup 14 times, Ohio-Indiana open 14 times. In 17 appearances in the Championship Division of World Tournament play he won 495 and lost 83, while averaging over 80% ringers. Of 149 tournaments between 1960 and 1976 he hit 80% or over in 130 of them. He holds several world records. Home: 1200 East Washington Street, Frankfort, IN 46041.

DAY, PAUL, b. December 30, 1954. W. Kathy. Industrial Engineer. S. Allen; t. three quarters reverse, right handed. Has pitched horseshoes for 22 years. Began playing in tournaments at the age of seven. Winner, Midwest Ringer Roundup, 1973, with a record of 6-1-79.7%. Indiana City Open Champion, 1978, 1979. Voted Outstanding First Year Player in Men's Division of World Tournament, 1974. With Mark Seibold, set several world records for juniors in World Tournament, 1969. Highest tournament average, 80.8%; highest single game, 90%. Home: 714 Sam Ralston Road, Lebanon, IN 46052.

DEAN, BOB, b. October 19, 1919. W. Cindy; children—Lorna, Kenneth, Deanna, R. Lynn. Mechanical Clerk. S. Allen; t. one and a quarter, right handed. Brought NHPA tournaments to the Shenandoah Valley. Started a Valley League in 1967. Winner, Virginia State AAU Championship, 1966. Winner, with wife Cindy, Virginia State Doubles Title, 1970. Winner, with Charles Price, State Doubles Championship, 1975. Winner, Gypsy Hill Open, 1975. Winner, State Fair meet, 1978. Winner, New Hope Open, with a record of 7-0-58.6% and a high game of 69.5%. Won Intermediate Class B World Championship in World Tournament, with a record of 7-0-62.3% and a high game of 72%. Home: Route 2, Box 198A, Elkton, VA 22827.

DEAN, CINDY, b. December 24, 1924. H. Bob; children—Lorna, Kenneth, Deanna, R. Lynn. Realtor Associate. S. Allen; t. one and a quarter, right handed. Win-

ner, Virginia State Championship, nine times, between the years 1966 and 1978. Set Virginia State record with 73.7% in 1978 contest. Has won many tournaments, including Winchester Ladies Cash, Apple Capital Open, Mountaineer Open, Russell Robery Open, Buena Vista, World Tournament Warmup, Frye Memorial, Hill City Open, and Boo Henson Open. With husband Robert, won the Virginia Doubles Championship; with Juanita Phelps, won State Doubles Championship. High qualifying score, 75%; high game, 82.6%. Secretary, Twin Valley Club. Member, Rules and By-Laws Committee of the State Association. Fourth Vice-President, NHPA, 1971, 1972. Virginia State Secretary, 1969, 1970, 1971. Vice-President, Virginia State Association, 1975–1978. Served on Advisory Committee of the Virginia State Association. Inducted into Virginia State Hall of Fame, 1978. Home: Route 2, Box 198A, Elkton, VA 22827.

DEAN, LOUIS, President, NHPA, 1949–1951. High School Superintendent. In World Tournament play, Championship Division, compiled a record of 242 wins, 129 losses, ringer percentage of 71.8 and an average qualifying score of 504. Finished seventh in World Tournament, Salt Lake City, 1947, with a record of 27-8-72.1%. Resident of Pamona, CA.

DEAN, WILLIAM E., Sr. Leading figure in horseshoe pitching activities in the Maritimes. Has promoted contests, helped organize clubs, and has run tournaments. Received special ward in 1978 as "Mr. Horseshoes" of the Maritimes. Home: Box 748, 152 North Foord Street, Stellaton, Nova Scotia, Canada.

DECKER, CAROLINE SCHULTZ, 1982 Member NHPA Hall of Fame, 1933 and 1934 Women's World Champion, b. July 6, 1912. H. John, deceased. S. Ohio; t. one and a quarter, right handed. Never defeated in 25 year career. Won 1933 World Championship with 5-0-73.8% a world record, and in 1934 with 7-0-81.3% to again set a world record percentage. Her 1934 qualifying round of 388 points in 150 shoes was a world record. With her sisters, Charlotte and Helen pitched exhibitions for years as the Schultz Sisters with Barnum & Bailey Circus and many others. Won several Cook County championships beginning in 1926, the 1932 Central States and the 1933 Mid-West. Home: Mt. Washington Care Center—Room 239, 6900 Beechmont Avenue, Cincinnati, Ohio, 45230.

DECKER, ROBERT, Winner, Colorado State Championship, four times—1934, 1938, 1939, 1942, with a high ringer percentage of 68.7.

DEEM, ANDY, Sr., b. June 10, 1918. W. Burnadean; children—Andy, Jr., Lee, Michael, Roger, Dorothy, Carolyn, Kathleen, Marlene, Deborah. Factory Worker. S. Allen; t. one and a quarter, right handed. Pitched horseshoes for 50 years. Winner, West Virginia State Championship, 1963, 1966. Holds West Virginia State qualifying record of 87 ringers; 272 points of 100 shoes. Has won several open tournaments. Highest tournament average, 77%; highest game, 89%. Hit nine four-deads and 38 consecutive ringers in tournament competition. Served as President of his local club for several years. Inducted into West Virginia State Hall of Fame, 1980. Enjoys fishing, hunting, bowling. Home: 2213 6th Avenue, Parkersburg, WV 26101.

DEHART, THOMAS R. "RUSS," b. April 24, 1926. W. Betty; children—Judy Swank, Cynthia Yoder, Nancy Hey. Retired Maintenance Man. S. Allen; t. one and a quarter, right handed. Has pitched horseshoes for 45 years, 28 in league and tournament competition. Winner, AHPA Indiana State Championship, 1971. Has won the following tournament championships: Johnson County Fair, Martinsville Fall Festival, 1967, 1968; Smith Valley, 1969; Jasonville Open, 1970; Marion County Open, Scottsburg Open, Scottsburg Fall, 1971; JCHC, 1972; Gem City Open, 1973; Martinsville Fall Festival, 1974; Plant City, FL, Open; Western Indiana Open; Indiana-Ohio Open, 1977. Average above 70% ringers. High game, 92%. Home: 1422 West Curry Road, Greenwood, IN 46142.

DELEARY, PAULINE E. "PAT," (dec.) 1908-1081). H. Stanley; children—Jerry, Joe, Shirley. S. Gordon; t. one and a quarter, right handed. Winner, Women's World Title, 1950, with a record of 9-0-51.2%; 1953, with a record of 7-0-35.7%.

DELEARY, STANLEY, b. July 20, 1914. W. Pauline (dec.); stepchildren—Jerry, Joe, Shirley, Construction Worker and Railroad Employee. S. Gordon; T. one and a quarter or one and three quarters, right handed. Played tournament horseshoe for 30 years. Winner, Massachusetts State Championship, 1936, 1939. Winner, New England Championship. Winner, Arizona State Championship, 1949, and nine more times. With Ted Allen, set a World Tournament record, combining for 12 consecutive four-deads. Finished sixth in 1948 World Tournament, with 25-6-77.5%. Complied a career record of 140 wins, 66 losses, a ringer percentage of 74.3, and a qualifying average of 514 points. Home: 929 North Delaware Drive, Space No. 9, Apache Junction AZ 85220.

DENNY, JIMMIE, Winner, Missouri State Championship, 1937, with a record of 14-1-67,3%.

DEUSTER, BOB, b. February 2, 1963. Marine Mechanic. S. Imperial: t. one and a quarter, right handed. Winner, Carl Steinfeldt Heritage Handicap, with 56% average. Winner, Heritage Club Class Championship. Came in second in World Tournament. Class B. High tournament average, 71.1%; high game, 88.8%. Home: North Road, Hampton Bays, NY 11946.

DEUSTER, LISA, b. February 2, 1963, Twin sister of Bob Deuster. Student S. Gordon; t. flip, right handed, Winner, Class B, Junior Girls World Tournament, 1977. Winner, Women's Division, Heritage Christmas Classic. Highest Tournament, 54,7%; highest game, 61,1%. Enjoys traveling and meeting people. Home: North Road, Hampton Bays, NY 11946.

DEUSTER, VIVIAN, H. Walter; children—Lisa, Bob. S. Gordon; t. flip, right handed. Winner, Class A. Championships— Vermont State Open, 1979; Orlando, FL, Open; Heritage National, in Massachusetts; Winner, Class F, World Tournament, Des Moines, IA, 1978. Finished ninth in Championship Division of World Tournament in Huntsville, AL, 1980. Finished third in New York State Tournament, 1980. Highest tournament average, 71%; highest game, 80%. Recipient, AAU Award of Achievement in horseshoe pitching. Home: North Road, Hampton Bays, NY 11946.

DEUSTER, WALTER, b. January 17, 1923. W. Vivian; children—Lisa, Bob. Building Contractor. S. Gordon; t. flip, right handed. Winner, Essex County Open, with a record of 7-0-60%, 1978. Winner, Sebring, FL, Open, with a record of 6-0-63%, 1980. High tournament average, 65.7%. Home: North Road, Hampton Bays, NY 11946.

DEWEESE, JOHNNIE K., b. February 13, 1909. W. Ivanell. Retired. S. Ohio; t. one and a quarter, right handed. Played horseshoes for 30 years, 25 years in tournaments. Played in state, national, and open tournaments. Has won trophies in Class A, Class B, and Class C competition. Has also played baseball and softball. Home: 550 High Street, Washington Court House, OH 43160.

DILGARD, GEORGE A., b. December 1, 1908. W. Geneva; children—Betty, Kenneth, Larry. Plastering Contractor. S. Ohio; t. one and three quarters, right handed. Has pitched horseshoes for 42 years, 23 years in tournament play. Has conducted many tournaments. Has won over 40 trophies. Among his Class A Championships are: Pickaway Ringer Classic, 1963; Bradenton Suncoast Open, 1965; Northwest District, 1966. Winner, Ohio State Class B Championship, 1959. Winner, Eastern National Class B Championship, with a record of 74.7%, ringers, 1962. Highest game, 92%. President, Crestline Horseshoe Club. Has constructed six horseshoe courts in his back yard. Home: 926 East Main Street, Crestline, OH 44827.

DINIUS, MEL, Elected Second Vice-President, Nevada Horseshoe Pitchers Association, 1980. Home: 250 East Seventh, Sun Valley, Sparks, NV 89431.

DISINGER, FRANK A., Inducted into the New York Horseshoe Pitchers Association Hall of Fame, 1979. Home: 6741 East High Street, Lockport, NY 14094.

DITMER, WANDA, b. March 2, 1911. H. Pete; child—Carolyn Sacks. Practical Nurse. S. Allen; t. three quarters, right handed. Winner, Indiana State Championship, 1962, 1967. Winner, Florida State Championship, 1970. Winner, Indiana State Fair Tournament, 1970. Finished second in World Tournaments, 1962, 1963. Won Greenville Classic, 1963; Indiana-Ohio Open, 1963, 1965, 1966; Desota Classic at Bradenton, FL, 1970. Highest tournament average 69.9%; highest game 82%. Home: 2401 Indianapolis Road, Lot 6, Hillcrest Mobile Court, Crawfordsville, IN 47933.

DITTMAN, ART, Winner, Utah State Championship, 1940.

DIXON, DALE, Married; has two children. Former General Contractor. T. one and three quarters. Participated in national horseshoe pitching events for over 50 years. Winner, Iowa State Championship, 11 times, between the years 1941 and 1959. Won many Class A Championships. In World Tournament Championship competition, has composite record of 69.7% and an average qualifying score of 500. Pitched games in the 80–90% bracket. Designed and manufactured a pitching shoe called the Dixon Victory Shoe. Built portable courts. Served as President, NHPA, 1953–1955. Became member, National Hall of Fame, 1973.

DOBLE, RICHARD F., b. August 21, 1936. W. Eleanor; children—Judy, Richard. Professor, Keene State College. Has Ph.D. degree. S. Allen; t. one and a quarter, right handed. Best tournament, 52%; high game, 62%. Has pitched horseshoes for 30 years, the past 17 in the NHPA. President, New England Horseshoe Pitchers Association. President, New Hampshire State Association. Has served as President and Tournament Director, Keene Horseshoe Club. Has run many tournaments, including the Keene Open, the New Hampshire State Tournament, and the New England Tournament. Has organized and run handicapped league. Has helped conduct several horseshoe clinics, where games of horseshoes was taught. Organized and directed New Hampshire's first Hall of Fame Committee. Has served as a member of New England Hall of Fame Committee. Home: 33 Wheelock Street, Keene, NH 03431.

DODGE, MELVIN B., b. February 15, 1924. W. Norma; children—Susan, Dana, Tom. Director, Columbus, OH, Department of Recreation and Parks. S. Gordon; t. one and a half, right handed. Has pitched horseshoes for 35 years. Chairman, State of Ohio AAU National Horseshoe Committee. Has been responsible for many tournaments and leagues in his area. Home: 5011 Heathmoor Drive, Columbus, OH 43220.

DOLAN, HARRY, S. Gordon; t. one and three quarters, right handed. Winner, Class B World Championship, Murray, UT, 1954. Winner, Senior Championships in California, 1952, 1953. Hit 69.5% in 1953 State Tournament. Resident of Fontana, CA.

DOLLEVOET, STELLA, Winner, Wisconsin Women's State Championship, with a record of 8-1-22.3%, 1969. Home: 810 East Lincoln, Little Chute, WI 54140.

DOLTER, JOSEPH, J., b. January 27, 1930. Wife (dec.); children—Steven, Joanne, Mary Kay, Robert. Commodity Pool Operator. S. Allen or Imperial; t. one and a quarter, right handed. Regional Director, Northwest Iowa. Organized the Dubuque (IA) Horseshoe Pitching Association, 1979; serves as Treasurer. Promoter of Key City Classic tournament. Plays in local tournaments and leagues. Highest tournament average, 58%; highest game, 75%. Home: 577 West Locust, Dubuque, IA 52001.

DOMER, RALPH L., b. July 1, 1911. Married; has two children. Stone Mason and Rancher. S. Allen and Ohio; t. one and three quarters, right handed. Has played horseshoes for 53 years. Began tournament play in 1966. President, Western Montana, HPA. Home: Box 541, East Helena, MT 59635.

DOMEY, BARBARA, b. July 30, 1962. Student. S. Allen; t. three quarters, right handed. Winner, Massachusetts Girls' State Championship, 1975 and 1976. Winner, New England Girls' Championship, 1976. Won eight tournaments in 1975; won three tournaments in 1976. Tied for 1975 Girls World Championship, lost playoff to finish second. Highset tournament average, 57.5%; highest game, 85%. Home: Stone School Road, Sutton, MA 01527.

DOMEY, EDWARD A., b. April 12, 1934.

W. Anne; children—Paul, Barbara, Janice. Contractor. S. Imperial or Hohl; t. one and a quarter, right handed. Has pitched horeshoes for 32 years, 12 years in tournament play. Winner, Massachusetts State Championship, 1975, 1976, 1978. Winner, New England Championship, 1974, hitting 74.4%. Won 7 consecutive Class A tournaments and 53 consecutive games. His 526 qualifying round in 1975 World Tournament is highest posted by a New England player. Highest tournament average, 83.5%; highest game, 92.4%. Owns and operates the Heritage Recreation Center in Sutton, MA, where leagues play and monthly tournaments take place. Wife and three children also pitch horseshoes. Home: 46 Stone School Road, Sutton, MA 01527.

DOMEY, JANICE, b. December 18, 1963. Student. S. Gordon; t. flip, right handed. Began pitching horeeshoes at the age of nine. Winner, Massachusetts Girls' State Championship, 1977, 1978, 1979. Winner, New England Championship, 1976, 1977, 1980. In 1980 contest, made a record of 6-0-48.7%. Won the Heritage Turkey Shoot, 1978; Franklin (NH) Warmup, 1977; Heritage Anniversary meet, Heritage January Thaw, Franklin Warmup, 1976; Franklin Warmup, 1975; Greater Lowell Invitational, 1974. Highest tournament average, 66.4%; highest game, 81.2%. Home: 46 Stone School Road, Sutton, MA 01527.

DOMEY, ROBERT C., b. July 20, 1937. W. Bonnie; children—Monica, Michelle. Mechanical Engineeer—Teacher. S. Imperial; t. one and a quarter, right handed. Has pitched horseshoes for 30 years, 20 years in tournament play. Winner, Rhode Island State Championship, 1975, 1976, 1977. Winner, New England Championship, 1978. Has won a number of tournaments, including Tournament of Champions at Sutton, 1977; January Thaw, 1978; Turkey Shoot, 1978; Greater Lowell Mixed, Turkey Shoot,

and Landry Memorial, 1979. In Landry Memorial meet, had record of 6-0-80.8%. Serves as State Secretary of State Association. Home: 6 Georgianna Avenue, North Smithfield, RI 02895.

DONNELL, SHIRLEY, SR., (dec.) (1904–1979). W. Anita; children—Shirley, Jr., Evans, Ben, Marilyn, Diane, Kathryn. Worked as Salesman of Classified Ads and Real Estate. S. Allen; t. three quarters. right handed. Competed in league and tournament play for 60 years. Winner, Texas State Championship, 1935, 1937. Family Residence: 1654 Dayton, Wichita Falls, TX 76301.

DORMAN, HUNTER LANE, b. November 28, 1937. W. Ruth Ellen; children—Hunter, Pamela, James, Daniel, Margaret, Elizabeth. General Electric Factory Worker. S. Allen; t. one and three quarters, right handed. Has played horseshoes for 20 years, 18 years in tournaments. Winner, AAU National Championship, AAU Indiana State Championship, 1980. Winner, Indiana-AHPA Travel League Championship, 1974, 1977, 1980. Winner, AHPA "Mr. Horseshoes" Award, 1978. High game, 93% ringers. Manager, Jasonville (IN) Travel League; President, Jasonville Horseshoe Club; Member, Board of Directors, Indiana-American Horseshoe Pitchers Association; Secretary, AHPA Travel League. Enjoys bowling and fresh water fishing. Home: Route 1, Box 240, Jasonville, IN 47438.

DOUGLAS, DONALD, b. November 10, 1938. Janitor. S. Ohio O; t. one and a quarter, right handed. Has pitched horseshoes for 16 years. Winner, North Carolina State Championship, 1974, 1975. Has won several open tournament titles. Home: Route 8, Box 91, Statesville, NC 28677.

DOUVILLE, MICHELLE, Winner, Canadian Junior Girls Championship, 1978,

1979. In 1979 contest, had record of 4-0-43.2%. Resident of Delmas, Saskatchewan.

DOVE, LINWOOD J., b. July 26, 1922. W. Frances; children—Donald Lee, Carol Ann, Barry Lynn. Salesman. S. Allen; t. one and a quarter, left handed. Has pitched horseshoes for 45 years, 38 years in league and tournament play. Winner, Virginia AAU State Championship, singles and doubles, 1951, posting his highest average, 66.4% and a high single game of 68%. Tied for third place in National AAU Tournament, 1952. Has won several local tournaments. First President of Virginia NHPA Chapter. Has served several terms as President of Hill City Horseshoe Club. Home: P.O. Box 10217, Lynchburg, VA 24506.

DOWNER, ELIZABETH A., b. May 23, 1931. H. Kenneth; child—Tommy. Inspector. S. Gordon; t. flip, right handed. Winner, Vermont State Championship, six times. State Tournament record in 1980 was 6-0-55.5%. Has won 20 tournaments—three Vermont Open titles. Was runnerup in New England Tournament, 1978, 1979. In 1978 tournament, made highest record—69% ringers; her single game high, 84%. Home: Route 2, Box 75, Bristol, VT 05443.

DRAPER, JACK, b. July 19, 1925. W. (dec.); children—Jackie, Jeanette, Jeff, Jim. Linotype Operator. S. Allen; t. one and a quarter, right handed. Has played horseshoes for 40 years, 25 years in league and tournament pitching. Received the Most Improved Player Award of the Iowa Hawkeye Horseshoe Pitching Association, 1968. South Central Iowa Regional Director. Served as Secretary of the World Tournament Committee of the IHHPA, 1978. Best game 70%; best tournament 58%. Home: 8113 Dema Drive, Des Moines, IA 50315.

DRURY, KEN, SR., b. April 12, 1913. W. Beatrice; children—Ken, Jr., Ron, Dane, Brenda. Bowling Establishment Proprietor.

S. Deadeye or Allen; t. one and a quarter, right handed. Winner, Michigan-Ontario Junior Championship, 1926. Winner first Canadian National Junior Championship, 1928. Winner, Canadian Senior Championship 50 years later, 1978; again in 1980. Won Bronze Medal in Canadian Olympic-type horseshoe competition, 1977. Won the first Pro-Am Tournament held in Niagara Fall, 1977, with a record of 10-1-76.7%. In NHPA Sanctioned League Program, had fourth highest game in nation, a 133-84% game. Best qualifying round, 513-80%, in 1977 World Tournament. Best Class A game, 80.46%. Shares a Senior Division world record with Carl Steinfeldt—96 ringers out of 120. Has won 17 tournaments and 80 trophies. Has taken part in many horseshoe pitching exhibitions and has pitched on television three times. Recipient, Sarnia City Award of Merit. President, Sarnia HPA. Home: 379 Talford Street, Sarnia, Ontario, Canada N7T 1R2.

DUBIE, JOSEPH N., (dec.) Played horseshoes for 70 years. Winner, Montana State Championship, each year from 1925–1935, except for 1933. In 1940 averaged 75% in Illinois state tournament and finished 17th in World Tournament. Winner, Georgia State Championship, 1967, at age of 81. Taught horseshoe pitching in Butte, MT, schools, 1930–1932. Organized the North Georgia Horseshoe Club (NHPA), 1965. Served as Georgia State Secretary, 1970–1971. Served as President, North Georgia Club. Organized Old Timers Club for horseshoe pitchers. Inducted into the Montana State Horseshoe Pitchers Hall of Fame, 1980. Was also a champion ice skater and roller skater and a skillful bowler.

DUCHARME, RITA, Winner, Massachusetts Women's State Championship, 1967, with a record of 3-0-48.7%; 1968, with a record of 2-0-59.4%.

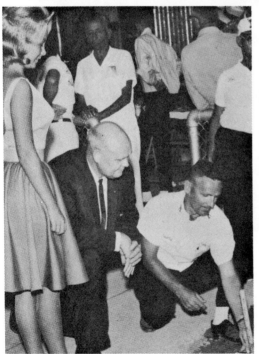

Top, 1952 New England Championship team. Porter Clark is second from right in top row. *Center,* Southgate Courts, with world tournament in progress. *Bottom, left,* Harold Craig, NHPA president, judges a close one at Southgate. *Center,* Phyllis Dahl. *Right,* Curt Day.

Top, left, Stanley Dahl, Canadian Champion. *Right,* Charles Davis, World Champion, with runner-up Duryee. *Center, left,* Paul Day. Bob and Cindy Dean. *Bottom,* John Davis (extreme right, second row) at Bradenton club tournament in 1965.

DUDEK, JOHN, Winner, Connecticut State Championship, 1960, with a record of 11-4-58.8%.

DUGLE, ARTHUR, Retired Postal Clerk. S. Allen; t. one and a quarter, right handed. Winner, Illinois State Championship, 1958, with a record of 11-0-81.6%; 1962, with a record of 11-0-79%; 1963, with a record of 10-1-75.1%. His 81.6% in 1958, an Illinois State record. Finished third in World Tournament at Murray City, UT, 1959, owns a composite record of 95 wins, 80 losses, 71.3% ringers and a 505 qualifying score average. Home: Oak Forest Hospital, Ward F-11, Bed 13, 15900 South Cicero Avenue, Oak Forest, IL 60452.

DUMONT, GARY G., b. May 12, 1962. Hardware Salesman. S. Allen; t. one and a quarter, right handed. Winner, Class C Junior World Championship, 1976, hitting 50.8% for the tournament and 62.5% in high game. Winner, Massachusetts State Boys Championship, 1978. Also takes part in backpacking and water skiing and likes hi fidelity music. Home: 506 Nashua Road, Dracut, MA 01826.

DUMONT, WILLIE, Resident of Saint Laurent, Manitoba, Canada. President, Manitoba Horseshoe Players Association—elected 1978.

DUNCAN, GRACIE, Winner, Ohio Girls State Championship, 1975, with a record of 3-0-18.6%.

DUNKER, LEIGH, b. March 23, 1915. Farmer. S. American; t. one and a quarter, left handed. Winner, South Dakota State Championship, 28 times between 1934 and 1976. Received Sports Illustrated award on winning his 24th title. Has won 35 open tournaments. High qualifying percentage, 84%, a record for his state. Highest tournament average, 79.4%; highest single game, 90%. Has served as President and as Secretary-Treasurer of the South Dakota Horseshoe Pitchers Association. Home: Warner, SD 57479.

DUNLEARY, GARY, Winner, Connecticut State Boys Championship, 1961, with a win-and-loss record of 7-0.

DUPUIS, CHARLES, Member, Board of Directors of Canadian Horseshoe Pitcher's Association. Past President, New Brunswick Horseshoe Players Association. Has actively promoted horseshoe pitching by holding clinics and staging tournaments and exhibitions. Home: 10 Roxbury Drive, Apt. 1, St. John, N.B., Canada.

DURFEE, RAY, Winner, Washington State Boys Championship, 1974, with a record of 7-0-68.5%.

DURHAM, JENE F., b. February 6, 1928. Hospital Equipment and Table Maker. S. Imperial; t. one and three quarters, right handed. Winner, Maryland State Championship, 1961. Winner, AAU Championship, 1951. Won New Jersey Open, 1960, with 7-2-67.8%. Won Rosselet Memorial, 1962, with 7-0-70%. Finished second in Winston-Salem Open, 1960, averaging 72%. Finished third in Pennsylvania State Tournament. Highest tournament record, 11-4-75.2%, with a high game of 88%. Also bowls. Home: 414 South Bentalou Street, Baltimore, MD 21223.

DURR, HENRY, (dec.) S. Gordon; t. one and three quarter, right handed. Winner, Class C World Championship, 1970, hitting 69.6%. Finished third in Class C of World Tournament, 1964, with 70.6%; finished sixth in Class B, 1966, with 67.6%. Attended many world tournaments. Averaged in the 60–70% range as a Class A pitcher. Was a resident of California.

DURYEE, BERT, Winner, Ohio State Championship, 1930, 1931, 1932. In 1931 tournament, had a record of 23-1-71.5%.

Winner, Kansas State Championship, 1924, 1934. His 1934 record—7-0-74%. Pitched widely known game in 1928 with C. C. Davis, that went 132 shoes. Davis record: 100 ringers for 75.7%; Duryee's record: 96 ringers for 72.7%.

DUTREMBLE, FERNAND, President, La Federation des Clubs De Fers Du Quebec, Inc. Named to post of Provincial Director, 1965. Has been active, with his wife Henriette, in staging Canadian National Championships and the "Horseshoe Canada" annual reunion. Home: 290 Fisel, Sorel, Quebec, Canada, J3P 3R1.

DUTREMBLE, HENRIETTE, Secretary-Treasurer, La Federation des Clubs De Fers Du Quebec, Inc. Named Provincial Secretary in 1971. Active with her husband Fernand in staging horseshoe pitching events in Canada. Home: 290 Fisel, Sorel, Quebec, Canada, J3P 3R1.

DYER, DEBORAH, b. May 15, 1966. Student. S. American; t. one and a quarter, right handed. Winner, New Hampshire State Girls Championship, 1979, with a record of 2-0-13.3%; winner again in 1980. Winner, Keene Warmup, 1979. Home: 12 Harold Road, Keene, NH 03431.

DYKES, RALPH E., b. November 21, 1913. W. Delores; child—Jimmie Joe Hixon. Retired Factory Worker. S. Ohio O; t. one and a quarter, right handed. Has pitched horseshoes for 45 years. President, NHPA, 1967–1973. President, Illinois Horseshoe Pitchers Association, 1948–1968. President, Chicago Horseshoe League, 5 years. Serves as aide to World Tournament Director. Winner, Garfield Park Class A Championship, 1954. Member, Center Club Winners of Chicago Horseshoe League, 1946–1949. Has played in World Tournament competition, Championship Division. Highest tournament, 68%; highest game, 78.5%. Recipient, Stokes Memorial Award of NHPA, 1968; Il-

linois HPA Award, 1968; NHPA Achievement Award, 1978. Inducted into NHPA Hall of Fame, 1973. Made Charter Member, Illinois NPA Hall of Fame, 1977. Home: 433 West North Avenue, Lombard, IL 60148.

DYSON, MARK, b. August 9, 1967. Grandson of Flake Dyson, a horseshoe pitcher. Winner, Junior Boys World Championship, at age 11, 1979, with a record of 9-2-73.6%; 1980, with a record of 11-0-82.1%. Winner, Frye Memorial Tournament in Winchester, VA; averaged 80% ringers. Winner, Stateville Dogwood, 1979; averaged 71.8% ringers. Winner, Elmont, Va. Open, 1979; averaged 79.8% ringers and hit highest game, 86.8%. Winner, North Carolina State Title, 1980, with a record of 5-0-78%. Has appeared on Kids World and P. M. Magazine television programs. Home: Route 5, Box 428, Taylorsville, NC 28681.

E

EACHUS, FRANK, (dec.) Winner, Ohio State Championship, 1916. Won medals, ribbons, and cups for horseshoe pitching activities.

EAKER, H. R., Won the Tennessee State Championship, 1924, becoming the first Tennessee State Champion. Became first Vice-President of the Tennessee State Horseshoe Pitchers Association when it was organized in 1928. Resident of Chattanooga, TN.

EARLEY, TERRANCE, Has played in Championship Division of World Tournaments in Murray City, UT, and Keene, NH. Has won several Class A honors. Defeated World Champion Ted Allen in a game. Averages about 70% ringers. Home: 2180 Ryer Avenue, Bronx, NY 10468.

EATON, PATRICIA L., b. June 12, 1931. H. Eldon; children—Jerry, Mickey, Bill. S. Ohio; t. flip, right handed. Winner, Wisconsin State Championship, 1976–1980. Other winnings include: Eau Claire City and County, Boyceville Open, Mountain Open, Goldendale Open, Combined Locks Open, and League—Class A. High tournament average: 72.9% ringers in Boyceville Open, 1979; high game: 88.9% in Greenville World Tournament, 1977. Tournament Director for the Annual Eau Claire Open. Selected as Athlete of the Year by *The Leadership Telegram* of Eau CLaire, WI, 1977, 1978, 1979. Home: 3027 Saturn Avenue, Eau Claire, WI 54701.

EBERHART, DR. DALE R., b. December 6, 1906. W. Phyllis; children—David, Marilynn Van Doren, Janis Kocanowski, Connie Nicolay, Quentin, Kathleen Senders, Gary. Research Chemist. S. Ohio; t. one and a quarter, right handed. Has played horseshoes for 50 years, 14 years in NHPA tournaments. Winner, with Ron Vogel, New Jersey State Doubles Championship, 1971. Winner, Class A Championship, John Rosselet Memorial Open, 1974. Winner, Class B New Jersey State Championship, 1971, 1974. Highest tournament average, 53.3%; highest game, 68%. President, New Jersey State HPA, 1973. Has served as Regional Director, NHPA, for New Jersey, Delaware, and Maryland. President, Middlesex Horseshoe Club, 1969–1971. Inducted into Middlesex Hall of Fame and New Jersey HPA Hall of Fame, 1977. Home: 319 Beechwood Avenue, Middlesex, NJ 08846.

EBERLY, DARRYL L., b. February 6, 1961. College Student. S. Imperial; t. one and a quarter, right handed. Winner, Pennsylvania State Boys Championship, 1977. Highest tournament average, 37.8%; Highest game, 53%. Home: 2373 Cottonwood Road, York, PA 17404.

EBERT DARLENE, b. December 8, 1933. H. Dan; child—Greg, foster child—Kip. S. Gordon; t. flip, right handed. Has played horseshoes for about 25 years. Winner, Wisconsin State Championship, 1972, with a record of 7-0-51.3%; 1973, 1974, 1975. Has served as Secretary, Fillmore Men's Horseshoe League, Fillmore Couples League, since 1968. With husband, maintains a foster home for boys. Home: 684 Highway 84, R1, Fredonia, WI 53021.

EDMONDS, JOHN R., b. February 22, 1926. W. Margaret; children—Donna, Iris, Doug, Mike, Jeff. Self-Employed—Home Improvement. S. Imperial; t. one and a quarter, right handed. Has pitched horseshoes for almost 50 years. Winner, with partner, North Carolina State Doubles Championship, 1979, 1980. Won the following Class A tournaments: 1980 NBHC Spring Open, with 7-2-67.6%; NBNC Invitational, with 4-1-69.3%; May NBHC, with 4-1-72.7% in regular round robin play and 70.9% in a playoff. Received national recognition for high average award—106.15 points per game, NHPA Sanctioned League Play, 1979. High tournament average, 71.7%; high game, 88.9%. League Director, NHPA Sanctioned League; Secretary, North Buncombe Horseshoe Club; Buncombe County Director. Home: Route 3, Box 308, Weaverville, NC 28787.

EDMONDSON, LOWELL, Finished 18th in 1948 World Tournament, with a record of 20-11-75%. Qualified at 511. Resident of Plainfield, IN.

EDMONDSON, G. H. "GERRY," Married, with two children. Operator, KOA Kampground. S. Gordon; t. one and a quarter, right handed. Served as President, Alabama Horseshoe Pitchers Association, 1969–1975; served as Vice-President, 1966–1968. Hosted State Tournament at Lillian, AL, 1969. Served as President of Foley JC's, hosts of tournament at Gulf Shores. Home: Route 1, Lillian, AL 36549.

EDWARDS, DOUG. Winner, Iowa Boys State Championship, 1967, with 8-0 record.

EDWARDS, MYRNA, b. April 2, 1927. H. Francis; children—Doug, Randy, Laurie, Melinda. S. Allen; t. flip-modified, right handed. Winner, Iowa State Women's Championship, 1979. Winner, with husband, Iowa State Mixed Doubles, 1978, 1979. Winner, Cedar Falls, IA, Open, 1979, with a record of 4-0-48%. Won Clay County Fair titles, 1977, 1978. Highest tournament, 5-0-50.5%. Serves as Secretary-Treasurer of local horseshoe club. Home: Route 2, Newell, IA 50568.

EGDOM, DAWN, Winner, New York Girls State Championship, 1974.

EHLERS, ALAN, b. November 14, 1959. Student; United Parcel Service Employee. S. Allen; t. reverse three quarters, left handed. Winner, Illinois Junior State Championship, 1977. Highest tournament, 58%; highest game, 70%. Home: 4125 Winston Drive, Hoffman Estates, IL 60195.

EHLERS, ROGER M., June 4, 1936. W. Barbara; children—Alan, John, Julie. Tool and Dye Maker. S. Allen; t. one and a quarter, right handed. Has played horseshoes for 28 years, 24 years in league and tournament competition. Winner, National AAU Championship in Winston-Salem, NC, 1961. Winner, with partner, National AAU Doubles Championship, 1959, 1960, 1961. Has won several Class A Championships in Illinois and Wisconsin. Highest tournament, 67%; highest game, 84%. Has pitched horseshoes on television. President and Secretary, Northern Illinois Horseshoe League. Home: 4125 Winston Drive, Hoffman Estates, IL 60195.

EHRESMAN, EUGENE and ELAINE, Husband and Wife Horseshoe Team. Inducted as team into South Dakota Horseshoe Pitchers Association Hall of Fame, 1979.

Have been active in promoting horseshoe pitching in state of South Dakota.

EISEMAN, FARRON, b. July 23, 1955. Farmer-Trucker. S. Imperial; t. one and three quarters, right handed. Has been playing horseshoes since he was eleven. Winner, Junior Boys World Championship, 1967, with a record of 6-0-73.6%; 1968, with a record of 7-0-78.5%. Held or shared 13 world records in 1967 tournament. Won Wyoming Boys' State titles, 1966, 1967, 1968. Has won numerous local titles. High tournament average, 85.1%; high game, 90%. Home: North Portal Route, Riverton, WY 82501.

ELKINS, JOHN, b. September 29, 1909. W. Hazel; child—Alma Raines. Farm, Recreation Department and School Employee. S. Ohio; t. one and a quarter, right handed. Played horseshoes for 57 years. Winner, Missouri State Championship, six times between 1949 and 1960. Won over 40 Class A tournaments, including Ozark Opens and Missouri Opens. His combined world tournament record, 88-82-69.1% ringers; highest individual record, 7-0-73%. Served for several years as Secretary, Missouri State Horseshoe Pitchers' Association. Home: 1006 Randolph, Neosho, MO 64850.

ELLER, DARRELL, Winner, North Carolina State Championship, 1965, with a record of 9-0-70.2%. Won several Class A tournaments; averaged over 70% ringers.

ELLIOTT, JACK, Winner, Kentucky Boys State Championship, 1971, with a record of 7-0-39.9%.

ELLISON, MARVIN RUDOLPH, b. December 12, 1941. W. Sharon; children—James, Charlotte, Tammy. Employee, Saskatchewan Provincial Championship, 1979, hitting 62.9% ringers and a high game of 76.5%. Finished fourth in Canadian National, 1979, with a record of 3-4-60.4%.

Has won many Class A Championships in local tournaments. Hit 14 consecutive doubles in tournament play. Recipient, Best Player in Saskatchewan Award, 1980. Home; Box 441, Raymore, Saskatchewan, Canada S0A 3J0.

ELLISON, SHARON LEA, b. December 7, 1949. H. Marvin; children—James, Charlotte, Tammy. S. Ohio; t. three quarters and single flip, left handed. Winner, Class B Ladies Championship in the Canadian Nationals, 1977. Has hit seven consecutive doubles. President, News Editor, Saskatchewan Horseshoe Pitchers Association. Has published a Saskatchewan Hall of Fame booklet. Has been active in promoting an Intermediate Ladies Division in Canada. Home: Box 441, Raymore, Saskatchewan, Canada, S0A 3J0.

ELMERSON, HARVEY, b. March 23, 1904. W. Virginia; children—Carla, Marlene. Retired International Harvester Employee. S. Ohio; t. one and a quarter, right handed. Has pitched horseshoes for 68 years. Winner, Wisconsin State Championship, nine times between 1926 and 1943. His 1931 record: 11-0-69.8%. In World Tournament, Championship play, made record of 114 wins, 51 losses, 63.9% ringers, and average qualifying score of 490. Runnerup for 1935 World Championship with a record of 19-4-72.1%. Has pitched 18 doubles in a row. Became Charter Member, Wisconsin Hall of Fame, 1976. Home: 110 Pleasant View Drive, Wisconsin Rapids, WI 54494.

ELVIG, KEN, b. January 14, 1913. W. Margaret; four children. Laundry Manager. S. Allen; t. one and a quarter, right handed. Has pitched horseshoes for 25 years, 20 years in tournament play. Winner, Whatcoma County Championship, four times. Has won many class titles and trophies. In top ten in ringer percentages in state of Washington, 1976-1980. Has served as Presi-

dent and Secretary, Bellingham Horseshoe Club. Writes poetry. Home: 1225 Roland Street, Bellingham, WA 98225.

EMERSON, BEN, Winter, Michigan State Championship, 1925.

ENDERS, CYRIL C., b. May 18, 1900. W. Margaret; children—Dorothy, William, Charlene, Wilbert, Evelyn. Furnace Operator (for 48 years). S. Allen; t. one and a quarter, right handed. Has pitched horseshoes for 74 years. Winner, Class C, Brady's Run Park Tournament, 1980. Winner, Class B Seniors World Championship, at Erie, PA, 1969. Has won many class championships. Has pitched in leagues for many years, beginning with the Aliquippa League, 1933. Bowls, sings in a chorus, and gardens. Home: 52A Street, Van Buren Homes, Beaver, PA 15009.

ENGBRECHT, KEITH, Winner, South Dakota Boys State Championship, 1977, with a 35% average.

ENGEBRETSON, ART, (dec.), (1908–1977). Was Burlington Railroad Employee. Winner, North Dakota State Championship, 16 times between 1928 and 1968. Set state record with his 71.2% average in 1961 meet; set state record for high game, 81.2%, 1932; set state record for most qualifying points, 469, 1959. Won 37 championships, 21 open tournaments. Managed tournaments in North Dakota. Served as Director, North Dakota Horseshoe Pitchers' Association. Served as official in Fargo, ND, horseshoe club for 35 years. Recipient of a number of awards for horseshoe pitching. Named "Mr. Horseshoe Pitcher of North Dakota" by North Dakota State Association, 1971. The Art Engebretson Open named in his honor, 1973.

ENGLEMANN, GEORGE, b. February 22, 1913. W. Violet; children—Bonnie, Bruce, Robert. Farmer and Part-time Government Employee. S. Allen; t. one and a quarter, right handed. Has pitched horseshoes for 60 years, 20 years in tournament and league competition. Pitched in World Tournament, Des Moines, IA, 1978. Highest tournament average, 50%; highest game, 72%. Accrued 119 points in a 50-shoe count-all game, Buena Vista County Fair, 1965. Active in promoting, originating, and overseeing operations of horseshoe pitching meets. Received Quad-County Horseshoe Association award for his services, 1975. Assistant Regional Director for Nebraska and Iowa. First Vice-President, Iowa Hawkeye Horseshoe Pitchers Association. Member, Iowa Hawkeye Horseshoe Pitchers Association Hall of Fame. Home: Rural Route 1, Storm Lake, IA 50588.

ENGERSOLL, PAUL, Winner, Illinois State Championship, 1941, with a record of 14-1-73.3%.

ENGLAND, RAY, Winner, Indiana Men's Senior State Championship, 1957.

ENGLE, OSCAR "BUCK," S. Imperial; t. one and three quarters, right handed. Winner, Class B World Championship, 1974; averaged 72.6% ringers. Winner, Pennsylvania State Championship, 1968, with a record of 14-1-75.6%; 1971, with a record of 15-1-80.2%; 1974; 1975. Finished 12th in World Tournament, 1969. Has pitched in Eastern National, Winchester, and Lynchburg tournaments; in open tournaments in Pennsylvania and Ohio. Home: 1525 Rockland Avenue, Pittsburgh, PA 15216.

ENGLISH, CLAYTON, S. Allen; t. one and a quarter, right handed. Winner, Canadian National Championship, 1976, hitting 57.3% ringers. Winner, Class C Championship, World Tournament, 1977, hitting 67.4% ringers. Resident of Sourin, Manitoba, Canada.

ERICKSON, ARNOLD, b. April 20, 1912.

W. Helen; children—Carol, Robert, Nancy, Gene, Terry. Retired Electrical Operator. S. Allen; t. one and a quarter, right handed. Has pitched horseshoes for 50 years, 15 years in NHPA. High tournament average, 61%; high game, 72%. Has been active in organizing, promoting, and directing horseshoe pitching meets. President, Rapidan Club. Vice-President, Apache Trail League. Has served as Director, Minnesota State Tournament, 1978; President, East Horseshoe League; Second Vice-President, Minnesota Gopher State Association; Director, Southwest Minnesota League; Chairman, Minnesota Hall of Fame Committee for three years. Received Rapidan Man of the Year Award, 1971–1976. Became Member, Minnesota Horseshoe Pitchers' Hall of Fame, 1974. Home: Route 1, Box 299A, Mankato, MN 56001.

ERICKSON, CHRIS, Finished 12th in World Tournament, 1922, with a 3–12 record. From Beresford, SD.

ERICKSON, GENE C., b. June 8, 1946. W. Jan; children—Damon, Sean. Machinist. S. Allen; t. one and a quarter, right handed. Has pitched horseshoes for over 20 years. High tournament, 47.6%; high game, 66%. Minnesota State Tournament Director, 1979. Secretary-Treasurer, Rapidan Horseshoe Club. President, East League. Director, Southwest Horseshoe League. Named "Man of the Year" by Rapidan Horseshoe Club, 1974. Has indoor horseshoe pitching court in basement of home. Home: Route 2, Box 14, Good Thunder, MN 56037.

ERICKSON, JAN, b. March 24, 1951. H. Gene; children—Damon, Sean. Bookkeeper. S. Allen or Deadeye; t. one and a quarter, right handed. Winner, Women's Division Championship, Southwest Horseshoe League, 1976. Winner, Class A Championship in Bertha Harvest Festival, 1979, with a record of 7-0-38.4%. High tournament average, 38.4%; high game, 54%. Secretary-Treasurer, Minnesota State Horseshoe Pitchers Association, since 1977. Formed a Women's Horseshoe Pitching League in Rapidan. Home: Route 2, Box 14, Good Thunder, MN 56037.

ERICKSON, VERNE, Winner, South Dakota State Championship, 1926, 1927.

ERICKSON, CHRIS, Winner, Massachusetts Boys State Championship, 1973, with a record of 6-0-63.3%.

ERMATINGER, H. L., (dec.), President, NHPA, 1925–1933. Plaque in his honor in Florida Hall of Fame. Was resident of St. Petersburg, FL.

ERNEST, MIKE, Winner, Nebraska Boys State Championship, 1977, with 56.8 ringer percentage; 1978, with 63.6 ringer percentage.

ERWIN, JACK (dec.) (1916–1980). Pitched horseshoes for over 50 years. Winner, Missouri State Championship, 1932, at age 16; 1946, with average of 71% ringers. Home of widow, Edith Erwin: 3613 South Crane, Independence, MO 64055.

EUTSLER, DAN, Winner, Indiana Boys State Championship, 1964.

EVANS, JAMES, Winner, Georgia State Championship, 1968, with a record of 7-0; 1969, with a record of 7-1; 1972, with a record of 11-0-50%.

EVERITT, ALVINA, Winner, Saskatchewan Provincial Women's Championship, 1962, 1963, 1965, 1968, 1969. Winner with Sverre Holm, Mixed Doubles Championship, 1960; with Stan Everitt, 1963, 1964, 1965, 1966, 1969.

F

FAHEY, JACK, b. October 5, 1945. Clerk. S. Allen; t. one and a quarter, right handed.

Winner, Kentucky State Championship, five times. Made following records in Kentucky State Tournament play: Hit seven consecutive four-deads, 1977; qualified with 90% ringers and 279 points, 1978; had a high game of 90%, with 27 out of 30; posted 32 consecutive state tournament victories, 1978, 1979, 1980. Won 15 of 16 tournaments played in Florida circuit, 1978. Highest qualifier, World Tournament, 1977, with 554 points; 1978, with 92%. Highest tournament, 7-0-83.5%; highest game, 96.5%. Served as Vice-President, Georgetown, KY, Club, 1973. Home: 124 Paris Avenue, Lexington, KY 40505; 2808 18th Street West, Bradenton, FL 33505.

FALES, DONALD E., b. October 10, 1925. W. Marjorie; children—Kenneth, Donna. Plant Manager. S. Allen; t. one and a quarter, right handed. Has pitched in tournament play for over 15 years. Highest tournament average, 57%. Organizer and promoter of horseshoe pitching events. Became Member of New Hampshire State NPA Hall of Fame, 1980; New England HPA Hall of Fame, 1980. Director, New England Horseshoe Pitchers Association, since 1976. Served as President, New Hampshire State Horseshoe Pitchers Association, 1969–1971; 1973–1976. Key figure in establishing Franklin Horseshoe Club; served as President, 1970–1975. Enjoys fishing. Home: P.O. Box 247, West Franklin, NH 03235.

FALES, KENNETH EUGENE, b. October 9, 1963. Student. S. Allen; t. one and a quarter, right handed. Winner, New Hampshire Boys State Championship, 1978, with high game of 96% ringers. Enjoys fishing and motorcycle riding. Home: P.O. Box 247, West Franklin, NH 03225.

FALOR, HAROLD, (dec.) Youngest player to win a World Championship, at age 15, in St. Petersburg, FL, 1923. Finished 8th in World Tournament, 1921; finished 8th in

1922; finished 10th in 1928. Also played in Midwestern tournaments. In 156 games in World Tournament competition, won 97, lost 59, and averaged 52.7% ringers.

FARNSWORTH, GARY, S. Allen: T. one and three quarters reverse, right handed. Winner, Illinois Boys State Championship, 1957. Finished 11th in Championship Division, World Tournament, 1966, with a record of 8-9-79.3%. Has won many major tournaments, averaging over 80% ringers in several. Home: 1515 Kilarny Street, Greenville, IL 62246.

FECHT, LOIS JANEA, b. October 5, 1961. Waitress. S. Diamond Tournament; t. three quarters, right handed. Winner, Nebraska Girls State Championship, 1977, 1978. Winner, Valentine Open; a number of Class A Championships. Highest tournament average, 43.8%; highest game, 50%. Home: Route 2, Box 75, Berwyn, NB 68819.

FELICCIA, VITO, Pfizer Chemical Company Employee. T. One and three quarters. Pitched tournament horseshoes for 40 years. Won over 100 Class A tournament titles. Winner, New York State Championship, 1936, 1949. Made 75.2% in 1936 tournament, a record at that time. Played in Eastern Open and in New Jersey, Pennsylvania, and Connecticut Opens. Played in Ft. George and De Kalb Clubs of Brooklyn, NY. Member, New York State Hall of Fame.

FENDER, WALTER. Married; one child. Retired Self-Employed Tinsmith. S. Allen; t. one and a quarter, right handed. Has been involved in horseshoe pitching and in promoting horseshoe events in Greenville, OH, since the 1950's. President and a founder of Greenville Horseshoe Club. Is an antique buff.

FENICCHA, STEVE, (dec.) Gardener. Married; two children. S. Allen; t. one and three quarters, right handed. Winner, New York State Championship, 1963, with a record of 6-1-69.9%. Played in Championship Division of many New York State and World Tournaments. In 1969 Eastern National, hit 52 consecutive ringers; hit ten consecutive four-deads twice in a game; made 99% in a game. Was a gourmet cook and bowler. Home: 627 Rumson Road, Rochester, NY 14616.

FERGUSON, CAROL, b. March 24, 1942. H. Max; children—Judi, Bechi. Waitress. S. Diamond; t. flip, right handed. Has played tournament horseshoe pitching for 18 years. Winner, Wyoming Women's State Championship, 1966, with a record of 6-0-39.2%; 1967, with 8-0-48.4%; 1969, with 15-3-49%. Has won city league and Rocky Mountain Open championship trophies. High tournament game, 66.5%. Home: Paradise Valley Route, Box 2425, Riverton, WY 82501.

FERGUSON, JUDY, b. November 29, 1964. Student. S. Diamond; t. flip, right handed. Winner, Wyoming Junior State Championship, 1980, with a record of 5-0-21%. Won trophy for high junior percentage. Home: Paradise Valley Route, Box 2425, Riverton, WY 82501.

FERGUSON, MYRON, Winner, Ohio State Championship, 1942. Placed 5th in Class B of World Tournament, 1935, with a record of 17-6-63.8%. Resident of Columbus, OH.

FERGUSON, RICHARD E., b. June 27, 1930. W. Helen; children—Steven, Carol, Terri. Teacher. S. Ohio Pro; t. one and a quarter, right handed. Has pitched horseshoes for 20 years. Winner, Seminole Open, with a record of 4-1-57.1%. Winner, Chris Hanson Open, 1979, with a record of 5-1-58.7%. Highest tournament average, 65%; highest game, 78.1%. Editor, Florida Horseshoe News. Secretary-Treasurer, Sarasota

Club. Served as President, Florida State Association, 1974–1977. Served as Assistant NHPA Regional Director. Enjoys bowling and bicycling. Home: 4337 Midland Road, Sarasota, FL 33581.

FESTA, JOSEPH L., b. February 9, 1923. W. Mary. Security and Air Force Protection Worker. S. Allen; t. one and a quarter, right handed. Has played 15 years of tournament horseshoe pitching. Has won several local and New England Class B Championships. Made 65% in McDonnell Memorial. Served as President, New Hampshire Horseshoe Pitchers Association, 1972. Home: 70 Benham Street, Hamden, CT 06514.

FEUDNER, A. L., Served as Vice-President, Minnesota State Horseshoe Pitchers Association, 1920. Resident of Hopkins, MN.

FICKBOHM, CHRISTINE, b. September 23, 1918. H. Walter (dec.); children—Diane, Paul, Warren. Factory Worker. S. Gordon and Allen; t. one and a quarter, right handed. Has pitched horseshoes for 20 years. Winner, South Dakota Women's State Championship, 1968, with a record of 5-0-31.7%; 1969, with 5-0-27.4%. Highest ringer percentage, 56. Served on South Dakota Board of Directors and on 1980 Hall of Fame Committee. Enjoys sewing and fishing. Home: 408 Union, Box 191, Alcester, SD 57001.

FICKBOHM, LUVERNE R., b. August 11, 1919. W. Klara; children—Kenneth, Mary. Farmer. S. Allen and Gordon; t. one and three quarters, right handed. Has pitched horseshoes for 30 years, 25 years in tournament play. Winner, Westfield Championship, 1967. Winner, Orton, MN, Class A Championship, 1977. Finished second in Class A Division, State Tournament, 1974, 1976, 1978; finished third, 1977. Finished second in Brookings Open, 1980. High tournament game, 80%. Served for many years as manager or co-manager, Spink Local Team

in the Sioux Valley League. Enjoys hunting and fishing. Home: Route 1—Box 56, Burbank, SD 57010.

FICKBOHM, WALTER, (dec.) (1917–1978). Widow, Christine; children—Diane, Paul, Warren. S. Allen; t. one and a quarter or one and three quarters, right handed. Played tournament horseshoes for 22 years. Winner, South Dakota State Championship, 1962, with a record of 11-0-64.5%; 1968, with 11-1-59.3%. High game, 89.6%. Vice-President, South Dakota Horseshoe Pitchers Association, several years; member of Board of Directors. Managed local team in league play. Inducted into South Dakota HPA Hall of Fame, 1976. Home of Widow: 408 Union, Alcester, SD.

FIELDS, BEN, b. December 15, 1922. W. Hilda; children—Rod, Tim. Builder. S. Allen; t. flip, right handed. Has pitched horseshoes for over 30 years. Has won following Class A Championships: Colorado Springs Open, 1975; Crested Butte Open, 1977; Crested Butte Ringer Tournament, 1978. High tournament average, 58%; high game, 78%. Vice-President, Colorado Horseshoe Pitchers' Association. President, Colorado Springs Club. Home: 2309 Patrician Way, Colorado Springs, CO 80909.

FINNIE, COLIN, b. September 3, 1963. Student. S. Imperial; t. one and a quarter, right handed. Winner, Saskatchewan Junior Boys Championship, 1980. Winner, British Columbia Junior International Open Championship, 1980. Finished second in Canadian Championship meet. Highest tournament average, 63.5%; highest game, 88.5%. Has hit 7 consecutive doubles. Home: General Delivery, Nut Mountain, Saskatchewan, Canada, SOA 2WO.

FINNIE, IRVAN, b. January 1, 1929. W. S.Ruby; children—Colin, Karen, Cherellee. Farmer and School Bus Driver. S. Imperial; t. one and a quarter, right handed. Has pitched horseshoes for 35 years. Winner, Alberta Open Championship, 1974; finished second in this event, 1980. With wife and son, played in World Tournament, Huntsville, AL, 1980. Highest tournament average, 60%; highest game, 63.3%. Home: General Delivery, Nut Mountain, Saskatchewan, Canada, SOA 2WO.

FINNIE, RUBY, b. June 23, 1940. H. Irvan; children—Colin, Karen, Cherellee. S. Ohio; t. three quarters, right handed. Winner, Saskatchewan Championship, 1976, 1978. Winner, Alberta Open, 1979, 1980. Winner, Saskatchewan Open, 1978. Won Class B Championship in the Canadian Nationals, 1980. Finished second in the British Columbia International Open. Highest tournament average, 54.9%; highest game, 70.6%. Home: General Delivery, Nut Mountain, Saskatchewan, Canada, SOA 2WO.

FISH, HELEN, Winner, New England States Championship, 1963. Resident of Keene, NH.

FISH, REGINALD, Past President, Keene (NH) Horseshoe Club. Played major role in staging 1965 World Tournament in Keene, NH. Resident of Keene, NH.

FISHEL, EDWARD W., b. April 11, 1915. W. Maxine; children—Dale, Phillip. Quality Control Coordinator—Timber Cutting. S. Allen; t. one and a quarter, right handed. Has pitched horseshoes for 48 years, 35 years in tournament play. Winner, Washington State Championship, 1959, with a record of 15-0-78.2%; 1963, with 15-0-76%. Winner, Northwest Championship, 1961, 1963, with 15-0 both years. Winner, Bryant Memorial, 1955, with 7-0; 1956, with 7-1. Hit 78.4% in World Tournament at Greenville, OH, 1964. Highest game, 96.7%. Became Member, Washington State NPA Hall of Fame, 1975. Home: P.O. Box 12, Neilton, WA 98566.

FISHEL, PHILIP E., Winner, First Washington Boys State Championship, 1954, with 50.9% ringer average; 1955, with 53.6% ringer average. Home: P.O. Box 435, Juneau, AK 99802.

FISHER, MEL, b. January 20, 1931. W. Kathy; children—Sandra, Heather, Glenn. Farmer. S. Dean; t. one and a quarter, right handed. Has pitched horseshoes for over 30 years. Has coached junior players. First Vice-President, Charter Member, Alberta Horseshoe Pitchers' Association. Charter Member, Edmonton Horseshoe Club. Served as Chairman of Alberta Summer Games. Home: Route 1, Morinville, Alberta, Canada TOG 1PO.

FISHER, ROLAND, Winner, Vermont State Championship, 1957, with a record of 8-1-57.2%.

FITE, RANDY, Winner, Iowa Boys State Championship, 1970.

FITZMORRIS, PAT. H., b. October 10, 1907. Brick Industry Worker. S. Allen; t. one and a quarter, right handed. Started pitching horseshoes in 1922; in tournament play since 1969. Has played in many tournaments in Kansas, Missouri, Texas, and Oklahoma. Has played in three World Tournaments. Winner, Oklahoma City Handicap Championship, 1969. Played semi-pro baseball for about 20 years. Home: 604 Kingston Place, Yukon, OK 73099.

FITZPATRICK, LEO J., b. November 22, 1917. W. Bertha. Supervisor, Goodyear Tire and Rubber Company. S. Deadeye; t. one and a quarter, right handed. Has pitched horseshoes for 15 years, 8 years in tournament play. Winner, Class A Jackson County title, 1979. Winner, Michigan Class B title, 1976; Class B, Sarasota Bee Ridge Open; Class B, Manatee County Open; Class B Sarasota Open. Home: 1214 Hamlin Place, Jackson, MI 49201.

FLAGG, ELAINE, Winner, Maine Women's State Championship, 1975, with 40.5% ringers; 1976, with 38.5% ringers.

FLAHERTY, W. R., Winner, Virginia State Championship, 1959, with a record of 11-1-52.2%.

FLANN, JIM, b. September 8, 1961. Student. S. Allen; t. one and a quarter, right handed. Has pitched horseshoes for 10 years, 5 years in NHPA tournament play. Winner, Minnesota Boy's State Championship, 1978, with a record of 7-0-57.4%. Highest game, 70%. Member of Championship Team in West Central Horseshoe League for three consecutive years. Home: Box 87, Lake Lillion, MN 56253.

FLANN, NEWELL L., b. January 6, 1916. W. Elaine; children—Darryl L., Bonnie Rae Day. Sheet Metal Journeyman. S. Allen; t. one and a quarter, right handed. Has won many tournaments. Highest tournament average, 76%; highest game, 88%. Made 36 ringers in a row. Past Secretary-Treasurer, Orange Horseshoe Club, Southgate Horseshoe Club. Home: 5111 Rotherham Circle, Westminster, CA 92683.

FLEHARTY, RALPH, (dec.) (1916–1978). Widow, Pearl Davis; children—Raymond Joe, Nita Nichols. Worked in Refrigeration field. S. Allen; t. three quarters and one and a quarter, right handed. Pitched horseshoes for over 25 years. Played in Colorado, Arizona, Nebraska, Missouri, and other states. Served in positions of President, Vice-President, and Secretary-Treasurer, Nebraska State HPA. Served as NHPA representative on Hall of Fame Committee. Member, Nebraska Hall of Fame. Fleharty Award established in his name. Home of Widow: 520 West 11th Street, Cozad, NB 69130.

FLEMMING, JAN W., b. June 17, 1945. W. Lois; children—Brian, Suzanne. Farmer. S. Allen; t. one and three quarters, right handed. Has pitched horseshoes for 20 years. Has won two Iowa Hawkeye Horseshoe Pitchers Association Class A tournaments and many local tournaments. Youth Director, IHHPA, since 1980. Has served as Chairman, IHHPA Hall of Fame Committee. Has served as Secretary-Treasurer, Southwest Iowa HPA for four years. Home: RR—Box 128, Minden, IA 51553.

FLESHMAN, DONALD CURTIS, SR., b. 1938. W. Hazel Ida; Children—Donald Curtis, Jr., James Martin, Linda May, Gary Lee, Kimberley, Philip, Steven and Curtis Michael. Griffith Consumers Oil Company employee. s. Ohio pro, t. one and three quarters, right handed. With Fred Beeman won Maryland state doubles championship. Four generations of his family played tournament horseshoes. Averages 65% ringers. Home: 3805 58th Avenue, Hyattsville, Maryland, 20784.

FLESHMAN, EVA—b. December 28, 1909 d. April 20, 1979. H. Levy Frank "Lee"; children—Frank, Jr., Donald Curtis, Wilbert Douglas and Robert Lemuel. S. Ohio; T. three quarters, right handed. Runnerup for Washington D. C. Women's Championship in 1934. Home: 3803 58th Avenue, Hyattsville, Maryland, 20784.

FLESHMAN, LEVY FRANK "Lee", SR. b. April 28, 1906. d. January 19. 1964. W. Eva May; children—Levy Frank, Jr., Don Curtis, Wilbert Douglas and Robert Lemuel. Owner and operator of Fleshman's Fuel Oil and Ice. S. Ohio; t. one and three quarters, right handed. Won Maryland state championship ten times including five in a row, 1937–41. Won 1933 Metropolitan Washington D.C. singles leagues with a 36-6-62% record, Brentwood Sweepstakes and McLean Classic. Helped build and maintain horseshoe courts in The Monument grounds in Washington D. C., Magruder Park in Hyattsville and Turkey Thicket in Brentwood. Was an exhibition pitcher and coach of beginning players. Home: 5008 54th Avenue, Rogers Heights, Maryland.

FLEURY, BUTCH, Winner, Manitoba Men's Singles Championship, 1974, 1976. With Shane Smith, won Men's Doubles title, 1975. Has won several Class A tournament championships.

FLOWERS, CAROL, Winner, Women's West Virginia State Championship, 1974. Has pitched in West Virginia tournaments. Has served as officer and as director for West Virginia tournaments. Home: Box 115, Lumberport, WV 26386.

FLOWERS, MARSHALL, Has pitched in West Virginia tournaments. Has served as officer and as director for West Virginia tournaments. Past Secretary, West Virginia State Horseshoe Pitchers Association. Home: Box 115, Lumberport, WV 26386.

FLOYD, VERA, b. December 19, 1926. H. Edward; children—Ron, Larry, Jim. Aide to Instructor of Mentally Retarded Children. S. Diamond; t. flip, right handed. Took up horseshoe pitching at age 53. Played in 13 tournaments in 1979, with a record of 55-22-40.7%. played in 20 tournaments in 1980, with a record of 104-24-54.7%. Winner, Alameda County Fair Invitational, 1980. Runnerup, California State Championship, 1979, with 54.7%; 1980, with 63.2%. Highest game, 76%. Has hit 14 consecutive ringers; had 11 four-deads in one game. Women's Representative for Northern California Horseshoe Pitchers Association. Home: 4461 Porter Street, Fremont, CA 94538.

FOCHT, EMMA, H. Paul. Beautician. A non-player who has been very active in horseshoe pitching field. Has helped organize and run many world, state, and district tournaments. Statistician, Ohio Buckeye HPA, 1950–1970; Assistant Statistician, 1947–1949. Member of Board of Controls, 1952–1970. Statistician, National AAU, 1953. Recipient, with husband Paul, of Special NHPA Award, 1969. Inducted into Ohio Buckeye NPA Hall of Fame, 1978. Home: 1051 West Dorothy Lane, Dayton, OH 45409.

FOCHT, PAUL, b. October 24, 1910. W. Emma. Retired. S Ohio Pro; t. one and three quarters, right handed. Has pitched horseshoes for 56 years; has been an NHPA member for 32 years. Winner, World Championship, 1962, with a record of 32-3-81.8%. Winner, Ohio State Championship, 1953, with a record of 24-1-71.9%; 1962, with 10-1-79%; 1963, with 11-0-82.5%. Runnerup, Ohio State Championship, 10 times. Winner, Montgomery County Tournament, 11 times. Has won many other meets, including: Southwest Ohio District, 6 times; Lakeside Open, 7 times; Greenville Spring Open, 5 times; Ohio State Fair; Norwood Invitational; Greenville Ringer Classic; Piqua Open; Wilmington Open; Pennsylvania Open; Corn Belt Open; Indiana-Ohio Open; Midwest Ringer Roundup; Ann Arbor Invitational; Kentucky Capitol Open; Avon Capitol Open; Avon National National Open, and the 1968 Eastern National averaging 85%. Has averaged over 80% in some 50 Class A tournaments. Hit 95.4% game in 1965 World Tournament. High qualifier in World Tournament play, 1962, with 546—86.5%. Set world record, with Floyd Toole, for longest game, 1961 World Tournament. Set world record, with Marvin Craig, for highest combined average for two players, 1965 World Tournament. Hit a 95.4% game in 1965 World Tournament. Won 385 and lost 161 in championship division of 16 world tournaments. Recipient, Governor's Award, 1952; Best Dressed Award, 1960; Sportsmanship Award, 1960, 1965, 1966; Carlings Sports Award, 1963;

Special NHPA Award, 1969. Has served as President or VIce-President of Buckeye Association (for over 20 years) and NHPA. Member, Ohio HPA Hall of Fame; NHPA Hall of Fame. Home: 1051 West Dorothy Lane, Dayton, OH 45409.

FOELSKE, WILBERT F., b. April 15, 1929. W. Grace; children—Diane, Donna, Daniel. Farmer. S. Allen; t. one and a quarter, right handed. Winner, with Ralph Simon, Iowa State Doubles Championship, 1979, 1980. Has won many tournaments in Iowa. Holds these championships: Farmers State Championship, 1980; NHPA State Class B Championship, 1980; Eau Claire Class B Championship, 1980. Best tournament percentage, 61.9%; has hit over 80% in individual games. Home: Route 1, Box 115, Denver, IA 50662.

FOGAL, DOUGLAS, Winner, New Jersey State Championship, 1958, averaging 67.5% ringers.

FOOKES, ALEX, b. 1907. Winner, Saskatchewan Men's Championship, 1965, 1967. Winner, Senior Men's title, 1976, 1977. With Bill Spilchen, won Doubles Championship, 1968. Winner in Old Timers Division meet. Inducted into Saskatchewan Horseshoe Pitchers Hall of Fame, 1977.

FORBES, HAROLD T., Winner, New York State Championship, 1928, with a record in the finals of 10-1-56.2%. Resident of Gloversville, NY.

FORD, DENVER, S. Ohio; t. single flip, right handed. Pitched horseshoes in Fayette, OH, and Bradenton, FL. First flip shoe pitcher to make the Championship Division of the World Tournament. In later pitching, averaged about 55% ringers. Hailed as a great flip shoe pitcher of his time.

FORGUES, JOE, b. March 19, 1964. Student. S. Imperial; t. one and a quarter, right handed. Winner, Vermont State Boys Championship, 1978, with a record of 6-0-63%. Has won a number of tournaments, including Father's Day Open, 1978, with a record of 6-0-49%; Northern Vermont meet, 1976, with 7-0-44%; 1978, with 8-0-56%. Highest tournament, 63%; highest game, 74%. Member, Sodbusters Club of Middlebury, VT. Recipient, President's Award for his performance. Home: Route 3, Box 81, Bristol, VT 05443.

FORGUES, RICHARD A., b. March 25, 1965. Student. S. Allen; t. one and a quarter, right handed. Winner, Vermont Boys State Championship, four times. Winner, New England Championship, three times; Runnerup, one time. 1980 New England Championship record: 5-0-76.5%. Highest tournament, 77%. Member, Sodbusters Horseshoe Club of Middlebury, VT. Home: Route 3, Box 81, Bristol, VT 05443.

FORSSTROM, RALPH, b. July 28, 1909. W. Nanette; children—Beverly Ann Coon, Michael McMillan (stepson). Retired Toolmaker. S. Ohio; t. one and a quarter, right handed. Has spent more than 50 years pitching horseshoes and organizing horseshoe pitching events. Held B Division title of the New England Tournament. Highest tournament average, 60%; highest game, 75%. Has held many state and regional offices. Played an important role in running World Tournaments in 1965, 1968, and 1972. Served as Tournament Director for the New England Championships and state championship tournaments. Inducted into National Hall of Fame, 1972. Charter Member, Massachusetts Hall of Fame. First organizer to be inducted into the New England Hall of Fame, 1968. Has served as NHPA Regional Director; Member of NHPA Hall of Fame Committee; Vice-President and Secretary, Massachusetts HPA: Chairman, Northeastern Association; Vice-President and Secretary, West Side Club. At present, is Member of the Executive Board of the State Association; Chairman of the New England Hall of Fame Committee; President, Sanctioned Ten Team League of the West Side Club of West Springfield, MA. Home: 358 Wilbraham Road, Hampden, MA 01036.

FORSYTHE, L. W., Winner, Wyoming State Championship, 1961, with a record of 8-2-62%.

FORT, CHARLES, Winner, District of Columbia Championship, 1929.

FORTENBERRY, CHARLES E., b. May 27, 1917. W. Rachel; children—James, Brenda, Charles, Sandra, Cathey, Karen, Rickey, Randy. Loom Exchange Technician. S. Allen; t. one and a quarter, right handed. Pitched horseshoes for 20 years. Winner, Tennessee State Championship, 1960, 1962, 1963, 1964, 1965. Played in Championship Division of World Tournament, 1962, 1964. Highest state tournament, 1963, with a record of 6-0-76.3%. Played semi-pro baseball. Home: Route 8, Curtis Road, Knoxville, TN 37914.

FOSS, BILL, Winner, Washington State Championship, 1974, with a record of 12-2-67.6%. Winner, Seattle Turkey Shoot, 1974, with a record of 7-0-68.1%. Home: 4809 North 25th, Tocoma, WA 98406.

FOSTER, JOSEPH A., b. May 26, 1896. W., deceased; child—Kenneth J. Packing House Employee. Pitched horseshoes for 48 years, 25 years in NHPA play. Traveled extensively to pitch horseshoes in many tournaments. Winner, Nebraska State Championship, 1953. Won 14 Omaha City Championships and several open tournaments. Averaged 72.2% for 11 games in his highest tournament; highest game, 90%. Recipient, Sports Illustrated Trophy, 1963. Participated in boxing, baseball, pool, and rifle sports. Home: 5025 Bancroft Street, Omaha, NB 68106.

FOURCADE, MARTIN E., b. November 12, 1918. U.S. Postal Clerk. S. Lattore or Anchor; t. one and a quarter, right handed. Pitched horseshoes for 22 years. Winner, Northern California Championship, 1939, with 66.6%; 1940, with 63%. Winner, Golden Gate Classic, at San Francisco Mission Club, 1940, with 72%. Undefeated in 1938 team league play. Hit 12 doubles in a row in one game. Historian for Northern California Horseshoe Pitchers Association. Became Member, Northern California Horseshoe Pitchers Association Hall of Fame, 1979. Has played in table tennis exhibitions. Home: 851 Capistrano Drive, Salinas, CA 93901.

FOURMAN, JAMES C., Married; has three children. Retired Sales Representative. S. Allen and Ohio Pro; T. one and a quarter, right handed. Horseshoe pitcher and promoter of the sport. Third Vice-President, Florida Horseshoe Pitchers' Association. President, Highlands County Horseshoe Club of Sebring (FL). Recipient, Florida's Outstanding Player Award, 1978–1979. Homes: Winter: 2832 Bolin Lane, Sebring, FL 33870. Summer: 4319 Gordon-Landis Road, Arcanum, OH 45304.

FOWLER, FLOYD, (dec.) Winner of many horseshoe pitching tournaments. Record in Championship Division of World Tournament play: 133 wins, 161 losses, 72.1% ringers, and 498 points qualifying. Winner, Greenville Open, 1962, with a record of 9-0-80.3%. Was resident of Greencastle, IN.

FOX, MARGARET, b. January 8, 1917. H. Wesley; children—Ann Nielsen, Ronald. Postmaster. S. Gordon; t. flip, right handed. Winner, Nebraska Women's State Championship, 1972, 1978. Placed fourth in Class C, World Tournament in Des Moines, IA, 1978. Best tournament average, 51%; best game, 75%. Has won over 30 trophies. Husband Wesley also a horseshoe pitcher. Home: Box 16, Kilgore, NB 69216.

FRAGALE, AUGGIE, Winner, Nevada State Championship, 1979. Has won several tournaments and Class A titles in Nevada. Home: 1840 Auburn Way, Reno, NV 89502.

FRAKES, RON, Winner, Nevada-Missouri Open, 1979, with a record of 7-0-68.3%. Played in Class A competition for years in Missouri and surrounding states. Home: 830 North Prospect, Springfield, MO 65802.

FRALEY, GEORGE, Winner, Kentucky State Championship, 1965. Helped organize the Kentucky State Horseshoe Pitchers Association.

FRANCIS, ALAN, b. December 10, 1969. Son of Larry and Joyce Francis. S. Deadeye; t. reverse three quarters, right handed. Winner, at age 11, Missouri Boys State Championship, 1980, with a record of 5-0-66.4%. Hit 9 consecutive doubles and a high game of 86.3%. In 1980 also won Frank Jackson Open, Kellerton, IA; Midland Open, St. Joseph, MO; Missouri State Fair meet. Plays baseball and basketball. Home: Route 1, Blythedale, MO 64426.

FRANCISCO, MAYME, Winner, Women's World Championship, five times, from 1922–1929. Composite record for ten World Tournaments: 76-12-46.7%. Total of 76 wins in Championship Division play; sixth on all-time winners' list.

FRANICH, JOHN J., Served as State Secretary, Oregon State Horseshoe Pitchers Association. Home: 12103 Southeast Sequoia Avenue, Milwaukie, OR 97222.

FRANKE, HENRY F., b. May 19, 1900. W. Goldie; child—Roy. Occupations: Carpenter, Farmer, Bus Driver, Salesman. S. Deadeye, Allen, Hohl; t. one and three quarters, right handed. Has pitched horseshoes for 67 years, 54 years in league and tournament play. has won 325 trophies and other awards. Holder or Co-holder of 7 World Tournament records in the Senior Division, 1972. Placed second in Senior Division, World Tournament, 1975; placed third four times. Tied for third place in Illinois State Tournament, 1971. At age 79, placed in 41 tournaments, finishing in top three 28 times. Highest tournament average, 72.1%; highest game, 45 ringers of 50 shoes, for 90%. Has pitched horseshoes on radio and television. Inducted into National Horseshoe Pitchers Association Hall of Fame, 1975. Member, Illinois Horseshoe Pitchers Association Hall of Fame. Home: 525 East Fifth Street, Centralia, IL 62801.

FRASER, BILL, (dec) (1910–1969). S. Allen; t. one and a quarter, right handed. Pitched horseshoes for some 20 years. Winner, California State Championship, 1964, with a record of 13-2-70.4%. Placed second in Class B of World Tournament, 1963. Played in Championship Division of World Tournament, 1953.

FRASER, KEN, b. May 19, 1961. Son of Bill Fraser. S. American; t. one and a quarter, right handed. Began pitching horseshoes at age of four. Winner, at age 15, Class B, Men's World Championship, 1976, with 72.9%. Winner, Class C, Men's World Championship, 1978, with 71.6%. Placed second in Pacific Coast Open, 1976, with a record of 6-1-80.6%. Placed second in May or Douglas Open in Vallejo, CA, 1977, with 4-1-81.3% Played in Men's Championship Division of World Tournament at age 16, 1977. Home: 443-A Hoffman Avenue, San Francisco, CA 94114.

FRAZIER, GENEVA, Winner, Oregon Women's State Championship, 1969, with a record of 4-0-25.0%; 1970, with 3-0-32.7%

FRAZIER, R. R., Winner, Montana State Championship, 1923.

FRAZIER, DR. RALPH, b. August 9, 1902. W. Mildred; child—Isabella Reed. Physician and Surgeon. S. Ohio or Lee; t.

one and three quarters, left handed. Has pitched horseshoes for 70 years; active in leagues and tournaments. Has won more than 25 trophies. Served as Vice-President, Logan Horseshoe Club. Inducted into the West Virginia State Horseshoe Pitchers Association Hall of Hame, 1978. Is an accomplished bowler. Home: Box 230, Hilltop, WV 25801.

FREDERICKSON, LLOYD, b. October 2, 1919. W. Norene; children—Cathleen, Karen, Patty, Priscilla, Wendy, Brian, Ida, Peter. Printer. S. Allen; t. one and a quarter, right handed. Winner, Minnesota Class B State Championship, 1972, 1979. Winnings in the Wazata Championship and the Loring Park Team Championship several times. Highest tournament average, 68%; highest game, 81%. Recipient of a number of trophies and awards, including the National Award for Outstanding Achievement, 1976. Member, National Publicity Committee. Has served as President and Treasurer of Wayzata Club, Public Relations Committee. Chairman, Tournaments Committee, for four years; served as its Vice-President, 1968; President, 1970; Chairman of its Hall of Fame Committee, 1970–1973. Served as a Regional Director, 1973–1979. Member, Crystal Horseshoe Club; St. Paul Club. Originator of the National Hall of Fame Scrapbook; kept Scrapbook from 1974–1978. Home: 1010-D Garland Lane North, Plymouth, MN 55447.

FREEMAN, MARK J., b. April 8, 1915. W. Virginia; children—Sally Jo Swadling, Mark O. Retired. S. Allen; t. one and three quarters, right handed. Winner, Michigan State Seniors Championship, 1977. Played in Championship Division of World Tournament at Keene, NH, 1974. Highest tournament, 74%; highest game, 92.6%. Served as President, Lapeer Horshoe Club. Member, Board of the Woverine State Horseshoe

Pitchers Association. Home: 1410 22nd Avenue Drive West, Bradenton, FL 33505.

FREY, LESTER, Winner, Indiana State Championship, 1924.

FRYE, CARL, Son of Raymond B. Frye, past Virginia State Champion. Sponsor of Raymond B. Frye Memorial, annual horseshoe tournament held in Winchester, VA. Home: Route 3, Box 341, Winchester, VA 22601.

FRYE, RAYMOND L., Winner, Virginia State Championship, 1934, 1935, 1937, 1950. Outstanding exhibition player. Played in town and country fair in the Virginia, Washington, DC, and Maryland area for many years. In a Metropolitan Open in Washington, DC, scored 5-2-75.6%.

FULFORD, DEBORAH PICKERING, b. March 28, 1956. H. Bruce; children— Brandon, Alia. S. Allen; t. one and a quarter, right handed. Winner, New Hampshire State Championship, 1972, 1973, 1974, 1977, 1980. Set state record, 1977, with 68.7% ringers; scored 70% ringers, 1980. Winner, New England Championship, 1977, with 74.4% ringers. Runnerup, New England Championship, 1980. In Keene Warmup, 1980, scored high game of 89.9%. Has won more than 50 horseshoe trophies. Hobbies include writing, softball, and bowling. Home: 24 East Diane Circle, Keene, NH 03431.

FULLER, J. B., b. August 7, 1926. W. Willie Mae; child—Patty. VA Hospital Maintenance Foreman. S. Imperial; t. one and a quarter, right handed. Has pitched horseshoes for over 30 years. Winner, North Carolina State Championship, 1979. Regional Director for North Carolina and South Carolina. Home: Route 2, Box 660, Ashville, NC 28805.

FULLER, M. Z. L., First President, Tennessee State Horseshoe Pitchers Association.

Top, left, Lee R. Davis, Hall of Fame member. *Center,* Pat DeLeary, World Champion. *Right,* Stan DeLeary, Indian representative and world record holder. *Center row, left,* Wanda Ditmer. *Right,* Dale Dixon and Casey Jones, both Hall of Fame members. *Bottom,* World Tournament group. Louis Dean is at extreme left in third row.

Top, left, Domey's indoor courts in Sutton, Massachusetts. *Right,* Ed Domey, proprietor. *Center row, left,* Leigh Dunker. *Center,* Mark Dyson, Boys World Champion. *Right,* Ken Drury, Sr., Class A World Champion. *Bottom,* Paul Focht, World Champion.

Elected in 1928. Resident of Chattanooga, TN.

FULLER, WILLIAM, Member, New York Horseshoe Pitchers Association Hall of Fame. Inducted in 1979.

FULTON, JOHN E., b. May 6, 1915. W. Mary. Retired. S. Allen; t. one and three quarters, right handed. Has pitched horseshoes for 48 years, 44 years in NHPA play. Winner, Pennsylvania State Championship, ten times, between 1936 and 1960. Won John Rosselet Memorial Tournament, five times; Eastern Pennsylvania Open, 1937; Lewistown Open, 1937; Hyattsville Open, 1950; Lakeside, OH, Open, 1955; Lynchburg, VA, Open, 1966. Highest tournament, 77.5%; highest game, 93.2%. First Member, Pennsylvania Horseshoe Pitchers Association Hall of Fame; inducted in 1976. First Member, New York County Horseshoe Pitchers Hall of Fame; inducted in 1976. Home: Route 7, Box 182, Carlisle, PA 17013.

FUNK, OSCAR, H., b. August 5, 1902. W. Luella; children—Elva Oaks, Irene Losee, Sonja Ross. Department Manager, Wholesale Hardware Company. S. Diamond Tournament; t. one and a quarter, right handed. Winner, Murray Open, 1969, with a record of 5-1-69.9%. Played in World Tournament, 1956, 1959. Highest game, 31 ringers of 32 shoes, for 96.9%. NHPA Member for 30 years. President, Utah State Horseshoe Pitchers Association, for six years. President, Murray City Horseshoe Club, for ten years. Home: 3860 McCall Street, Salt Lake City, UT 84115.

FUTRELL, ROLLIN, b. June 7, 1921. W. Alice; children—Les, Sally, Neal. Accountant, S. Allen; t. three quarters, right handed. Has pitched horseshoes for 45 years, 22 years in NHPA play. High tournament, 56%; high game, 78% ringers. Has been active in promoting the sport. Has served sev-

eral terms as Secretary, Treasurer, or Vice-President of Darke County Horseshoe Club. Recipient, Stokes Memorial Award, 1972, for service as Coordinator, 1972 World Tournament, staged in Greenville, OH. Home: 3468 Brumbaugh Road, Greenville, OH 45331.

G

GABRIELSON, CLIFTON KIPP, W. Elda; children—Brenda, Karen, Neil. Elementary School Principal. S. Allen; t. three quarters, right handed. High tournament, 43%; high game, 68%. Past State Secretary, Montana Horseshoe Pitchers Association. Son Neil also a horseshoe pitcher. Home: 810 Ninth Street Southwest, Sidney, MT 59270.

GADOURY, RUSSELL A., b. August 22, 1935. W. Edith; children—Jocasta, Robin. Hydrologist. S. Allen, Ohio O., Imperial; t. one and a quarter, right handed. Winner, Class A. Championship, Heritage Recreation Center's Club Tournament. Highest tournament, 68.4%; highest game, 88.3%. Secretary-Treasury, Massachusetts Horseshoe Pitchers' Association. Coordinator, NHPA and State Sanctioned League-Club Program. Has served as President and Publicity Director, St. Moritz Horseshoe Club of Quincy, MA. Wrote the complete guide for the Sanctioned League-Club Program. Originated Handicap Tournament of Champions, 1973; stages event each year. Has served as a delegate to national horseshoe conventions. Recipient, Stokes Memorial Award, 1979, for his work in sanctioned-league play. Home: 44 Edward Road, Watertown, MA 02172.

GALL, JOHN F., b. June 30, 1931. W. Emma; children—Tony, Andy, Steve, Mark. Machine Operator. T. one and three quarters, right handed. Has pitched horseshoes for 40 years, 15 years in tournament competition. Winner, Indoor Championship, with a record of 67.8% ringers. Won 1980 Indiana Class BB title, with 60.1%. Highest game, 88%. Served as Secretary-Treasurer, Indiana State Horseshoe Pitchers Association, 1973–1976. Served as President, Anderson Horseshoe Club. Home: 2117 East Fourth Street, Anderson, IN 46012.

GALL, EMMA, H. John; children—Tony, Andy, Steve, Mark. Served as Secretary, Indiana State Horseshoe Pitchers Association, for several years. With husband John, has actively promoted horseshoe sport in Indiana. Home: 2117 East Fourth Street, Anderson, IN 46012.

GANCOS, LOUIS J., b. November 18, 1919. Married; children—Louis, Patricia. Senior Housing Inspector. S. Allen; t. one and a quarter, right handed. Has pitched horseshoes for 50 years, 29 years in NHPA play. Has won 131 trophies. Among his championships are: Long Island State Park Commission Tournament Championship, 1951; Long Island Championship, several times; National AAU Championship, 1968. Average in high 60's. Secretary-Treasurer, New York State Horseshoe Pitchers Association. Inducted into the New York Horseshoe Pitchers Association Hall of Fame, 1980. Home: 436 69th Street, Brooklyn, NY 11220.

GANDY, ALVIN, Winner, Kansas State Championship, 1935, 1938, 1939, 1940. In Championship Division of World Tournament, won 198 games, lost 156 games; averaged 70.5% ringers; 494 qualifying score. Resident of Topeka, KS.

GANZ, HOWARD ("HOWIE"), b. April 25, 1914. W. Luella; children—Sharon, Bill. Millwright. S. Allen; t. one and three quarters or one and a quarter, right handed. Has pitched horseshoes for more than 50 years. Has won 75 titles. Winner, Minnesota State Championship, 1960, with a record of 10-1-67.9%; 1961, with 10-1-70%. High game, 86%—43 ringers of 50 shoes. Inducted into Minnesota Horseshoe Pitchers Association Hall of Fame, 1975. Home: Backus, MN 56435.

GARCIA, MICHALL, b. October 1, 1967. Son of Waldo and Irene Garcia. Student. S. Ohio Pro; t. reverse one and a quarter, right handed. Winner, New Mexico Boys State Championship, 1980, with a record of 5-0-31.4%. Winner, P. D. Riley Spittoon Championship. Won Junior Title in the fourth Ringer Only Tournament. Runnerup, New Mexico State Tournament; Albuquerque Boys Singles, 1979. Placed second in Class B, New Mexico State Fair meet, 1981. Placed third in P. D. Riley Spittoon Tournament, 1981. Placed fourth in Los Altos Open, 1979. Founder of horseshoe club. Plays baseball and basketball. Home: 10704 Constitution Northeast, Albuquerque, NM 87112.

GARLAND, JIM, b. November 17, 1918. Owner and Operator of Garland Enterprises. S. American; t. two and a quarter, right handed. Has pitched horseshoes for 40 years. Active in promotion of the sport and the sponsorship of teams, many of which have won league championships. Member, Ohio State Championship Team, 1962. Home: 7080 Roundelay Road, Reynoldsburg, OH 43068.

GARNER, JOHN, Winner, Illinois State Fair Championship, 1979. Home: Route 1, Quincy, IL 62301.

GARNER, KENNETH M., b. October 4, 1910. W. Florence; children—Duane, Philip, Cheris, Louise. Retired Postal Employee. S. Allen; t. one and a quarter, right handed. Has pitched horseshoes for 16 years, 10 years in NHPA play. Winner, Nebraska State Championship, 1974. Has won a number of tournament Class A Championships. Highest tournament, 68%: highest game, 84.5%.

Instrumental in organizing the Siouxland Horseshoe Pitchers Association. Home: 815 East 20th Street, South Sioux City, NB 68776.

GARVEY, JOHN, Winner, Iowa State Championship, 1935. Played in World Tournament in Moline, IL, 1935. Resident of Boone, IA.

GARVEY, WILLIAM, Placed fourth in World Tournament in Moline, IL, 1935, with a record of 17-6-62.9%. Resident of Boone, IA.

GASEAU, NORMAN A., b. February 7, 1913. Married; has one child. Accountant. S. Allen; t. one and a quarter, right handed. Horseshoe pitcher and promoter of the sport. Secretary-Treasurer, Florida Horseshoe Pitchers Association, for past six years. President, Clearwater, FL, Horseshoe Club, sponsor of Sun 'N Fun Festival annual tournament. Member, Florida State Horseshoe Pitchers Association Hall of Fame. Home: 1908 Nugget Drive, Clearwater, FL 33515.

GASTON, JEFF. b. March 18, 1941. President, Texas Horseshoe Pitchers Association. W. Priscilla; children—Bennie and Clair. Teacher. S. Imperial; t. one and a quarter, right handed. Pitched for eight years. Texas Class B Champion in 1974 and 1977; Received Texas Sportsmanship Award 1977; helped local club grow from two members in 1973 to 200 in 1980 in league and tournament play; Past President, 1976, 1977 and 1978 Arlington Ironbenders Horseshoe Club; Hobbies, wood work, carpentry, collecting antique tools. Home: 3117 Harvard, Irving, Texas, 75062.

GATEWOOD, RAY, World Tournament record, championship division: 132-78-73.4%, qualified at 495 average. Hit 93 ringers out of consecutive 100 shoes, and 66 out of 67 with lone miss a bounce-off at the twenty-third pitch, Los Angeles Park Horseshoe Club, July 7, 1946, against Dean Brown. Home: Lennox, California.

GAUTHIER, JEAN, 1977-78 Quebec Provincial Champion. Teamed with Louis Tardiff to win doubles title, 1979. Home: Victoriaville.

GAYET, LOUIS V., b. March 26, 1912. Qualifying record, 1970 World Tournament, Southgate, California: 413-56.5%, then posted a 4-3-48.7% record. Children—Lee Thornhill, Joann Gow. Retired. S. Gordon; t. one and a quarter, right handed. President of local horseshoe club; high tournament, 45.5%; high game 54.6%; served as judge at two World Tournaments; won Class C championship, Northern California HPA, 1969; played in Canadian International Western Open, Penticton, British Columbia, placed second in Class D, May 1980. Home: 2664 Coffey Lane, Santa Rosa, California 95401.

GEMMELL, LLOYD, Manitoba Provincial Champion, 1966, 1971, 1973, 1975, 1977, 1978. Won doubles title, with Ken Robinson, 1970, with Bob Henderson, 1976, 1977; Gemmell-Henderson won several large doubles tournaments in Western Canada; Gemmell against Butch Fleury for singles title each year considered one of the best matches. Home: Portage La Prairie.

GEORGE, MERWIN, 1927 Pennsylvania State Champion. Member, Pennsylvania HPA Hall of Fame. Home: Grove City, Pennsylvania.

GEORGINA, LESTER, b. June 25, 1908. Vice-president, Vermont HPA. W. Linda; four children. Retired mill worker. S. Ohio; t. one and a quarter or three quarters, right handed. Served as president or vice-president, Vermont HPA, fifteen years; third vice-president, National Horseshoe Pitchers Association, 1965–66; president, Brattleboro Club, ten years; inducted into

New England Hall of Fame as "Mr. Horseshoes of New England," 1970–71; high tournament, 47%; pitched more than thirty years in NHPA tournament and league play, Vermont, New Hampshire; served as tournament director and promoter. Home: Stage Road, Chesterfield, New Hampshire 03443.

GEORGINA, MALCOLM L., b. April 9, 1933. 1949 Vermont Boys State Champion, 1979 Member, New England Hall of Fame. W. Cynthia; children—William, Daniel, Susan, Diane. General manager, Wholesale Paper Company. S. Ohio; t. reverse three quarters, right handed. Secretary-Treasurer, New England HPA; secretary-treasurer, Keene Horseshoe Club, as well as having served in every office in Keene Club; served two terms, vice-president, New Hampshire State HPA; publicity chairman for 1965 and 1968 World Tournaments in Keene; pitched for thirty-two years; high tournament, 34%, Southern Vermont Tournament, c. 1950; high game, 62.5%, league play, 1949; Vermont Junior State runnerup, 1950, 1951; inducted into New Hampshire HPA Hall of Fame as organizer, 1978. Home: 41 Bent Court, Keene, New Hampshire 03431.

GERBRAND, GLENN O., b. June 1, 1922. Thirty-year Member, Lakewood Club, Ohio. W. Ruth; child—Glenn. Eaton employee. S. Ohio; t. one and three quarters, right handed. Won Class B singles championship, Lakewood Tournament, 1962; memorable game against Bob Cash, 112–134 (loss), c. 1950; Gerbrand's team won annual tournaments in Seven Hills, Independence, Lakewood. Home: 16365 Heather Lane, Middleburg Heights, Ohio 44130.

GERMAN, LAVERN J., b. December 15, 1920. Wyoming State Champion, 1973, 1974, 1977. Child—Mrs. William Murray. Salesman. S. Ohio O; t. one and a quarter, right handed. Third vice-president, Wyoming HPA; helped acquire ten lighted courts, Highland Park, Casper, Wyoming, 1978, site of 1979, 1980 state tournaments directed by German; high tournament, 56%; high game, 68%; won local city championship, 1977 most improved player, and 1979 Wyoming Winter Title; won game against Ted Allen, 1974 Tri-State meet. Home: P.O. Box 9207, Casper, Wyoming 82609.

GERRISH, CHARLES, b. 1888, deceased. New England Champion, 1932. Won Maine State Title, 1931, and again in 1960, 9-0-64.5%, high game for state record, 79.4%; won five other titles, 10-1-58.2%, 1950, 11-0-65.7%, 1951, 11-0-65.5%, 1952, 12-1-61.2%, 1953, 11-0-63.27%, 1957; inducted into Maine HPA Hall of Fame, 1972. Home: Kittery, Maine.

GETCHELL, LEWIS, Member, Washington State Hall of Fame. Washington State Champion 1945, 13-2-61%, 1946, 15-0-70%, 1948, 12-3-67.1%, 1950, 13-2-66.2%, 1951, 15-0-71.2%. Home: 3715 Freeman Road, Puyallup, Washington 98371.

GETCHELL, ROY (dec.), Tied with brother Lewis for Washington State Championship. Won title 1933, 14-1-65.1%, 1934, 12-3-68.5%, 1935, 23-8-69.1%; won Oregon title, 1948, 1951, 1952, 1953; won Portland, The Bremerton Open, and Northeast (Yakima) championships many times; placed eighth, Class A World Tournament, 1952; placed first, Class B over field of 24 men, World Tournament, 1951, average 60.5%; ringer average, 70%. Home: Tigard, Arizona.

GIACOMMINI, SARAH, 1972 Washington Women's State Champion, 6-1-54.2%. Home: 7986 Sidney Road, Port Orchard, Washington 98366.

GIBBY, BILL, 1971 South Carolina State Champion, 7-0-47.5%.

GIBSON, PAUL O., b. May 30, 1926.

NHPA Regional Director for Illinois-Indiana-Michigan. W. Barbara; children—Linda, Bob, Barbara, Mike, Alice, Rose. Painter for Illinois Central Gulf Railroad. S. Allen; t. one and three quarters, right handed. President, Centralia Club; past Illinois vice-president, six years, and president, four years; helped organize World Tournament religious program; pitched thirteen out of twenty years in NHPA; high tournament, 50%; high game, 65%. Home: 30 Ridge Road Drive, Centralia, Illinois 62801.

GIBSON, RICK, 1971 Missouri Boys State Champion, 5-0-35.4%.

GIBSON, TOM, 1980 Oregon Boys State Champion, 7-1-25%. Home: Oregon City, Oregon.

GIDDES, JACK, b. April 2, 1931. New Jersey State Champion, 1967–68, 1971–72, 1974. S. Allen; t. one and three quarters, right handed. Qualified in 1971 World Tournament, Middlesex, N.J., championship division, 9-26-71.3%, 30th place; hit 72.6% to win Bound Brook Invitational; set two state records: 94.4% game, 15 consecutive doubles, 1972; high tournament, 70.8%; won 1970 Rosselet Memorial Open, 7-0-67.3%; won New Jersey Open, 7-0-72.3%, 1970. Home: 81 Dock Watch Hollow Road, Warren, New Jersey 07060.

GILES, CLARENCE W., b. March 12, 1916. Utah State Champion 1974, 1976, 1979, Charter Member. W. Clarissa; children—Mary Lou Mangum, James C., Allen R. Retired. S. Allen; t. one and a quarter, right handed. Championship record: 1974, 11-0-64.1%, 1976, 8-1-59.5%, 1979, 11-0-70%; pitched twenty-seven out of thirty-five years in NHPA competition; won Class A titles: Stokes Memorial, Moesinger Memorial, Wahlin Memorial, Deweyville Town Days, Riverton Town Days, Steel Days; best season, 1979, played eleven tournaments, won nine, finished second in two for season record of sixty-five wins, three losses; won Senior Olympic state championship, 1979; high tournament, 70%; high game, 81.8%, twice; received Lee Jolley award for outstanding promotion; inducted as charter member, Utah State Hall of Fame; chairman, Utah State Hall of Fame Committee, Senior Olympics committee, Riverton Town Days, Riverton Stake L.D.S. (Mormon) Church, and Shoe Tossin at Mountain Man Rendezvous, St. Bridger, Wyoming; served three terms president, Utah HPA, three years as secretary, five years as chairman, Intermountain A.A.U., and tournament director, 1960 Junior World Championship, Muncie, Indiana. Home: 13480 South 1700 West Riverton, Utah 84065.

GILES, STAN, Manitoba Provincial Champion, 1938, 1953. Won Armed Forces Championship of Great Britain, 1918; doubles with Ted Lozanski during 1950s and 1960s; inducted into Manitoba HPA Hall of Fame, 1979. Home: Calgary, Alberta, Canada.

GILLESPIE, GLENN S., b. April 2, 1943. Played Class A since 1977. Won Class D, 1977. W. Judy; children—Glenn, Jr., Debbie. Taxidermist. S. Allen; t. one and a quarter, right handed. Average, 65%–72%. Home: Route 2-Box 85, Jane Lew, West Virginia 26378.

GIORGETTI, GUIDO, b. May 8, 1903. Connecticut State Champion 1933, 11-0-42.7%, 1934, 1948, 10-1-55.6%. W. Florence; child-Robert. Retired. S.Ohio; t. one and a quarter, right handed. Pitched for forty-eight years, thirty years of tournament play; average, 62%; won Class B New England title, 70%, 1939 (won title twice); record in Connecticut State League, 125-1-62%, 1939; high game, 92.8%. Enjoys duck pin and rifle shooting. Home: 78 Eldridge Street, Manchester, Connecticut 06040.

GLANT, C. A., Alabama State Champion 1920–1930. Billiards. World Tournament record: 1919, 30-24, placed eighth, 1920 (W), 11-13, placed fifteenth, 1920 (S), placed 23rd, 1921 (W), 8-13, placed fifteenth; helped organize National League of Horseshoe and Quoit Pitchers of the United States, St. Petersburg, Fla., 1919; elected vice-president in its first slate of national officers (original organization between Grand League American Horseshoe Pitchers and NHPA of America); no Alabama championship records available. Home: 412 South Lincoln, Huntsville, Alabama, 35805.

GLASS, WILLIAM L., b. July 22, 1921. Wisconsin State Champion seven times since 1968. W. Lois; children—Steven, Jade, Felicia, William, Crystal. Farmer. S. Gordon; t. one and three quarters, right handed. Winning percentages between 59% and 73%; high tournament, 76.5%; high game, 92%; record for 1980 state title, 6-1-71.4%. Home: Route 1, Box 191, Vesper, Wisconsin 54489.

GLASS, MARVIN L., b. April 7, 1917. Kentucky Doubles Champion (with J. W. Hilton). W. Virginia; child—Carol Glass Williams. Clinical research technician in narcotics; S. Allen; t. one and a quarter, right handed. Won several doubles titles with K. W. Sinkhorn (d.); won Daniel Boone Festival Class A Championship, Barbersville, Ky., 1980; won the only tournament game Jack Fahey (Kentucky State Champion) lost in 1980; finished fourth in Kentucky singles; pitched for thirty-one years. Enjoys golf, bowling. Home: 106 Fordland Drive, Georgetown, Kentucky 40324.

GOBLE, GARLAND, b. 1911. Minnesota State Champion 1937–38. W.; two children. Highway foreman. Played in Mid-West Nationals, 1937–38. Home: Mondamin, Iowa.

GODDARD, GUY, b. November 14, 1885. Pitched for ninety years. W. Leona (d.); children—George, Mary. Retired school executive/Merchant. S. Ohio; t. one and three quarters, right handed. Past president, Oklahoma State HPA; won trophies in Oklahoma tournaments 1952, 1957, 1959, 1962, 1965, 1969; attended 1957 World ment, Murray, Utah. Enjoys bowling, geneology. Home: 825 Northwest 35th, Oklahoma City, Oklahoma 73118.

GOFORTH, JAMES T., b. August 10, 1935. Past Secretary-Treasurer, North Carolina State HPA. W. Nancy; children—Robert, Jane. Mechanic. S. Ohio Pro; t. one and a quarter, right handed. Dedicated to administration and promotion, 1972–78 (years of office). Home: Route 4, Box 140, Statesville, North Carolina 28677.

GOFORTH, ROBERT J., b. January 26, 1958. North Carolina State Boys Champion 1971–74. Student. S. Ohio; t. one and a quarter, right handed. Won 1971 Southeastern Classic boys title; entered men's division, won Greensboro Open and North Carolina doubles championship with James Scotten; high tournament, 68.4%; high game, 92.8%. Home: Route 4, Box 140, Statesville, North Carolina 28677.

GONZALES, JESSE G., b. May 25, 1932. Northern California Association Class A title, four times. World Tournament record 132-96-75%, 530 qualifying points. W. Sylvia; children—Nancy Browning, Lisa, Sylvia, Jesse, Jr., Sarah. Groundman, Parks Department. S. Gordon; t. one flip, right handed. Inducted into California Hall of Fame, 1976; received sportsmanship award, 1977; averaged 77.2%, California State Championship, 1978; hit 80% tournament with high single flip; called "master of flip flop from forty feet"; hit 80% tournament, Eureka, 1972; averaged 80.5% for 35 games, World Tournament, Greenville, Ohio, 1964; high game, 92%, Mosswood, 1971. Home: 440 Lilac Drive, Los Osos. California 93402.

GONZALES, LISA, b. August 10, 1966. 1980 California Girls State Champion. Student. S. Gordon; t. flip, right handed. Won San Jose Junior Open Horseshoe title, 1980; championship average, 38%. Enjoys track, baseball, basketball. Home: 440 Lilac Drive, Los Osos, California 93402.

GOOD, PAUL W., b. May 31, 1919, Virginia State Doubles Champion. W. Josie; children—Joyce, Judy. Retired from Merck & Co., Inc. S. Allen; t. one and a quarter, right handed. Teamed with Charlie Price for championship and three second place finishes; high tournament, 71%; high game, 92%; won three Class A tournament championships, Winchester, 65–70%; finished third, Frye Memorial, 12-3-69.7%, beating Dale Carson, Jim Solomon, Stan Manker, and Al Zadroga in succession; hit 38 consecutive ringers against A. Plank in an 87.6% game, 90% against Dale Carson, Boo Henson Open; pitched 45 years, 16 in NHPA play. Home: P.O. Box 227, Stanley, Virginia 22851.

GOODIER, HAROLD E., b. July 20, 1918, Maine State Champion, 1935, 1938; Member, Maine HPA Hall of Fame, 1976. W. Donna Mills; children—Lee, Kerry, Lawrence. Controller, Deering Ice Cream Corp. S. Gordon; t. one and three quarters, right handed. Championship record: 9-2-59.4%, 1935, 8-0-63.6%, 1938; won six consecutive Cumberland County titles, 1935-40; high tournament, 81%; with Ted Allen, hit five consecutive doubles in exhibition game; state runnerup, 58.6%, 1936 and 59%, 1937, 5-6-62.1%; finished third, 50.2%, 1939 state tournament, 1940 runnerup, 57.4%, 1941, fourth, 52.7%; finished second, 8-3-57.1%, 1950 state tournament; finished fourth, 7-4-58.3%, 1951 state tournament; pitched exhibition games, 1935–50, including one against Ted Allen, Deering Oaks, Portland, Oregon. Home: D-12 Juniper East Yarmouth, Maine 04096.

GOODLANDER, SAM, d. December 6, 1971. Secretary-Treasurer, Ohio Buckeye HPA. W. Zena. Recruited members from all Ohio districts, worked with local tournament directors on county and district events. Home: Reading.

GORDON, JOHN, Designer and Manufacturer, Gordon Spin On pitching shoe. Member, NHPA Hall of Fame, 1971; sixth member inducted into California Hall of Fame; Served as promoter, organizer, patron and sponsor of horseshoe pitching; shoe still manufactured by Queen City Forging Co., Cincinnati. Home: (daughter's address) 1600 Cedar Avenue, Apt. 1, Long Beach, California 90800.

GORE, BOB, 1964 Massachusetts Boys State Champion, 4-0-30.9%.

GORE DONALD W., b. May 13, 1936. Nevada HPA Vice-President. W. Sonnia; children—Mike, Terri, Jo Dee. Draftsman. S. Deadeye; t. one and a quarter, right handed. Won Class C, Nevada state tournament, 1978; won Class B, Nevada state tournament, 1979; moved into Class A, 1980; averages 40–50% high game, 60%. Home: 1435 Clemson Road, Reno, Nevada 82502.

GOULD, CYRUS, Vice-President, Maritime Provinces HPA, elected 1968. Home: 11 Beacon Street, Amherst, Nova Scotia, Canada.

GOURVENAC, JOHN, 1931 Washington, D.C., Champion (not to be confused with the Championship of Metropolitan Washington, D.C., won by Harry F. Saunders).

GRADY, DONN, New Jersey State Champion. Elected State Secretary, New Jersey HPA, 1980. Home: RD 18 Glen Road, Flemington, New Jersey 08822.

GRAHAM, BOB, b. March 28, 1929, 1971, 1976 Texas State Champion, Member, Texas Hall of Fame, 1976. W. Elizabeth; children— James, Larry, Keith, Robert, Kelly. Personnel administrator. S. Allen or Ohio Pro; t. one and a quarter, right handed. Joined NHPA, 1963; pitched in 138 consecutive Texas tournaments, 1963–79; won forty-three Class A tournaments in Texas; holds twelve state records: high single game, 91.5%, high single tournament, 76.3%; competed in Class A, World Tournament, 1977; served six years, president of Texas chapter, two years as secretary, two years as editor; chairman of the NHPA Board of Regional Directors, 1975–78. National Vice President. Home: 5926 Darlinghurst, Houston, Texas 77085.

GRAHAM ERNEST G., JR., b. November 13, 1927. Secretary, New York HPA. W. Dorcas; children—Ernest III, Sandera, Steven. Garbage collector. S. Ohio Pro; t. one and a quarter, left handed. Founded local club by building eight courts in his backyard; served as past president of local club; served as League secretary-treasurer; averages 40%. Enjoys bowling and fishing. Home: 8713 State Route 13, Camden, New York 13316.

GRAHAM, HENRY, 1930 Oregon State Champion.

GRANT, DESSIE MOSSMAN, Finished fifth, 3-4-58.6%, 1934 World Tournament; sister of World Champion Putt Mossman.

GRANT HERBERT, 1930 New York State Champion, 49.2%.

GRAVES, EARL, R. b. March 16, 1916. Colorado State Champion 1955–56, 1976. W. Ruth; children—Jean, Lynda, Retired. S. Ohio; t. one and a quarter, right handed. Served as vice-president, Colorado State HPA, 1972; championship state records: 13-0-72.7%, 1955, 12-1-71.1%, 1956; runnerup for Illinois state title, 1945; won Colorado-Wyoming-Nebraska Tri-State, 1956–57, 1971; defeated Ted Allen, Rocky Mountain Open, 80%, 1957; pitched string of nineteen

consecutive doubles, 1956 tournament. Enjoys bowling. Home: 3460 Otis Street, Wheatridge, Colorado 80033.

GRAY, FLOYD, W., b. July 22, 1925. Washington State Doubles Champion. W. Caroline; children—Dennis, David. Animal Science Dept., Oregon State University. S. Allen; t. one and a quarter, right handed. Teamed with Ridge Leggett for doubles title, 1979–80. Home: Route 1, Box 303A, Corvallis, Oregon 97330.

GRAY, LOWELL, 1936 California State Champion. World Tournament championship division record: 114-84-72%, qualifying average, 504. Home: Long Beach.

GREEN CLYDE, d. Played one World Tournament, Senior Division 4-4-56.4%; averaged over 60% in tournament play; Clyde Green Memorial annual tournament conducted by Indiana HPA. Home: Route 1, Portland, Indiana.

GREEN, KEN, 1979 Maryland State Doubles Champion. Home: 421 Tuxedo Street, Baltimore, Maryland 21211.

GREEN, SHERMAN, d. 1973. 1965, 1968 Connecticut State Champion, 5-0-69%, 5-0-70%, respectively. Won New England Championship, 70%, 1967; as a youngster, helped Ted Allen in exhibition pitching; played Class B, World Tournament, 1965, 62.9%, and 1968, 5-2-69.6%. Home: Rocky Hill, Connecticut.

GREENER, GEORGE, 1933 Utah State Champion.

GREENLAW, RAYMOND A., b. December 5, 1919. Founded Eastern Pennsylvania HPA. W. Hazel; child—Rita. Self-employed—Ray's Towing. S. Gordon and Allen; t. one and three quarters, right handed. Pitched for forty years, competed with First Army, 1950–60; served as president, Eastern Pennsylvania HPA and president of Bristol Township HPA; headed construction (with NHPA Regional Director Peter Shepard and officers) of 24 new courts in Bristol; hosted 1976 World Tournament after squelching injunctions filed in Bucks County Court to prevent the tournament. Home: 28 Balsam Road, P.O. Box 699, Levittown, Pennsylvania 29058.

GREGSON, ARCHIE, d. 1965. Member, NHPA Hall of Fame, 1966. Served as president, NHPA, 1958, and as national secretary, 1941–47. W. Katie. Considered one of the most valuable husband-wife teams in history of NHPA; member, California HPA Hall of Fame; served as player, administrator, organizer, tournament manager, master of ceremonies at NHPA functions. Home: Crestline, California.

GREGSON, KATIE, 1954 Women's World Champion. H. Archie, d. Joint recipient with husband of Stokes Memorial Award, 1959; championship play-off, 6-1-52%; tied for World Championship, 1955, 1958, each year lost play-off, finished second; competed in World Tournaments nine years, 41-15-42.5%. Home: Crestline, California.

GRIER, H. C., 1921 Colorado State Champion.

GRIFFIN, LARRY W., b. November 20, 1947. 1975 Illinois State Champion. W. Connie; children—Mickey, Timothy. Foreman, Hercules, Inc. S. Allen; t. one and three quarters, right handed. Won several open tournaments and finished eleventh, World Tournament, 1975; finished thirteenth, 1977 World Tournament; high tournament, 86%; started a sanctioned tournament game, Newport, against Jim Weston, with 58 consecutive ringers, missed the 59th, hit rest to finish at 95%. Enjoys softball. Home: Box 407, Newport, Indiana 47966.

GRIGGS, ELLIS, b. September 3, 1911. Illinois State Champion ten times. W. Emma.

Grocery store operator. S. Imperial; t. one and three quarters, right handed. Member, NHPA; won over 100 Class A tournaments; inducted into Illinois State Hall of Fame, 1978; hit 48 out of 50 ringers in count-all game, Quincy Horseshoe League; hit 37 out of 38 in a 50–3 win over Charles Rhodes, Illinois State Tournament; averaged 78.6% for eleven games. Illinois State Tournament, 1967; set state record, 736 ringers in state tournament, 1940; won first state title 1935, his tenth in 1970. Home: Box 56, Plainville, Illinois 52365.

GRIGGS, LONNIE, 1971 Washington Boys State Champion, 5-1-51.6%.

GRIGGS, STAN, b. November 2, 1963. 1978–79 Missouri Boys State Champion. Student. S. Gordon; t. one and a quarter, right handed. Championships: Pony Express Doubles, 1976, Pony Express Singles, 1977, Pony Express Team, 1978, Mound City Open; 1978–79, St. Joseph Open, 1978–79, Atchison Open, 1978, 1980, Midland Open, 1979, 1980, Pony Express Doubles, 1980. High tournament 71.5%; high game 85%. Enjoys gospel singing (member, The New Generations Singers), bowling, cheerleading, school theatrical productions. Home: 4702 Valley Lane, St. Joseph, Missouri 64503.

GUENTHER, PETER J. b. December 16, 1922. Canada—Representative. W; five children. Carpenter. S. Ohio and Allen; t. one and a quarter, right handed. Played organized competition since 1961; won Class B doubles championship, Alberta. Home: 2236 45th Street Southeast, Calgary, Alberta, Canada T2B 1K2.

GUIER, NELSON, 1974 Missouri Boys State Champion.

GULLICKSON, WILL, b. December 11, 1927. NHPA Publicity Director and Vice-President. W. Syblann; children—Glenn, Roger, Tedd. Sports writer. S. Deadeye, Imperial, and Diamond; t. one and three quarters, right handed. Received Arch Stokes award; promoted Danny Kuchcinski of Pa.; served as secretary, Fargo League; set up first cash-prize tournament still in existence at Moorhead American Legion Park Board complex; served as pitcher and officer, Minnesota HPA, mid-1950s; formed several tournament fields at North Dakota Winter Show, Valley City; organized junior league, Fargo; participated in more than 160 tournaments, including World Tournaments at Greenville, Keene, Des Moines, Fargo, North Dakota, Salt Lake City, Statesville, North Carolina, and Huntsville, Alabama; maintained 50–60% average in leagues and tournaments; hit 70% and 72%, Aberdeen, Lloyd Swartwout Open, 1978; pitched Preimesberger Fall Open, Class B, 56%, 1978; won Class A championship against Willis Wilger, Minot, 1967; contributor of articles to NHPA News Digest and the Minnesota horseshoe newsletter; has been among top four or five average pitchers for more than twenty years, Fargo-Moorhead leagues; high game, 77%, against Harold Diiro; defeated Leigh "The Champ" Dunker, 52–47, Fargo tournament, Oak Grove Park, 1979 (Dunker won a four-way tie to win play-off); brought Walter Ray Williams and Walter Ray "Deadeye" Williams to Fargo for exhibition games after Deadeye wqon 1978 World Tournament; distributor of Deadeye and Diamond horseshoes; published "Double Ringer" with sponsors including George Clark (of Diamond Horseshoe and Tool Company, Duluth). Home: 1608 17th Street South, Moorhead, Minnesota 16160.

GUNDERSON, JAMES M., 1977 Class A Champion, South Dakota, 61.5%. Farmer. S. Deadeye; t. one and three quarters, right handed. Won Class C state title, 43.7%, 1974. Enjoys bowling, golf, woodworking. Home: Route 2, Box 362, Crooks, South Dakota 57020.

GUNYON, HELEN DAIRE, b. July 19,. 1921. First Vice-President, Indiana State HPA. H. Max; four children. Housewife. Served as scorekeeper at every World Tournament since 1973; elected "Number One Helper" at Clinton Country Club, 1978; works tournaments for Indiana HPA each year. Enjoys piano, scouting and church work. Home: 409 Brightwood Drive, Frankfort, Indiana 46041.

GUNYON, MAX, President, Clinton County (Indiana) Horseshoe Club. W. Helen; four children. Won first place, Class V, World Tournament, 1979. Home: 409 Brightwood Drive, Frankfort, Indiana 46041.

GUY, JOSEPH R., b. February 6, 1922. President, Massachusetts HPA. Child— Robert. S. Gordon; t. three quarters, right handed. Served as recording secretary, West Side Horseshoe Club, five years. Home: 30 Washington Avenue, Agawam, Massachusetts 01001.

GUYETT, JAMES, b. 1920. New Hampshire State Champion 11 times, 1978 New Hampshire Hall of Fame. Won state championship at age fifteen, 50%, 1935, 55%, 1936, 60%, 1937, 62%, 1938, 65%, 1939, 70%, 1941, 60%, 1946, 65%, 1949, 65%, 1950, 11-0-67%, 1953, and 68%, 1955; retained state title 1942–45; no record available, 1940; "only man to beat Guyett" was Howard White. Home: Portsmouth.

H

HACKETT, JIM, b. August 2, 1946. President, Iowa Hawkeye HPA. W. Michelle; children—Mike. General manager, Arnold Tool and Die Works, Council Bluffs, Iowa. S. Allen or Deadeye; t. one and a quarter, right handed. Founder and public relations representative, Southwest Iowa HPA; invented and manufactured the "Port-a-

Court," a portable pitching indoor or outdoor court (featured in "The New York Times," March 1979 and approved by NHPA; high tournament, 43% high game, 52%. Home: Route 2, Box 109, Neola, Iowa 51559.

HAFNER, BYRON, Class A pitcher, Home: Route 2, Letts, Iowa 52754.

HALCOMB, LYNNE HARRISON, b. November 1, 1957. 1974 Girls World Champion. H. Gregory; child—Sarah Lynne. Housewife. S. Allen; t. one and a quarter, right handed. Began pitching at age 6, first tournament, Greenville Classic; won Ohio Girls State Championship and Girls World Championship, 1973; won Greenville Ringer Classic, Statesville Dogwood Festival (twice), Fort Hamilton Days; won high league average in local league; won Ohio Class B Championship, (women's division) 1975; high game (against Linda Patenaude, 70.8%; holds state record with Kathy Melling for four-deads (four), 1974; plays in Franklin, Ohio league since 1960s, and Day-Bel, Kentucky leagues since 1970s; awarded medal by South African delegation visiting World Tournament for outstanding achievement. Home: 1101 Ford Boulevard, Hamilton, Ohio 45011.

HALE, GEORGE W., b. December 28, 1917. 1980 Member, New York State HPA Hall of Fame. W. Marilyn Gould. Owner/operator, Hale's Sunoco Gas Station. S. Ohio Pro; t. reverse one and three quarters, right handed. Pitched horseshoes in tournament play for twenty-five years; served as president, New York State HPA and president, Falconer Horseshoe League; won Class B title, New York, 1966, 1971, 1975, Class C title, 1962, 1979; won Class B championship. DeSota Open, Plant City, Fla., 1969; won Class A championship, Chatanqua County Tournament (twice), and Falconer Rod and Gun League; won Falconer

league doubles with Virgil Williams nine times; elected "Player of the Year," Falconer Club, 1980. Enjoys bowling, golf, rifle shooting. Home: 129 Willow Avenue, Jamestown, New York 14701.

HALL, ERNIE, 1976 California Seniors State Champion.

HALLER, JIM, JR., b. May 21, 1962. Kansas State Boys Champion 1975, 1977, 1978. Student. S. Deadeye; t. one and a quarter, right handed. Finished second, Kansas Boys State Tournament, 1976, 1979; high tournament average, 66.5%; high game, 90%; finished second, Class C, World Tournament junior division, 1979. Home: 2008 Emerald Drive, Lawrence, Kansas 66044.

HALLICKSON, HENRY MANFUL, b. September 24, 1907. 1977 Member, South Dakota HPA Hall of Fame. W. Marie; children—Bert, Shari, Carpenter. S. Ohio; t. one and three quarters, right handed. Pitched for sixty-five years, forty-five in tournament play; vice-president, local club; known as "Grand Old Man of Horseshoes"; built courts at McKinnon Park, Sioux Falls, with help of prison inmates. Home: 405 North Lewis, Sioux Falls, South Dakota 57103.

HALLOCK, DEL, 1957 Michigan State Champion.

HAMBIDGE, GEORGE HAMILTON, b. September 30, 1920. South African Sports Administrator. W. Jacoba; children—Elizabeth, Joan, Marina, Eleanor. Retired local secretary, Old Mutual Insurance Co./Senior clerk, Early Bird Farm Pty., Ltd. S. American Professional; t. one and a quarter, right handed. Elected sports administrator for Standerton (in South Africa's Eastern Transvaal), 1979; built regulation horseshoe courts, Standerton Jukskei Park, Klerksdorp, Springs, and Kroonstad; initiated play between United States and South Africa, Kroonstad and Standerton, 1972–74,

1979–80. Enjoys jukskei (South African sport), and is active in politics, school, church, and community affairs; serves as treasurer, Standerton Constituency of the Nationalist Party and as an Elder, Dutch Reformed Church. Home: P.O. Box 516, 2430 Standerton, South Africa.

HAMILTON, BUD, b. March 22, 1921, 1977, 1979 Oklahoma State Champion. W. Kathleen; child—Kay E. Harper, Employee, B.F. Goodrich. S. Allen; t. one and a quarter, right handed. Won Class D, Oil Capitol tournament; won Class C, Oklahoma Open; finished third, Class B, state tournament; won Class B state title, 1974; defeated World Champion Opal Reno, Ponca City exhibition, 84%, 1978; high tournament, 64.2%; hit eight consecutive doubles in tournament play; elected vice-president, Oklahoma State HPA, 1974; was professional steer roper until 1968. Home: 31 E Street, S. W. Miami, Oklahoma 74345.

HAMILTON, DAVID, Illinois Boys State Champion, 1960, 6-1-43.5%, 1965, 7-0.

HAMILTON, HOWARD, Kentucky State Champion, 1967, 10-1-53.4%, 1970, 9-1-63.5%.

HAMMAN, GILBERT C., Past Oregon State Secretary. Home: P.O. Box 5000, Salem, Oregon 97302.

HAMMAN, WILLIAM, 1938 New York State Champion. Home: White Plains, New York.

HAMMOND, JUNIOR, 1977 Oklahoma Boys State Champion. Home: P.O. Box 294, Columbus, New Mexico 88029.

HAMPTON, ART, Iowa State Champion, 1968, 11-0-73.8%, 1969, 11-0-76.8%, 1971, 10-1-70.6%. Won Des Moines Open, 5-0-64.2%, 1979. Home: 1836 7th Avenue Court, Iowa City, Iowa 52240.

HAMPTON, BRYANT "BARNEY," b. September 24, 1905. Oregon State Champion 1954-55, 1980 Member, Oregon HPA Hall of Fame. W. Agnes; children—Lynda Havlik, Michelle. Longshoreman. S. Allen; t. one and a quarter, right handed. Won seven Portland city championships, five Veronia Opens, four Bremerton Opens; high game, 94% including sixteen doubles out of seventeen pitches; set Oregon state qualifying record for fifty shoes hitting 142 points; pitched fifty years, thirty-five in tournament play. Enjoys pool. Home: 5903 Southeast Holgate, Portland, Oregon 97206.

HANANIA, HAL, Recipient, Stokes Memorial Award, 1971. Police Sergeant. Founder and organizer, Middlesex Horseshoe Club, which hosted 1971 World Tournament; served as first vice-president, Middlesex Horseshoe Club, 1971, held other offices thereafter; elected vice-president, NHPA, 1969. Home: 448 Runyon Avenue, Middlesex, New Jersey 08846.

HANES, DON, b. September 2, 1928. Past State Secretary, New Mexico HPA. W. Marilyn; children—Ronald, Wade, Steven, Trent, Michael. TWA Airline ramp serviceman. S. Imperial; t. one and a quarter, right handed. Won City Championship, Albuquerque, 1978, hit high tournament, 62%; high game, 72%, against Al Cherry, 1976 World Tournament, Levittown, Pa.; sent by U.S. Department of Interior to Ft. Chaffee, Arkansas, to teach Cuban refugees to pitch horseshoes. Home: 10608 Constitution NE, Albuquerque, New Mexico 87112.

HANES, MARILYN, b. August 30, 1934. New Mexico State Secretary-Treasurer, New Mexico State Champion, 1970–71. H. Donald; children—Ronald, Wade, Steven, Trent, Michael. Housewife. S. Imperial; t. three quarter flip, right handed. Won Albuquerque City Championship three times; attended five World Tournaments as delegate to National Convention. Home: 10608 Constitution NE, Albuquerque, New Mexico 87112.

HANES, STEVEN, b. December 1959. New Mexico Junior Boys State Champion, 1975–77. Student. S. Deadeye; t. one and a quarter, right handed. Won three consecutive city championships (boys division), Albuquerque, 1975–77; won Class A Championships (men's division), Morarity Open, The Spittoon, and Albuquerque City Championship; born with bone disorder (vertical talus) for which horseshoe pitching and swimming are theraputic exercises. Home: 10608 Constitution NE, Albuquerque, New Mexico 87112.

HANGEN, RUTH, b. May 4, 1916. Women's World Champion five times, 1975 Member, NHPA Hall of Fame. H. Harry; children—Harry, John, Ruth, Ester. Waitress. S. Gordon; t. flip, right handed. Inducted into New York State Hall of Fame, 1974; won New York State Championship eight times; inducted into Amherst's Avenue of Athletes, 1979; won Greenville Ringer Classic seven times; won Eastern National seven times; won Mid-West Ringer Roundup five times; won Lockport League seven times; won West Virginia Professional, twice; won Carolina Dogwood Festival, twice; won Michigan Water Wonderland, the National AAU, and the Massachusetts Open; World Tournament records of forty-two consecutive ringers and a 95% game (listed in Guinness Book of World Records); set world records for a seven-game tournament, 582 shoes pitched, 448 ringers, 172 doubles, for a single game, 105 ringers, 43 doubles, for longest game, 134 shoes against Debbie Michaud, 1977, and for shortest game, 20 shoes, against Esther Williams, 1973; holds high tournament percentage of 82% for New York State and 84.7% for Eastern National; appeared on "Today" program, "Virginia Graham Show," "What's My Line?," and "Mike Douglas Show"; member, National Hall of Fame Committee; has been instrumental in increasing amount of prize money, number of participants, size of classes for women in the World Tournament; served as NHPA's fourth vice-president. Enjoys gardening. Home: 630 Heim Road, Getzville, New York 14068.

HANKINS, JOHN R., b. March 16, 1942. Past Kentucky State Secretary. W. Joanne; children—Tamara Jo, John, Jr., Tony, Nocole. Regional manager, Coppercraft Guild. S. Allen; t. one and a quarter, right handed. Won Oldham County Class A title, 5-0-47.7%, 1979; averaged 53.6%, Yellowstone WAMZ tournament, Louisville, 1979; high game 70.6%; came back from 49-12 deficit in Greenville, Ohio, tournament, 1971, hitting 16 ringers in a row to win 50-49. Home: 12117 Springmeadow Lane, Prospect, Kentucky 40059.

HANSEN, CLIFFORD, 1945 Iowa State Champion.

HANSEN PEGGY, 1966 Washington Women's State Champion, 7-0-35.1%.

HARBURN, FRED, Canadian National Champion, 1936-37, 1939. Finished ninth, Class B, 15-8-60%, World Tournament, Moline, Illinois, 1935. Home: Ontario, Canada.

HARING, WALTER N., b. December 18, 1907. 1964 New Jersey State Champion. Single. Retired. S. Allen; t. one and a quarter, right handed. Served as secretary-treasurer, New Jersey HPA; won Class B State Championship five times; pitched 38 out of 40 years in tournament play. Enjoys motorcycling, swimming, CB radios. Home: Box 12, Middleville, New Jersey 07855.

HARLAN, STANLEY, 1921–22 Minnesota Boys State Champion.

HARLAN, TED, 1942 Iowa State Champion.

HARPER, HENRY, Compiled world tournament record of 99-157-63.4%, 469 points qualifying. Defeated Louis Dean, Tommy Brownell, Dean Brown, Hansford Jackson in many years of play. Home; Monterey, California.

HARPER, SCOTT, 1975 Indiana Boys State Champion.

HARRIS, ARLO E., b. November 18, 1910. Indiana State Champion, 1937, 1948, and 1949. President, NHPA. W. Byrnece; children—Carolyn, Sharon, Arlene, Larry, Kathy, Jerry. Quality control engineer. S. Harris or Allen; t. one and three quarters, right handed. Played horseshoes 58 years; member, NHPA since 1930; only person to serve as president of both NHPA and American HPA (1950–51); served as secretary-treasurer, AHPA; won NHPA Indiana state titles, 1937, 75%, 1948, 76%; won AHPA Indiana State titles, 1950, 80%, 1952, 74%, 1958, 73.9%; won Indiana Fair Tournament, 1964, 77%, 1970, 78%, 1973, 77%; high tournament, 80.9%; high game, 92.3%, 1948 World Tournament, Milwaukee; ranked among ten best in the world, 1937–48; played World Tournaments, 1946, 1948; selected "Mr. Horseshoes" of Indiana, 1958; hit 96%, 48 out of 50, 144 points, Indiana State Fair; won Class A Championship, Lake Worth, Florida, Spring Festival Horseshoe Tournament, 1980; designed and manufactured the Harris pitching shoe, sanctioned by NHPA; known as "father of count-all system". Home: 5515 Maplewood Drive, Speedway, Indiana 46224.

HARRIS, BERT, 1930 Kansas State Champion, 10-1-62%. Home: Minneapolis.

HARRIS, DONALD R., b. January 18, 1922. Played in Championship Division, World Tournament, three times. W. Fern; children—Rhonda, Rachel, Rebecca, Barbie. Sheet metal mechanic, TWA. S. Allen; t. three quarter reverse, right handed. Qualified for Class A, World Tournament play, 1976; qualifying percentages in World Tournaments: 1976, 73%, 1978, 75%, 1979, 76.5%; high tournament, 72%; high game, 85.2%; hit 33 consecutive ringers, June 5, 1973; defeated high qualifier Al Zadroga, 50-45, 1978 World Tournament; Class A tournament titles include: Springfield, Mo., Tournament of Champions, Higginsville Open (twice with 69.8% and 67%), Mound City Open, St. Joseph Open, Gower Centennial, Platte City Fair eight times, Kearney's Jesse James Days seven times, Plattsburg Fall Festival, Leavenworth's Buffalo Bill Days, Buffalo County Fair, Parkville Festival; finished third and fourth in Missouri State Tournaments, losing one year by three points (one point to Charles Kilgore and two points to Ronnie Frakes). Home: Route 2, Box 61, Smithville, Missouri 64089.

HARRIS, JAMES W., b. May 7, 1931. President, Alabama HPA. W. Maxine; children—Rhonda, Jim. Supervisor, P.P.G. Ind. S. Ohio Pro; t. one and a quarter, right handed. Served as secretary-treasurer, Huntsville HPA; finished fourth, Class E, 1980 World Tournament. Enjoys bowling. Home: 3031 Holiday Drive Southwest, Huntsville, Alabama 35805.

HARRIS, ORVILLE, d. October 23, 1968. 1951 AHPA Indiana State Champion. S. Allen; t. one and three quarters, right handed. Member, 1948–49 World Championship Team; high tournament (Indiana State), 80%; played horseshoes from age twelve; played in Championship Division, World Tournament, 1933, 1948; designed (with Arlo Harris) Harris Professional Shoe, built and paid for dies for 5,000 pairs, sanctioned though production was discontinued; served as president of state HPA, active in AHPA.

HARRIS, P. VIRGIL (Rev.), 1933 Vice-President, NHPA. Home: Holden, Massachusetts.

HARRIS, SIDNEY, b. 1908. Nebraska State Champion, 1933, 1937–41. Interior decorator. World Tournament record: 81-31-74.8%, qualified at average of 501 points; hit 24 consecutive doubles and 93 out of 100 shoes. Home: Minden, Nebraska.

HARRIS, TED, b. October 16, 1909, d. January 18, 1981. Class A Player, 1972 World Tournament. W. Alma, d.; children—Bertha, Phyllis Hargo, Dianne Hampton, William. Bookstore clerk. S. Allen; t. one and a quarter, right handed. Won about 200 trophies; high tournament, 77%; high game, 88%; won Class B title, Ohio State Tournament, played in Class A three times; member of winning teams in league play at New Rome and Madison County, won Class A championships in tournaments in Bainbridge, London, and Greenfield; qualified for Class A Division with 510 and 7-28-69.3%, 1972 World Tournament, Greenville, Ohio, finished 34th; one of seven victories was over 1976 World Champion Carl Steinfeldt. Home: 94 Riley Avenue, London, Ohio 43140.

HARRISON, DONALD F., b. February 6, 1915. Past President, Massachusetts and Connecticut HPAs. W. Martha; children—Robert, Frances, Barbara, James, William. Crops Enterprize salesman, Agway Inc. S. Allen; t. one and a quarter, right handed. Pitched league and tournament horseshoes forty-four years; served as secretary-treasurer, Litchfield County Horseshoe Club, 1937–42; president, Connecticut State HPA, 1963–64; president, Massachusetts HPA, 1971–75; with Frank Wagner, reorganized Connecticut horseshoe pitchers; finished second, Class B, Connecticut State Tournament, 1936; finished fourth, Class A, state tournament, 1948; won Class B state title, 1949; high tournament, 58%, 1954; high game, 75%; won doubles championship with Ray Dulmaine in tournament with 21 teams participating, Heritage, 1975; inducted into Massachusetts HPA Hall of Fame, 1977. Home: 7 Glen Street, RFD 3, Westboro, Massachusetts 01581.

HARRISON, ELMER, b. September 9, 1933. Trustee, Fort Hamilton Horseshoe Club. W. Katherine; children—Esther Lynne, Ella Bernice. Chemical operator, Water production, City of Hamilton. S. Allen; t. one and a quarter, right handed. Won Class A title, Eli Reno Memorial; qualified and played in championship division, World Tournament, 3-32-61.3%, 1973. Enjoys car racing. Home: 1921 King Avenue, Hamilton, Ohio 45015.

HARRISON, KATHERINE, b. February 25, 1936. Ohio Women's State Champion, 1969, 1970, 1971, 1976. H. Elmer; children—Esther Lynne, Ella Bernice. Housewife. S. Gordon; t. flip, right handed. NHPA Regional Director for Ohio and Kentucky; first vice-president, Ohio Buckeye HPA; director, Southwest District; lifetime member, Fort Hamilton Club; finished fourth, Class A, World Tournament, Middlesex, N.J., 1971; Class A record, 15-31-58.4%. Enjoys sewing, making and arranging artificial flowers. Home: 1921 King Avenue, Hamilton, Ohio 45015.

HARRISON, TROY, b. May 31, 1924. Florida State Champion, 1979, 66%. W. Janet; child—T. J. Sheet metal mechanic, Cape Kennedy. S. Ohio O; t. one and three quarters, right handed. Won Class A titles including: 1979 Polk County Open, 1974 Seminole Pow Wow Open, 70%, Strawberry Open, Plant City, 1977, 72%; high game, 86%; organized Melbourne Club, Fla.; competed in NHPA games for 26 seasons; served as second vice-president, West Virginia, 1965; served as president or secretary, Melbourne Club, since 1971. Home: 5702 Jacaranda Avenue, Lakeland, Florida 33805.

HARTON, R.A., One of Founders, National League of Horseshoe and Quoit Pitchers of the United States, 1919, and served as vice-president in original slate of officers. Home: Lansing, Michigan.

HARVEY, ELDON, Oregon State Champion, 1956, 1961, 1963 (73.2%). Won Class B, state tournament, 1954; was runnerup for state title 1957–60, 1964; finished 20th, championship division, World Tournament, Salt Lake City, 1957; won eleven Clakamas county titles, two Bryant Memorials, and two Willamette Valleys. Enjoys coaching Little League Baseball.

HASKINS, BRAD, 1978, 1979 Oregon Boys State Champion (4-1-21.1%). Home: P.O. Box 356, Merrill, Oregon 97633.

HASTINGS, WALTER, Idaho State Champion, 1970, 7-0-54.5%, and 1972, 8-0-54.4%. W. Helen. Shipping clerk, Speer Bullet, Inc. S. Allen; t. one and a quarter, right handed. Won fifty trophies, including Lewiston city championship, local titles, Inland, Empire, John Monasmith championships; high game, 72%. Home: 702 12th Avenue, Lewiston, Idaho 83501.

HATTON, ROD, 1973 Class B World Champion, 1973 Texas State Champion. W. Celia; child—Steve. Reconstructor of stringed instruments. S. Allen or Ohio; t. two and a quarter, right handed. Won Boys State Championship, Indiana, 1955; won more than 100 trophies for Class A tournament titles; longest string of consecutive doubles, 20, Garfield Park, Indianapolis; pitched several games above 90% in league and tournament play; promoted three days of round robin play, San Antonio stock show (sponsored by Dr. Pepper) with six state champions participating, 1972. Home: P.O. Box 12272, San Antonio, Texas 78212.

HAUGE, HAAKEN, 1925, 1944 Minnesota State Champion. t. one and a quarter. Was also baseball pitcher. Home: Hawley, Minnesota.

HAWKINS, LAVERN, 1968 Kentucky State Champion, 10-1-52.8%. Served as president, Kentucky Chapter; helped reorganize state chapter, late 1960s.

HAWLEY, GROVER, Ohio State Champion, 1941, 15-0-73.8%, 1943, 1944, 1945, 1949. Finished ninth, World Tournament, 14-9-63.9%, 1933. Home: Bridgeport, Ohio.

HAY, (MRS.) A. FRED, Played two World Tournaments, 10-9-31.4%. Home: Minnesota.

HAY, A. FRED, 1921, 1924, 1927, 1936 Minnesota State Champion. t. one and three quarters. Druggist. Home: Minnesota.

HAYDEN, W. H., Oregon State Champion, 1924, 1925, 1926, 1927, 1929, 1940.

HAYES, HARVEY, b. January 25, 1938. Vice-President, Western Pennsylvania HPA. W. Rose Marie; children—Leanne, Keith Allen. Owner/operator, Hayes Antenna & Sound. S. Imperial; t. one and a quarter, right handed. Active member, Erie Horseshoe Club; high game, 61.9%; pitched NHPA horseshoes eleven years. Home: 4129½ Essex Avenue, Erie, Pennsylvania 16504.

HAYNES, HARRY G., chief Organizer/First President, National Horseshoe Pitchers Association, February 26, 1919, organization that bridged the gap between Grand League American Horseshoe Pitchers Association and the present National Horseshoe Pitchers Association of America. President, Kenmore Banking Company, Akron, Ohio; vice-president, Akron Realty Company; sponsored 1920 national tournament, Akron; worked with Dr. E. C. Beach, St.

Top, left, Ralph Dykes, NHPA president from 1967 to 1973, with other NHPA officers. *Right,* Henry Franke, Hall of Fame member. *Center row, left,* World Tournament finalists in Des Moines, Iowa, 1922. Frank Lundin, World Champion, is at left in front row. Harold Falor is at extreme right in top row. *Right,* Golden Gate Park, San Francisco, Paul Mori, Guy Zimmerman, Don Titcomb, Bill Fraser, and George Callas. *Bottom,* Presentation of awards at the Metropolitan Tournament, Washington, D.C., 1934. Raymond L. Frye is at right in front row.

Top, left, Ralph Forsstrom, Hall of Fame member. *Center,* 1962 Ohio State Fair championship team. Jim Garland is at left in top row. *Right,* Jesse Gonzales. *Center row, left,* Malcolm Georgina. *Center,* Sam Goodlander (left) with his Ohio State Tournament team. *Right,* Bob Graham. *Bottom, left,* Guy Stoddard. *Right,* John Gordon, Hall of Fame member.

Petersburg, Fla., Art Headlough, William Weis on new association; pitchers and representatives from twenty-nine states participated in association in 1919, national tournament held in St. Petersburg (Williams Park), under auspices of St. Petersburg Board of Trade; through association published first book of constitution, by-laws and rules; elected president, National League of Horseshoe and Quoit Pitchers of the United States, recognized as chief organizer. Home: Akron, Ohio.

HEADLOUGH, ARTHUR L., b. June 20, 1884. d. June 18, 1944. 1982 member NHPA Hall of Fame. National Secretary, NHPA. Fire chief. Wrote early history, "Official Horseshoe Guide and Blueprint"; wrote with William Weis, standard rules for pitching, 1920; originated NHPA magazine, "Barnyard Golf"; incorporated NHPA and the Buckeye State HPA, office of the Secretary of State, Columbus, Ohio, May 21, 1921; served as secretary, Buckeye HPA; helped run winter tournaments in Florida (worked with Dr. E. C. Beach); helped bring World Tournament to Akron, 1920. Home: Akron, Ohio.

HEALY, LAWRENCE, 1928 Utah State Champion. Served as vice-president, Murray Horseshoe Club.

HEBERT, RAYMOND, 1979 New Brunswick Provincial Champion, 60%, the fifth consecutive year Hebert won the title. Won doubles championships with brother Albert, 1975–79; won doubles championship with Edgar Richard, 1974; won men's title, Maritime Championships, 1972, 37%, 1974, 47.2%, 1975, 58.2%; won Maritime Doubles Championship with brother Albert, 1973, 1977, with Henry McGraw, 1974, 1975; won five consecutive Loyalist Days tournaments, St. John, beginning 1974; won 1979 Canterbury Open, Notre Dame, and Atlantic National Exhibition. Home: Moncton, New Brunswick, Canada.

HEIST, L. E. "SHADY," b. November 25, 1899. Past President, Nebraska HPA. W. Bethel, d.; child—Janice Buhr. Owner/manager, Heist Implement Company. S. Allen; t. one and a quarter, right handed. Pitched horseshoes sixty-three years, sixty-one in tournament and league play; won county championship many times; played in five World Tournaments; finished third, Senior Division, World Tournament, Fargo, North Dakota, 1967; was oldest competitor in World Tournament, Greenville, Ohio, 1977; won more than 100 trophies; averages 50–60%; recipient, Community Citizen Award, sponsored by DeWitt Grange No. 429, 1978. Home: 204 South Quince Street, DeWitt, Nebraska 68341.

HELBERG, VAUGHN, b. November 16, 1946. 1977 Nebraska State Champion. Single. Rancher/registered Hereford breeder. S. Allen; t. one and a quarter, right handed. Served as president, Nebraska HPA one year; won doubles and team championships with Gary Glendy, University of Nebraska, 1966–67; state title record, 66.4%, also high tournament, winning title from Don McCance who was defeated by only three men in 23 years; high game, 90%, most consecutive doubles, 9; played in Class C, World Tournament, 4-1, lost last game 47–50 (and played with broken toe), 1978; graduate, University of Nebraska, 1968; taught high school science, five and a half years; serves as high school football official. Home: Rural Route 1, Oconto, Nebraska 68860.

HELGASON, SIMBI, b. September 21, 1906. 1978 Member, Saskatchewan Hall of Fame. Won Men's Singles Championship, Saskatchewan, 1960; won Senior Men's title, 1972; won doubles championships with Geiri Helgason, 1960, with Les Widenmaier, 1972. Home: Mozart, Saskatchewan.

HELMS, JOE, New Mexico State Champion, 1962, 7-0-60.8%, 1963, 3-0, 1964, 6-1-64.5%.

HENN, WILLIAM, b. June 18, 1924. Kentucky State Champion seven times. W. Audry; children—Jack, Judy, Joyce, Bob, Peggy, Donald. Bus driver. S. Allen, Ohio Pro; t. one and three quarters, left handed. State title record, 1969, 1971–76; finished 15th, World Tournament, 21-15-74.3%, 1973; high tournament, 75.4%, Day-Bell March Tournament, 1974; high game, 91.4%, 1975 state tournament; served as secretary, Bellevue Vet's League, and secretary, Day-Bell Thursday League, 1965–80; helped form Don Moore's indoor courts, Dayton, Kentucky, and indoor club, Cincinnati, Ohio; helped revive Kentucky NHPA chapter, 1964. Home: 206 Prospect Street, Bellevue, Kentucky 41073.

HENN, HARRY J., b. March 29, 1895. d. March 20, 1951. Kentucky State Champion, 1935–36. W. Catherine; children—Bill, Chick, Clif, Dolores, Velma. Shoe factory employee. S. Gordon; t. three-quarter flip, right handed. Sold shoes for friend, John Gordon, who designed and manufactured Gordon shoes; held office in Kentucky State Association, 1940s; competed in championship division, World Tournament; pitched twenty years.

HENRY, W. W., One of founders of National League of Horseshoe and Quoit Pitchers of the United States, 1919, and was vice-president in original slate of officers. Home: St. Petersburg, Florida.

HENSON, CLAYTON C. "BOO," b. October 4, 1912. Virginia State Champion fifteen times, Charter Member, Virginia State HPA Hall of Fame. W. Anna May, d.; children—Clayton, Jr., Richard, Kenneth, Patricia. Building contractor. S. Allen; t. one and three quarters, right handed. Won Metropolitan Washington, D.C., Championship 34 times; set state record, game 92.9%, 1975;

set state record for tournament, 79%, 1942; set world qualifying records, Intermediate Division, World Tournament, 84 ringers, 265 points in 100 shoes, and 35 doubles (tied world record), 1976; averaged 80.2%, District of Columbia Tournament, 1941; member, Virginia Hall of Fame Committee; served as first vice-president, NHPA, 1941; suffered stroke, early 1970s; exhibitions with Raymond Frye, Jimmie Risk, Ted Allen, Bill Kolb, Jimmy O'Shea drew large crowds and publicity for the sport. Home: 3915 9th Street South, Arlington, Virginia 22204.

HENSON, ROGER, b. December 5, 1945. Champion, U.S. Army support command, Saigon, Vietnam 1967. W. Laurie; first child expected September 1981. Owner/operator, Roger Henson Landscaping. S. Ohio; t. one a quarter, right handed. Claims to have only log home in the world with a professional indoor horseshoe court; won several Class B trophies in New England; averages 60%. Home: 98 Patton Road, North Haven, Connecticut 06473.

HENTON, GLEN "RED," b. September 3, 1920. Iowa State Champion fifteen times, Member, NHPA Hall of Fame. W. Bernice; children—Judy, Nancy. Entertainer. S. Allen; t. one and a quarter, left handed. Member, Iowa State Hall of Fame; tied for World Championship, Greenville, Ohio, lost playoff to Elmer Hohl, 1977; recipient, "Pride of Iowa" award, Iowa Jaycees, 1976; pitched exhibition games, Kroonstad, South Africa, 1974; pitched a record game with Ray Martin, World Tournament, Keene, New Hampshire, 194 shoes, 1965; retired from Post Office Department; won Galesburg Tournament more times than any other player. Hit many tournaments over 80%. Home: Route 2, Maquoketa, Iowa 52060.

HENTON, NANCY, Iowa Girls State Champion, Runnerup for Women's World

Championship at age fifteen. Home: Route 2, Maquoketa, Iowa 52060.

HERFURTH, BERNARD, b. June 1, 1911. 1980 Member NHPA Hall of Fame, New England States' Hall of Fame. W. Violet; child—Robert. Piano instructor. S. All brands; t. one and three quarters, right handed. Won Western Massachusetts Championship, 1927, 1977; won first championship at age fourteen, July 4, 1924, 9-0- win over all-adult field, pitching from 40-foot men's distance; won Massachusetts State Championship 1973, 1974, 1976, runnerup many times since 1935; played in ten of thirteen World Tournaments since 1966; high tournament, Providence, Rhode Island, 77.1% for seven games, four of which went more than 100 shoes, 1940; chairman, NPHA Hall of Fame Committee since 1972; member, NHPA Publicity Committee; organizer and chairman, Massachusetts State Hall of Fame Committee; served as publicity director, Massachusetts State Association, since 1974; wrote guidelines for Massachusetts "Junior Achievement Award"; originated NHPA Appreciation Award; recipient, Stokes Award, 1975; won 1980 Massachusetts State 7-2-71.3%. Home: 17 Fort Street, Northampton, Massachusetts 01060.

HEROUX, PETER, Member, New England Hall of Fame, 1976. Won 1933 Rhode Island Junior Championship, finished second in Men's State Championship at age thirteen; won Rhode Island Men's State Championship, 67%, finished third in New England meet; 63%, 1935; won Rhode Island Open, 10-1-64%; won Rhode Island State Championship over Ken Hurst, 1940; finished 8th, New England meet, 60%, 1941; won Rhode Island State title seven times, 64–70%, 1947-56; won New England Championship, 11-0-69.5%, 1950; in five consecutive years, averaged 69-72% in New England meets, and in eleven years, won once, finished third three times, fourth once, fifth

four times, sixth once, eighth once in 12-man classes; won Rhode Island Open 1935, 1947; won Connecticut Open, 1953; won Dover, New Hampshire, Centennial, 1955; high game, New England Championship tournament, 91.9%, 1954. Home: Providence, Rhode Island.

HERREMAN, D. E. "MONTE," b. January 5, 1913. Director, South Dakota HPA. W. Barbara; two children. Colonel, U.S. Army, retired. S. Deadeye or Allen; t. one and a quarter, right handed. Won South Dakota Class B Championship, 6-1-49.5%, 1976; recipient, Sportsmanship Award, Ringers Horseshoe Club, Rapid City, 1977; vice-president, Rapid City Ringer Horseshoe Club; past president, South Dakota HPA, 1979; past president, Ringers Club, 1978–79. Home: 611 St. Patrick Street, Rapid City, South Dakota 57701.

HERRICK, KEN, First President, Alberta HPA. Won Alberta men's singles championship, 1973; won Klondike Days, 1972; member, Edmonton Horseshoe Club; serves as pitcher and promoter. Home: Edmonton, Alberta, Canada.

HERRMANN, WILLIAM C., b. October 12, 1924. Secretary-Treasurer, New Jersey State, 1971–73, 1978–79. W. Florence; children—Janice, William. Sheet metal mechanic. S. Allen; t. one a quarter, right handed. Won 1978 New Jersey Doubles Championship with Al Ravencraft, finished second in singles, 1977; past president, Elizabeth Indoor Horseshoe Pitchers Club, 1977–79. Home: 3 Orchard Terrace, Clark, New Jersey 07066.

HESKETT, JOE, 1920–21 Illinois State Champion (in the first two known tournaments).

HIATT, S. L., 1927 California State Champion.

HILL, JEFF, 1965 Minnesota Boys State Champion, 4-1-47.4%.

HILL, LAUREN,. b. August 6, 1938. 1964 Oregon State Champion, 7-1-71.4%. W. Priscilla; children—Faye, Darrell, Diane, Brian, Melanie. Computer storage supervisor, Safeway Grocery Warehouse. S. Allen; t. reverse one and a quarter, right handed. Won Portland City Championship three times; won Portland Club Championship four times; won twenty-one Class A championships in Oregon and Washington; won Oregon Junior State Championship, 1954; hit 80% and 82% to defeat the state champion twice to win 1964 state tournament; high game, 89.4% (twice); served eight years as secretary-treasurer and seven years as president of Portland Horseshoe Club. Home: 43255 Southeast Elmer Road, Sandy, Oregon 97055.

HILL, LEROY, b. August 8, 1909. Ohio AAU State Champion, 1962-63, 1965. W. Cecile Naomi, d.; children—Anna Marie, George Leroy, Howard, Shirley, Susie. Employee, State Highway Department. S. Ohio; t. one and a quarter, right handed. Won Milford Center Sesquicentennial Championship, 1966; finished third in nationals, Salisbury, Maryland, 1963; high tournament, 73%; pitched many games over 80%; won over Sol Berman in National AAU finals, 80%; played league and tournament horseshoes since 1933. Enjoys coon hunting. Home: 19740 State Route 245, Marysville, Ohio 43040.

HILL, RAYMOND, b. April 20, 1919. 1973, 1974 Michigan Upper Peninsula Champion, W. Leona; children—Andrew, Leslie, Fia. Mine mechanic. S. Allen; t. one a quarter, right handed. High tournament, 71.5% for seven games. Home: Route 1, Box 340, Wakefield, Michigan 49968.

HILL, RUSSELL ROOD, b. October 27, 1902. 1979 Nebraska Senior State Champion. W. and children, d. Retired. S. Allen; t. one and a quarter, right handed. Pitched horseshoes fifty-nine years, thirteen in tournament play; director, Pop Corn Days, annual tournament for junior players; won last four classes, B and C, averaging over 50%; hit qualifying round, state tournament, 66%, 220 points, missing Class A by one point, finished third in Class B. Enjoys bowling, checkers, gardening. Home: Box 54, North Loup, Nebraska 68859.

HILL, TRINA KAY, b. January 23, 1958. Kentucky State Champion, 1976, 1979. S. Allen; t. single flip, right handed. Won Girls State Championship, 1974; averaged 59.8%, 1979 state tournament; high game, 70%; won 1974 Millville Couple League, with Tony Wash; won James Gaines Open, and Millville Warmup, 196; won Christine Kelley Memorial, 1978, 1979; won Metro Open, 1979; graduate, Eastern Kentucky University; teacher, Hazard. Home: 254 Hawkeegan Park, Frankfort, Kentucky 40601.

HILL, WILSON, 1937 North Carolina State Champion.

HILLBURN, RALPH, Connecticut State Champion, 1955, 11-0-44.1%, 1956, 11-0-57.2%, 1957, 8-1-50.3%

HILST, GEORGE J., 1923 Illinois State Champion. Served as secretary, Illinois State HPA, 1929.

HILTON, JENEAN, Played in six World Tournaments, 14-16-35.4%. Home: Murray, Utah.

HILTON, RODNEY J., b. July 10, 1945. 1957 Junior Boys World Champion. W. Vicki; children—Mark Allen, Nanette Susan, Misty Ann. Aerospace engineer. S. Gordon; t. one and three quarters, right handed. Took two hitches, NHPA tournament and organized league play, 1955-60, 1973-74. Home: 3015 Johnston Avenue, Redondo Beach, California 90278.

HILTON, STAN, b. June 20, 1935. Publicity Chairman, Burbank Horseshoe Club. W. Alice; children—Linda, Larry, Stephanie. Drywall contractor. S. Gordon or Allen; t. one and three quarters, right handed. Past president, Burbank Horseshoe Club, 1978–79; served as secretary, Salt Lake City Horseshoe Club, 1950, 1961–62; competed in 1947 World Tournament Junior Division, Salt Lake City; pitched Class B, Men's Division, World Tournament, 1953; member, NHPA, since 1947; won second place, 1951 Junior World Tournament; won Class D World Championship, 1973; finished second, Class C, World Tournament, 59.9%, 1970; high tournament, 62.7%, high game, 74.8%; listed in Guiness Book of World Records for 120-hour horseshoe marathon, South Gate, California. Home: 424 South Sparks, Burbank, California 91506.

HILTON, VIOLA, Played in six World Tournaments, 13-23-25%. Home: Murray, Utah.

HITE, LESTER E., b. October 11, 1923. Third Vice-President, Ohio Buckeye HPA. W. June; children—Sonya, Ray, Glen, Beth. Gravel pit foreman. S. Allen; t. one and a quarter, right handed. President, Licking County Club; chairman, Central District of Ohio; served as fourth vice-president, OBHPA and secretary, Licking County Club; high tournament, 52.4%; high game, 73.3%. Home: 7915 Loudon Street, Johnstown, Ohio 43031.

HITT, BOB, b. January 1, 1922. Michigan State Champion 1936, 1937, 1938. W. Eleanor; children—Lowell, Julie, Janice. Step-children, Cinny, Marty, Debbie, Randy. Milkman. S. Lattore; t. one and a quarter, right handed. Led Jackson Club to International Association championship; record for state title (which he won at ages 14, 15, and 16), 25-2-68.4%, 1936; called "Boy Wonder"; pitched two games at age 12

against Ted Allen, averaging 74%, losing 50–35, 50–46; considered one of best professional bowlers, competed in televised matches, 1950s and 1960s, rolled nineteen perfect 300 games; stopped playing horseshoes while in his twenties. Home: 440 Ross Street, Plymouth, Michigan 48170.

HIX, FLOYD, JR., b. September 21, 1941. Past Secretary, Virginia HPA. W. Ruth; children—Franklin Andrew, d., Deborah Renee, Sonja Gayle, Floyd Eugene, Tonya Monette, Kara Jean, Karl William. Machinist. S. Deadeye; t. one a quarter, right handed. President, Elmont Club played in many Class A and other tournaments against top pitchers in country; pitched 62.7%, Class B, Frye Memorial, Winchester, Virginia, 1979, with high game, 75.5% against C. C. Henson; played for 31 years, 21 in NHPA tournament. Enjoys bowling, jukskei, checkers. Home: Route 1, Box 15S, Ruther Glen, Virginia 22546.

HIX, DEBORAH RENEE, b. March 23, 1966. 1980 Virginia Girls State Champion. Student. S. Imperial; t. one and a quarter, right handed. Finished fifth, Women's Division, 1980 Frye Memorial, Winchester. Home: Route 1, Box 15S, Ruther Glen, Virginia 22546.

HOBLYN, PAT, b. February 7, 1951. Nebraska Women's State Champion, 1974, 1976. H. Jim; child—Kelli. Teacher/housewife. S. Ohio Pro; t. flip, right handed. High tournament, 44%; high game, 72%. Home: Rural Route 1, Ansley, Nebraska 68814.

HODGES, CLINTON, b. September 22, 1921. President, New Rome Horseshoe Club, Organizer, Promoter. W. Gertrude. Superviosr, Timken Roller Bearing Company. S. Ohio; t. one and three quarters, right handed. Won playground championship, Sunshine Park, Columbus, Ohio, 1937; Class A Champion, AAU, Detroit, Columbus; organized Central Ohio Horseshoe League, 1960; captain, Garland Equipment team which won Ohio league, averaged 66.4%; member, Old Timers (Beatty Park Horseshoe Club); has had winning teams sponsored by Garland Enterprises in Whetstone Park, Hilliard Recreation Park, Sunshine Park, Waverly league, New Rome winter and summer league; had Post Office Leagues for intercity weekend play, Springfield, Centerbury, Columbus, Johnstown, Cincinnati, Toledo, Dayton, 1956–57; member, Royal Arch Masons, St. Mark's Lodge No. 7, Johnson Chapter No. 3, Herald Council No. 3, Taylor Commandery No. 6; past president, National Alliance of Postal Employees. Home: 410 South Wayne Avenue, Columbus, Ohio 43204.

HOEKSEMA, JACK, 1932 Michigan State Champion, Battle Creek (Ed Walls won championship in Pleasant Ridge due to a split in Michigan membership creating two charters). Played in Championship Division, World Tournament, Chicago, 2-21-53.8%, 1933; served as vice-president, Wolverine State HPA.

HOELZLE, RUTH ALLEN, b. June 8, 1919. 1974 Member, New York State Hall of Fame. H. John, d.; children—John, Robert, Linda. Suffolk County school crossing guard. S. Lattore and Ohio; t. one and a quarter, right handed. Finished second, Long Island Open Tournament, 58%, 1937, finished third, 1938; became first and only woman pitcher to compete in official New York State Tournament with men at 40 feet, 1938; won Nassau County Championship three times, 63.5% at 40 feet, which enabled her to be the first woman ever to pitch at Syracuse State Fair Agricultural Tournament, 1938; received New York State Championship Award for women at 40-foot distance, 1938; competed in international exhibition between New York City and Toronto (held in Canada), won four games,

58%, 1939; finished third, Long Island Open, 1940–41; won Long Island Open, 64.7%, 1942; past member, West Hempstead Club, 1935; considered one of great woman pitchers in the East. Home: 414 Pecan Street, Lindenhurst, New York 11757.

HOFFMAN, WILLIAM G., b. January 20, 1945. Vice-President, Shasta Horseshoe Club. W. Marleen; children—Danny, Kara. Cabinet maker. S. Ohio Pro; t. one a quarter, right handed. Finished 66th, NHPA percentage rankings, 67.1%, 1980; won AA Reno, Nevada, Open and Rio Del Scotia Open, 5-0-67.7%, 1977; won Shasta VI Open, 4-2-73.7%, Vallejo Major Curtola Open, 6-1-67%, October Open, 73.9%, 1980; high tournament, 73.9%, 1980; high game, 84.8%. Home: 1593 Lloyd Lane, Anderson, California 96007.

HOGAN, JOHN J., 1922 Illinois State Champion. One of principal members, Tournament Committee, World Tournament, 1933. Home: 768 Uhland Street, Chicago, Illinois.

HOGG, ARNOLD, Second Vice-President, Alberta HPA, elected 1968. Home: Didsbury, Alberta, Canada.

HOHL, ELMER, b. January 16, 1919. Men's World Champion, 1965, 1968, 1972, 1973; 1975, 1977, Member, 1966, Hall of Fame, Canadian Champion seventeen times. W. Hilda; children—Sandra Roemer, Susan Graff, Richard, Karen Ehnes, Stephen. Carpenter. S. Elmer Hohl; t. one and three quarters, right handed. Considered by many to be the greatest horseshoe pitcher who ever lived; set world record, 88.5% for 35 games, 1968 World Tournament; set world record for qualifying, 572 points out of possible 600; holds world record game, 100%, against Wes Kuchcinski; holds world record for 15 consecutive four-deads, with Carl Steinfeldt, 1964; pitched in Championship Division, World Tournament, 1960–80, with record of six titles, six seconds, two thirds, five fourths (three were ties), one fifth, one seventh, 20-year record: 619-93-83.3%, 159 ringers out of 57,854 shoes; from 1962–79, missed only 1978 Eastern National, won eleven, finished second five times, fifth once, won Canadian National Championship 1957, 1958, 1959, 1961, 1962, 1963, 1964, 1965, 1966, 1968, 1970, 1972, 1975, 1977, 1978, 1979; won Ontario Championship every year from 1957–79, except 1968, when he did not compete; pitched on "Mike Douglas Show," Philadelphia, 1966; received Canadian NHPA Special Award—"Horseshoe Pitcher of the Decade," 1970; Regional Athlete of the Year, C. H. Y. M. Community Foundation, 1975; won gold medal, Ontario Summer Games, 1977; received Queen's Medal, commemorating Queen's Silver Jubilee, for excellence; won Greenville, Ohio, Classic seven times; designed and built the Elmer Hohl shoe; executive member, Canadian HPA and Ontario Association. Home: R. R. 1, Wellesley, Ontario, Canada NOB 2TO.

HOHL, STEPHEN, b. November 21, 1962. Canadian Boys Champion, 1973, 1975, 1977, 1978, Boys World Champion, 1978. S. Elmer Hohl; t. one a quarter, left handed. Won Canadian Junior Boys Championship, Ontario, defeating defending champion Billy Zinger, 1973, and won the championship again in 1975, 1977, 1978; entered Men's Division, 1979; won Boys Ontario Championship, 1974, 1975, 63.5%, 1976, 69%, 1977, 72.8%, 1978, 79.9%; world championship record: (Des Moines, Iowa) 84.1%, posting eleven consecutive wins; qualified, Men's Division, Statesville, North Carolina, with 450 in B Division, 69%, 6-5, 1979; won Boys Championship, Greenville Classic, 6-0-69%, 1976, and 7-0-78.5%, 1977, finished second, 79.5%, 1978; received Gold Medal, 1977 Ontario Summer Games; high tournament, 87.1%, 1978 Canadian Championship; high game, 96.1%, 1977 Canadian

Championship. Home: R. R. 1, Wellesley, Ontario, Canada NOB 2TO.

HOHMANN, SID C., b. October 24, 1914. Charter Member, North Dakota HPA Hall of Fame. W. Jeanne R.; children—Kenneth, Douglas, Dale, Dean. United States Government Civil Service employee. S. Allen; t. one and three quarters, right handed. Received special sportsmanship award signed by four former North Dakota state champions (Morris Wold, Ernolf Roland, Wally Rislou, Phil Prescott), state champion Will Gulickson, and world champion Danny Kuckcinski; served as president, league organizer, Minot Club, since 1934; played 22 years in tournaments and leagues. Home: 416 Hillcrest Drive, Minot, North Dakota 58701.

HOLDING, DONALD JOSEPH, b. 1962. 1972, 1974 Kansas Boys State Champion. W. Kay. Farmer/construction worker. S. Gordon; t. flip, right handed. Home: Route 1, Walnut, Kansas 66780.

HOLLAND, WILLIAM ANTHONY, b. July 8, 1955. 1970 Junior World Champion. W. Carolyn. Computer operator. S. Imperial; t. one and three quarters, left handed. Championship record: 79.7%; won Class B championship, World Tournament, 72.2%, 1977; serves as assistant regional director, Indiana; president, Metro Horseshoe Club, Indianapolis, 1976–78; won Class A championships, second and third place finishes; high tournament, 83%; high game, 96%. Home: R.R. 1, Box 35A, Stilesville, Indiana 46180.

HOLLIN, GLEN, Oregon State Boys Champion, 1963, 4-0-32.4%, 1964, 5-0-33.1%, 1965, 4-0-36.3%.

HOLLIDAY, DESSIE, b. March 22, 1934. Wyoming Women's State Champion, 1965, 5-0-25.5%, 1968, 9-3-46.3%, 1970, 9-0-40.5%, 1972, 6-3-48.9%, 1973, 6-0-38.9%. H. Herbert; children—Rodney, Miles, Beverlee. Office manager, Fremont Co. Radiological Associates. S. Allen; t. three quarters, right handed. Won Fremont County titles and Wyoming Winter Fair Open; placed, Rocky Mountain Open; won Class B titles. Murray, Utah, and Fargo, North Dakota, World Tournament play; served as president, vice-president, secretary-treasurer, local horseshoe club. Enjoys softball, bowling. Home: Paradise Valley Route, Riverton, Wyoming 82501.

HOLLIDAY, HERBERT, b. February 7, 1932. Won Fremont County Championships. W. Dessie; children—Rodney, Miles, Beverlee. Self-employed maintenance engineer. Albertsons. S. Allen; t. one and three quarters, right handed. Won Shoshoni Open Championships; placed, Wyoming Winter Fair Open. Enjoys softball, bowling. Home: Paradise Valley Route, Riverton, Wyoming 82501.

HOLLIDAY, MILES, b. January 5, 1957. 1972 Wyoming Boys State Champion. W. Sherrie; child—Tera Rae. S. Allen; t. one and a quarter, right handed. Won Fremont County Championships; placed, 1976 World Tournament, Fargo, North Dakota; state championship record: 4-1-23.3%. Enjoys trapping, fishing, hunting. Home: Paradise Valley Route, Riverton, Wyoming 82501.

HOLLIDAY, RODNEY, b. July 26, 1953. Won Fremont County Championship. W. Jeannie; child—Jessica, step-children—Shannon, Dianna, Brock. Driller, Vierson-Cochran. S. Allen; t. flip, right handed. Played in Junior Division, 1966 World Tournament, Murray City, Utah. Enjoys softball, hunting, fishing. Home: General Delivery, Big Piney, Wyoming 83113.

HOLLISTER, KEVIN, b. October 30, 1957. Vermont State Champion, Boys: 1972, 1973, 1974; Men's, 1975, 1976, 1978, 1979, 1980. W. Judy. Appliance salesman, Montgomery Ward Co. S. Ohio Pro or Deadeye;

t. one and a quarter, right handed. Finished seventh, 72%, World Tournament, 1974; won Oxford County Fair, 8-0-76%, 1979; finished second, 13-2-76%, New England Tournament, 1980; pitched three games above 90%, 1980 season; high tournament, 82.5%. Enjoys bowling, motorcycling, hunting. Home: Chapel Road, Bennington, Vermont 05201.

HOLM, SVERRE, b. 1902. Member Saskatchewan Horseshoe Pitchers Hall of Fame, 1977; Teamed with Ben Meberg, Doubles Champion 1957, 1958; Won mixed doubles, teamed with Alvina Everitt, 1960.

HOLMBERG, EDWIN W., b. March 23, 1919. Montana State Champion, AAU, 1962, 1963, 1965, 1966, 1967, 1969; Montana State Champion, NHPA, 1966, 1970, 1971, 1972, 1973, 1974, 1978. W—Donna Mattison Holmberg; children—Jeanette, William, Robert. High School math teacher. Allen or Deadeye; t. one and a quarter, right handed. Secretary, Big Timber Horseshoe Club; Won 60 Class A Championships in AAU or NHPA play from 1962 and 1980; 1962 National AAU Doubles Champion teamed with Art Olsen; Member Western Montana HPA Hall of Fame, 1977; Hit best tournament average, 71.7%, to win 1971 Montana NHPA Championship on dirt courts; Hit high game, 77.6%, at same tournament. Home: Box 462, Big Timber, Montana 59011.

HOLTER, ARTHUR N., b. February 1, 1910. Member Minnesota HPA Hall of Fame, 1974. W—Loretta; child—Karen Langsam. Employee, Federal Reserve Bank of Minneapolis. S. Ohio O; t. one and three quarters, right handed. Qualified six times for Intermediate Division of the World Tournament, in 1970 with 7-0-64.8% and in 1971 with 7-0-59.3%; Placed second in the Minnesota State Tournament in 1971, his best finish; highest tournament average, 69%; highest game, 88%, 44 out of 50.

Home: 4417 Brunswick Avenue, Minneapolis, Minnesota 55422.

HOOD, CHUCK, JR. 1979 and 1980 Illinois State Boys Champion. Maintenance worker—McDonald's. S. Ohio; t. one and three quarters, left handed. Illinois State Fair Boys Champion, 1978, with 11-2-62%; Illinois State Boys Champion, 1979, with 7-0-65%, NHPA event, and 1980, with 6-1-38.5%; Highest game, 78%; best tournament, 68%. Home: Route 1, Box 67 Mazon, Illinois 60444.

HOOK, JIMMIE. 1947 Ohio Boys State Champion.

HOOLEY, WALTER J., b. August 20, 1919. 1974 Westchester County Champion with 57%. W—Margaret, deceased; children—Owen and James. Supervisor of Micrographies, New York City Banking Organization. S. Allen; t. one and a quarter, right handed. Member of Hall of Committee of NYHPA; past president and vice president of both NYHPA and Westchester County HPA; other interests—walking, canoeing, swimming. Home: 21 Glenwood Drive, Montrose, New York 10548.

HOPE, OSCAR. Senior Michigan State Champion, 1978. Home: 1008 Carwood, Lansing, Michigan.

HOPKINS, CHARLIE; HOPKINS, LUCILLE, served as workers, promoters, officers for many years on all levels. Both deceased. Home: 124 South Cherry Street, Ottumwa, Iowa 52501.

HOPKINS, HARRY ALVIN, b. February 9, 1920. Won Class B, George Smith Memorial, Sidney Fair. W—Catherine; children—Charlotte, Patricia, Barbara, and Roger. Machinist—Universal Grinder. S. Allen; t. one and a quarter, right handed. Trustee, Piqua Horseshoe Club; 65% average, 1975 Piqua League; best tournament, 62% at Class B, Sidney Fair; best single game, 84.2%,

1977 Ohio state tournament; collects Indian artifacts; active member Archeological Society of Ohio. Home: 7385 North Troy-Sidney Road, Piqua, Ohio 45356.

HOPKINS, LUCILLE, died November 20, 1976. Member Iowa Hall of Fame; Vice President 1962 N.H.P.A.; Iowa Secretary-Treasurer for 20 years; member of the National Executive Committee.

HORE ROY. 1977 and 1978 Ontario Senior Provincial Champion. W. Leone. Retired from Union Carbide. S. Imperial; t. one and a quarter, right handed. Won singles championship in Niagra district three years in a row; Highest tournament game, 75% in Toronto. Home: Route 1, Welland, Ontario, Canada L3B 5N4.

HORN, CARL M. Montana State Champion 1959, 6-1, 49.7%; 1960, 9-0, 55.3%; 1961, 6-1, 55.7%.

HORNBACK, MABLE. 1980 Kentucky Women's State Champion. H—Russell; children—Mona, Debbie, Martha, Steve, Marty and Robbie. Employee Hardin County Board of Education. S. Allen; t. reverse three quarters, right handed. Won the Kentucky 1980 championship with a record of 6-2-41.8%; Class E runnerup, 1980 World Tournament; softball player; den mother for children's baseball club. Home: Route 2 Elizabethtown, Kentucky 42701.

HORNER, WALTER "BUD", deceased. Played in Senior Division of the World Tournament with a record of 5-2-66.2%, also in the regular men's division, 1961 World Tournament with a record of 15-20-70%. S. Ohio; t. one and a quarter, right handed. Home: Farmersburg, Indiana; retirement in Florida.

HOSFIELD, GORDON, b. May 15, 1911. Chairman, Minnesota Hall of Fame. W—Esther; children—Edith, Helen and Roger. Farmer. S. Ohio and Gordon; t. one and a quarter, right handed. Chairman, Minnesota H.P.A. Home: Route 1 Medford, Minnesota 55049.

HOSIER, ERVIN. Played in championship division of World Tournament several times, winning 117, losing 154, averaging 67.6% and 470 points qualifying.

HOSTAK, AL, b. January 7, 1916. Won Washington State Open, Class B. W. Rose; children—Terry and Phil. Security officer. S. Allen; t. one and three quarters, right handed. High tournament—59%; high game—76% with six doubles in a row; won Class B titles at Washington State Open, Tacoma Daffodil Open, Gilbo Open, Bremerton Open and Skagit Open. Plays golf. Formerly professional boxer and a title contender in his weight class. Home: 10436 21st Avenue SW, Seattle, Washington 98146.

HOTTINGER, LISA. 1975 and 1977 Virginia Girls State Champion, in 1977 with a 62.5% ringer percentage. Home: 4901 Courthouse Road, Chesterfield, Virginia 23832.

HOWARD, MELVIN, b. March 24, 1930. North Carolina NHPA State Champion 1962, 8-1, 70.0%; 1963, 7-2, 70.5%; 1964, 11-0, 70.2%. W—Faye; children—Randy, Dreama and Scott. Employee of Prudential Insurance. S. Allen; one and a quarter, right handed. Won 1962, 1963, and 1964 AAU North Carolina State Champion; Won a national AAU doubles championship and several state doubles championships. Won the 1962 Southeast Classic averaging over 80% ringers for 15 games and defeated World Champion Harold Reno. Home: 3401 Garrell Street, Archdale, North Carolina 27263.

HOWARD, RAYMOND B. 1966 inductee as charter member of NHPA Hall of Fame. Former vice president of NHPA. Secretary-treasurer of NHPA for 7 years. Published "The Horseshoe World" from 1920 to 1940, the first monthly publication in the history of the sport. Worked in the office of the Ohio Secretary of State at Columbus and renewed the charter of the NHPA, an Ohio corporation.

HOWE, PERCY D., b. September 23, 1919. 1977 member New England Hall of Fame. W—Rita; children—Ronald, James, Linda, Rhea, Marsha, Karen, Shirley, Robert and Richard. Drill press operator and assembler. S. Gordon, Diamond, Ohio "O" and Deadeye; t. one and three quarters, right handed. Past president, Massachusetts HPA. Served for 26 years as secretary of the Twin County Horseshoe League. Home: 76 Brookside Road, Orange, Massachusetts 01364.

HOWE, RICHARD A., b. November 26, 1961. Massachusetts Junior State Champion 1974, 7-0, 83.1%; 1975, 5-0, 84.8%; 1976, 5-0, 78.3%; 1977, 7-0, 71.0%. W—Lesley. Toolmaker. S. Imperial; t. one and a quarter, right handed. Played a world record game of 190 shoes and hit 172 ringers, the most ever hit by a junior in one game. In 32 world tournament games, won 20, lost 12 and hit 79% ringers. Highest world tournament average, 85.7%. New England Junior Champion, 1975, 1976. Other interests—hockey, basketball, and bowling. Home: 159 Park Street, Athol, Massachusetts 01331.

HOYER, JAY, b. August 30, 1920. Won over 100 trophies. W—Lois Latson; children—Terri Morse and Karen Hodge. Farmer. S. Allen; t. one and three quarters, right handed. In 1967, hit highest game of 85% with tournament averages in the sixties. Played against Wilbur Kabel, Clarence Bellman, Mark Seibold, Bill Holland, Harold Anthony, Ken Jensen, Doc Maison, Roy Smith. Played in the World Tournament, county and open tournaments in surrounding states. Home: Box 303 Pleasant Lake, Indiana 46679.

HOYT W.A. First President, California HPA, 1920. Active in organizing the state association. Member of Long Beach Tourist Horseshoe Club since it was formed in 1900.

HUDSON, ALBERT S. 1925 Rhode Island State Champion with a 40.8 ringer percentage. Home: 15 Broad Street, West Warwick, Rhode Island 02893.

HUFFMAN, SAMUEL H., b. July 13, 1933. President Rushville Outdoor Horseshoe Club. Factory Worker. S. Allen; t. reverse three quarters, right handed. In 23 tournaments, won 13 trophies. Highest game, 75%. Highest tournament 50% for 7 games. Has had five tournament games of 70% or better. Home: 116 East 10th Street, Rushville, Indiana 46173.

HUGHES, DAVID, b. July 29, 1961. Ninth Place in the World Tournament, 1979, with 78% ringers and finished tenth in 1980 with 17-14-74.1%. Printer. S. Imperial; reverse one and three quarters, left handed. Best tournament—1979 Minnesota State Tournament with 80.6%. Highest game—94%, 47 out of 50, against Clayton Gage of St. Paul, Boyceville Open. Won Class A tournaments: Boyceville Open, 6-0-77%; Big Fork, 7-0-78%; Rapidan, 4-1-73.6%; Minneapolis Open, 6-1-75%. In 1979 League Play hit three games of 90%. Most improved Player, 1976–1979. Home: 8414 10th Avenue; South Bloomington, Minnesota 55420.

HUGHES, JAMES. 1971 Wyoming boys State Champion with a record of 5-1-10.5%.

HUGHES, JOHN, b. January 29, 1919. Won the 1977 Pinecrest Open at Elwood, Indiana and the 1979 Hamilton, Ohio Open each with a record of 6-1-70%. W—Gertrude; children—Larry, Bob, Patricia, Deborah, Tom, and Karen. Machinist. S. Ohio Pro; t. one and three quarters, right handed. Best game, 86.4%. Best finish in the Ohio State Tournament, Eighth Place in

1978. Twice made the championship division of the Greenville Classic. Home: 3431 Craig Avenue, Cincinnati, Ohio 45211.

HULSHOF, WILLIAM, b. February 20, 1906. First Vice President-Oregon HPA. W—Edyth; children—Carol. Plasterer. S. Allen; t. one and three quarters, right handed. President- Oregon HPA, 13 years. President- Portland HPA. Best game- 75.2%. Best tournament average- 54.6% Editor, Oregon Ringer Review. Member of Oregon HPA Hall of Fame. Home: 670 Southeast 146th Avenue, Portland, Oregon.

HUMMEL, DAVID, b. June 9, 1938. Class C Champion Ohio State Tournament, 1975. W—Sandra; children—Steven David and Philip Wayne. Maintenance Foreman. S. Allen; t. one and a quarter, right handed. Best tournament, 66.4%. Best game, 81.8%. Won the 1976 Bellville Street Fair Championship and the 1976 Licking County League Championship. Vice- President, Licking County Club. Home: 5099 Fallsburg Road Northeast, Newark, Ohio 43055.

HUMMEL, PHILIP W., b. November 19, 1962. 1979 Ohio Boys State Champion. Single. Student. S. Allen; t. one and a quarter, right handed. Won the 1979 Championship over all other Ohio boys with 3-0- 73.2%. Won the 1979 Licking County League Championship with 5-0-76%, the '79 Hebron Open Junior Championship with 2-1-67.4%, and The Licking County Men's Championship with 5-0-66.1%, the first year he competed. 1980 Licking County Men's Title—holder with 64.8%. Licking County Junior Champion, 1973 and 1974. 1976 Hebron Open Junior Champion. Secretary, Licking County Horseshoe Club. Home: 5099 Fallsburg Road Northeast, Newark, Ohio 43055.

HUNSAKER, OSCAR FITZALLEN, b. July 18, 1896, deceased. 1932 Utah State

Champion. W—Susie M; children—Marcus L., Rhea, Karma, June, Oscar J., Robert M., George R., A. Irwin, Betty Jean, Norma Dean, Max Dee, and Grant Kay. Merchant and Farmer. S. Spaulding and Gordon; t. three quarters, right handed. Utah's first recognized champion. Home: 547 South 3 East Salt Lake City, Utah 84111.

HUNT, JAMES B. Governor of North Carolina. Pitched the opening shoe at the 1979 World Tournament at Statesville.

HUOTARI, BERNICE, b. October 3, 1940. Nine times Michigan Upper Peninsula Champion. H—Waino; children—Tammy, Terry (deceased), Tina, Todd, Tracy and Tricia. Ontonagon County Clerk and Register of Deeds. S. Gordon; t. flip, right handed. Michigan Upper Peninsula HPA Secretary for eleven years. Won Michigan Upper Peninsula Women's championship 1970, 1971, 1973-1979. High tournament, 72% in 1978. High game, 78%. Hit nine consecutive four-deads against her daughter Tammy, in which they both hit 68%. Managed a softball team 1976-1978. One of the top ten bowlers in her league. Home: Route 1 Box 66, Mass City, Michigan 49948.

HUOTARI, TAMMY J., b. December 22, 1959. Six times Michigan Upper Peninsula Girls Champion. Single. College Student. S. Allen; one and three quarters, right handed. Won her six championships from 1970 through 1975. Played in three world tournaments, as a junior finishing fourth in 1972, second in 1974 and seventh in 1975 with a three year record of 8-11-36.5%. In a 1977 game against her mother hit nine consecutive four-deads and averaged 68%. 1977-78 season, All Upper Peninsula in basketball and state honorable mention. In 1979 slow pitch softball tournament game pitched a no-hitter. Home: Route 1 Box 66, Mass City, Michigan 49948.

HOUTARI, TERRY ANNE, b. February

11, 1961; deceased, May 26, 1979. Fourth Place in the 1974 Girls' Division of the World tournament 1975 runner-up in Class B World Tournament. Home: Route 1 Box 66, Mass City, Michigan 49948.

HUOTARI, TINA, b. February 2, 1962. 1976 and 1977 Michigan Upper Peninsula Girls' Champion. S. Gordon; t. flip, right handed. Third in Class B 1975 World Tournament. Home: Route 1 Box 66, Mass City, Michigan 49948.

HUOTARI, TODD, b. April 1, 1964. 1978 Michigan Upper Peninsula Boys' Champion. Student. S. Allen; t. one and a quarter, right handed. Participated in the 1974 and 1975 World Tournaments. American Legion baseball player. Home: Route 1 Box 66, Mass City, Michigan 49948.

HUOTARI, WAINO, b. November 2, 1930. First Champion, Michigan Upper Peninsula, 1970. W—Bernice; children—Tammy, Terry (deceased), Tina, Todd, Tracy and Tricia. Totally disabled. S. Allen; t. three quarters and one and a quarter, right handed. 1970-1971 Champion Michigan Upper Peninsula, averaged 62% both years in the playoffs. Home: Route 1 Box 66, Mass City, Michigan 49948.

HURST, ALFRED L. Past President, Rhode Island HPA. Child—Ken Hurst.

HURST, KENNETH, b. 1922. Rhode Island State Champion, 1936-1940, averaging over 70% in those years. t. one and a quarter, right handed. In five State championships, hit 6-1-69.1% in 1936; 71.3% in 1937, scoring 472 points in four games with the 50 shoe count-all scoring system; 73.5% in 1938; 9-0-72.6% in 1939; and a record-breaking 75.8% in 1940. Competed in National AAU tournament.

HYLAND, WILBERT B., b. February 16, 1911. Member New York State Hall of Fame. W—Frances; children—Nan Louise

Barrett, Carol Ann Clark, Bruce Loy Hyland, and Stephen Arthur Hyland. Retired from Ingersoll-Rand Company, S. Allen; t. one and a quarter, right handed. Past President, Steuben County Magistrates Association. Town Justice for Hornby, New York. Member, Hall of Fame Committee, State of New York, President, 1959-1960, New York HPA. President, Corning Horseshoe Club. Tournament Director, Elmira Doubles. High tournament average, 57%. High game, 85%, 17 of 20. In track, won the National High and Prep School Cross County Championship, 1931, and with a time of 4:32 won the New York State Mile Championship. Organized the "Coral Islanders", a group that specialized in Hawaiian music on local radio stations. Contestant on Ted Mack radio and television shows as an imitator. Home: Route 3, Box 167, Corning, New York 14830.

HYMER, RANDY, b. April 7, 1962. Top contender in junior division play, 1976, 1977, 1978, Class A, World Tournament. Student. S. Allen; t. one and a quarter, right handed. First world Tournament game 1976, hit 84% to defeat Massachusetts Champion, Rick Howe. Averaged between, 75% and 80% ringers, as a junior, with a 79% tournament in the Fort Hamilton days and 80% tournament in Hamilton County. Highest game, 94%, Southwest Ohio District tournament. In 1977 World Tournament, lost 50-49 to Jeff Williams in a 122 shoe game; Williams hit 87.7%; Hymer hit 86.6%, with ten consecutive four-deads pitched at 49-49. At present in the men's division, hits from 60% to 70% ringers. Home: 340 Heaton Street, Hamilton, Ohio 45011.

I

INGE, BETTY, b. October 18, 1943. Secretary, Virginia HPA 1975-1978. H—Tommy; children—Mark and Robin. Employee, Virginia State Department of Conservation and Economics. S. Gordon; t. flip, right handed. Runner-up for Virginia State Title. Pitched in the 1977 World Tournament at Greenville, Ohio. Home: Route 1, Box 206A, Ashland, Virginia 23005.

ISAAC, JACOB D., b. October 26, 1911. Vice- President, Nebraska State HPA. Single. Bridge Welder. S. Allen; t. one and a quarter, right handed. Namesake of Isaac Horseshoe Courts, Fairbury Park. High tournament average, 66%; high game, 70.1%. Home: 1208 Third Street, Fairbury, Nebraska 68352.

ISAIS, FERNANDO, b. December 20, 1914. Eight times World Champion, 1941, 1947-1952, 1958; eight times California State Champion, 1931, 1932, 1933, 1937, 1940, 1941, 1952, 1953. W—Hope; child—Linda. S. Gordon; t. one and three quarters, right handed. 1966 Charter Member, National Hall of Fame. National Champion of Mexico. Pitched a perfect game, 1952 California State Tournament. Hit 41 of 42 against Ron Cherrier in World Tournament play. One of Mexico's best tennis players. Home: 41927 Park Avenue, Hemet, California 92343.

J

JACKSON, CARROLL. Son of World Champion, Frank Jackson of Kellerton, Iowa. Won 142 games, lost 118, averaged 53.9% and qualified at an average of 462 in world tournament play. Finished in 16th place in 1922.

JACKSON, DONALD. 1950 Massachusetts State Champion with 5-2-68.6%.

JACKSON, FRANK B. b. 1870, d. 1955. First Recognized World Champion, 1909. 1966 Charter Member, National Hall of Fame. W—Alma; children—Herbert, Hansford, Carroll, Vyrl, Vera, Mrs. Clarence Townsley, and Mrs. Newman. Farmer. T.

two and three quarters, later in 1926 one and three quarters, right handed. World Champion- 1909, -1914 (recognized champion), 1915 (24-1-97 ringers), 1920 (36-0-850 ringers), 1921 (512 ringers), 1925 (31-0-59.5%), 1926 (24-6-61.4%), 1927 (33-1-63.1%). Other world tournament play; 1922, 2nd place, (13-2-389 ringers); 1923, 4th place (26-3-48.5%); 1923, 4th place, (11-4-54.2%); 1923, 4th place, (28-4-54.9%); 1924, 2nd place (21-2-61.7%); 1925, 3rd place, (42-13-60.5%); 1926, 4th place, (29-3-62.4%); 1927, 3rd place, (22-3-61.3%); 1927, 4th place, (25-8-64.4%); 1927, 2nd place, (26-7-61.1%); 1928, 5th place, (23-6-59.7%); 1928 5th place, (17-16-61.1%); 1934, 4th place, (20-3-72.3%); 1935, 5th place, (17-6-72.9%. 517 wins, 89 losses in world tournament play- 4th on all time victory list. Averaged 60% ringers. Iowa State champion, 1921, 1927, 1928, 1930, 1932, 1933. Charter member Iowa Sports Hall of Fame. Annual tournament held on the Frank E. Jackson Courts in Kellerton. Home: Kellertown, Iowa.

JACKSON, GRACE., H—Carroll Jackson. 1934 World Tournament, Third Place, 5-2-67.7% 1933 World Tournament, Fifth Place, 1-4-38.1%. Home: LaGrange, Illinois.

JACKSON, HANSFORD. 1931 Iowa State Champion. Son of Champion Frank Jackson. In world tournament play, won 132, lost 131, averaged 56.2% and qualified with 454. Best game, 47 out of 50. Home: Kellerton, Iowa.

JACKSON, LELAND REX, b. January 13, 1930. First president, Frank Jackson Memorial Horseshoe Courts Association. Worked with Iowa Hawkeye Horseshoe Pitcher's Association to initiate the Frank E. Jackson Open. W—Betty Elaine; children—Sherry, Barry, and Roland. Builder. Home: Route 1, Kellerton, Iowa 50133.

JACKSON, STEVE. Washington Boys'

State Champion, 1964, 38.7%, and 1965, 39.2%.

JACKSON, VYRL, b. 1907. Pitched in exhibitions with his father, Frank Jackson. W. Machinist. S. Gordon. 161 ringers in one game. Home 11903 McGirk Avenue, El Monte, California 91700.

JACOBS, WILLIAM SHIRLEY "JAKE", b. Marsh 23, 1929. President Kentucky State HPA 1972-1974. Single. Printing Analyst, Department of Finance. S. Allen; t. flip, right handed. Secretary Millville Horseshoe Club. Vice-President, Kentucky HPA 1978 and 1979. Best tournament average, 46%, 1973 Millville 50 Shoe count-all. Highest game, 59.4%, Scott County Open. Received Kentucky Golden Horseshoe Award for outstanding service. Home: Route 3, Frankfort, Kentucky 40601.

JACOBS, JOSEPH V., b. July 19, 1932. Secretary, Rosedale Horseshoe League, 1969- 1971. W—Mary; child—Joseph. Garment worker. S. Rogers; t. one and a quarter, right handed. Board of Directors Eastern Pennsylvania HPA. Member of the Rosedale team champions 1969 and 1971.

JACOBS, LEE, b. February 24, 1906. Michigan State Champion 1934, 1944, 1955. Member Michigan Hall of Fame. W—Helen; children—Lee, Jr., Robert, and Dianne. Auto worker. S. Diamond Super Ringer; t. one and three quarters, right handed. Played in World Tournament, 1927, 1928, 1933, 1935, 1940, 1947, 1950, 1963-1980, with the exception of 1968 and 1976. Best finish in world tournament play was 1940, seventeenth, 14-17-74%. In 1944, won National AAU championships. Member, Michigan AAU All-Sports Hall of Fame. Defeated World Champion Putt Mossman, 1927 World Tournament. Highest tournament, 74%, 1946, with two 87% games. Hit a 93.3% game in a Detroit City tournament. Hit 32 consecutive ringers against Bob Hitt.

Sings the national anthem to open the World Tournament each year. Held every office in the Michigan HPA. Secretary-Treasurer, NHPA. As National Secretary, ran the 1940 World Tournament. Put together the *Horseshoe Compendium*, published by the NHPA. Owns the Lattore Horseshoe Company. Home: 11105 Quirk Road, Belleville, Michigan 48111.

JACQUES, BEVERLY. New Hampshire Women's Champion, 1970, 5-1-59.2%; 1971, 6-0-54.3%. New England Champion.

JALLEN, HELMAR, b. 1905 d. 1977. 1976 Member North Dakota Hall of Fame. W—Mary; child—Gale. Operator of watch repair shop. S. Allen; t. one and three quarters, right handed. Captain, Sons of Norway Team; won Red River Valley League championship. Worked at Fargo in hosting the 1967 World Tournament. 1976 Charter Member, Minnesota HPA Hall of Fame. Home: 723 North River Road, Fargo, North Dakota 58102.

JAMES T. ESTHER. 1935 Women's World Champion with 5-0-63.6%. 3rd place, World Tournament, 1933 with 3-2-58.3%. World records set 266 points, 86 ringers in 100 shoes; 14 consecutive doubles inqualifying.

JAMES, MARVIN. 1960 Iowa Boys State Champion, 3-0.

JAMES, WILLARD, b. March 31, 1915. 1980 Iowa HPA Hall of Fame. W—Veida; children—Willard, Jr., Marvin, and Gary. Railroad conductor and farmer. S. Allen and Gordon; t. reverse one and three quarters, right handed. 1956 Iowa State Champion. 1956 Four States Open Champion. Highest game, 92.6% in Omaha. 1979-1980 Captain, Lost Dutchman Horseshoe Team at Apache Junction, Arizona. Expert in eight ball pool. Missed the championship division of the 1957 World Tournament by a single point.

Home: Route 1 Box 39A, Underwood, Iowa 51576.

JARNIGAN, CHARLES. 1968 Tennessee State Champion, 5-0-73.8%. Dealer in fresh produce.

JARRELL, TEMPLE R. State Champion, Maryland, 1935 and 1936; Tennessee and Florida, prior to 1938. Director of Parks and Recreation. Prepared Management Aids Bulletin No. 71., Horseshoe Pitching, 1967, for the National Recreation and Parks Association. Averaged over 70% ringers. S. Ohio. Champion fast-pitch softball player. Home: 4101 Gallatin Street, Hyattsville, Maryland 20781.

JARRETT, E.Z. 1922 North Carolina State Champion.

JEFFERS, JOHN, b. October 6, 1963. 1978 West Virginia Boys Champion, 6-1-43.5%. Student. S. Allen; t. one and a quarter, right handed. Member Moundsville Club. Bowls. Plays golf. Home: 2415 Kanawha Street, Moundville, West Virginia 26041.

JENKERSON, RON. 4th, 1979 Canadian National Tournament, 4-4-65.3%.

JENKINS, LEON. 1931 Oregon State Champion.

JENKINS, STEVE. 1966 Illinois Boys State Champion, 7-0-45.8%.

JENSCHKE, TERRI, b. June 10, 1965. 1980 Texas Girls State Champion. Student. S. Diamond Super Ringer; t. single flip, right handed. 1980 Junior State Player of the Year. Vice-President, Lakeside Juniors Horseshoe Club. Plays golf and softball. Home: 5867 Oak Run, San Antonio, Texas 78247.

JENSEN, HERMAN. Past Montana State Secretary. Home: Box 187, Culbertson, Montana 59218.

JENSON, IRA O., b. December 20, 1922. Montana State Champion, 1965 and 1969.

National AAU Champion in 1962. W— Christine, Farmer. S. Allen or Ohio; t. one and a quarter, right handed. Highest tournament, 63.2%. Highest game, 80%. President, Eastern Montana Chapter NHPA. President and Secretary, Culbertson Horseshoe Club. Home: Route 1 Box 40, Culbertson, Montana 59218.

JENSEN, KEN. Michigan State Champion, 1958, 1959 (his best- 8-0-70.8%), 1961, 1966 and 1976. S. Imperial; t. one and three quarters, right handed. 15th Place, 1962 World Tournament, Greenville, Ohio, 21-14-75%. Home: 410 Church Street, St. Joseph, Michigan 49085.

JOHNS, LAURENCE. Provincial Director, Alberta HPA. Brought pitchers of Northern Alberta and British Columbia together into one organization, the Peace Country Horseshoe Club.

JOHNS, MARGARET. 1979 Peace Country Women's Champion. 1977 Secretary Treasurer, Peace Country Horseshoe Club. H—Laurence.

JOHNS, WILLIAM F., b. July 22, 1919. Sunday Handicap Individual League Champion, 1979, 1980. Funeral Director. S. Ohio; t. one and a quarter, right handed. Captain, winning team, New Rome leagues. Best Dressed Pitcher, Columbus Leagues. Highest tournament, 55%; best game, 112, count-all play. Home: 1050 East 19th Avenue, Columbus, Ohio 43211.

JOHNSON, EARLE W., b. July 15, 1903. 1978 Florida State Hall of Fame. W—Eunice Mae; children—Glenn and Shirley Bailey. Dairyman. S. Lattore; one and a quarter. Secretary-Treasurer, Bradenton Horseshoe Club. Highest tournament, 37%; highest game, 60%. Home: 3031 Twelfth Avenue East, Bradenton, Florida 33508.

JOHNSON, ELWOOD, b. March 12, 1923. 1980 Class A Champion, Pima County Tournament. W- Murtis; children- Ricky, Kathy, and Dean. Farmer. S. Allen; t. reverse three quarters, right handed. High game, 80% with eight consecutive doubles; high tournament, 62.3%. President, Elmore Horseshoe Club. Home: Route 1, Elmore, Minnesota 56027.

JOHNSON, GEORGE. 1959 Indiana Senior State Champion. Home: 1218 East Perry, Indianapolis, Indiana 46200.

JOHNSON, JAMES, b. April 19, 1929. First Vice-President, Alabama HPA. W— Elnora; children- Lisa, Karen and James. Carpenter. S. Deadeye; t. one and a quarter, right handed. Current Ringer percentage- 45%. Coaches and plays softball and basketball. Home: 3109 Hillsboro Road, Huntsville, Alabama 35805.

JOHNSON, JAMES H. "Pop", b. July 8, 1909. 1945 National Amateur champion. Kentucky State Champion, 1947-1950. 1974 Intermediate World Champion. W— Genevieve, deceased; child- Betty Jean Dauwe. Postal worker, retired. S. Ohio Pro; t. one and three quarters, right handed. World tournament career record., 149 wins, 190 losses., 70.4% ringers; qualifying average, 504 points. Two appearances, Intermediate Division, 9-5-67.7%. 1950 World Tournament, in consecutive games, defeated Fernando Isais and Ted Allen. 1948 World Tournament, defeated Ted Allen, 50-42, 84.9%; 107 ringers out of 126 shoes. 1949 Kentucky State Tournament, hit 82.5%, a personal and State record. 1957 Midwest Ringer Roundup, hit a 94.4% game, 34 ringers out of 36 shoes. 1945 National Amateur Championship, 19-1-58.5%. Home: 8370 Pippin Road, Cincinnati, Ohio 45239.

JOHNSON, NORMA K., b. January 25, 1934. Kentucky Women's State Champion, 1969 and 1978. Children- Kathy, Paul, Ronnie, and Lewis. Administrator- Management and Personnel. S. Gordon; t. single flip,

Top, left, Archie Gregson, Hall of Fame member, second from left, poses with Miss Utah 1959. Others are Robert Pence, Reiny Backer, and Ottie Reno. Just below is Ellis Griggs, flanked by Ellis Cobb and Ralph Dykes. *Top, right,* Ruth Hangen, World Champion and Hall of Fame member. *Bottom row, above, left,* Elmer Harrison (front) with group, several Class A contenders. *Right, above,* Arlo Harris, President of both NHPA and AHPA. At right are Will Gullickson, Katie Gregson, World Champion, and George Hambidge of South Africa.

Top, Statesville, North Carolina, 1978 Dogwood Festival. Left to right, Helen Roberts, Ruth Kirk, Ruth Hangen, Janet Reno, Katherine Harrison, Jean Myers, Opal Reno (who was the winner). *Center row, left,* Clayton C. Henson, with sons Richard and Kenneth. *Right,* Glen Henton, Hall of Fall member. *Bottom,* Bernard Herfurth.

1977. W. Shirley; children—Sheila, Donald Jr., Raymond, Joel. Traffic Maintenance, Police Department. S. Ohio O; t. three quarters, right handed. Won city championship ten times, Western Massachusetts championship seven times, New England States Champion, once, state grange champion four times; won Class C World Championship, 66%, 1965; averaged 66.8%, Class B, World Tournament, 1968; won state championship with 71.4% for seven games; high game, 100%; high tournament, 78%, 1966 state tournament, finishing second to Ed Landry. Home: 60 Highview Street, Fitchburg, Massachusetts 01420.

KAHLE, GERALD R., b. June 30, 1929. Past President, Oklahoma State HPA. W. Vivian; children—Leslie, Lisa, Gretchen, Research chemist and manager. S. Allen; t. one and a quarter, right handed. Served as Regional Director for the Southwest, president of local club, and vice-president and secretary, Oklahoma State HPA; holds PhD, Ohio State University; high tournament, 59%; high game, 77%. Enjoys woodcarving, fishing. Home: 2017 Skyline Drive, Bartlesville, Oklahoma 74003.

KALLBERG, EDNA, Played one World Tournament, 16-4. Home: Minneapolis, Minnesota.

KAMMAN, ARTHUR, b. May 6, 1909. Arizona Champion eighteen times. Child—Sharon Terfehn. Retired farmer. S. Ohio O; t. one and three quarters or one and a quarter, right handed. State title record (since 1957), 81%; hit 82.5% game against Ronnie Simmons, 1970 World Tournament; hit 36 consecutive ringers against Clarence Cummins, Midwest Ringer Roundup, 1967; served as president, Arizona State HPA, eight years; played NHPA tournaments for the last 54 years; won tournament titles including Mesa City Open (eight times), Tempe Open, seven times, Phoenix Open,

six times, Valley of the Sun, five times, 1974 Elmer Beller Open, 1967 South Gate Ringer Roundup, 1968 Alemeda County Fair, 1968 Iowa Open, 1967 Union County, Iowa, Open. Home: 523 South Hobson Street, Mesa, Arizona 85204.

KAMPS, JERRY, b. December 29, 1930. Instrumental in establishing horseshoe pitching in Combined Locks, Wisconsin. W. Rosemary; children—Debbie, Amy, Steve, Jay. Tavern owner. S. Allen; t. flip, right handed. Installed horseshoe court, 1960, which grew into the only covered horseshoe facility in the state; Combined Locks Horseshoe Club organized in 1967; first NHPA sanctioned state tournament held at Kamps Kovered Kourts, 1967, other state tournaments hosted there in 1969, 1973, 1976, 19769; women pitched in Wisconsin state tournaments for first time, Combined Locks, 1969; won many trophies in tournament and league play, averaging 35%. Home: 101 Kamp Court, Combined Locks, Wisconsin 54113.

KANGAS, DON, b. June 25, 1955. Michigan Upper Peninsula Champion, 1978. Single. Warehouseman. Empire Mine. S. Gordon; t. reverse one and a quarter, left handed. Won Junior Boys Championship, 3-0-34%, 1970, and 6-0-49%, 1971; pitched against four state champions, Sault Ste Marie tournament, in final round he was seeded number one after hitting 128 points, 84% in 50 shoes, finishing third, 1980. Enjoys tennis, won conference championship, 1972, 1973. Home: P.O. Box 830, Gwinn, Michigan 49841.

KAPKE, JERRY, 1974 Nebraksa Boys State Champion.

KAPP, JOHAN W., b. December 3, 1949. First South African Player to Compete in Round Robin Play, World Tournament. W. Tiette; child—Morne. Farmer. S. American Professional; t. one and a quarter, right handed. Hit qualifying round of 53 ringers,

193 points, in 200 shoes, World Tournament, Keene, New Hampshire, 1974, played in Group R3, 30-shoe game, 2-3-23.3%; won 15-12 over Floyd Hix, 16-15 over Ed Sell, lost 16-26 to Fred White, lost 7-36 to Phil Zozzaro, lost 14-26 to Chuck Roball. Enjoys jukskei; is top player in South Africa. Home: Leeufontein, P.O. Platrand, 2435, South Africa.

KARASCH, SANDRA, b. May 15, 1952. Won Preimesberger Halloween Open, 7-0-62.8%, 1980. H. Richard. children—Trent, Jay, Tracy. Housewife. S. Gordon; t. flip, right handed. High tournament, 67.15%; high game, 82%; won 1980 Class A Championship, Preimesberger Arena October tournament. Home: Route 1, St. Joseph, Minnesota 56374.

KARR, CLARK, b. April 14, 1912. 1978 Illinois Senior State Champion. W. Lillie; children—Ed, Ellen Campbell. Farmer. S. Allen; t. one and three quarters, right handed. Member, NHPA, and Champaign-Urbana Horseshoe Club; won Class C, Intermediates, World Tournament, 5-1-51.3%; 1976; won Will Bruens Open Class B, Hoopeston, 6-1-61.5%, (high tournament), 1972; high game, state championship, 77.4% against Ross Sornberger, 1978. Home: 335 South Cherry, Paxton, Illinois 60957.

KAUFFMAN, PRESCOTT, d. Oregon State Champion, 1944.

KEENE, ELOISE, b. September 27, 1936. West Virginia State Champion, 1976, 1978, 1980. H. Jim; children—Danny, Melissa. Dietary Department, Greenbriar Valley Hospital. S. Gordon; t. flip, right handed. 1980 record for state title, 6-1-35.3%. Home: 506 Spruce Street, Ronceverte, West Virginia 24970.

KELLEY, CHRISTINE, b. January 15, 1925. d. July 14, 1977. Kentucky State Champion, 1970, 1971, 1972, 1973, 1974. H. Nathan; child—Karlyn. Musician/songwriter. S. Ohio t. three-quarter, right handed. Won Class A titles in Bluegrass Fair, 1973, Hillville Sportsmen Tournament, 1973, Class A Maggie & Jiggs state championship, with Simon Kelley, 1973; high tournament, 78%; high game, 84%; honored by Governor Louis B. Nunn as outstanding Kentucky citizen, presented gold horseshoe by Kentucky chapter, NHPA; helped establish Lexington Bluegrass Army Depot Horseshoe Club, served as secretary, three years; member, "The Kelley Family," a band which played mountain music, bluegrass, gospel, did radio and television performances, cut record album, "The Early Days of Bluegrass Music."

KELLY, CHAR, b. August 10, 1947. Won Duluth City Championship, 1979. H. Thomas; children—Tami, Jodi. Housewife/waitress. S. Diamond Tournament; t. flip, right handed. Won Cloquet Tournament, and Pine City (twice); for three years has won high ringer percentage award, Duluth Women's League, serves as secretary; in Hjalmer's tournament, pitched a shoe for a ringer that would have completed a four-dead, circled the stake near the top, spun around and nestled on top of stake with caulks hanging down. Enjoys biking, cross country skiing, fishing. Climbed to third place in state where many women pitch, and where state champion is 1979 World Champion, stands 31st in top 40 in country. Home: 55 Daniels Road, Duluth, Minnesota 55811.

KELLY, JOE, Class A player in state tournaments. W. S. Diamond; t. one and three quarters, right handed. Won 1959 Eastern National Class B title and many Class A events in Michigan, Florida and other states; played World Tournament, senior division, 4-7-57.1%; averaged 60%; traveled with Lester Peary, Carl Lundgren, Irwin Carlberg to pitching events. Home: Highland Park, Michigan.

KELSVEN, L. O. "LUCKY KEL," 1925 North Dakota State Champion. Charter member, North Dakota HPA Hall of Fame; one of top promoters of early twenties. Home: Minot.

KELTS, SOPHIE, 1979 Alberta Women's Provincial Champion. Home: Red Deer, Alberta, Canada.

KEMPFE, WILLIAM, 1959 Missouri State Champion, 11-0-73.1%.

KEMPLE, JAMES, b. July 24, 1916. Past President, Rusville Club. W. Gladys; children—Phillip, Warren. Farmer. S. Allen; t. one and a quarter, right handed. Played 38 years, NHPA; hit 74% to win Marvin Christman Open; finished second, Rushville Indoor, 1980, with 76.4%; tournament high at Winchester, 77%; high game, 92%, set record at Franklin, Indiana; member, Fortville, Indiana team, won championships three years in a row in 1950s; played many times in Class A Indiana State Tournaments and World Tournaments. Home: Route 6, Box 48, Rushville, Indiana 46173.

KERR, HARRY "DOC," Editor, Akron Press, 1920; credited with originating term "Barnyard Golf."

KERSHNER, IRVIN, b. March 15, 1911. Vice-President, Western Montana HPA. W. Darlene; children—April, Kent. Rancher. S. Deadeye; t. one and a quarter, right handed. Won four Class A titles including State Fair, Billings, and has competed in state tournaments for last six years; attended World Tournament, 1974, 1978; high tournament, 55%; high game, 72%; president, Gallatin Ringer Club. Home: 3282 Blackwood Road, Bozeman, Montana 59715.

KETTLESON, EARL, b. September 27, 1944. 1960 Washington Boys State Champion. W. Gina; children—Gina, Eydie, Ellisa. Food broker. S. Allen; t. one and a quarter, right handed. Championship record, 1960, 25.9%. Home: 13623 East Eighth, Spokane, Washington 99216.

KIBEE, MIKE, 1976-77 New Hampshire Boys State Champion, averaged 64.9% (1977).

KIENIA, DOUG, Maine Boys State Champion, 1970-73, 1974 Boys World Champion, 7-0-81.2%. Home: Portland Street, North Berwick, Maine 03906.

KILGORE, LLOYD R., b. April 9, 1938. Historian, Oregon HPA. W. Judith; children—Kevin, Connie, Linda. Bookkeeper/freelance writer. S. Gordon; t. flip, right handed. Serves as media director, Emerald HPA; treasurer, EHPA, 1979; won two firsts, four seconds in nine sanctioned tournaments in lower classes; high tournament, 32.2%; high game 46.7%; originated Connolly Harvest Classic, Eugene, 1978, Mother's Day City, Springfield Championship, 1980; currently developing a point system for OHPA tournaments to result in state team championship race. Home: 83230 Rattlesnake Creek Road, Dexter, Oregon 97431.

KILINSKY, FRANK, b. October 4, 1907. Won County and Club Championships. W. Mae; children—Frank, Mary Ann. Railroader. S. Ohio; t. one and three quarters, right handed. Pitched for 20 years; high tournament, 70%; twice threw qualifying rounds of 87 ringers out of 100 shoes for 87%, and hit 38 consecutive ringers. Enjoys bowling. Home: 10 Township Road, Pittsburg, Pennsylvania.

KILINSKY, MAE, b. July 11, 1915. Pennsylvania Women's State Champion, 1970, 1971, 1972; Member, Pennsylvania HPA Hall of Fame. H. Frank; children—Joan, Alberta, Charlotte, Joyce, Ronnie. Housewife.

S. American; t. flip, right handed. Has pitched in tournament for 10 years, during that time won club championship once, the county championship twice. Enjoys swimming and bowling, Home: 10 Township Road, Pittsburg, PA 15229.

KILLGORE, CHARLES, b. August 5, 1930. World Class B Champion, 1978, 70.7%; Missouri State Champion, 1975. W. Marieta; child—Scott. Farmer and Operator-Manager for Retail and Wholesale Fertilizer and Chemical Company. S. Allen; t. one and three quarters, right handed. Attended Martin Grammar School and William Jewell College in Liberty, Missouri; has been playing since high school and has played in tournaments for 22 seasons; President of Missouri State Horseshoe Pitchers Association; has served as Vice-President of MHPA and NHPA Regional Director for Missouri and Kansas; has played in championship division of world tournament 5 times; averaged 77% through the entire world tournament in 1977. While serving in United States Army in Korea was one of General Gavin's honor guard. Is a member and elder in the First Christian Church. Enjoys basketball and golf. Home: Route 2, Plattsburg, MO 64477.

KIMBALL, GILBERT, b. July 20, 1911. Michigan State Treasurer for 7 two year terms; Member, Michigan HPA Hall of Fame, 1974. W. Iva Mae; child—Virginia Barrix. Oldsmobile Division of General Motors, 43 years of service. S. Detroit Flyer and Ohio O; t. three quarters, right handed. Has played for about 20 years in organized horseshoes; is Treasurer of his local club; won class championship in Michigan tournament in 1970 and several other trophies; contribution to horseshoe pitching has been mostly in office; worked five world tournaments as well as host to Michigan tournaments; received NHPA Special Achievement Award in 1975. Has pitched softball for about 20 years and has worked in the tournament office of the Michigan State Bowling Association for past 20 years. Has scored in 6 bowling propietors all-star tournaments for top bowlers on the pro tour. Is Secretary-Treasurer of 3 bowling leagues, one for 18 years. Home: 141 East Washington, P.O. Box 231 Diamondale, MI 48821.

KING, WALTER, b. Indiana. (dec.) North Carolina State Champion. 1959 and 1971. Average in 1959 11-0-66.4% and in 1971 8-1. Started playing as a child; in 1970 he tied with Gurney York for championship at 7-2 and was runnerup, in their play-off game York won 50-42 hitting 58 of 80 for 72.5% and King getting 56 of 80 for 70% ringers; won the National AAU championship in 1963 and then teamed with Glynden Moore to win the doubles title; in singles competition averaged 68.3% and hit a high game of 85.3%.

KINGMA, ERIC PAUL, b. March 18, 1965. Indiana Boys State Champion 1980, with 5-0-71.4%. S. Allen; t. one and a quarter, right handed. Started playing tournament horseshoes at 10. The Kingmas are a horseshoe pitching family. Grandfather, George Kingma founded the Lafayette Horseshoe Club. All 6 sons, including Eric's father Fred pitched horseshoes as does his brother, Fred, Jr. Has won about 30 trophies, most are Class A championships; won the Paul Cunningham Memorial Northwest Open, Lafayetts GLA, Huntington Open, Hoosier Hills and Reynolds Open and was second in Indiana State Tournament in 1978; in Lafayette GLA averaged 70.9% ringers including games of 84.4% and 81.2%; in Huntington Open he averaged 71.1%; in 1979 won the Indoor State Championship and the Marvin Chrismam Open with 70.2% mark and high game of 83.3%, then added the Ora Pearman Memorial, Ben Shores Memorial, Pioneer Days, Midwest Ringer Roundup, Rose Festival, Wabash

Valley Open and Greenville Ringer Class where he posted his highest tournament average of 75.4%, in World Tournament at Statesville, North Carolina in 1979 he won 6 and lost 5 in the Championship Division averaging 64%. Enjoys playing piano, drums, basketball, baseball, bowling, pingpong and swimming. Home: 2205 Sauk, Lafayetts, IN 47905.

KINSER, VERNON, b. July 7, 1909. Designed and Manufactures the Detroit Flyer shoe. Single. Machinist. S. Allen; t. one and three quarters, left handed and right handed. Has played for 30 years, pitching from 40% to 60% at diffrent times, winning several dozen trophies, most of them in Class C tournaments. Studied engineering at Wayne University. Home: Route 1 Box 157A, Jenkins, MO 65677.

KIRK, RUTH, b. November 26, 1917. Open Tournament Champion. H. Aaron; children—Wayne (dec.), Juanita, Shirley, Maxine; 8 grandchildren. Retail clerk. S. Gordon; t. single flip, right handed. Current ringer percentage 63%. Started paying at the age of 54 in 1972; first play was NHPA sanctioned Ostrander tournament where she lost, to return 7 years later to win the Class A Championship; finished second in Ohio Buckeye Association tournament in 1975; won 9 Class A championships in open tournaments: Ronceverte, West Virginia Mountaineer in 1977; Statesville, North Carolina Autumn Open 3 times, 1974, 1976, 1978; Ostrander, Ohio, 1970; Xenia Ohio Memorial Day Open, 1979; Daybel Winter Classic, 1974, 60% and New Rome Club Tournament, 1980 with 60.8%; in New Rome league play posted high single game in count-all play hitting 86%, 43 ringers out of 50 shoes and 136 points; highest sanctioned tournament average is 63.3% in Xenia Memorial Day Open in 1979; has participated in 4 world tournaments, 1975, 1977, 1978, 1979; League titles are New

Rome, 1975, 1979; Ladd Ridge, 1978, and Pike Indoor, 1978. Home: 4616 Camp Creek Road, Lucasville, OH 45648.

KISSICK, MYRNA, Canadian National Women's Champion 1976, with record of 6-0-46.3%; defending her crown in 1977 she improved her performance to 4-1-56% but lost in a playoff to Mary Archer.

KLEINHAUS, PATRICIA THOMAS, b. April 7, 1953. New York Junior Champion, 1970, only girl ever to win. H. Kevin; child—Jonathan. Hairdresser and Housewife. S. Gordon; t. flip, right handed. Patricia Thomas Kleinhaus is the daughter of Paul Thomas, New York Hall of Fame member, and Lorraine Thomas, a two-time Women's World Champion. Home: Route 7, Box 36, Statesville, NC 28677.

KLEMENT, ARTHUR J., b. June 1888; (dec. July 2, 1962), Served as President of Wisconsin Horseshoe Pitchers Association from 1926 until his death. W. Ruth; children—Robert, Jon. Salesman; in retirement he was part time City Recreation Department employee. S. Ohio; t. three quarters, right handed. Played for 40 years; contracted to hold the state tournament during the Wisconsin State Fair in 1926, and this was done for 40 years; spent much of his time promoting horseshoe pitching, helping other clubs and running tournaments; for several years ran a tournament at Jefferson County Fair, promoted the first TV show for horseshoes in Wisconsin, and boosted team play; helped organize the Wisconsin HPA in 1925; after serving as President of Wisconsin HPA for 36 years, his son Robert was chosen to succeed him and his son Jon was named Vice-President, the office was in Klement family for 49 consecutive years; Klement helped draft the rules and regulations for the National Association in 1924 in Miami, Florida; started and operated the Fort Atkinson Horseshoe Club; for last few years of his life was a part-time employee of City of Fort Atkinson in charge of horseshoe pitching and shuffleboard activities in Jones Park. Was a good baseball player and played several years. Home: Fort Atkinson, WI.

KLEMENT, JON, Wisconsin HPA Vice-President. Klement's father, Art and brother, Bob both served as President of Wisconsin HPA for a combined total of 49 years. Home: Black Hawk Island Road, Fort Atkinson, WI 53538.

KLEMENT, ROBERT H., b. December 29, 1914. Served as President of Wisconsin Horseshoe Pitchers Association for five years, following 8 years as Secretary-Treasurer. Single. Retired. S. Ohio; t. one and three quarters, right handed. Has played for 30 years, 4 years in tournament play. His father Art was State President for 36 years, his brother Jon, was Vice-President for 5 years and a niece, Bonnie was Secretary-Treasurer for 5 years. Home: 1745 Jefferson Street, No. 1, Hollywood, FL 33020.

KLINE, GARY T., b. February 22, 1948. NHPA Historian, Stokes Award Winner, 1980. W. Lorraine. Factory worker—G.M. Union alternate health and safety representative. S. Allen; t. one and a quarter, left handed. Has played for 27 years, the last 10 in NHPA tournaments; won the Montgomery County Junior Championship from 40 feet in 1964 with 8-0-65%; became Miami County champion with 5-0-55.8% in 1974 and repeated with 6-1-68% in 1977; won the Anna, Ohio Invitational with 5-0-66% in 1979; highest tournament average is 68% and highest single game 80.6%; was the recipient of the Stokes Memorial Award at the 1980 world tournament in Huntsville, Alabama, signifying that during the preceeding year he had done more to promote the sport than any other single person in the sport. Is also a statistician for world tournaments; is the statistician and schedule maker for East Dayton

Horseshoe Club, Publicity Director for V.F.W. 5434, tournament director of Ohio Champion of Champions. Ohio historian and statistician, Chairman of Ohio Hall of Fame Committee and member of NHPA Publicity and Promotion Committees; he is the youngest person ever named state or national historian or chairman of a Hall of Fame Committee, first to tabulate the history of the NHPA World Tournament, and first to index the state and world tournament career of individuals and to compile an all-time state and world tournament victory list. Home: 108 Calmont Farms Circle, Union, OH 45322.

KLOEPPER, GERRY L., b. August 21, 1934. President, Southern California Horseshoe Pitchers Association, was Vice-President prior to becoming President. W. Nancy; children—Kim, Donn, Brad, Brian. Carrier Maintenance Man for General Telephone Company of Southern California. S. Allen or Deadeye. t. one and a quarter or one and three quarters, right handed. Has played for 10 seasons, 6 in NHPA competition; President of San Bernandino Horseshoe Pitchers Club; highest tournament average is 56.6% and best game 68.8%; was one of 6 persons who in June, 1977 set the marathon pitching record for the Guinness Book of World Records. Home: 35672 Ivy Avenue, Yucaipa, CA 92399.

KNAUFT, HENRY, b. August 4, 1923. Washington State Champion 11 times, and Pacific Northwest Champion 10 times. W. Anita; children—Diane, Cheryl, Jason. Partsman. S. Bronze Lee and Allen; t. one and a quarter, right handed. Has been playing for 32 years; finished 3rd in World Tournament, and in 1970 4th; highest tournament average was 83.2% and highest single game 94.1%; record for consecutive ringers is 52; is presently Chairman of Washington State Hall of Fame Committee and a member of that select group; past First Vice-President of

WSHPA, 1973; record in Washington State Championship 1980 was 13-1-79.9%. Home: 2110 North Morton Street, Spokane, WA 99207.

KNISLEY, JIM, b. December 22, 1942. Ohio State Champion 1968, 1974, 1977, 1979, 1980; Runnerup for World Title, 1968, 1979. W. Mary; children—Jamie, two stepsons, Scott, Mike. Owner and Operator, Classic Billiards—Sheet metal worker. S. Imperial; t. one and a quarter, right handed. Started played around 1960; constructed 6 outdoor and 3 indoor courts and conducted tournaments and leagues in Bremen which attracted many top pitchers from out of state as well as all over Ohio; in 1980 Ohio state championship averaged above 80%, then went to 13-0-83.4%; Class A championships are numerous, as are his games above 90%, the long list of consecutive ringers, the four deads and his 80% tournaments; highest percentage game was 97%, hitting 33 out of 34 against Levi Miller in Hebron Open, 1980. World Tournament Record:

Year	Finish	Won	Lost	Ringer %
1968	2nd	31	4	82.8
1969	11th	23	12	78.1
1970	17th	20	15	72.1
1971	11th	23	12	78.6
1973	17th	20	15	74.9
1974	15th	20	15	78.5
1975	8th	24	11	80.1
1976	9th	24	11	79.3
1977	6th	20	6	83.8
1978	6th	28	7	78.1
1979	2nd	26	5	82.3
1980	7th	24	7	80.4

Home: 233 Bartlett, Bremen, OH 43107.

KNUTSON, HART, b. April 14, 1910, Minesota State Champion 1963, winning 10 of 11 games with 67.8%; Minnesota HPA Hall of Fame 1970. W. Myrthle; children—Richard, Marilyn, William, Stephen. United States Treasury Agent (retired) S. Gordon; t. one and a quarter, left handed. Has played for 30 years, 25 years in NHPA competition with a 65% ringer percentage; highest single game is 80%; other championships include Class C World Championship at Fargo, North Dakota in 1967, Duluth Open, 1963 with 5-1-63.5%, Cloquet Open with 10-1-64%, Quint City Open 6-1-63%, and the 1964 St. Paul A League with 66.7% Home: 4003 Holly Drive, East Holiday, FL 33590.

KOHLENBERGER, HARVEY C., b. November 18, 1914. Member, Illinois HPA Hall of Fame, 1980. W. Eulalia; children—Delores Rahn, Vicki Williams, Marsha, Sue. Accountant—Peabody Coal Company. S. Allen and Imperial, t. one and three quarters, right handed. As a pitcher played for 40 years, and 35 in organized league or tournament play; played in NHPA events for 25 years; in Illinois state tournaments finished 2nd in 1977 and 3rd in 3 other years; hit a 74.2% in 1976 through the Intermediate Division of the World Tournament; tied or set 7 intermediate world records; in 1963 in Sharpshooters' Club in Washington, Missouri had a 100% game hitting 36 consecutive ringers and was on the cover of the October, 1963 Horseshoe Pitchers News Digest; has won city titles in Altamont, Mascoutah, Millstadt, Pinckneyville, East St. Louis and Highland; has won Eastern Missouri Open, St. Louis Open and St. Louis County Open; now holds offices of Vice-President of Millstadt Club and Chairman of Illinois Hall of Fame Committee; was President of Millstadt Club for 25 years; was Illinois State HPA President for 8 years, and Vice-President for 15 years prior to that. Home: 210 West White Street, Millstadt, IL 62260.

KOLB, WILLIAM A., b. April 17, 1914. 14 times New Jersey State Champion, between 1941–1980, hitting in sixties and seventies. Member of New Jersey HPA Hall of Fame. W. Ann. Painter. S. Allen; t. one and a quarter or one and three quarters, right handed. Has played for 45 years, 42 in NHPA competition; Treasurer of Inter-City Horseshoe Club of Clifton, and past Tournament Director of New Jersey several times; in New Jersey State qualifying rounds, 1942 he set a state record hitting 283 ringers out of 350 shoes for 81%; hit 135 ringers in a three game match against Joe McCrink, out of 150 shoes for a 90% average, and in the 3rd game of that match hit 48 of 50 for 96% including 34 straight to open the game with McCrink hitting 70% and failing to score; among many tournament titles is Eastern United States Open; record in 1980 New Jersey state tournament was 11-0-63.1%. Home: 120 Rutgers Street, Belleville, NJ 07109.

KOSO, DONALD, b. March 7, 1919. President, Nebraska Horseshoe Pitchers Association. W. June; children—Dennis, Linda Long. Retired, Seed and Nursery. S. Imperial; t. three quarters, right handed. Has

pitched horseshoes most of his life, until becoming disabled and works to boost the sport although is not able to pitch any longer; Regional Director in charge of the sale of game-related items; Secretary of Falls City Club; State Secretary for 10 years and president most of the other years for 25 years; since 1956 has been Tournament Director for 4 Nebraska State tournaments with close to 100 entries, and Tournament Director every year since 1958 of Annual Falls City Open; reached height of game as pitcher in 1962 with 64.0% average for season; helped to organize the Nebraska Hall of Fame, and was its first member; has helped to start new clubs and sends information to schools and colleges. Home: 803 East 12th Street, Falls City, NE 68355.

KRAFT, ROLAND, b. Feb. 7, 1912, d. Feb. 23, 1982. 10 times Kansas State Champion. W. Christine; children—Dennis, Nancy. Postmaster S. Gordon; t. one and three quarters, right handed. Pitched in 31 Kansas state tournaments, winning 9 and retained the title a 10th year when no tournament was held and finished 2nd in 12 others; winning 7 in succession from 1955 to 1961; started pitching in state tournaments in 1930 until 1961; pitched for 45 years and played tournaments for 43 of them; in world tournament play compiled 189 wins, 135 losses, hit a ringer percentage of 72.2% and averaged qualifying at 494 points, all in championship division; finished 15th in 1940 and 6th in 1941 averaging 78% ringers; in Kansas state tournament play established state record with 94.1% in 1952 and combined with Alvin Dahlene to establish another with 120 shoes pitched in 1938; served as Secretary of Kansas State Horseshoe Pitchers Association. Having been a polio victim at age 7 and had a left arm which was useless this made his achievement all the more remarkable; a kidney ailment ended his pitching in 1961.

Enjoys fishing and gardening. Home: Box 6, Lecompton, KA 66050.

KRAJICEK, JOE III, Nebraska Boys State Champion, 1972 with a record of 4-0-40.5%.

KRENTZ, FREDERICK, b. January 27, 1940. W. Leona; children—Lyle, Lynn, Lisa. Farmer. S. Allen; t. one and a quarter or one and three quarters, right handed. Has been pitching organized play for 8 years, all but one in NHPA: hit high game of 82% and high tournament average of 68%; won Class A championship in Le Sueur Open, 1980 with 5-0-59.2%. He advocates that pitching distance for women and juniors be increased from 30 to 35 feet and performs a juggling act with 3 horseshoes. Home: Route 2—Box 106, Belle Plaine, Minnesota 56011.

KRIMBILL, GEORGE E. First Secretary of California Horseshoe Pitchers Association. On June 12, 1920 the Golden State Association of Horseshoe Pitchers of California was organized. The first slate of officers elected was:

President: W. A. Hoyt, Long Beach
Secretary: George E. Krimbill, Long Beach
Assistant Secretary: H. L. Smith, Pasadena
Treasurer: T. Holman, Glendale

If any one man is to be called the Founding Father of the California Horseshoe Pitchers Association it would have to be George E. Krimball. Was formerly secretary of Long Beach Tourist Horseshoe Club, the largest in the United States with over 600 members representing 29 states and Canada. It was through his efforts that the Golden State Horseshoe Association was formed after many months of gathering data from the Buckeye Association and holding meetings.

KROWEL, WALTER, California State Champion, 1929.

KRUG, JOE, Washington State Champion, 1973 with a record of 13-1-75.5%. Is a friend and long time pitching companion of World Champion, John Monasmith. Home: 2813 Frazer Way, Yakima, WA 98902.

KRYDER, HARVEY, The National Horseshoe Pitchers Association was incorporated in 1921, and in that year Harvey Kryder of Akron, Ohio was elected a vice-president.

KUCHCINSKI, DAN. b. 1949 World Champion, 1967, 1969, 1970; Member of National Hall of Fame. W. Sue. Entertainer; Owner of Health Spa. S. Allen; t. reverse one and a quarter, left handed. In world tournament play hit 66 consecutive ringers, hit 97.1% ringers in best game, 84.9% for an entire tournament and 92.5% for a 200 shoe qualifying round; won Pennsylvania state championship in 1966 and 1967 with percentages of 82.7% (a state record), and 82.3%; with wife Sue Gillespie he put together an exhibition act which combines trick horseshoe pitching with acrobatics. They have toured the United States, Canada and Japan playing successfully to thousands of people, billed as "Mr. and Mrs. Horseshoes". They have appeared on local, regional and national television, making appearances on the Johnny Carson Tonight Show, Mike Douglas Show, Merv Griffin, "What's My Line", To Tell the Truth and The World Surprise Show in Japan. The Dan and Sue Show uses portable equipment and combines talent, costuming, music and showmanship. Along with his wife he helped to form a Professional Horseshoe Pitchers Association and serve as tournament directors. World Tournament Record:

Year	Finish	Won	Lost	R%
1965	10th	27	8	79.3
1966	2nd	23	5	80.2
1967	1st	34	1	84.4
1968	3rd	30	5	82.3
1969	1st	35	0	84.7
1970	1st	34	1	84.9
1971	9th	25	10	80.0
1972	5th	29	6	81.8
1973	11th	22	13	75.6
1974	22nd	15	20	74.3
1975	9th	24	11	78.1
1979	6th	23	8	77.7
1980	14th	17	14	70.6

Is a Penn State graduate. Home: Box 526, Portland, IN 47371.

KUCHCINSKI, DON. Qualified in Class A of 1979 World Tournament in Statesville, North Carolina. During the first 3 days of competition he defeated most of the top 20 then became ill and had to withdraw from the tournament and forfeit those wins. In New Castle Spring Fling, 1980 he averaged 79.8% for 7 games against good competition and included games of 89.5% and 87.5%. Home: Erie, PA.

KUCHCINSKI, EDWARD JOSEPH. b. June 1, 1926. W. Dorothy; children— Karen, Ed, Steve, Paul, Rob. Independent Trucker. S. Ohio Pro; t. one and three quarters, right handed. Has played since childhood, and in tournaments for 20 years; Director of Erie Horseshoe Club; averaged about 60% ringers; won Erie County Championship, 1976 with 60.9% ringers; won the Erie County Class B title in 1980 with 60.4%; was Class B champ in Erie County, 1979 with 58.9%, and Class D champ in New Castle with 59.7%; high game is 76% and longest string of consecutive doubles 11. Enjoys golf and bowling. Home: 2322 Fairmont Parkway, Erie, PA 16510.

KUCHCINSKI, RONALD, b. June, 23, 1952. Erie County Championship, 1968,

1980. W. Vicky Lynn; child—Amie. Assembler—painter. S. Allen; t. one and a quarter, right handed. Made championship division of World Tournament in 1969, finishing 26th with a record of 14-21-74.8%; highlights of his pitching are 30 consecutive ringers and a high game of 91.8%. Other hobbies include back packing, camping and bowling. Home: 1820 Wagner Avenue, Erie, PA 16505.

KUCHCINSKI, SUE GILLESPIE, b. 1947. Women's World Champion 1962, 1964, 1965; National Hall of Fame Member, 1976. H. Dan. Entertainer, Owner of health spa. S. Allen; t. one and a quarter, right handed. Was 13 when she took up the sport and became champion in 2 short years when she was only 15 years old, winning the world title, the youngest ever; hit 81.3% for entire 1964 world tournament, making this a world record until 1978; hit a 93.3% game in world tournament play, hit 30 consecutive ringers and an 83% qualifying round. Along with her husband she helped to form the Professional Horseshoe Pitchers Association and act as tournament director for the PHPA. She and her husband put together an exhibition act which has toured the United States,

Canada and Japan, they are billed as "Mr. and Mrs. Horseshoes". They have appeared on local, regional and national television, including Johnny Carson's Tonight Show, Mike Douglas Show, Merve Griffin, What's My Line, To Tell the Truth and The World Surprise Show in Japan.

She is a graduate of Purdue University and won the Indiana State gymnastics championship while at the school; is a dancer as well as an acrobat. Home: Box 526, Portland, IN 47371.

Sue Kuchcinski's World Tournament record:

Year	Finish	Won	Lost	R%
1961	4th	4	1	42.4
1962	1st	7	0	65.3
1963	3rd	4	2	59.9
1964	1st	7	0	81.1
1965	1st	6	1	75.9
1966	3rd	5	2	61.3
1967	4th	4	3	58.5

KUCHCINSKI, WESLEY. Is a Class A pitcher; in World Tournament at Keene, New Hampshire, 1965 had a record of 9-26-69.5% for 27th place; in 1968 was 6-29-70.9% for 33rd place, and in that tournament was joined by Henry Pergal as the only 2 men ever to have a perfect game pitched against them in World Tournament play. Elmer Hohl hit 30 ringers out of 30 shoes in their brief encounter. Has won city, county and open tournament titles with a 70% ringer average. Home: 2630 Van Buren Avenue, Erie, PA 16504.

KUGLER, KEN, b. August 5, 1929. W. Margaret; children—Marlene Hacker, Barbara Vessely. Bookkeeper. S. Ohio "O"; t. one and three quarters, right handed. Started to pitch horseshoes in fall of 1965 and entered first tournament in 1966; from 1966 through 1980 pitched every year in Ohio State Tournament; hit 47% in 1966, but since then has been above 60% every year; highest finish is 3rd in 1978; tied for third hitting 75.4% in 1980, making this his best state tournament average; highest tournament was Hamilton May Open, 1980 with 76.5%; has

a 92% game at Day Bel and a 90% game at Greenville and both games came against Gary Kline; has been in 5 World Tournament games, 1972, 1976, 1977, 1978, and 1980, 3 of these games in the Championship Division, once in B and once in C; defeated Mark Seibold 52-18 hitting 87.9% in World Tournament, 1977; won Southwest Ohio District, 1980 hitting over 72% and 4 other tournaments; in 1973 in London after winning Class B was invited to replace Glen Riffle in Class A after Riffle went to Eureka to participate in World Tournament and he then won Class A also. Also likes to bowl, averaging above 190, and averaged above 200 in 1961-62 season. Home: 176 Cambridge Drive, Hamilton, OH 45013.

KUHNE, MILDRED, b. December 6, 1917. Washington State Champion, 1968, 1969, 1970, 1971. H. Earl; children—Danny, Darla; three grandchildren. Beautician. S. Gordon; t. three quarters flip, right handed. Won Northwest Championship 4 times and Billingham twice. In Northwest tournament at Yakima hit highest game of 84.6% and highest tournament in 1967 with

71%; has been NHPA member since 1966 and is presently Secretary of Tacoma Horseshoe Club; participated in World Tournament at Eureka in 1970; set state records with 71.1% tournament game and 59% tournament average in 1969; her 40 ringers, 12 doubles, 4 consecutive four-deads versus Myrna Bailey were all state records. Home: 3740 North 29th, Tacoma, WA 98407.

KUTIL, ROBERT, South Dakota Boys State Champion, 1978 with 30% ringers.

L

LABBE, GERALD "GERRY", b. August 22, 1921. Colorado State Champion 5 times; 1951 with 11-0-70.9%, 1958 with 11-0-70.6%, 1960 with 10-1-69.2%, 1961 with 11-0-72.1% and 1962. W. Maxine; children—Evangeline, Mary Beth, Doreen, Kevin, Robert. Mechanical Engineer. S. Gordon; t. one and a quarter, right handed. Has played in tournament competition from 1938 to 1980; won New England States Open Championship, 1940; member of Melrose, Massachusetts state championship team in 1945; won New England States championship at Keene, New Hampshire, 1948; won Nebraska Open, 1960; played in Class A division of World Tournament, 1948 in Milwaukee hitting 7-25-64.7%, 1950 and 1951 at Murray, Utah; hit 87 ringers out of 100 shoes in 1940; hit 88.9 in Colorado state tournament, 1960; in past years served as President of the Colorado State Horseshoe Pitchers Association; other highlights include match competition against Jimmie Risk, Casey Jones, Ted Allen, Fernando Isais; greatest memory was playing in February 1942 in Sulphur Springs, Florida with Frank Jackson; while stationed in Italy won the "Fifth Wing 15th Air Force Championship". Out of Gerry's scrap book comes a duplicate score sheet signed by Guy Zimmerman of the first perfect game in World Tournament play pitched against Henry Pergal in August 19, 1948. Enjoys amateur radio and woodworking. Home: 2338 South Utica, CO 80219.

La BROSSE, BILL, b. March 19, 1951. Minnesota Boys State Champion 1963 and 1967. Surveyor for St. Louis County, Minnesota. S. Allen; t. one and three quarters, right handed. Played four years in Class A Junior Boys division of the World Tournament finishing fifth in 1964, third in 1965, and second in both 1966 and 1967. World Tournament record 20-15-61.1%. Home: 1619 Third Avenue East, Hibbing, Minnesota, 55746.

La BROSSE, JERRY, b. May 4, 1956. Three times Minnesota Boys State Champion, 1969, 1970 5-0-59.8% and 1971 4-1-40%. W. Debra; children—Jeremy and Jessica. Machine shop Manager. S. Allen; t. one and a quarter, right handed. Highest finish in Boys World Tournament play, fifth place. Home: 220 East 45th Street, Hibbing, Minnesota, 55746.

LACY, CLARE, Washington D.C. Champion, 1940 with 72.3% average, which is a record for the state, as are his 1940 qualifying marks of 247 and 78% ringers; won Maryland state championship, 1942 with a record of 13-2-63%.

LACINSKI, GWEN, b. April 19, 1967. Michigan Girl's State Champion, 1978. Single. Student. S. Ohio; t. flip, right handed. Started pitching at age 10; won her own club championship. Enjoys softball, volleyball and basketball. Home: 515 South Gorham, Jackson, Michigan 49203.

LACKEY, RALPH, b. August 11, 1905 (dec.) March 6, 1976. Ohio State Champion, 1948, won 18, lost 1, record 76.2%—1950, won 18, lost 1, record 72.4%—1951, won 17, lost 2, record 70.6%—1952, won 12, lost 3, record 70.3. Farmer and Armco Steel.

S. Allen; t. one and a quarter, right handed. Home: West Middletown. OH.

LaCOILLE, KEN, New Hampshire Boy's State Champion, 1972 with a record of 6-0-50.6%. Home: 294 Roxbury Street, Keene, NH 03431.

LACROIX, LEO. Rhode Island State Champion, 1957, averaging 60.2% and 1958 averaging 59.7%.

LACROSSE, PAUL, b. November 4, 1939. Colorado State Champion, 1979 with 10-1-58.4% and 1980 with 10-1-61-4%. W. Judy. Chemical Sales. S. Allen; t. one and three quarters, right handed. Pitched in first state tournament in Maine, 1957; threw qualifying rounds at World Tournament 1964, 1967; from 1964 played leagues in Cloquet and Duluth, Minnesota, Denver, Colorado and Kansas City, Missouri; was Secretary-Treasurer of Colorado State Horseshoe Pitchers Association from 1974 through 1977 and Publicity Director of the Denver Metro Club in 1978 and 1979; after pitching in state tournament in Maine he pitched in Minnesota State Tournament in 1969 finishing in 4th place with 68.8%; best tournament average ever was 71.2% in Fruita Open, 1980; best game was 82.4% in Speakeasy Open in Denver, 1980; in Rocky Mountain Area, 1980 won 6 of 7 tournaments. Home: 12433 Green Mountain Circle, Lakewood, CO 80228.

LAMKIN, LINDA SMITH, b. August 16, 1951. Michigan State Girls Champion, 1967. Single. Shipping Clerk—Howmet Corporation. S. Lattore; t. one and a quarter, right handed. Has played since childhood and in organized competition since 1965; won the Holton Centennial in 1971. Home 2290 Johnston Road, Twin Lake, Michigan 49467.

LANDRUM, BOBBY L. New Mexico Champion 1978, with 47% ringers. Home: 1121 Kentucky Southeast, Albuquerque, NM 87108.

LANDRY, EDGAR, d. February 15, 1975. Massachusetts State Champion, 1952-53, 1956-59, 1962, 1964-66. Won Class B World Championship, 78.4% (Highest ringer percentage since Class B competition started in 1951), 1964; won New England Championship, 73.9%, 1951, and nine more times, averaging at least 72% overall (record in 1955 meet 11-0-72.9%); broke 500 in qualifying round, 1964, the only year in history when 500 failed to make championship division; held state high record high game, 93%; won Northeast Tournament five times, 71.2%-79.7% (the record for that meet); considered best pitcher in New England, 1951-67; inducted into New England Hall of Fame, 1971; was charter member, Massachusetts HPA. Home: Fall River, Massachusetts.

LANDRY, ESTELLE, 1977 Manitoba Pronvincial Women's Champion (with no losses). Home: Morris.

LANE, LESLIE, Secretary-Treasurer, Connecticut HPA, 1935-44. Helped with organization of state assocation and promoted state and industrial leagues and tournaments.

LANE, SAMUEL C., Connecticut State Champion, 1929-32, 11-2, and 1937, 11-1-58.6%. Pitched twice in New England championships averaging 50%.

LANE, WALTER, 1929 Indiana State Champion.

LANG, PEGGY, b. July 7, 1946. 1980 Alabama Women's State Champion. H. James A.; children—Wayne, Rhonda. Employee, Huntsville Manufacturing Co. S. Deadeye; t. flip, right handed. Home: Box 163 Little Mountain Road, Huntsville, Alabama 35803.

LANG, RHONDA, B. December 9, 1966. 1980 Alabama Girls State champion. Student

S. Americans; t flip, right handed. Won Annistion Open. Home: 163 Little Mountain Road, Huntsville, Alabana 35803.

LANG, WAYNE, b. June 21, 1965. 1980 Alabama Boys State Champion. Student. S. Deadeye; t. three quarters, right handed. High game, 69%; now averaging 50%. Home: 163 Little Mountain Road, Huntsville, Alabama 35803

LANGE, MARION W., b. November 2, 1912. Vice-President, Iowa State HPA, 1978 Member, I.H.H.P.A. Hall of Fame. W. Pauline. Farmer. S. Allen; t. one and three quarters, right handed. Serves as fourth vice-president, I.H.H.P.A.; pitched for fifty-five years, fifty-two in organized competition; joined Des Moines club, 1928; won Class A titles; Four-State Opens (Iowa-Kansas-Nebraska-Missouri), 1962, 1964, Iowa Farmers state championships (70%, 1949), Iowa Open (70% in 1971), 1970-71, and Greater Des Moines League, 1976; awarded NHPA Achievement Award, 1977; high game, 88%, Omaha Open; high tournament, 75%, 1964 Four-State Open; superintendent, Iowa State Fair Horseshoe program, 1974-80; co-chairman, 1978 World Tournament, Des Moines. Home: 701 North East Ninth Street, Ankeny, Iowa 50021.

LANHAM, (MRS. C.A.), Women's World Champion, 1922-25, 1927-28, 1971 Member NHPA Hall of Fame. Played in seven world tournaments, won six, finished second, 1923; established world record of 70.8% for one game, 1923 World Tournament; composite record for seven tournaments. 79-4-54.6%, and her 79 wins are fourth on all-time victory list; became thirteenth member, NHPA Hall of Fame, the second woman to be inducted. Home: Bloomington, Illinois.

LANKHORST, CAROLYN, 1967, 1969 New Hampshire State Champion. Record for state titles: 5-1-46.7%, 1967, 7-0-65.5%,

1969; qualified twice for Championship Division, World Tournament, with record of 7-7-61.5%.

LARAWAY, KELLY, b. June 29, 1908. Member, Washington State Hall of Fame. W. Gussie; child—Terry. Puget Sound Civilian Navy Yard Rigger, retired. S. Imperial; t. one and a quarter and one and three quarters, right handed. Won Northwest Open, 55%, 1927; won Kitsap County and Bremerton City Championships several times; hit thirteen consecutive doubles and five consecutive four-deads; competed in tournament play for fifty-six years; played semi-pro baseball. Home: 306 North Cambrian, Bremerton, Washington 98310.

LA ROSE, GEORGE "FRENCHY," b. January 16, 1912. 1976 Member, New York HPA Hall of Fame. W. Catherine; child—George, Jr. Punch press operator. S. Imperial and Allen; t. one and three quarters, right handed. Served as president, New York HPA; won Syracuse City Championship thirteen times, Syracuse County Championship twelve times; made seven appearances in New York State Tournament with finishes of third, fourth, fifth (twice), sixth, eighth, seventh, hit 36 consecutive ringers and 93 of a running 100, 1938; pitched for fifty-two years; played with friend of 45 years Carl Steinfeldt in 1935 state tournament. Home: 504 Clinton Street, Fayetteville, New York 13066.

LARSON, WILMA, Alberta Provincial Doubles Champion 1979 with Margaret Johns. Won 1977 Women's Singles Championship at Alberta Summer Games.

LASH, SID. British Columbia Provincial Champion. Finished fifth, Class B, World Tournament, 6-5-68.7%, 1973; won gold medal, British Columbia Summer Games, Richmond, 7-1-56.5%, 1979; won British Columbia Men's Singles title, 60.5%, 1970, 62.7%, 1971, 69.4%, 1972, 67.3%, 1973;

Top, left, Members of the "Pythian Drug" team, which in 10 years won at least six tournaments in Ohio. *Right,* Bill Holland, World Champion. *Second row, left,* Stephen and Elmer Hohl of Canada, World Champions. *Right,* Waino and Bernice Huotari, and their six children, a horseshoe pitching family. *Bottom row, left,* Fernando Isais, World Champion and Hall of Fame member. *Center,* Lee Jacobs. *Right,* Johan Kapp of South Africa. *At Right,* Gary Kline.

Top, left to right, Jim Johnson, world record holder; Wilbur Kabel, Hall of Fame member; Jim Knisley; and Due and Dan Kuchcinski, both in the Hall of Fame and World Champions. *Center,* 1942 match between Bill Kolb, New Jersey champion, and Bob Henson, Virginia champion. *Bottom,* 1965 World Tournament at Keene, New Hampshire, with a star roster of state and world champions. *At right,* Gerald Labbe and Guy Zimmerman at the 1948 World Tournament in Milwaukee.

finished fifth, Canadian National Championship, 1976.

LASKO, JOE, Michigan State Champion thirteen times, 1929, 1939-41, 1943, 1945-51, 1954. Served as vice-president, Wolverine State HPA. Home: 619 Fox Street, Flint, Michigan.

LATHROP, NOAH, Secretary-Treasurer, Vermont HPA. W. Katherine; two children. Lumber mill worker. S. Gordon; t. three quarters, right handed. President, Sodbusters Club of Middlebury; disabled by lumber mill accident; pitched for more than twenty years. Home: 126 North Street, Bristol, Vermont 05443.

LATIMORE, FOSTER D., b. November 28, 1901. 1977 Ohio Senior State Champion. W. Gladys; children—Richard, Jean Reasoner. Machinist. S. Deadeye; t. one and a half, righ handed. Member, NHPA, 15 years; member, Marion Horseshoe Club; won 42 trophies, attended five world tournaments. Home: 1565 Marion-Marysville Road, Marion, Ohio 43302.

LATINO, MONTE, b. December 27, 1916. Horseshoe Hall of Fame (Northern California HPA), 1975, Fast Pitch Softball Hall of Fame, 1979, Soccer Hall of Fame, 1980. W. Mildred; children—Susan, Monte, Tom, Joe. Railroad worker. S. Allen; t. one and a quarter, right handed. Won Northern California Championship, 1975; won Intermediate World Championship, 1980; high tournament, 78%; high game 86%; hit seven four-deads in a row and 15 consecutive doubles in tournament competition; qualified for Championship Division, World Tournament, 1970, 1973; third vice-president, Northern California chapter, NHPA, 1980. Home: 4317 46th Avenue, Sacramento, California 95824.

LATTORE, LEO G., Designer of Lattore pitching shoe. Pitched average of 65%;

finished 16th, 9-14-64.8%, World Tournament, Moline, Illinois, 1935. Home: St. Petersburg, Florida.

LATTRAY, LOUIS PAUL, b. August 31, 1916. Missouri State Champion, 1938, 1957, 1962-65. W. Anna Mary; children—David, Darryl. Artist. S. Allen; t. one and three quarters, right handed. Finished tenth, 25-10-81.1%, World Tournament, 1964; holds state record for high tournament, 79.9%, and highest percentage qualifying, 90% with 90 ringers out of 100 shoes; high tournament average, 83.5% (hit 453 ringers out of 542 shoes in Eastern Missouri tournament); hit 325 of 394, 7-0-82.4%, Gascondale County Fair; past president, Municipal Athletic Association, and Municipal HPA; has pitched exhibitions; with Marvin Craig, hit 12 consecutive four-deads to tie world record set by Ted Allen and Stan DeLeary, World Tournament, 1964. Home: 201 West Glendale Road, Webster Grove, Missouri 63119.

LAUER, ORVILLE, 1941 Colorado State Champion, 14-2-68.4%.

LAUGHLIN, LEE, b. March 21, 1903. Wyoming State Champion, 1964, 1969, 1975. W. Ruth; child—Robert. Farmer/mechanic. S. Allen; t. one and three quarters. Competed in NHPA for 25 years; vice-president, Wyoming Chapter, NHPA; titles include 1952 Southeastern Wyoming-Cheyenne Club, 1952 Larimie County, 1951, 1953, Cheyenne City, 1954 Wybraska Interstate, 1952 Southeastern Wyoming. Home: 3118 Dillon Avenue, Cheyenne, Wyoming 82001.

LAVERS, CLARENCE "SWEDE," b. May 27, 1935. 1959 Connecticut State Champion. Child—Lori. Laboratory technician. S. Ohio or Allen; t. three quarters, right handed. Title record: 7-2-54.3%; other tournament titles include Fairfield County, Stratford City, Y.M.C.A. (four times), North Haven Fair (twice), Bridgeport and Connecticut State Open; high game, 94% (hit 47 of 50); hit 37 in a row in 46 out of 50 game; high tournament, 75%; pitched 35 years, six in NHPA tournament play; inactive for last twenty years. Home: 160 Peck Street, Stratford, Connecticut 06497.

LAVETT, FRED, b. May 31, 1920. 1967 Northern California Champion, 10-1-70.8%. W. Genevieve. Disabled veteran, WWII, Okinawa. S. Allen; t. one and a quarter or one and three quarters, right handed. President, Seaside Club, held office in this club for 18 years; director for junior boys, Northern California, 1975; won 14 consecutive Monterey County Championships, 1966-79, the Ole Hansen Open, and the Los Gatos Open; posted highest tournament average, 71.7% for 36 games, World Tournament, Eureka, California, 1973 (in 24th round hit highest game, 85.4%); recipient, Special NHPA Award, 1973 World Tournament; attended 12 World Tournaments; served in 77th U.S. Infantry Division, WWII, wounded by mortar shell, May 23, 1945, Okinawa. Home: P.O. Box 266, Seaside, California 93955.

LAVETT, GENEVIEVE McNALLY, Statistician, Organizer on Local, State, and National Levels for 25 Years. H. Fred. Worked statistics for two World Tournaments for National Secretary Bob Pence, Middlesex, N.J., and Greenville, Ohio, 1971 and 1972, respectively; filled in for resigned state secretary three years, and served as secretary-treasurer, Seaside Club, four years; donates money to California money tournaments; works Americon Legion and VA organizations to promote Fort Ord Army Tournaments (including junior tournaments); worked with city officials in Seaside, replaced seven courts with ten new ones; played first tournament, 1980, and won it with 33.8% average. Home: P.O. Box 266, Seaside, California 93955.

LaVOIE, ERNIE, Oregon State Secretary, Editor, state brochures, local publicity; held every office, Hillsboro Horseshoe Club; called "Mr. Horseshoes" by local press; instrumental in forming Hillsboro Club (with now-deceased Ted Chirstiansen and Ed Karlbom), and with help of city Parks and Light Departments constructed twelve lighted, fenced courts; promoted televised tournaments, Portland, starting 1959, and by 1965 they hosted three tournaments a year and received bid for 1966 state meet; published brochures covering 1965, 1966 state meets; averaged 35-40%, won five trophies. Home: 1820 Orchard Avenue, McMinnville, Oregon 97128.

LaVOIE, JACK, Oregon Boys State Champion, 1966, 26.1%, 1967, 45.2%, 1968, 3-0-50.1%. Son of Ernie LaVoie. Pitched in 1966, 1967 World Tournaments, finished third, Class B, 11th in tournament, and hit high game of 66.7%, 1967, Fargo, North Dakota. Home: San Francisco, California.

LAW, GERTRUDE SELBY, "GERTSIE LOU," 1957 World Champion. S. Allen, t. one and a quarter, right handed. Tutored by Ted Allen; pitched against women while still a junior because there was no junior girls division; started World Tournament play, 1953; finished 8th, 0-7-14.8%,1953, second, 4-1, 1954, fourth, 2-3, 1955, second, 5-2, 1956, first, 3-0-42.4%, 1957; tied for title in 1954 and 1956, lost play-offs. Home: 2009 Pueblo Court, Plano, Texas 75074.

LAWSON, WILLIAM, 1980 Massachusetts Doubles Champion (with Francis Norman). Home: 87 Nicholas Avenue, Boyeston, Massachusetss 01505.

LAYES, FRANCIS E., b. August 2, 1939. Vice-President, Nova Scotia Horseshoe Association. W. Anne Pauline; children— Sheila, Shirley, Margaret, Frances, Robert. Laborer. S. Diamoind; t. flip, right handed. President, Avon League; played league and tournament competition six years, NHPA for four years; ringer average 35%; won first place trophy, B Class, two first place trophies, C Class. Home: Route 1, Monastery, Antgonish County, Nova Scotia, Canada BOH 1WO.

LeBOW, JOHN, d. 1946 Tennessee State Champion. Brother of Oscar D. LeBow. S. T.J. Octigan; t. one and a quarter, right handed.

LeBOW OSCAR, 1958, 1959 Tennessee State Champion. Owner/operator, Lebow's Garage and Wrecker Service. S. Allen; t. one and a quarter, left handed. Hit 70%, 1959 tournament, then teamed with George Bell to win doubles title; won Statesville Autumn Open, 1976, and several Class A tournament titles in Tennessee area. Home: Route 23 Foster Lane, Knoxville, Tennessee 37920.

LECKY, JAMES O., Arizona State Champion 22 times, 1927–48. Starred in five-minute film for television program, "You asked For It," the film a trick pitching exhibition.

LECLERC, SOLANGE, 1979 Quebec Women's Provincial Champion. Won Class B Championship, Canadan National Tournament, 6-1-48.8%, 1979. Home: St. Hyacinthe.

LEE, MARY, 1969 Junior Girls World Champion. Secretary. S. Allen; t. one and three quarters, right handed. Played first World Tournament, Keene, New Hampshire, 1968; first girl to average 50% ringers, when she won 1969 World Championship, Erie, Pennsylvania, high game, 55.5%; finished second to Jennifer Reno, with 57% to Reno's 59.7%, World Tournament, Greenville, Ohio, 1972; won three consecutive tournament classes in Middlesex, N.J., all men's tournament classes D, C, and B, pitching from 40 feet, 55% average; qualified with 71%, 242 points, Southeastern Classic,

Winston-Salem, North Carolina, 1973; hit 17 consecutive doubles in one game; began pitching when nine years old, 1965, working out with James Mauney, who noticed that her swing was strong enough at the start for her to pitch from 37 feet; during 1967–74 in New York Metropolitan Area, there were no junior girls, junior boys, or women's pitching from thirty feet to compete with, and she adjusted to competition with men. Home: Manhattan.

LEE, NAVACE C., b. October 18, 1918. Past Secretary-Treaurer, Alabama HPA. W. Elinor; children—Lois L. Miller, Vance David, Dean Clayton. Electronic equipment specialist. S. Allen; t. one and a quarter, right handed. Was Class A contender, atttended 1980 World Tournament; pitched 42 years in Minnesota, South Dakota, Wisconsin, Alabama, thirty years in league or tournament play, ten years as NHPA member; helped build Huntsville club, which hosted four state tournaments and the 1980 World Tournament. Home: 3200 Berkley Street, S W Huntsville, Alabama 35805.

LEE, OSCAR, 1939 Washington State Champion, 13-2-59%.

LEE, RUEBEN G., b. July 20, 1911. Northern California HPA Hall of Fame, 1978. W. Bernadine; children—Bryce, Gary, Susan Maiers. Operating engineer in construction. S. Allen; t. one and a quarter, right handed. Won Class B California State Championship, 1977; member, Mt. Vernon, Washington, Horseshoe Club, ten years; president, Arroyo Viejo Club, Oakland, 1964–67; organized and served either president or secretary-treasurer, San Lorenzo Club; president, Gold Country Horseshoe Club, Grass Valley-Nevada City area, since 1977; organized Gold Country Club, a family club of mostly beginning players, which was a subject of the President's Message in the 1979 November issues of "Horseshoe

Pitchers' News Digest"; won a number of Class A tournament championships; high tournament, 72.9%; high game, 92%; pitched 45 years, 18 as NHPA member. Home: 15893 Turquoise Place, Grass Valley, California 95945.

LEIGHTON, BEN, d. NHPA Founding Father, Hibbing, Minnesota. W. Louise, d. School teacher/Park and Recreation supervisor, Hibbing, Minn. Organized and promoted World Tournament, Ramsey County Fairgrounds, St. Paul, Minn., 1921, a meet sanctioned by the two existing horseshoe leagues, the Grand League of American Horseshoe Pitchers (organized 1915, Missouri) and the National League of Horseshoe and Quoits Players; elected president, set in motion the merger of two groups, completed at Winter World Tournament, Lake Worth, Fla., 1925, when the National Horseshoe Pitchers' Association of America was named; worked with Raymond Howard, Ohio, publisher "Horseshoe World"; served on various committees, NHPA, 1925–34; developed ringer percentage charts (still used by Diamond Horseshoe Co, Duluth); wrote article, "How to Organize a Horseshoe Club and Promote the Game," copyright, Diamond Horseshoe Co., copies of which in shoes sold today; promoted 1933 World Tournament game into Chicago Century of Progress World Fair (Ted Allen's first world title); helped formulate a revised constitution during 1933 tournament, and was appointed chairmen of NHPA Advisory Committee. Home: Baraboo, Wisconsin.

LEMOND, JOHN W., b September 16, 1917. Indiana Class A State Title, 1975. W. Mary; children—Kirby, Darryl. Factory worker. S. Gordon; t. one and a quarter, right handed. Hit 64.9% for eleven games, championship division, Indiana State Tournament, 1980; won League club championship five times; one of four-man committee which governs local club; high game 90%.

Home Route 7 Box 261, Anderson Indiana 46011.

LENZ, HUGO A., b March 5, 1931. President, Wyoming State HPA. W. Martha; children—Travis, Hugh. State Farm Insurance agent . S. Allen; t. one and a quarter, right handed. Vice President, Wyoming State HPA, 1977–80; served as Wyoming's delegate to World Tournament, Levittown, Pa., 1976, and Des Moines, Iowa, 1978; won Class B, Denver Speakeasy Open, 1975, Western Nebraska Open, 1976, and Rocky Mountain Open, Boulder, Colo., 1978; runnerup, Class A, Wyoming Cowboy Open, 1978, Wyoming State Tournament, 1979; finished third, Class A, Wyoming State Tournament, 1980. Enjoys snow skiing, snooker, pool. Serves as hydrant or plugman, Wheatland City Fire Dept., 21 years, whose drill team won state championship five times. Home: P.O. Box 458, Wheatland, Wyoming 82201.

LEONARD, DAVID T., First recognized State Champion of New York, 1921. New York State Champion, 1924–27, 19-1-34.9%, 47.3%, respectively; World Tournament record: 101-125-41.8%, Championship Division. Home: Adams Basin, New York.

LEPPER, BERNIE, b. October 2, 1934. Director British Columbia Association, "Horseshoes B.C.," and Director, Greater Vancouver Horseshoe Club. W. June; children—Arlene, Brian. Printer. S. Imperial; t. one and a quarter, right handed. Serves as representative of British Columbia to "Horseshoes Canada"; serves as assistant provincial advisor for horseshoes in British Columbia Summer Games; played in Classes B and C, won a few Class A titles in local tournaments; won Class C Championship, 66.7%, 1975 Canadian Championships; hit fourteen consecutive doubles, interclub match between Vancouver, British Columbia, and Bellingham, Washington. Home: 34 North Howard Avenue, Burnaby, British Columbia, Canada, V5B 1J5.

LESTER, ARNOLD, b. October 4, 1909. 1975, 1976 Illinois Senior State Champion. W. Rebecca; children—James, Richard, Eugene, Kathy Young. Conductor, Burlington and Northern Railroad. S. Ohio Pro; t. one and a quarter, right handed. Member, NHPA, 18 years; joined Galesburg Horseshoe Club, 1959; won 75 trophies in 18 seasons, including senior state championship, 10-0-65%; has been a Knox County Champion, posted high single game, 84%. Home: 1247 East Knox, Galesburg, Illinois 61401.

LEWIS, GEORGE C., b. April 3, 1927. Contender in Tennessee. W. Mildred; children—George, Michael, Jerry, Chris. Grader operator. S. Allen; t. reverse one and three quarters, right handed. High game, 84%; tournament average, above 60%; pitched horseshoes 30 years and in tournaments for 20 years. Enjoys hunting, fishing. Home: Route 6—Strauplains Pike, Knoxville, Tennessee 37914.

LEWIS, LORI BROWN, 1977 Illinois Women's State Champion, 9-0-43.4%. Right handed. Won Loraine Illinois, Open, 5-0, 1977. Home: Loraine, Illinois 62349.

LEYK, ROSIE, b. December 27, 1941. League Secretary. H. Richard. Operator of service station and tavern. S. Diamond Tournament; t. flip, right handed. Operates Leyk's Three and One Courts for horseshoe pitching; finished third, Women's Division, Minnesota State Tournament, 62.3% (high tournament), 62.5% (high league), 1980; won Ramsey County Championship; high game (league play), 80%, hit 22 consecutive ringers, 32 out of last 34. Enjoys snowmobiling, motorcycling, bowling. Home: Route 1, Sauk Rapids, Minnesota 56379.

LIBBY, WILLIAM, 1965, 1966 Maine State Champion, 9-0-62.2%, 8-1-64.1%. Home: Limerick, Maine.

LICHTY, MERV, Secretary-Treasurer, Ontario HPA. Serves as regional director of Zone Three. Home: Route 1, Box 73, Waterloo, Ontario, Canada, N2J 4G 8.

LIEDES, ARTHUR, b. August 16, 1909. 1974 Member, Washington HPA Hall of Fame. Single, Retired furniture factory foreman. S. Gordon; t. one and a quarter, right handed. State secretary, Washington HPA, six years; secretary, Grays Harbour County HPA, 20 years; recognized for promotion efforts by Hall of Fame, 1974; won county championship, 1932; won Aberdeen City Title, 1938; 45% average; averaged 66.7% in 52-game league. Home: 505 North "F" Street, Apt. 714, Aberdeen, Washington 98520.

LINDMEIER, JOHN C., b. December 2, 1917. Illinois State Champion, 1948–50, 1955. W. Marylou; children—John, Mary Ann, Bonnie, Richard. Carpenter/cabinet maker. S. Allen; t. one and three quarters, right handed. Hit 78.9%, 1950 state tournament; pitched 50 years, 45 in league and tournament competition; averaged 500 points in qualifying rounds, World Tournament, with composite record of 168-97-73.4%; finished seventh, 20-11-75.2%, World Tournament, Milwaukee, Wisconsin, 1948; finished fourth, 25-10-74.8%, World Tournament, Murray, Utah, 1951. Enjoys pool, fishing, bowling (bowled 300 game, 1963). Home: 207 South Wolf Road, Northlake Illinois 60164.

LINDSEY OLLIE, b. March 6, 1920. Vice-President, Utah HPA. 1975–80. W. Leah; children—Sheldon, Randall. Coal miner/athletic equipment manager, Brigham Young University. S. Gordon; t. one and a quarter, right handed. Won Class B Utah State Championship, 1978; high game, 69%; averaged 52% for state meet; pitched for 45 years, seven in tournament play. Enjoys hiking. Home: 849 North 750 West Street, Provo, Utah 84601.

LINDQUIST, ALLEN, 1963 Minnesota Boys State Champion, 6-0. Home: Tower, Minn.

LINDQUIST, ANNA, b. February 12, 1901. d. February 5, 1968, 1949 Women's World Champion. H. Arner; children—Elna, Arne. Teacher. S. Gordon; t. one and a quarter, right handed. Helped organize West Virginia Chapter NHPA, 1947, served as secretary-treasurer, 1948–63; World Tournament record: 6-1, W. C., 1949, 8-1, 2nd, 1950, 5-2-47.7%, 3rd, 1951, 5-2-39.6%, 3rd, 1952, 6-1-46.7%, 2nd, 1953, 5-1-48.2% (lost play-off), 2nd, 1960, 4-1-61.2%, 3rd, 1961, 4-3-53%, 4th 1962, 1-6-55.8%, 8th, 1964.

LINDQUIST, ARNER, b. December 21, 1895. West Virginia State Champion, 1949–50, 1953, 1956–57. W. Anna, d.; children—Elna, Arne. Glass engraver. S. Gordon; t. one and a quarter, right handed. Member, West Virginia HPA Hall of Fame; campaigned 23 years as NHPA member; averaged 70%, won many Class A championships; pitched several times in Class A, World Tournament, composite record: 154-210-67.4%, average qualifying score, 491. Home: 305 Sixth Street, Morgantown, West Virginia 26505.

LIPOVSKY, DALE, b. April 22, 1955. Minnesota State Horseshoe Pitching Crown, 1973-76, 1978. W.; child—Dale, Jr. Police work. S. Allen; t. one and a quarter, left handed. Won Eau Claire Open twice, St. Paul Open twice, and many other Class A championships; pitched several exhibitions, including one with Walter Ray "Deadeye" Williams at the 1976 Farmfest; past historian, Minnesota HPA; past member, Minneapolis Horseshoe Club Board; averaged 75% in

1978 state title. Enjoys baseball, bowling. Home: Pompano Beach, Florida.

LIPOVSKY, LEONARD, b. December 7, 1926. Vice-President, Minneapolis Horseshoe Club. W. Renea; children—Carole Frey, Dale. Tool room machinist. S. Allen; t. one and a quarter, right handed. Past president, Minneapolis Horseshoe Club; member, Hall of Fame selection committee; won Class A crown, Boyceville, Wisconsin, 1980; won several Class B championships; high tournament, 66.7% (at Eau Claire, defeating Glen Henton, Frank Stinson and Bill Glass, June 1980); pitched 20 years, 13 in tournament play. Home: 8339 12th Avenue South, Bloomington, Minnesota 55420.

LISEY RUSSELL, b. 1906. Finished 13th, Championship Division, 1920 World Tournament, Akron. Was Wayne County Champion; hailed as one of best pitchers in U.S.; a three best of five games match between Lisey (14 years old) and Willie Witt (16), Summit Beach Park, Akron, attracted 2500 spectators, May 24, 1920; Lisey won match in three straight games, 50-37, 50-39, 50-34. Home: Marshallville, Ohio

LITTLE, T. R., b. February 22, 1919. President, Tennessee State HPA. W. Lorene; child—Judith Ann. Senior serviceman, Tennessee Valley Authority. S. Ohio Pro; t. one and three quarters, left handed. President, Cleveland local club, since 1965; instrumental in construction and maintenance of 12 outdoor courts, Cleveland; won Bradley County Championship, 1930; his high average, 74.8%, Bull's Gap open tournament, 1974; high game, 90.5% in a Cleveland tournament, 38 ringers out of 42 against Rogers Norwood, May 1980; won four open tournament Class A titles. Home: 2785 Patterson Road, Cleveland, Tennessee 37311.

LOMBARDI, LEONARD, d. 1936 Maine State Champion, 11-0-62.8%.

LONG, LESLIE, b. April 3, 1914. 1975, 1977, 1979 Illinois Senior State Champion. W. Wilma; children—Leonard, Vernon, Wedon, Warren. Farmer. S. Allen; t. one and a quarter, right handed. President/tournament director, Bradenton Horseshoe Club (Florida); President/director, Rock River Valley Club, Illinois, and secretary/director, Twin City Club; conducted 44 NHPA open tournaments, 25 on Labor Day, 19 on Memorial Day; started a 50 shoe count-all play in Northern Illinois, which now prevails; won Plant City Class A title three times, Orlando Open twice, Miami Open, once (for which he won a three-day vacation in Bahamas); finished second, Class B, World Tournament; finished second, missing title by two points, Illinois state meet, 1970; suffered stroke, 1972, but came back to a 60% average and won three Senior State titles thereafter. Was fast-pitch softball player. Home: Route 1, Sterling, Illinois 61081.

LONG, S., 1980 Tennessee Women's State Champion, 5-0-23.6%.

LORD ALBERT, b. February 7, 1929. Maine State Champion nine times. Single. Son of Orrin and Gladys Lord. Machinist's helper. S. Imperial; t. one and three quarters, right handed. Won New England Championship three times; finished 8th, World Tournament, out of field of 503, posting a record of 21-10-73%; won Maine Spring Roundup, 1967; won first Maine state title, 1968, during following ten years won eight championships and two seconds, in a ten-year period of 60 tournaments, averaging 70% or better in 18 of them; high tournament, 79.6%, Maine State Tournament, 1974; averaged 77.6%, 12-1, 2nd place finish, New England Tournament, 1974; pitched in Championship Division, World Tournament, 71.6%, 1974, 13-10-71.4%, 1977, 1980, Class B, 64.8%, 1964; won Maine Open, Maine State, Vermont Open, averaging 75%, 1978; finished second, Keene Open, New England Championships, 1978; won Maine Spring Roundup, 82.2% for five games, Maine Open, 69.3%, New England Championship, 78.6%, 1979; won Keene Open, 77.3%, 1980; high game, 93.2%, 41 out of 44 against Mike Patenaude. Home: 60½ Elm Street, Mechanic Falls, Maine 04256.

LOSETH, OTTO, North Dakota State Champion, 1934, 10-1, 1946, 9-0, 1947, 9-0, 1955, 7-1.

LOUCKS, DAVE, b. June 1, 1937. Junior Boys World Champion, 1951, 1952, 1953. W. Cathie; children—Garth, Susan, Mark, Ryan. Owner/operator, "What's the Score" Baseball-Softball Slo Pitch Scorebooks. S. Allen; t. one and three quarters and one and a quarter, right handed. 1951 record, 15-0-47.9%, 15 wins in one tournament for all-time high; high game, 86.5%, San Francisco Youth City Tournament, 1951; past secretary-treasurer, Northern California HPA, four years; pitched 30 years; member, NHPA, 25 years. Home: P.O. Box 1055, Cupertino, California 95015.

LOUDERMILK, CONNIE S., b. December 19, 1945. West Virginia State Champion, 1973, 1975. H. Kyle; children—Jeffrey, Dana. Housewife. S. Imperial; t. flip, right handed. Won league championship, Ronceverte, 1975; high tournament, 40%; high game, 60.2%; pitched in all men's Pioneer Days Parade, Marlinton, W. Va. Home: Box 101, Frankford, West Virginia 24938.

LOVELACE, STANLEY P., b. October 21, 1926. Finished second, three times, state tournament. W. Gladys; children—Terry, Tony. Machinery operator, Binding Standard Publishers. S. Allen; t. one and a quarter, right handed. High tournament, 73.3%; pitched 22 years. Enjoys bowling, averaging 203. Home: 825 Crescent Avenue, Covington, Kentucky 41011.

LOVELADY, ROBERTA, 1977 California Girls State Champion, 26.4%. Home: No. 5 Herbert Court, Pacifica, California 94044.

LOY, CANDY, b. November 29, 1934. 1977 Indiana State Champion, 1976 Indoor State Champion. H. Gene; children—Teresa, Trudy, Jimmie, Kitty, Shelley. Factory-Sheller-Globe. S. Gordon; t. flip, right handed. Tournament wins include: 1969 Clyde Green Memorial, 1973 Ben Shores Memorial, Eastern Indiana and Indiana-Ohio Open, 1975 Ohio-Indiana-Illinois Open, 1976 Indiana Indoor State, Ben Shores Memorial, Bicentennial and Midwest Ringer Roundup, 1977 Rose Festival and Newcastle Open, 1979 Eastern Indiana and Ohio-Indiana Opens, and 1980 Connersville Open; qualified for Championship Division, World Tournament, 1977; high tournament, 73%; high game, 80%. Home: 826 Hickory Street, Union City, Indiana 47390.

LOZANSKI, TED, b. 1926. d. 1976. Manitoba Provincial Champion, 1955, 1956, 1963, 1964, 1967, 1968. Won Doubles title with Sifton Rasmussen, 1971; organizer and promoter of horseshoe pitching; served as executive, Manitoba Horseshoe Players Association, 1948; inducted into Manitoba HPA Hall of Fame, 1979. Home: Brandon, Manitoba.

LUCAS, AL, Past State Secretary, Louisiana State HPA. Home: 621 27th Street, Kenner, Louisiana 70062.

LUCAS, JEFF, 1974 Alabama Boys State Champion, 3-0-18%.

LUND, MARGARET, 1923 Minnesota Women's State Champion.

LUNDGREN, CARL, Finished second to Bobby Hitt, 1937 Michigan State Tournament. Pitched 60 years; hit 8-3-56.7%, World Tournament, Senior Division; won Class A tournaments, had many games in 80% bracket. Home:Detroit, Michigan.

LUNDIN, FRANK, b. March 27, 1900. 1922 World Champion, Member, National Hall of Fame, 1978. W. Lola. Shoe repair- and salesman. S. National Standard; t. one and three quarters, right handed. Won World Championship, 1922, with 14-1, 424 ringers; won Iowa State Championship, 1922, 1923; finished second, 28-1-51.5% (losing only to Harold Falor), World Tournament, 1923; shoulder injury ended pitching career at age 23; won several county tournaments; inducted into Iowa Hawkeye HPA, 1976. Home: 300 South Walnut Street, New London, Iowa 52645.

LUNSFORD HOWARD, b. August 8, 1915. 1973 North Carolina State Champion. W. Anna Lee; children—Charles Howard, Becky Forrest, Linda Robinson, William Herschel, Vicki Gail. Maintenance employee, Thomasville Furniture Industries. S. Allen; t. one and a quarter, right handed. Won North Carolina State AAU Championship, 1972; averaged 65%; won game in Southeastern Classic, Winston-Salem, over World Champion Harold Reno; won Greensboro Open, 1972. Enjoys bowling. Home: 6411 Robin Hood Road, Pfafftown, North Carolina 27040.

LUOMA, WAYNE H., SR., b. November 28, 1927. Director, Northeast Ohio District of OBSHPA. W. Carolyn; children—Billie Marie, Wayne, Jr., Larry Martin, Glen Edward. Maintenance employee. S. Diamond Super Ringer or Imperial; t. one and a quarter, right handed. Won Burton Championship fourteen times; won Geauga County Fair and the Times Leader Tournament; president, Burton, Ohio, club; high tournament, 65%; high game, 133 in count-all league play; won 163 trophies, most are first place in his class; finished second, Class C, World Tournament, 1977; qualified in Class A, Greenville Classic, 1979. Home: 14035 Butternut Road, Burton, Ohio 44021.

LUOTO, PHIL, d. November 11, 1972. Member, Washington HPA Hall of Fame. Worked as promoter for World Tournament participants from Washngton.

LUTE, IVAN, 1948 Pennsylvania State Champion.

LYBECK, BILL, North Dakota State Champion, 1949, 10-1, 1950, 10-1, 1951, 8-1. Left handed.

LYKKEN, GENE, North Dakota State Champion, 1958, 10-1-61%, 1962, 9-0-64.3%. Won Red River Valley Open, 1964.

LYKKEN, RUDY, League and tournament coordinator. Made scoring devices and promoted the sport in North Dakota for many years; uncle of Gene Lykken.

M

McBRIDE, MATE, b. September 24, 1916. 1975 Utah State Champion. W. Merna; children—Shirley, Patty, Kathy. Civil Service employee. S. Deadeye; t. one and a quarter, right handed. Past secretary, Utah State HPA; won California Class B state title, 1979; won Northern California Seniors Championship, 1979; high game, 84%; pitched 30 years, 28 in tournament play. Enjoys playing in harmonica band. Home: 2308 Estrellita Way, Sacramento, California 95825.

McCAMEY, HARLEY, 1972 Tennessee State Champion, 69.9%, 10-1. Set state record with Dexter Stallings for most four-deads in one game with nineteen, and consecutive four-deads with seven, 1973 state tournament.

McCANCE, DON E., b. September 25, 1937. Nebraska State Champion, 20 times from 1957–79. W. Orva; children—Kent L., Karla A. Manager, Big Valley Building Center. S. Allen; t. one and a quarter, right handed. Won first title at age 20, entered Na-

tional Tournament, finished 17th; member, Nebraska Hall of Fame Committee; elected vice-president, 1958, 1964, president, 1970, NHPA; played in organized tournaments since 1953, pitched in state tournament 26 consecutive years; member, NHPA, 26 years; high tournament, 7-0-78.6%, Tri-State (Wyo-Colo-Nebr), 1979. Home: 953 West 11th, Lexington, Nebraska 68850.

McCANCE, KENT, b. February 21, 1960. Nebraska Boys State Champion, 1971, 1973, 1975. Single. Student. S. Allen; t. one and a quarter, right handed. Runnerup, state tournament, 1972; averaged 32.4%, 1973; high tournament, 44.7%, 1975. Home: 953 West 11th, Lexington, Nebraska 68850.

McCHARREN, ROBERT D., b. September 22, 1949. 1970 New Mexico State Champion, 6-1-48.9%. W. Michelle; children—Kristin, Maile, Robert, Marni. Manufacturer's sales representative. S. Deadeye or Ohio Pro; t. one and three quarters, right handed. Past editor, Texas HPA publication. Enjoys golf. Home: 6838 Desert Rose Lane, Houston, Texas 77086.

McCHESNEY, WALTER "ERNIE," b. June 20, 1918. d. November 10, 1977. 1964 Montana State Champion, 7-0-58.7%. W. Lois; children—Robert, Mary, Steven, Kathy. Farmer. Right handed. Won numerous trophies; died in automobile accident. Home: 626 9th Avenue SW, Sidney, Montana 59270.

McCLELLAND, CHARLES, 1924 Nebraska State Champion.

McCLINTOCK, BOBBY DEAN, b. December 31, 1964. 1979 West Virginia State Champion. Single. Student. S. Ohio Pro; t. one and a quarter, right handed. Home: 346 Poplar Avenue, Moundsville, West Virginia 26041.

McCLINTOCK, WAYNE, b. October 18, 1963. 1980 West Virginia State Champion, 8-

1-51.2%. Student. S. Gordon; t. one and three quarters, left handed. Won playoff over Charles Bertrand after 8-1 tie in regulation play. Home: 346 Poplar Avenue, Moundsville, West Virginia 26041.

McCOLLAM, LESTER, Kansas State Champion, 1931, 11-0-65%, 1932, 6-1-66%. Home: Kincaid.

McCOMBS, JACKIE, b. May 1, 1937. Class A Champion, North Carolina Dogwood Festival, and the Marion Open, 1977. H. James; children—James III, Jeanie, Cathi, David, Terri. Real estate salesperson. S. Ohio O; t. flip, right handed. Pitched in Class A, Ohio State Tournament her first year pitching; pitched Class A, World Tournament, Keene, New Hampshire, 1974 (second year of pitching); played in 1976 Farmfest with Ruth Hangen, Vicki Winston, Pat Eaton; served on Housing Committee, Greenville, World Tournament, 1972, 1977; sustained back injury, auto accident, 1977–79. Home: 774 Primrose Drive, Greenville, Ohio 45331.

McCOMBS, JIM, JR., b. August 30, 1935. President. Ohio Buckeye HPA. W. Jacqueline; children—Jeannie, Jimmy, Cathie, David, Terri. Realtor. S. Allen; t. one and a quarter, right handed. Finished second, Class A (one loss), high tournament, 67%, Snowball Tournament; won Class A Championship, Indiana Rosebud Festival, 64%; qualified in Class A, Ohio State Tournament, finished ninth, high game, 80%; received achievement award, promotion and staging of World Tournament, NHPA, 1977; vice-president, Darke County Horseshoe Club, six years, president, one year; opened Northeast District of Ohio (largest of five districts); pitched NHPA tournament since 1964. Home: 774 Primrose Drive, Greenville, Ohio 45331.

McCONNELL, CHET, d. July 10, 1980. Nebraska Centennial Brown County Cham-pion, 1958. W. Virginia. Served as president, Ainsworth Horseshoe Club (which he helped organize); chosen Man of the Year, 1978; conducted Brown County Fair Tournament every year. Home: Ainsworth, Nebraska.

McCORKENDALE, ARVEL, 1980 Missouri Senior State Champion, 7-0-53.7%. Home: P.O. Box 81, Camden, Missouri 64017.

McCOSKEY, HERBERT, b. August 10, 1917. Kentucky State Fair Champion, 1962. W. Clarice; children—Judy Jean Geddes, Sue Jane, Jan Darlene Hobson, Marshall. Farmer/custom operator. S. Bronze Lee, Allen, Ohio; t. one and a quarter, one and three quarters, right handed. Won 75 trophies, including three consecutive Scottsburg League titles, Browntown Sesquicentennial, 1966, Scott County Fair, Pekin July Fourth Open, 1971, New Albany Open, 72%, 1969, Campbellsburg Fall Festival, 1969; traveled two years with Scottsburg, A.H.P.A., two years with Bloomington team; high game, 92%, in qualifying round, Washington County Fair, 1965; averaged above 70% for several seasons. Home: Route 2, Pekin, Indiana 47165.

McCOY, ELMER, Kentucky State Champion, 1939, 1940, 1941.

McELDOWNEY, CHERYL, b. 1965. Finished third, Ohio State Tournament, 1980. Daughter of Tom and Rita McEldowney. Student. S. Gordon; t. flip, right handed. Runner-up, Class A, Greenville Ringer Classic, 1979; finished third, Class A, Ohio State Tournament, 1979; participated in World Tournament, 1979, 1980. Home: 5494 Horatio Harris Cr. Road, Greenville, Ohio 45331.

McELDOWNEY, LORI, b. 1968. Daughter of Tom and Rita McEldowney. Student. S. Gordon; t. flip, right handed. Competes in Ohio State, Greenville Classic and World tournaments, 40% ringers. Home: 5494 Horatio Harris Cr. Road, Greenville, Ohio 45331.

McELDOWNEY, TOM, b. March 21, 1940. Trustee, Darke County Horseshoe Club, nine years. W. Rita; children—Theresa, Cheryl, Dennis, Lori. Factory worker. S. Ohio Pro; t. one and a quarter, right handed. Won Knights of Columbus state championship, 1970, 1972, 1974; won 30 trophies; played Class C, once, Class B, three times, Class A, twice (best finish: ninth), Ohio State Tournaments; averages 65%. Home: 5494 Horatio Harris Cr. Road, Greenville, Ohio 45331.

McFARLAND, EDWARD J., b. November 20, 1916. Texas State Champion, sixteen times, Charter Member, Texas HPA Hall of Fame. W. Joyce M.; children—Thomas, Barbara Jeanne, David. Petroleum landman, Exxon Co., U.S.A. S. Allen; Ohio, Imperial; t. one and a quarter, right handed. High tournament, 77%; high game, 94%; pitched since 1934; first league play in Greater Pittsburg Horseshoe Pitching League (14 teams), 1936; member, NHPA, since 1948; played Championship Division, World Tournament, 1949, 1950, 1970; member, National Hall of Fame Committee; past treasurer, Texas State HPA; held office in three state associations: Pennsylvania, Texas, California. Home: 211 Wroxton Drive, Conroe, Texas 77304.

McFATRIDGE, GRAYDON, b. October 5, 1911. d. 1972. Indiana State Champion, 1949, 1950, 1951. S. Allen; t. one and a quarter, one and three quarters, right handed, pitched left handed at times. Pitched 51 years; averaged 75% right handed, 40% left handed; championship record, 18-1-75.3%, 1949, 15-0-71%, 1950, 14-1-73.3%, 1951; qualified 406 points, 91% ringers for 150 shoes, 1956; pitched Championship Divi-

sion, World Tournament, finished 11th, 22-13-76%, 1961, 10-25-70.8%, 1962. Was amateur baseball pitcher.

McFATRIDGE, HAROLD, b. December 13, 1905. Member, NHPA, 43 years. W. Joyce; children—Alvin, Eileen Hyatt. Retired. S. Ohio; t. one and a quarter, right handed. Pitched for 60 years since 1921; served as manager, Rushville Horseshoe Club; played in 30 state tournaments, one World Tournament; finished seventh, state tournament; qualified for Championship Division, World Tournament, 1961; high game, 80%, 104 shoes; averaged 65%. Home: East Third Street, Carthage, Indiana 46115.

McGARVEY, WALTER, Past State Secretary, Idaho HPA. Home: 1234½ Alder Avenue, Lewiston, Idaho 83501.

McGEE, WAYNE, 1926 North Dakota State Champion, 10-1, pitched 204 ringers.

McGRATH, LEO, b. July 18, 1903. Member, NHPA Hall of Fame, President, Ohio Buckeye HPA, 27 years. W. Eva; children—Raymond, Donald. Foreman, Plant's Eastern Construction District. S. Gordon and Allen; t. one and a quarter, right handed. Past first vice-president, NHPA; helped run World Tournaments, worked toward increased participation, more prize money, and involvement in decision-making; pitched 13 years; high tournament, 60%; high game, 80%; won Norwood League; promoted sport 42 years, 1938–80; received Stokes Memorial Award, 1969; inducted into Ohio BHPA Hall of Fame, 1969; served as tournament director and official judge. Enjoys serving as committee chairman, Boy Scout Explorers Post 127; worked with rifle clubs. Home: 1937 Lawn Avenue, Cincinnati, Ohio 45237.

McGREGOR, ROBERT ROY, b. March 18, 1922. Vice-President, New Mexico

HPA. W. Ruth; children—Robert Leroy, Richard, Rosemary, Ronelle. Teacher of masonry. S. Ohio; t. three quarter, right handed. Finished second, Class D, New Mexico State Tournament, high game, 36%; averaged 26%. Enjoys writing, collecting pens and pencils. Home: 5944 Carlos Rey Southwest, Albuquerque, New Mexico 87105.

McGREW, HENRY M., b. September 5, 1907. 1928 Oregon State Champion, Member, Oregon HPA Hall of Fame. W. Mabel; child—Jack. Retired. S. Allen; t. one and three quarters, right handed. Finished third, tied for first, state tournament, 1927; tied for first place, won first and third games to win title, averaged 45.5%, hit 70% in final game of playoff, state tournament, 1928; helped run several Lebanon tournaments, three state tournaments, several open tournaments in Oregon; pitched 57 years, tournaments for 30 years; past president, secretary-treasurer, Lebanon Horseshoe Club; won several Lebanon tournaments; high tournament, 60%; best effort for 100 shoes, 72 ringers. Home: 34841 Tangent Drive, Albany, Oregon 97321.

McGUFFIN, LINDA, 1969, 1970 Texas Women's State Champion, 6-0-31.7% (1969), 8-0 (1970).

MACIBORSKY, PETER, 1979 Peace Country Men's Champion. Pitched since the 1930s; won singles title, University of Alberta, 1946; won first place, Dunnegan Tournament, 1971. Home: Grand Prarie, Alberta, Canada.

McISAAC, GORDON, 1977 Nova Scotia Provincial Champion (first Men's Singles Champion, received Nova Scotia Cup). Teamed with Pat Burke to win doubles title, 1978; won Maritime Championship, 1971, 36.6%, 1978, 62.1%, 1979, 64.3%; won Maritime Doubles title, with Gordon Campbell, 1971. Home: New Victoria.

McILVENE, RICHARD, 1967 New Hampshire Boys State Champion, 5-0-31.3%.

MACK, VILKO, b. December 8, 1911. 1974 Louisiana State Champion. W. Margaret. Retired. S. Ohio Pro; t. one and three quarters, right handed. Pitched 40 years, eight in NHPA tournament play; average, 65%. Home: 3205 42nd Street, Metairie, Louisiana 70001.

McKEE, ESTA B., b. May 10, 1911. 1960 Women's World Champion, 5-1-54.1%. H. Clifford, d. Teacher/housewife. S. Gordon; t. flip, right handed. Finished second, World Tournament, 54.7% average, 1961; was undefeated in five games to win Indiana State Championship, 1961; pitched eight years; high game, 80%. Enjoys sewing. Home: Route 1—Box 10, Royal Center, Indiana 46978.

McLAUGHLIN, DEAN, Canadian national Champion, 13 times, Member, NHPA Hall of Fame, 1974. T. one and three quarters. Championship record: 60%, 1938, finished second to Elmer Hohl, 73.1%, 1980, averaged 91.6%, 1960, averaged 81.8%, 1968; hit several perfect games, won countless titles; conducts clinics for younger players. Home: 160 Cadillac Avenue South, Oshawa, Ontario, Canada.

MacLEOD, WILLIAM NEY, b. February 21, 1922. President, New Rochelle Horseshoe Club. Single. Machine operator. S. Hohl; t. one and three quarters, right handed. Recipient of award from Brooklyn Horseshoe Club for outstanding dedication; pitched 45 years, 12 as NHPA member; high tournament, 55%; served as president, New Rochelle club for the last ten years. Home: 12 Mount Etna Place, New Rochelle, New York 10805.

McMAHON, WILLIAM JOSEPH, b. January 1, 1928. Member, Massachusetts Hall of Fame Committee. W. Grayce Ann. Rigger. S. Ohio O; t. three quarters, right handed. Maintains state and Hall of Fame photo albums, prepare annual display at Heritage Recreation honoring all state champions; executive board member; won 50 trophies in ten years for first, second and third place finishes; played in Tournament of Champions every year from 1973–80. Enjoys singing with Boston Choral Society, Revere Men's Glee Club, American Federation of Men's Glee Clubs; has sung national athem at opening ceremonies at horseshoe tournaments including World Tournament, Lafayette, Indiana. Home: 98 Goodyear Avenue, Melrose, Massachusetts 02176.

McNAMARA, JOSEPH, Pitched for 70 years. Played in Class B, World Tournament, 1959, Murray, Utah; record for three World Tournaments, Senior Division, 4-26-36.7%. Home: 2135 Fair Park Avenue, Los Angeles, California 90041.

McNEECE, WILLARD, b. July 20, 1919. Class A Competitor, Indiana tournaments. W. Evelyn. Factory worker. S. Allen; t. one and three quarters, right handed. High game, 88%, Robinson Open; high tournament, 71%, Cayuga; hit 13 consecutive doubles in one game; began tournament play 1974. Home: P.O. Box 91, Patoka, Indiana 47666.

McNEILL, BARBARA R., b. April 18, 1946. 1980 Massachusetts Women's State Champion, 3-1-37.2%. H. Charles; children—Brenda, Charles, Jr., Barbara, Lisa, Denise. Machine press operator. S. Allen; t. three quarters, right handed. Most Improved Pitcher in Massachusetts and the Northeast, 1979, 1980; won four tournaments, high average, 46%; high game, 70%. Enjoys knitting, camping. Home: 37 Main Street, P.O. Box 124, Upton, Massachusetts 01568.

McNEAL, MELVIN, 1968 Missouri Boys State Champion, two out of three playoff.

McPHERSON, DEBBIE, 1980 Georgia Women's State Champion, 6-0-34.4%.

McSWANE, DOROTHY, 1975 Washington Women's State Champion, 61.9%.

McTAGGART, KEVIN, b. October 19, 1965. Georgia Boys State Champion, 1978, 1979, 1980. Son of James McTaggart. Student. S. Gordon; t. three quarters, right handed. Posted 72.8% ringers, 1979; undefeated in three years of championship; high sanctioned game, 78.2%; 1980 record: 2-0-51.8%. Home: P.O. Box 182, Nelson, Georgia 30151.

MADDOX, RALPH, b. October 23, 1922. 1980 member NHPA Hall of Fame West Virginia State Champion 25 times. W.; two children. Chemical operator. S. Ohio Pro; t. one and three quarters, right handed. Member, West Virginia Hall of Fame; was highest qualifier, 87%, World Tournament, 1961; finished ninth world torunament, Greenville, Ohio, 1964; established three world records for 34 games pitching 3476 shoes, 2903 ringers, 1173 doubles, 25-10, above 80%; pitched 45 years, 44 in organized competition. Home: Route 1, Box 83, Poca, West Virginia 25159.

MADSEN, ALMA A., b. July 3, 1911. Utah State Champion, 1969, 10-1-58.7%, 1970, 9-2-53.8%. W. Lois; children—Clifford, Don, Calvin, Colleen, Betty Jean, Annette. Meter superintendent, Utah Power and Light Company. S. Gordon; t. one and a quarter, right handed. Served as horseshoe tournament director, 35 years, American Fork Annual Celebration; secretary, Utah HPA, 1969–70, and acting president at death of President Carl Davis; won Utah County Championship 22 years out of 35 years that it has been conducted; won Class B State Championship, 1943, 1952, 1953, 1966; pitched 42 years, 40 in tournament competition. Home: 136 South 100 West American Fork, Utah 84003.

MADSEN, BOB, 1956 Boys World Champion (Murray City, Utah), 4-1-45.2%.

MAGNUSON, GUST, b. June 8, 1907. 1972 Minnesota State Champion. W. Renora, d.; children—Greta Shewstad, Grant. Farmer/maintenance man. S. Allen or Ohio; t. three quarter, right handed. Championship record, 10-1-73.4%; set two qualifying records in state tournament play, 91 ringers and 282 points in 100 shoes; won over 100 trophies; defeated Dan Kuchcinski, Red River Open, 84.2%, 1968; hit 90% game, 45 of 50, Fargo indoor league, and 90.2% for entire tournament, Toronto, South Dakota, 1935; served as treasurer, local league, 16 years; pitched 56 years in competition. Home: Box 15, Apt. 206, Northside Terrace, Hawley, Minnesota 56549.

MAHONEY, LAWRENCE F., b. September 19, 1919. New Jersey State Champion nine times, Member, NJSHPA Hall of Fame, 1972. W. Paula M.; children—Patricia M. Fowler, Barbara J. Special police officer/ school custodian. S. Gordon; t. one and three quarters, right handed. State title record: 1934-40, 1947-48, his 73.6% average for 1940 tournament still stands as state record; won 1934 Trenton State Fair, the Metropolitan Open, 1938 Hudson County Open, 8-1-78.4%, Central Jersey Open; in game against New York State Champion William Hamman, hit 111 ringers, Hamman 109, out of 132 shoes, hit 35 consecutive ringers, 17 consecutive four-deads exceed by two the record for world tournament play; hit 89.5% game against John Fulton, 28 consecutive ringers against Vito Feliccia, a three best of five win over Ted Allen (Jersey City), an avereage of 79.6% for five game match against Feliccia at Jersey City, won all games; captained a U.S. team which defeated a Canadian team before 6000 people, Exposition Stadium, Toronto, with Ken Hurst, 1937; defeated Canadian Champion Dean McLaughlin, 50-38; won Canadian Open, 11-1-75.4%, high game, 87%, Toronto, 1940; won Dominion Open, 77.9%; hit state record game, 12.85%, against Russell Ontko, New Jersey State Tournament, 1939; played in World Tournament, Moline, Illinois, 1940; underwent surgery, December 1979; served in U.S. Army, 1940–45. Home: 615 Newman Springs Road, Lincroft, New Jersey 07738.

MAISON, GERALD "DOC," b. September 15, 1915. Michigan State Champion, 1971, 1972, 1975, 1978, 1979. W. Winifred; five daughters. Chrysler Corporation employee. S. Allen and Imperial; t. one and three quarters, right handed. Won 200 tournaments; named Most Improved Player, 1971 World Tournament; high tournament, 82%; hit 38 consecutive ringers against Roy Smith for state crown. Home: 23574 Stewart, Warren, Michigan 48089.

MAITLEN, HARRISON, b. April 25, 1917. Selected to Indiana All-Star Tournament for television series "Championship Horseshoes." W. Jessie "Knuckles"; child—Darrell. Farmer/factory worker. S. Allen; t. one a quarter, right handed. Won more than 100 tournaments, including Adams County Championship, 15 times, Greenville, three times, 1956 Corn Belt Open, Celina Open, Northern Indiana Open, five times, Van Wert Open, five times, Ohio City Open; hit 99 ringers out of 100 shoes, and 100% game; set state record with Bill Nielson, 10 four-deads in a row, 1956 Indiana State Tournament; lost match game to Guy Binkley, 51-49, each averaged 92% in game featuring 22 consecutive four-deads and lasted over 200 shoes; served as president and secretary-treasurer, local club; attended International Business College. Enjoys bowling and promoting horseshoes as sport. Home: Route 2, Berne, Indiana 46711.

MAJEWSKI, DOMINIC J., b. March 11, 1919. 1963, 1964 Connecticut State Champion. W. Louise; children—Vincent John, Donna Louise Simao. Foreman. S. Allen; t. one and three quarters, right handed. Finished second, New England Tournament; high game, 80%; high tournament, 70%; won nearly 100 trophies; constructed regulation court in his home. Home: 24 Jay Street, East Hartford, Connecticut 06118.

MAKI, ARNE, 1928 Minnesota State Champion, St. Louis County Fair. Participated thirty years later, Minnesota State Tournament, Bennett Park, Hibbing.

MALVERN, JIM, 1967 Washington Boys State Champion, 5-0-64.2%.

MALVITZ, WILLIAM A., b. June 12, 1947. 1961 Michigan Boys State Champion. W. Marie; children—Emily, Laurel. Architect, registered in Michigan. S. Ohio, Allen; t. one and three quarters, right handed. Was runnerup, Michigan Boys State Championship, 1962; high game, 60%. Enjoys baseball, golf, bowling, racquetball, photography. Home: 38 Amherst, Pleasant Ridge, Michigan 48069.

MANCINI, JOSEPH J., b. November 9, 1919. Secretary-Treasurer, Pennsylvania HPA. W. Pauline; children—Joseph, Jr., Darlene. S. Imperial; t. one and three quarters, right handed. Secretary-treasurer, New Castle Club; member, Hall of Fame committee; won Class G, 1971 State Tournament, and Class E, 1978 Eastern National. Home: 1025 Dewey Avenue, New Castle, Pennsylvania 16101.

MANKER, STANLEY J., b. September 28, 1905. Senior World Champion, 1971, 1974, 1975, 1978, 1979, Member, NHPA Hall of Fame, 1977. S. Ohio; t. one and three quarters, left handed. Won Ohio State A.A.U. Title, 1942; finished third, National A.A.U. Tournament, 1942; organized local club, Wilmington, 1948 (oldest club in state); won Ohio State Title under NHPA sanction,

1955; recipient, first Sportsmanship Award given, World Tournament, 1959; played 25 years of World Tournaments, 13 years in Championship Division, five years in Class B, seven years in Senior Division (45-4); holds world records in Senior Division: high average, 74.2%, high game, 83.3%, high qualifying points, 271, high qualifying ringers, 86, high qualifying doubles, 38; built courts, organized play for boys, Lynchburg, Ohio; served as NHPA regional director; designed the Ohio pitching shoe; wrote article, "How to Build Horseshoe Courts," used in original NHPA Horseshoe Pitchers' Manual; provided drawings also; hit 92.8% game against Jim Knisley, Columbus, Ohio; hit 90% game against Dan Kuchcinski, Erie, Pa., pro tournament; hit 87.5% game against Carl Steinfeldt, Keene, New Hampshire World Tournament; won 50-46 over Elmer Hohl, Marion, Ohio, 1977; traveled 10,000 miles, walked 60 miles in game play, threw 20 tons of steel in a typical year; distributed Ohio Horseshoes for more than 40 years; considered "ambassador of good will" for horseshoes. Home: Box 214, Lynchburg, Ohio 45142.

MANN, HOWARD "BUCK," b. December 15, 1923. Chairman, West Virginia HPA Hall of Fame Committee. W. Maxine; children—Barbara Aidala, Coleen Ford, Linda Wheeler, Cinda Miller, Howard, Tina. Sales administrator, Bendix Corporation. S. Imperial; t. one and a quarter, right handed. President, West Virginia HPA, 1976; president, Mountaineer League; played in Class A in three state tournaments; played four World Tournaments; high game, 66.7%, against K. Stinchcomb, 1976 World Tournament; high tournament, 58.4%, Buena Vista, Virginia; pitched in 45 tournaments, won five, finished second five times; won 130 of 321 tournament matches, averaging 44%; longest game, 50-49 loss to Richard Wiseman, Glen Maury Open, 1976; won Class H, 1977, and

Class J, 1979, World Tournament; Most Improved Player, Player of the Year, recipient, Achievement Award, Mountaineer Horseshoe Club, Ronceverte, 1979. Home: 117 Goheen Street, Fairlea, West Virginia 24902.

MANN, NORA, 1973 Texas Women's Champion.

MARCUM, DANNY, 1963 Ohio Boys State Champion, 9-0-51.2%. Pitched in men's tournament play, averaging 65% or better. Home: 1132 Harmon Avenue, Hamilton, Ohio 45011.

MARCEVICH, CZAR G., b. March 5, 1916. Member, Northern California HPA Hall of Fame. W. Helen. Retired, Oakland Navy Supply Center. S. Gordon; t. one and three quarters, right handed. President, Northern Califronia HPA, ten years; NHPA regional director, for Pacific Coast, 1959–60; president, ten years, and vice-president, Mosswood Horseshoe Club (which awarded him lifetime membership for his efforts on its behalf); won Alameda County Championship, 1944–55; won Northern California Championship, Golden Gate Park, 1937; played in Class A, World Tournament, Murray, Utah, 70.6%, 1958; runnerup, California State Championship, Santa Clara Fair, San Jose; played against World Champions Ted Allen, Fernando Isais, Frank Jackson, Putt Mossman, Guy Zimmerman, Don Titcomb; hit 16 consecutive doubles, state tournament; helped Fleet Admiral Chester Nimitz build horseshoe court in his backyard, and played with Nimitz, Berley; a Czar Marcevich Open Tournament was staged to celebrate 50th anniversary of Mosswood Horseshoe Club (est. 1929), now an annual event; president, St. George Orthodox Church, 1970–73. Home: 622 Boulevard Way, Oakland, California 94610.

MARDENSEN, JANET CHRISTENSEN, 1975 and 1976 Iowa Girls State Champion.

H. Marty; child—Ryan. Bookkeeper, Atlantic State Bank; S. Gordon or Allen; t. flip, right handed. Home: Anita, Iowa 50020.

MARKLE, JEAN, Secretary-Treasurer, Canadian National HPA, since 1972. H. Larry. Vice-president, Ontario Provincial HPA, a 600-member association; does not pitch; makes game-related items, blankets, cushions, jewelry. Home: 705-1185 Fennel Avenue E, Hamilton, Ontario L8T 1S4 Canada.

MARLATT, MIKE, 1969 Wyoming Boys State Champion 9-3-32.1%.

MARONI, RICHARD, 1969 Class C World Champion, 71.5%. Class A contender for Pannsylvania State title; made championship division, World Tournament, winning ten games, averaging mid-60%, 1971, 1972. Home: 1914 Victoria Avenue, Arnold, Pennsylvania 15068.

MAROON, DELBERT, b. August 1, 1935. Past President, Illinois State HPA. W. Eleanora; child—John David. Public school administrator. S. Allen; t. one and three quarters, right handed. Member, NHPA, 20 years; high game, 86%; high tournament, 73%; member, Hall of Fame Committee, Illinois State HPA. Home: Route 1-Box 284, Altamont, Illinois 62411.

MARSH, BETTY MAE, b. May 23, 1932. North Carolina Women's State Champion, 1974, 1975, 1976, 1978, 1979. H. Fredrow; children—Roger Lee, Bobby Ray, Billy Gray, Richard Dale, Ronnie Eugene, Margaret Ann, Janet Mae, Sandra Kay. Housewife. S. American; t. flip, right handed. High tournament, 67%; high game, 78%. Enjoys fishing. Home: 2645 Shepherd Hill Street, Kernesville, North Carolina 27284.

MARSH, SANDRA KAY, b. May 1, 1962. 1975 North Carolina Girls State Champion. Single. S. Diamond; t. flip, right handed. Won Statesville July Fourth Open, 1975;

Top, left to right, Gertrude Law, World Champion; Mary Lee, World Champion; Anna Lindquist and Esta McKee, runner-up and winner of the 1960 Muncie, Indiana, World Tournament; Dave Loucks, World Champion. *Center, left,* Frank Lundin, World Champion. *Right,* 1980 World Tournament, Class A, Huntsville, Alabama. *At left,* Stanley Manker, Hall of Fame member.

Top, left, Jean Markle. *Center,* Ray Markle, Hall of Fame member. *Right,* Clyde Martz. *Left center,* George May, World Champion and Hall of Fame member. *Bottom row, left to right,* Loran A. May, World Champion; Deborah Michaud, World Champion; John Monasmith, World Champion and Hall of Fame member; Oren Mossman, World Champion and Hall of Fame member. *At right,* Edward Murray, Canadian publisher.

was junior champion and runnerup in women's division, North Carolina-South Carolina Tournament, 1975. Enjoys baseball, softball. Home: 2645 Shepherd Hill Street, Kernersville, North Carolina 27284.

MARTIN, CLYDE, b. May 29, 1937. Past Vice-President, Virginia HPA. W. Mary. children—Clyde, Jr., Gerald, Keith, Debbie Higgins, Kathy, Deedre. Sawyer. S. Allen; t. flip, right handed. Past president, Buena Vista Horseshoe Club; won one major Class A Championship; was contender in tournaments in Virginia, West Virginia, Maryland against Dale Carson, Cecil Monday, Ralph Maddox; underwent back operation, 1978. Home: 2230 Sycamore Avenue, Buena Vista, Virginia 24416.

MARTIN, RAY, b. October 19, 1928. 1980 Member NHPA Hall of Fame. Single. Concrete finisher. S. Ohio or Allen; t. one and three quarters, right handed. Won Danville County Fair tournament, age sixteen; won first individual open tournament championship, age 17; Illinois State Champion, 1964, 1965, 1973, 1974, 1976; runnerup, World Championship, Fargo, North Dakota, 1967; set Illinois state record with 81.6% average through 1964 state tournament; career record in Championship Division, World Tournament: 297-116-79.9%; won hundreds of Class A titles; played longest game ever pitched, against Glen Henton, World Tournament, Keene, New Hampshire, 194 shoes, 1965 (Henton hit 175 ringers, Martin 174, 63 times all four ringers were on stake). Enjoys bowling, member, Illinois Bowling Hall of Fame. Home: Route 1-Box 115, Philo, Illinois 61864.

MARTIN, RONALD M., b. September 6, 1927. Class A Donut Open Champion, 1979. W. Wanda. Employee, Beechcraft Corporation. S. Hohl, American or Allen; t. one and three quarters, left handed. Won Yukon, Oklahoma, Open, twice; finished

fifth, Pro Division, 5-4-66.1%, 1980; high tournament, 67.3%; high game, 85.7%; hit 12 consecutive doubles and nine four-deads in one game. Enjoys bowling. Home: 1830 East 52nd Street South, Wichita, Kansas 67216.

MARTIN, WOODROW W., b. April 8, 1913. 1977 Illinois State Champion. W. Frances F.; children—Mary, Joanne. Carpenter. S. Allen; t. one and three quarters, right handed. Won Intermediate World Championship, 1977; won many Class A championships in Illinois tournaments; played 22 years, tournament horseshoes; hit 72.9% for seven-game tournament, 430 ringers out of 590 shoes, 1977; hit 156 ringers, 63 doubles, 19 four-deads, with Harvey Kohlenberger; placed in top ten in Illinois for ten years; finished second for state championship, twice. Enjoys bowling, golf, hunting, fishing. Home: 1517 South Seventh Street, Pekin, Illinois 61554.

MARTINDALE, CAL, 1966 Washington Boys State Champion, 6-0-28.1%. Home: 209 North Acacia Avenue, Apt. A, Fullerton, California 92631.

MARTZ, CLYDE W., b. April 23, 1934. Pennsylvania State Champion, 1970, 1973, Manufacturer of Imperial Shoe. W. Lois; children—Susan, Holly, Cathy. Personnel manager. S. Imperial; t. one and a quarter, right handed. Advocated substitution of new substance for clay, changing scoring system to make it more attractive and understandable to spectators, attracting more money to the game, giving more decision-making power to horseshoe club officers; posted tournament average of 83%, Pike County, Ohio, Indoor Open, 1976; for state title, 1970, hit 81.6%, 1973, 81.6%; best finish in World Tournament play, fifth, 1971; hit one perfect game, 56 straight, against Jack Rainbow, Redmill; pitched since 1946, played in NHPA since 1952; past president and secretary, Pennsylvania State HPA. Home: 3726 Henley Drive, Pittsburg, Pennsylvania 15235.

MASON, ANN, b. July 18, 1922. 1960 New Hampshire Women's State Champion. H. Jess O; children—Michael, Carol Pakutha, Rita Whitney. Cashier, O.K. Fairbanks Supermarket. S. Gordon; t. flip, right handed. Championship record: 5-0-23.1%; first recognized state champion in history of New Hampshire HPA. Enjoys swimming, bowling, bicycling. Home: 46 Dale Drive, Keene, New Hampshire 03431.

MASSEY, ELAINE, 1977 West Virginia Women's State Champion.

MATHEWS, (MRS. J. R.), 1921 Women's World Champion, 1921 Minnesota Women's State Champion. World Tournament record for two years: 24-7; finished fifth, 6-5-26.2%, 1924; finished in four-way tie for title, 15-2, won three consecutive playoff games, 1921 tournament.

MATTINGLY, SAMUEL B., 1927, 1929 Kentucky State Champion. Runnerup, state tournament, 1926; finished third, 1928 state tournament. Home: 2103 West Lee Street, Louisville, Kentucky.

MAUNEY, JAMES, b. September 23, 1904. Coached Mary Lee to World Championship, 1969. W. Elizabeth. Retired. S. Allen; t. one and three quarters, right handed, left handed the last two years. Pitched 61 years, 45 in league and tournament play, 25 years in NHPA events; won Metroplitan New York City AAU Class C title, 50%, 1970; high tournament, 65%; high game, 75%; attended 25 World Tournaments, played in two. Home: 451 Casselman Street, Chula Vista, California 92010.

MAUNEY, ELIZABETH, b. 1908. Winner, SCHPA Women's Handicap, 1978. H. James. Housewife. S. Gordon; t. flip, right handed. Won 1977 Jerry Schneider

doubles, San Diego, 1979 SCHPA Double Your Money Tournament; finished second, Class D, World Tournament, 1979; high tournament, 35%; high game, 60%. Home: 451 Casselman Street-Apt. H7, Chula Vista, California 92010.

MAUZEY, ROBERT H., b. March 20, 1918. Won Sonoma County Championship, 1976, 1979, 1980. W. Yvonne; children—Wayne, Sherry French. Businessman. S. Allen; to. one and a quarter, right handed. Won Senior Championship, Northern California (Redding), 1980; president/tournament director of local club; defeated Jesse Gonzales, 74% game, and Don Titcomb, 70% or better game; high game, 82%; hit ten consecutive doubles, six consecutive four-deads in tournament play. Home: 1272 Ponderosa Drive, Petaluma, California 94952.

MAUZEY, YVONNE, b. May 25, 1925. 1979, 1980 California State Champion. H. Robert; children—Dewayne, Sherry. Retired. S. Diamond; t. flip, right handed. NHPA member, three years; won Northern California Championship, 84% high game and 64.6% tournament average, 1979; secretary/treasurer, Sonoma County Club; first vice-president, Northern California Association; won Grass Valley Invitational, 1980; Class A and tournament titles include: Golden Gate, San Jose, Vallejo, Sacramento, Stockton, Nevada City, Rio Del, Tri-Valley. Turlock, Shasta, Seaside; composite record, 43-9-34.96%, 1978;hit 2660 ringers out of 5036 shoes for 52,82%, 97-6, 1980; set state tournament record with high game, 78.3%, 7-1-62.6%, California State Championship, 1980. Home: 1272 Ponderosa Drive, Petaluma, California 94952.

MAXWELL, W. O., d. 1961 (age 81). 1960 Senior World Champion, Member, Ohio BHPA Hall of Fame, 1978. S. Gordon; t. one and a quarter, right handed. Oldest man ever to win Senior World Championship, 62.4% ringers; competed in Championship Division in World Tournament play with career record, 97-155-64.7%, average qualifying score, 475; in two appearances in Senior Division, 16-3-69.2%; won 109 games and was Class A contender, Ohio State Tournaments; pitched 66 years in tournament play. Home: Hicksville, Ohio.

MAY, BOB, b. September 22, 1922. Indiana State Indoor Championship. W. Nilah; children—Glenna, Jerry, Cynthia. Farmer. S. American; t. one and a quarter, right handed. Finished fourth, Indiana State Tournament, 8-3-70.4%, 1980; played in Championship Division, World Tournament, 9-22-66.5% (26th place finish), 1980; won outdoor Class B Championship twice; opened game with 18 consecutive doubles, hit 90% or better games, World Tournament, Keene, New Hampshire; best World Tournament performance, finished 16th, 19-16-78.6%, 1965; president, local Club. Home: Route 1, Box 221, Glenwood, Indiana 46133.

MAY, GEORGE, d. 1920, 1923 World Champion, Member, NHPA Hall of Fame, 1972. W. Blanche. Fireman. S. National Standard; t. one and a quarter. Generally credited for perfection of "open shoe," was first to use it effectively in World Tournament play, 1920; first man to average over 50% ringers—open shoe revolutioned game of horseshoes; World Tournament record, 131-34-54.4%; designed and manufactured National Standard shoe, with partners Loran May (nephew), Art Headlough, Cap Stair, shoe not available today; won Wayne County Fair title, 1919; taught by Hughie Palmer, 1918 Ohio Champion. Pitched baseball for Firefighters. Home: Akron, Ohio.

MAY, LORAN, b. March 27, 1906. 1924 World Champion, Ohio State Champion 11

times. W. Mary E. "Dolly," d. 1973; W. Virginia, 1977; child—L. E.; Retired. S. National Standard; t. one and three quarters, right handed. Won Ohio Championship, 1919, went undefeated in state championship play for eleven yeras; won championship crown, NHPA Tournament (as opposed to another national horseshoe pitchers association which existed at the time and also crowned champions in their tournaments; all groups consolidated into NHPA, 1925); won state title, 1920; partner with George May, Art Headlough, Cap Stair, manufacturers of National Standard pitching shoe, est. 1922 or 1923; signed contract with Ziegfeld Follies, 1925 season, performed horseshoe trick pitching shows with brother James Alvin, Will Rogers, W. C. Fields, Brook Johns, Ann Pennington, Edna Peterson, Keely Brothers; organized Firestone Horseshoe Team, which competed in Northeastern Ohio League and others, Firestone undefeated for fifteen years; pitched for President Calvin Coolidge; defeated World Champions Ted Allen, Blair Nunamaker, and Charlie Davis in exhibition games; high tournament average, 86%; hit 70% for 43 league games, 1936; pitched 72-game "marathon" in a state tournament at Mansfield. Played basketball, baseball; enjoys hunting, fishing. Home: 4692 Tahiti Drive, Akron, Ohio 44319.

MAY, MARVIN B., b. June 2, 1933. Virginia State Secretary, 11 years. W. Fay; children—David, Kevin. General contractor. S. Imperial; t. one and three quarters, right handed. Joined NHPA, was key man in establishment of Virginia State Chapter, 1959, served as state secretary, 1959–70; served as Southeastern regional director, three years; won Tri-County Championship twice; runnerup, Virginia State Championship, 1960; won several invitational tournaments and division titles; high game 85%; high qualifying score, 256, most consecutive ringers, 22, six consecutive four-deads. Home: 208 Pearson Drive, Lynchburg, Virginia 24502.

MAYLAHN, RALPH, 1972 Wisconsin State Champion, 6-0-73.1%. Home: 8661 West Ohio Avenue, Milwaukee, Wisconsin 53227.

MAYS, CHADWICK, b. April 27, 1915. Organized Tournament and League Play, Delaware, Ohio, 1948. W. Julia; children—Phyllis Rockhold, Patricia Davidson, Barbara Myers, Steven. Tool grinder. S. Deadeye; t. one and a quarter, right handed. Played in Ohio State Tournaments since 1955; high tournament, 58%, 1962; high game, 74%, Muncie, Indiana, 1961; best string of doubles, eight in a row to end a game; pitched 53 years. Home: 308 South Leighton Street, Kenton, Ohio 43326.

MEAGER, TOM, Missouri State Champion, 1921, 1924, 1925, 1928, 1929.

MEBERG, BEN, Charter Member, Saskatchewan Hall of Fame, 1976. Won Saskatchewan Championship, 1956.

MELISSA, JERRY, 1978 British Columbia Champion, 57.4%. Runnerup to Elmer Hohl, Canadian National Championship, 9-2-66.5%, 1975. Home: Duncan.

MELLING, KATHY, 1974 Ohio Girls State Champion, 3-0-33.5%.

MENDENHALL, EUGENE, b. September 4, 1912. Class B World Champion, 61.9%, 1958. W. Phyllis. Mail carrier. S. Allen; t. one and a quarter, right handed. Member, NHPA, 32 years, pitched fifty years, 34 in league and tournament play; elected Most Improved Player, World tournament, 1962; served as second vice-president, Indiana HPA; high tournament average, 75%; high game, 80% or better; best qualifying round, 284 for 100 shoes, Galesburg. Home: 1308 Division Street, Noblesville, Indiana 46060.

MENRCHIK, STEVE, 1934 Pennsylvania State Champion.

MERCHANT, E. M., 1922 Kentucky State Champion.

MEREDITH, ELLA H., b. September 13, 1921. Past Secretary, Nebraska State HPA. H. Ralph; children—Dennis, Robert. Cook. Right handed. Enjoys reading, sewing. Home: 1105 Seventh Street, Fairbury, Nebraska 68352.

MERRIT, JOSEPH, 1979 Massachusetts Doubles Champion. Home: 222 East River Street, Orange, Massachusetts 01364.

MERRIT, MELVIN, Member, New England Hall of Fame, 1975. Won New England Championship once, finished second twice, third once; won Massachusetts State Championship twice, finished second four times, third twice; won Massachusetts Open, Keene Open, Maine Open, averaging over 70% in ten tournaments; won Western Massachusetts, the New England, the Maine Open, averaging 72% for eight meets, best average, 76.3% for seven games; hit 7-0-63.4%, Massachusetts state title, 1961, 6-1-71.2%, 1967 (second title year); pitched since 1957. Home: 222 East River Street, Orange, Massachusetts 01364.

MERRYMAN, JOSEPH, 1931, 1932 Maryland State Champion.

METTLACH, LOUIS, 1942, 1943 Texas State Champion.

MEYER, NANCY, b. November 7, 1962. Indiana Girls State Champion, 1979, 1980. Daughter of Mr. and Mrs. Charles Meyer. High school student. S. Ohio; t. flip, right handed. Won Cambridge City Championship, five consecutive years; state championship record, 5-1-42.6%, 1979, 3-0-46.6%, 1980; second place, Women's Division, Cambridge City, 1980; finished third, Class A Boys Division, Rushville Indoor

Courts. Home: 610 South Fifth Street, Cambridge City, Indiana 47327.

MICHAEL, BILL, 1965 Iowa Boys State Champion, 11-0.

MICHALEK, FRANK, 1977 Member, New York HPA Hall of Fame. Won Binghamton City Championship, and Broome County title several times; averaged above 70%. Home: Route 1, Binghamton, New York 13901.

MICHAUD, DEBORAH M., b. December 21, 1946. 1977 World Champion. H. Leo; children—Hans, Shawneen. Registered nurse. S. Gordon; t. single flip, right handed. Won Women's World Championship, Greenville, Ohio, 1977; member, Heritage Recreation Center, since 1975; serves as women's representative, Massachusetts HPA Executive Board; won Massachusetts State Championship every year from 1972 through 1979; won New England Championship, 1973, 1974, 1975, 1976, 1978, 1979; most consistent and highest percentage pitcher in Massachusetts; inducted into Massachusetts Hall of Fame, 1978; high tournament, 78.1% (1978 Keene Open); high game, 95% (1978 Lowell Massachusetts Open); set world records in 1977 World Tournament, defeating Ruth Hangen, 75%: most ringers by a loser in one game, 104, most doubles by a loser in one game, 41, most shoes for a game, 134 (with Ruth Hangen), most total ringers, 209, cancelled ringers, 180, fourdeads, 30, doubles, 84 by both players in one game (with Hangen); World Tournament record: 3-4-63.8%, fifth, 1974, 4-3-71.9%, fifth, 1976, 6-1-75%, first, 1977, 7-4-71.7%, third, 1978, 5-6-65%, seventh, 1980; New England Championship, 4-2-75.3%, 1980. Home: 246 Nicholas Road, Raynham, Massachusetts 02767.

MILLIGAN, G. J., 1922 California State Champion.

MILLARD, DICK, President, Nevada HPA. Home: 47 South Gobi Circle, Sparks, Nevada 89431.

MILLER, BOYCE H., b. December 15, 1916. Nevada State Champion, 1972, 1973, 1974, 1975, 1976. W. Helen; children—Barry, Todd. Picture framer. S. Ohio; t. one and a quarter, right handed. Served as vice-president, Nevada State HPA; member, Board of Directors, Nevada State HPA; played tournament for 13 years, open play, 45 years. Home: 111 West Palizada—Suite 6, San Clemente, California 92672.

MILLER, DOROTHY, Wyoming Women's State Champion, 3-0-42.5%, 1962, 5-0-26.4%, 1963, 6-0-42.5%, 1964. Home: P.O. Box 1139, Saratoga, Wyoming 82331.

MILLER, JUDY, 1968 Oregon Women's State Champion, 21.6%. Home: 1903 28th, Forest Grove, Oregon 97116.

MILLER, LARRY DALE, b. January 13, 1964. d. January 3, 1980. 1977, 1979 South Carolina Boys State Champion. Son of Mr. and Mrs. Ronald Miller. Student. S. Imperial; t. one and a quarter, right handed. Member, school baseball and wrestling teams; died in hunting accident. Home: Route 1, Box 32 A-2, York, South Carolina 29745.

MILLER, LAWRENCE, b. January 20, 1915. Vice-President, Ross County Horseshoe Club. W. Edna. Retired. S. Allen; t. one and a quarter, right handed. Won Ross County Championship, twice; high tournament, 63%; high game, 82%, 1980; hit twelve consecutive doubles, five four-deads. Home: 618 East Second Street, Chillicothe, Ohio 45601.

MILLER, LESTER, 1972 Illinois State Champion, 13-1.

MILLER, LEVI M., b. January 6, 1907. 1975, 1976 Florida State Champion.

W. Emma; children—Mary, Melvin, Sarah Mae, Mose, Oris, Levi, Jr. Farmer. S. Allen or Ohio Pro; t. one and three quarters, right handed. Secretary-treasurer, Sarasota Club; played NHPA tournaments, ten years, pitched 60 years; championship record: 6-1-59%, 1975, 6-1-66.9%, 1976; reached Class A Division, World Tournament, 1976; high tournament, 73.5%; high game, 92.3%. Home: 10885 Lafayette-Plain City Road, Plain City, Ohio 43064.

MILLER, MAX, 1961 Wyoming Boys State Champion.

MILLER, NESTOR, Wyoming State Champion, 12-2-51.6%, 1966, 11-2-56.2%, 1968. Home: Box 1139, Saratoga, Wyoming.

MILLER, PAUL, b. November 11, 1930. 1979 Virginia State Doubles Champion. W. Virginia; children—Mickie, Mike, Charlie. Antique dealer. S. Allen; t. one and a quarter, right handed. Championship record: (with Alvin Perry), 6-1-62.4%; high tournament, 63%; high game, 75%; president, Twin Valley Horseshoe Club; elected second vice-president, Virginia State HPA, 1978. Home: Route 5, Box 92A, Staunton, Virginia 24401.

MILLER, RAY, b. August 15, 1903. 1972, 1973 Senior World Champion. W. Ada; child—Roger, Retired, International Harvester. S. Ohio; t. one and three quarters, right handed. Helped build courts (with Harry Moore), Goshen Park, Mechanicsburg, and courts for Buckeye Steel Casting, Columbus; helped organize local club, 1926, 33 players participated in this league, with Miller winning their only tournament; known as "The Red Fire Engine Kid"; promoted team leagues, International Harvester Company, last 28 of his working years; won Ohio State Fair Amateur Class Champion, 65%; won 42 Class Championships and trophies, averaging 65%, 1948–76; World Championship record: 69%, 1972, 62.5%, 1973; pitched 62 years; pitched 80% game, Class A, World Tournament, 1965; won Ohio State Fair, 1957, Michigan Water Wonderland, 1967, Madison County Classic, 1972, Urbana Open, 1962, Bellfontaine Open, 1963, Ross County Open, 1966, Piqua Open, 1972, Lakeview Open, 1976, Central Ohio District, 1923 (72%), 1924 (72%), 1925 (73%); played in leagues at Olentangy and Sunshine Parks, Columbus, 1922–23; won Midwest Ringer Roundup, 1968. Enjoys bowling; member, Masonic Lodge (past Patron, 1974–76). Home: 1422 Eastgate Road, Springfield, Ohio 45503.

MILLER, RON, b. September 21, 1937. Past President, Secretary-Treasurer, Portland Horseshoe Club. W. Karen; children—Rhonda, Billy, Bobby. Teacher. S. Allen; t. one and a quarter, right handed. Pitched 30 years, 20 as NHPA member; won Class A Championships including the Corvallis, the Portland Club, and the Hermiston Turkey Shoot (69%); high tournament, 70.9%; high game, 85%; defeated Bob West in 50-shoe game, 41-40. Home: 14707 Whiskey Hill Road NE, Hubbard, Oregon 97032.

MILLIGAN, G. J., 1922 California State Champion.

MINEER, HAROLD DUANE, b. May 28, 1923. First Vice-President, Texas HPA. W. Irene Margaret; children—Patricia, Robert. U. S. Army retired, Senior Army instructor, Junior Reserve Officer Training Corps. S. Deadeye or Ohio Pro; t. one and a quarter, right handed. Won VFW Class A Championship, 1978; was Class B runnerup, 1976, 1980, and Class B Champion, 1978, Texas State Tournaments; president, Lakeside Horseshoe Club, five years; second vice-president, Texas State HPA, 1979; high tournament, 52.6%; high game, 62.5%. Enjoys bowling, golf, gardening, working with young people (four drill teams, two first-aid teams, two orienteering teams, one color guard). Home: 2803 Littlejohn, San Antonio, Texas 78209.

MINNICH, JOE, Secretary-Treasurer, Kentucky HPA. W. Lillian. Salesman. S. Allen; t. one and a quarter, right handed. Pitched for 30 years, eleven in NHPA; publishes monthly mailer, "The Ringer," for Kentucky Chapter; publishes "Horseshoe News," for Louisville Metro Horseshoe Club. Home: Route 3, Box 426, Shelbyville, Kentucky 40065.

MINNICK, GARY, 1980 Arizona State Champion, 5-0-56.8%. Home: 6441 Calle Lunn Street, Tuscon, Arizona 85710.

MINOR, TAMMY, b. June 28, 1963. 1980 North Carolina Girls State Champion. Daughter of Grover and Carolyn Minor. Student. S. Ohio; t. one and a quarter, right handed. Enjoys track, playing guitar, writing gospel songs, singing. Home: 3811 Gilmore Drive, Greenville, North Carolina 27407.

MITCHELL, ED, 1923 Wisconsin State Champion (first recognized champion).

MITCHELL, GLENN, b. July 7, 1920. President, Ostrander Horseshoe Club. W. June; children—Bob, Bonnie. Trucker. S. Ohio Pro; t. one and a quarter, right handed. Pitched 15 years; served as secretary-treasurer, Ostrander Horseshoe Club; won first place trophy, Bainbridge Festival of Leaves, 1977. Home: 267 North Main Street, Ostrander, Ohio 43061.

MITCHELL, JOHN, 1931 Utah State Champion.

MITCHELL, STEVE, 1974 Oregon Boys State Champion. Home: 445 East Jennings, Hermiston, Oregon 97838.

MITCHELL, WILMA, 1964 Oregon Women's State Champion, 18.2%. Home: 445 East Jennings, Hermiston, Oregon 97838.

MOEFIELD, HOMER, Finished 22nd, World Tournament, 15-20-71.8%, 1963. World Tournament record, 6-29-66.7%, 1964.

MOESINGER, GILBERT "DOC," d. Member, Utah Hall of Fame.

MOGUS, ANDY, b. August 26, 1924. Oklahoma State Champion, nine times, 1961–65, 1969–70, 1972–73. W. Beth; children—Nida, Bud, Ben, Joe, David. Working foreman, Gas Service Company. S. Allen; t. one and a quarter, left handed. Pitched 44 years, 28 in NHPA; won 57 trophies and several ribbons; Class A Championships include Oklahoma Open, three times, Denton, Texas, Open, twice, nine city tournaments, Neosho, Missouri, Open, Oil Capitol Open, Vanita Invitational, Augusta, Kansas, Open, Coffeyville Centennial; high game, 87%; served as president and vice-president, Oklahoma State HPA. Home: 404 Mistletoe Lane, Bartlesville, Oklahoma 74003.

MOLER, DANA, 1973 Nevada Boys State Champion, 7-0-22%.

MONASMITH, JOHN, b. February 22, 1917. World Champion, 1963, Member, National Hall of Fame. W. Florence; children—Gary, Philip, Dianne. Retired hodcarrier. S. Allen; t. one and a quarter, right handed. Joined Yakima Club, 1947; won Washington State Championship 15 times; won 16 Northwest titles against Henry Knauft, Bob West, Ed Fishel, Cletus Chapelle, Roy Getchel, Eldon Harvey; went 10-1-75.6%, 1980 Northwest; averaged 82.3%, World Championship, South Gate, Ca., 1963; set state records: high game, 97.2%, high tournament, 84.7%, longest game, 124 shoes; highest tournament, 15-0-85%, Pacific Northwest; won Sportsmanship Award, 1963 World Tournament; member, Washington State Hall of Fame, 1964; composite record 1950–78: 169-69-76.9%, qualifying score, 515. Home: 212 North 28th Avenue, Yakima, Washington 98902.

MONDAY, AMY, 1974, 1976 Virginia Girls State Champion, 2-0-21%, 2-0-62%. Runnerup, Girls World Championship, to Tari Carpenter, 1976; set three girl's world records, with Tari Carpenter: both players in one game with 95 ringers, 35 doubles, 10 four-deads (Monday's tournament record, 6-1-61.5%), 1976.

MONDAY, CECIL O., b. 1929. Virginia State Champion, 12 times. S. Imperial; t. one and a quarter, right handed. Won State Championships, 1963, 1967, 1970–80, dethroning Alvin Perry, averaged 75% for 12 title years; hit 50 consecutive ringers against Mike Cochran, Frye Memorial, 1980; won many Class A titles; hit many 90% games, 80% tournaments; posted record of 13-22-72%, Championship Division, World Tournament, 1972; achieved top class, 1976 Philadelphia tournament. Home: 5141 Little Creek Lane, Richmond, Virginia 23234.

MONDAY, CECIL P., 1970 Virginia Boys State Champion. Son of Cecil O. Monday. Single. S. Ohio; t. reverse one and a quarter, right handed. Runnerup, Men's Class D, World Tournament, 1976; averaged 50% for championship, 1970; injured in auto accident. Home: 5141 Little Creek Lane, Richmond, Virginia 23234.

MONDAY, FRANK, 1968 Virginia State Champion, 14-1-63.9%. Father of Amy Monday; brother of Cecil Monday.

MONFEE, DAVID, 1975 Alabama Boys State Champion, 3-1-17.9%. Home: Boys Ranch, Alabama.

MONSON, JO ANN, 1979 North Dakota Women's State Champion, 5-0-50%.

MONTGOMERY, CARL, Class B. Tennessee State Champion, 1979. Suffered broken neck in construction site accident; averages 65%; helps in local club activities. Home: 2760 Patterson Road, Cleveland, Tennessee 37311.

MONTGOMERY, MELVIN R., b. April 17, 1921. d. Organized Linden Park Horseshoe Club, 1962, and Whetstone Club, 1968. W. Amanda; children—Richard, David. Special Service, assistant manager, Seven-Up Bottling Company. S. Ohio; t. one and a quarter or one and three quarters, right handed. Franklin County Champion, 1955; Central Ohio A.- A.U. Champion, 1964; Columbus Ringers Intramural Champion, 1962; Central Ohio NHPA District Champion, 1967; Kingston Festival Champion, 1968; member, league team champion ("Seven-Up" team), won Linden League, 1963, 1965, Columbus City League, 1961–62, and C. C. C. Horseshoe League, 1972; high game trophies awarded for Clintonville Conservation League, 1968, C. C. C. League (130 points), 1970, Whetstone League (121 points), 1975, (129 points), 1976, and Clintonville high scratch game, 1977; hit several 80% or better games; averaged 60%. Home: 1133 Pauline Avenue, Columbus, Ohio 43224.

MOON, GEORGE WILLIAM, b. February 17, 1944. Achieved Class B, 466 qualifying points, 1980 World Tournament. W. Sandra Lee; children—Gerald Duane, Pamela Deane, William Douglas. Electrician, Goodyear Atomic Corporation. S. Allen; t. one and a quarter, right handed. Won Clarksburg Field Day, 7-0-69.4%, two 78% games, 1978; won Ostrander Open title. 6-1-69.3%, high game, 78.3%, playoff game, 76%, 1979; hit 87.9% against Gary Kline, 51 out of 58, Xenia Open, 1980; hit 12 consecutive doubles, league game against Kenny Dawes; hit eight consecutive four-deads in tournament play, lost game against Frank Coursen with 72.9%. Home: 146 North Street, Greenfield, Ohio 45123.

MOON, JUSTIN, b. February 24, 1968. 1979 Oklahoma Boys State Champion. Son of Sandra Ostendorf. Student. S. Gordon; t. flip, right handed. Championship record, 5-0-24%; runnerup, junior title in San Jose Horseshoe Club, 1976; runnerup, Class B, Southern California State Tournament, 1976; finished third, Tom Brownell Open, and California State Class B, 1977; won NCHPA State Fund Open, and Auburn Horseshoe Club Tournament, 1977; recipient, Northern California's Most Improved Boy Award, 1978; finished third, Oklahoma State Tournament, 1980; finished second, third, in two Sallisaw tournaments; grandson of Lloyd Potter. Enjoys Little League baseball, fishing, hunting, model-making, and showing his registered Polled Hereford cattle in 4-H shows. Home: Route 1, Box 45, Sallisaw, Oklahoma 74955.

MOORE, DONALD C., b. March 22, 1930. Builder/Operator, Day-Bell Courts, 10 years. W. Janet; children—Donna, Gary, David, Debbie, Danny, Patty, Robbie, Darren. Printing manager. S. Allen; t. one and a quarter, right handed. Pitched 25 years, 15 in league and tournament play; closed Day-Bell courts, where many Ohio, Kentucky, Indiana players held tournaments. Home: 82 Viewpoint Drive, Alexandria, Kentucky 41001.

MOORE, GEORGE, Kentucky State Champion, 1933, 9-0-48.4%, 1937, 12-1-56%, 1938, 14-1-61.4%.

MOORE, GLYNDEN, 1961, 1977 North Carolina State Champion, 11-1-70% (1961).

MOORE, MIKE, 1980 Maine Boys State Champion, 6-0-51.8%. Home: Wells Street, North Berwick, Maine 03906.

MOORE, W. T., d. Member, Nebraska HPA Hall of Fame. Helped bring state tournament to Valentine, a central location for Nebraska pitchers. Home: Hay Springs, Nebraska 69347.

MOORE, WILLIAM, 1938 Illinois State Champion, 14-1-77.3%, tournament average a state record at that time.

MOORE, WILLIAM V., 1935–36 District of Columbia Champion.

MORALES, MATT, 1979 Player of the Year, Minnesota HPA. Home: 5252 Washburn Avenue North, Minneapolis, Minnesota 55430.

MORI, PAUL, b. 1895. Northern California Champion, 1955, 75.9%, 1956, 72%, 1957, 75.4%. S. Gordon; t. one and a quarter, right handed. Won Golden Gate Classic, 70%, 1961, 74.9%, 1955 Santa Rosa title, 1957, 67.9%, Almeda Fair; finished 25th, 14-21-65.2%, 1949 World Tournament, Championship Division, 1951, 10-25-66.2%, finished tenth, 9-8-72.5%, 1957; led with right foot, turn more a one and three eighths; pitched from 1936–70. Home: 840 Grand Avenue, South San Francisco, California 94080.

MORLEY, BILL, 1978 Member, Manitoba HPA Hall of Fame. Won Manitoba Senior title five times; has been Ringerama finalist more than once. Enjoys bowling, curling. Home: Dauphin.

MORRIS, GLENN E., b. September 9, 1911. 1953 South Dakota State Champion, Past Secretary-Treasurer, South Dakota HPA, Oregon HPA. W. Lucille. Milk bottling machine operator. S. Allen; t. one and a quarter, right handed. Won Strawberry Festival Tournament (Class A), Lebanon, Oregon; held office, South Dakota HPA, 1954–55, in Oregon, 1958–62; championship record, 13-0, 1953; pitched 53 years; high tournament, 69.5%, Oregon State Tournament, 1960; high game, 78.8%, Oregon State Tournament, 1960. Home: 338 South Columbia Drive. Woodburn, Oregon 97071.

MORSE, WILLIAM, 1922 Treasurer, NHPA. Home: Kansas City, Kansas.

MORTENSEN, LELAND, 1971 Member, NHPA Hall of Fame. Was leading organizer, promoter, and director of major Iowa tournaments; horseshoe historian of Iowa; conducted tournaments at Iowa State Fair; promoted and conducted annual Midwest National, Des Moines, when NHPA was unable to hold official World Tournaments, 1936–39, attended by top pitchers in country (Ted Allen, Fernando Isais, etc.); World Tournament came in on the success of Midwest Nationals, 1940; member, Iowa Hawkeye HPA. Home: Des Moines, Iowa.

MORTENSON, ARNOLD, b. January 12, 1917. NHPA Regional Director. W. Arlene; children—Leighton, Linda. Sheet metal mechanic. S. Diamond; t. one and a quarter, right handed. Tournament chairman, Burbank Club; worked with Trans World International, Inc., for "Challenge of the Sexes" program, CBS, in which Carl Steinfeldt and Kelley O'Brien pitched against each other, 1978; received California Sportsmanship Award from Jim and Emily Weeks, 1978; won Burbank Open, 5-0-63.5%, 1979; pitched against Frank Jackson in exhibition game, Stoughton, Wisconsin, scored six points against Jackson, 1932; finished second, 80.4% (which set state tournament record), 1980 California Seniors tournament; pitched 50 years. Home: 2713 Montrose Avenue, Number 12, Montrose, California 91020

MORTON, LARRY, b. February 11, 1929. President, Georgia State HPA. W. Virginia; seven children. Watchmaker. S. Allen; t. one and a quarter, right handed. Won several league and tournament titles in twelve seasons, hitting high tournament, 68.9%, high game, 85%; finished second, Kansas State Tournament, 1977; competed in Championship Division, World Tournament, 1979;

past president, Topeka HPA. Home: 4960 Basswood Drive, Columbus, Georgia 31904.

MOSER, JOANNE, 1977 Idaho Women's State Champion, 3-2-14.8%.

MOSNESS, ARNIE, 1978 Western Montana HPA Hall of Fame Member. Won Montana AAU State Championship and many other open tournaments. Home: 417 West Third Street, Big Timber, Montana 59011.

MOSSMAN, OREN "PUTT," b. July 8, 1906. World Champion, 1924, 1925, 1926, Member, NHPA Hall of Fame. W. Ethiel; one son. Showman. S. Mossman; t. one and a quarter, right handed. Designed Mossman pitching shoe, and with Frank Niven, patented, manufactured, and marketed it, first shoe with hooks to hold ringers on stake, later copied by Ohio, Gordon, Diamond; pioneer (or inventor) of one and a quarter turn. Sometimes called "Mossman twist"; played in 11 World Tournaments; performed a horseshoe trick exhibition in his road show; pitched in Africa, Europe, New Zealand, Australia, America, 60 years; won Hardin County Doubles Championship, Eldora, Iowa, with brother Warren, 1922; staged exhibition game, Maynard, Arkansas, Memorial Day, 1980; puts on 100–200 shows a year; championship record, World Tournament: 1924, 23-0-62.%% (S), 1925, 53-2-67.6% (WF), 1926, 31-1-67.4% (WP); finished second, World Tournament, 1925 (WP), 29-2-62.1%, 1926 (WF), 24-6-67.9% (lost playoff); finished third, World Tournament, 1924 (W), 19-3-48.5%. Performed as stunt motorcyclist, high kicker, boxer, wrestler, acrobat, musician, radio and TV artist, baseball and basketball player. Home: P.O. Box 71, Maynard, Arkansas 72444 and P.O. Box 13, Poynar, Missouri 63959.

MOUBRAY, CASEY, b. June 3, 1934. Michigan Wolverine HPA State Secretary. W. Wanda; child—Star. Factory worker. S.

Allen; t. one and a quarter, left handed. Assistant NHPA regional director for Michigan; past president, vice-president, secretary, Capitol City Horseshoe Club, Lansing; pitched tournament horseshoes 11 years; attended five World Tournaments, pitched in four, highest qualification, Class F, Des Moines, 1978. Home: 1516 Centennial Courtyard, Lansing, Michigan 48910.

MOUNTENAY, WILLIAM, b. September 19, 1892. Charter Member, Saskatchewan Hall of Fame. Right handed. Barber. Won Eiler Cup (representing championship of Southern Saskatchewan) 17 times; pitched as one of best players in Western Canada in Dominion Tournament preliminary, Regina, 87 ringers out of 100 shoes (55 in succession), 1931. Home: Bethume.

MROZAK, WALTER M., b. October 15, 1906. Past officer, New Haven Horseshoe Club, Past vice-president, Connecticut State HPA. W. Margaret; child—Margaret E. Electric lineman. S. Diamond Super Ringer; t. single flip, right handed. Served as league and tournament director, 18 years; won Class A title, Connecticut Open, 1976; Senior Class B champion, World Tournament, 1974, 1975; finished second, Class A, Intermediates, World 1971; averaged 56% in last four years; high game, 82% (New Haven Club Championship); helped construct lighted courts in West Haven, Northford, Brandford, New Haven; honorary life member, West Haven and Branford Clubs; billed as "Mr. Horseshoes of Connecticut," appeared on Radio WELI sports programs; monument with plaque installed at West Rock Park Courts honoring contributions to game as player and promoter; new club house named the Walter Mrozak Horseshoe Club by member of New Haven Club. Home: 95 Pleasant Drive, Hamden, Connecticut 06514.

MUIRHEAD, BILL, Oklahoma State Champion, 1966, 4-1-60.8%, 1967, 5-1-54.1%.

MULLEN, ALICE, 1977 Oklahoma Women's State Champion, 37.5%. Home: 823 West Garriott Road, Enid, Oklahoma 73701.

MULRY, NANCY, b. August 20, 1963. Wisconsin Girls State Champion, 1976, 1978, 1979, 1980. Student. S. Diamond; t. flip, right handed. Finished second, Wisconsin State Tournament (Juniors), twice; average, 40%; championship record, 1980, 5-0-46%. Home: 511 Janssen Street, Combined Locks, Wisconsin 54113.

MURPHY, CONRAD W., North Carolina State Doubles Champion, five times. W. Clara; children—Raymond, Frances Wiles. Core maker, Briggs-Shafner and Hayes, Albion. S. Allen; t. one and three quarters, right handed. Won state doubles title with Woody Thomas; won Winston-Salem City Championship, eight times, with Sid Welch; won Winston-Salem City Championship, twice; runnerup to Walt King, National A.A.U. title, Salisbury, Maryland; won National A.A.U. Doubles Championship, 1954, Marietta, Ga.; pitched 45 years; averaged 70%; best qualifying round, 80 out of 100 shoes. Home: 2627 Burgandy Street, Winston-Salem, North Carolina 27100.

MURRAY, EDWARD H., Editor/Publisher, Canadian Horseshoe Pitchers' Year Book. W. Margaret. T. one and a quarter, left handed. Formed horseshoe club, North Battleford, Saskatchewan, 1975, several other smaller clubs thereafter; established organized leagues, Saskatchewan, 1976, 1978; coaches women, junior girls (producing two national champions and others in Class A status); organized Saskatchewan HPA, serves as president since 1976; served as Saskatchewan representative, Executive Council of the Canadian National HPA; serves as information director, Horseshoe Canada; sportswriter, horseshoe columnist for several newspapers in Saskatchewan; wrote short stories, hobby articles for magazines from Texas to California; artist of comic books, nature and wildlife drawings. Home: Delmas, Saskatchewan, Canada SOM OPO.

MURRAY, HERBERT E., b. November 22, 1928. President, West Virginia HPA. W. Opal; children—David, Carolyn, Daniel, Cathy. U.C.C. Metals employee. S. Allen; t. one and a quarter, right handed. Secretary-treasurer, Wood County HPA, five years, president, two years; won about 40 trophies in various classes; high tournament, 57.4%, Marietta Open; high game, 84.6%; Class E Champion, state tournament, 1971; finished second, Class C, state tournament, 1978; pitched 35 years, played tournaments since 1971. Enjoys upholstery work, singing gospel music with The Murray Singers. Home: 1303 Clyde Street, Parkersburg, West Virginia 26101.

MURRAY, MARGARET, 1979 Canadian National Women's Champion. H. Edward. t. flip. Won Battlefords Fair, 1971–75; won Saskatchewan ladies' championship, 1977, 1979, runnerup, 1976, 1978; won Saskatchewan Provincial Mixed-Doubles Championship, with husband Ed., 1976, 1977, 1978, finished fourth, 1979; runnerup, Canadian National Championships, 1976, third, 1977; won every Alberta tournament to date with no losses; high ringer percentage, 90%, Consort, Alberta, 1976; average, 56%. Home: Delmas, Saskatchewan, Canada SOM OPO.

MYERS, JEAN, Class B Championships, 1978 Eli Reno Memorial, 1978 Ohio State Outdoor and Ohio State Indoor Championships. H. Charlie; children—Michael, Lori Ann. Assistant clerk, Court of Claims of Ohio. S. Ohio O; t. flip, right handed. Finished second, Silver Dollar Open, Lancaster, 1978, Marion Spring Fever, 1978, Hebron

Open, 1979, 1980; finished third, Class B, World Tournament, 1979; finished fourth, Class A, Carolina Dogwood Festival, 1980; high tournament, 56%; high game, 73.1%; participated in organized play since 1976. Home: 326 Rosslyn Avenue, Columbus, Ohio 43214.

N

NAPIER, JOHN, b. January 13, 1921. Greenville Club Champion, 1975. W. Beaulah; children—Brenda, Barbara, David. Turret lathe operator. S. Allen; t. one and three quarters, right handed. Achieved Championship Division, World Tournament, Lafayette, Indiana, 1975; hit 47 consecutive ringers against Elmer Harrison, 1975; high tournament, 68.4%, Day-Bel, Kentucky; high game, 84.2%, Piqua; posted record of 8-27, 1975 World Tournament. Home: 612 Prytania Avenue, Hamilton, Ohio 45013.

NAPPA, ANNE, 1972 Nevada State Girls Champion.

NASH, FRANK, 1979 Nebraska Boys State Champion, 3-0-50%. Home: Sparks Route, Valentine, Nebraska 69201.

NATALE, ANTHONY J., b. August 20, 1922. New York State Champion, 1959, 15-0-70.9%, 1961, 15-0-78.7%, Member, New York HPA Hall of Fame. W. Carmella; children—three. Layout inspector. S. American; t. one and a quarter, right handed. Pitched 38 years, NHPA competition; won Northwest Open Championship, twice, and Massachusetts Open; posted high qualification round, 91%, Eastern National, Clearfield, Pa; high tournament, 80% or better; high game, 92%. Home: 895 Glide Street, Rochester, New York 14606.

NAVARRO, RALPH, 1963 World Seniors Champion, 56%.

NAVE, A. J., b. October 18, 1925. South Carolina State Champion, three times. W. Frances. Meat cutter. S. Imperial; t. two and one quarter, right handed. Won North Carolina Dogwood Festival Tournament, Statesville, 70.4%, 1970; first vice-president, South Carolina HPA; played organized horseshoes since 1970. Home: 105 Mauldin Road, Greenville, South Carolina 29605.

NAVE, J. MIFF, b. July 3, 1901. d. November 12, 1977. Tennessee State Champion, 1934, 1935, 1936, 1937. W. Vada; seven sons, seven daughters. Factory worker, American Bemberg Corp. S. Ohio O; t. one and a quarter, right handed. Won a 51-0 shutout, 97.4%, over Carmen Cole, August 14, 1934; won Carter County Championship, 1923, and 21 times thereafter; pitched 50 years; performed exhibition games. Home: Elizabethtown, Tennessee.

NEEB, CLAYTON, Defeated Bob Redding, Class B contest, World Tournament, Greenville, Ohio, 1964. Home: Canada.

NEFF, BRIAN W., b. May 23, 1961. 1977 Junior Boys World Champion, 7-0-81.6%. Carpenter. S. Allen; t. one and a quarter, right handed. Won District title, 5-0, 1973; won Ohio State Championship, 1975, 3-0-66.7%, 1976, 7-0-71.2%, 1977, 3-0; won Greenville Ringer Classic, 1978; high tournament, 85%, high game, 90.9%, Men's Division. Home: 6527 Westfall Road, Greenville, Ohio 45331.

NEFF, GEORGE, b. February 28, 1936. Greenville Classic Tournament Director. W. Thelma; child—Brian. Building contractor. S. Allen; t. one and a quarter, right handed. Served as officer, Darke County Horseshoe Club, since 1962; won 30 trophies; high tournament, 61.8%; high game, 75%; recipient, NHPA Special Achievement Award, for service to sport, 1977; tournament director, Ohio State Championship. Home: 6527 Westfall Road, Greenville, Ohio 45331.

NEFF, THELMA, b. December 10, 1939. Class A Champion, Rushville, Indiana tournaments. H. George, Jr.; child—Brian. Retail buyer. S. Ohio Pro; t. flip, right handed. Won 30 trophies, including Darke County League championship; played in Class C, World Tournament, 1973, Class B, 1974, Class A, 1975 (Lafayette); played in championship division, Ohio State Tournament, with high game, 74%; served on housing committee, World Tournament, Greenville. Home: 6527 Westfall Road, Greenville, Ohio 45331.

NEGAARD, PHYLLIS, b. February 6, 1943. 1979 Women's World Champion. H. Ron; child—Randy. Owner/operator, Negaard's Lettering and Design. S. Allen; t. three quarter, right handed. Women's State Champion, 1976 (39.5%), 1977, 1978, 1979 (80.86%); hit 37 consecutive ringers in 90% game against Lynn Hughes, July 4, 1980; finished eighth, Class C, World Tournament, 1977, finished fifth, Championship division (Des Moines), 1978 (7-4-68.9%), finished first, 1979, (Statesville, N.C.) 10-1-70.2%, finished fourth, 1980, 72.2%, 8-3-72.2%; won 50 tournaments in four years of tournament competition, including Farmfest 1976, Eau Claire 1979–80, Rapidan Open 1976–79, St. Patrick 1979, Preimesberger July Open, 1978–80, Preimesberger November Open 1979, and Preimesberger October Open, 1979; won Minnesota State Championship, 11-0-78.1%, 1980. Home: Route 1, St. Joseph, Minnesota 56374.

NEILSON, WILLIAM, b. November 6, 1913. 1940 Indiana State Champion. W. Blanche Irene; children—Shirley Ann Hall, Reba Jeraldine Boyd. Retired. S. Gordon; t. one and a quarter, right handed. Pitched 27 years; played only in Class A and never placed lower than third; hit high tournament, 85%, 1939 Doubles Tournament, AAU, Andrson, Ind.; hit many games above 90%; won Norwood Open, 1959; won Indiana State Championship, 1940, 9-0-76.2%; played in American Association using count-all point system, 1954–62; led Indiana state in point average with as high as 125 points per game for an entire season; pitched against Curt Day (and other top pitchers), in one tournament won by Day, he and Day tied with 915 points for seven games, Day winning play-off. Home: Box 6, Dugger, Indiana 47848.

NELSON, CLARENCE, 1945 North Dakota State Champion, 7-2.

NELSON, WAYNE, b. 1921. Indiana State Champion, 1946–47, 1952, 1954. t. one and three quarters. Championship record: 10-0-76.3%, 1952, 11-2-75.3%, 1954; finished fourth, 32-3-80.7%, World Tournament, 1947, with 2080 ringers out of 2576 shoes, three losses to Ted Allen, 50-49-85.2%, Fernando Isais, 50-16, and James O'Shea, 50-34; hit games of 91.4% (against Henry Harper), 90.3% (against Alvin Gandy), 90.2% (against Ron Cherrier), 1947 World Tournament.

NELSON, WILLIAM A., b. March 10, 1903. Past State Secretary, Alabama, Alabama Hall of Fame Charter Member. W. Theresa; children—William A. II, Harriet Manning, Jacqueline Dominy, Thomas. Retired—35 years military service. S. Ohio; t. three quarters, right handed. Finished second, Alabama State Tournament, 1972, 4-1; finished second, Boys! Ranch July Fourth Tournament, 1976, 8-1; pitched in Sarasota Open, 1973, and in World Tournament, Greenville, Ohio, 1977; inducted into Alabama Hall of Fame, 1977; served as state secretary 1972–77; organized local clubs; built or helped build playing courts; hosted two state tournaments, Calera, 1973–74. Enjoys dancing, crafts, poetry, history, gardening,

cooking. Attended Massey-Draughon Business College. Home: P.O. Box 692, Calera, Alabama 35040.

NESSET, HAROLD, b. April 7, 1908. 1978 Member, Saskatchewan Hall of Fame. Won Saskatchewan doubles championship four times (with Melvin Nesset), 1964–67.

NESSET, MELVIN, b. September 29, 1910. 1978 Member, Saskatchewan Hall of Fame. Won Saskatchewan Men's Doubles Championship, 1964, 1965, 1967, 1969. Home: Preeceville, Saskatchewan.

NETHERTON, J. W., SR. 1923 Kentucky State Champion. Home: St. Mathews.

NEUBERGER, MARLOW, b. April 9, 1930. 1975 Member, South Dakota HPA Hall of Fame. W. Bonnie Ann; children—Katy, Candy, Mark. Fireman-Driver Engineer/proprietor of Neuberger's Honey Sales Bee Keeper. S. Allen or Ohio Pro; t. one and three quarters, right handed. Serves as NHPA Regional Director, District 8, and as commissioner, South Dakota HPA; past president, 1969–74; NHPA member since 1968; high game, 54%; high tournament, 36.5%; built four indoor courts, conducts winter leagues and tournaments; wrote first constitution, South Dakota Association, started banquets and business meetings in 1969 on day before each tournament; established South Dakota Hall of Fame. Home: 2500 East Austin Street, Sioux Falls, South Dakota 57103.

NEUHARTH, ALVIN, 1973 Member, South Dakota HPA Hall of Fame. Pitched first state tournament, 1957; active in leagues in Madison and Morrells and in tournament play in Sioux Valley since 1957; attended 1967 World Tournament, Fargo, North Dakota. Home: 2115 East Austin Street, Sioux Falls, South Dakota 57103.

NEUMILLER, GLEN, 1979 Wyoming

Boys State Champion, 6-0-19.9%. Home: 348 Socony, Casper, Wyoming 82601.

NEWELL, JOHN, 1941 New Mexico State Champion.

NEWHOUSE, JOLYNN MINNICH, b. January 15, 1966. 1974 Texas Girls State Champion. Employee, Kentucky Farm Bureau Insurance. H. S. Allen; t. reverse one and three quarters, right handed. Pitched in championship division, girls' world tournament, 1-6-22.3%. Home: Kentucky.

NEWKIRK, DEBORAH WILLIAMS, b. June 25, 1954. 1971 California Girls State Champion. H. Steven; child—Timothy. Housewife/graduate student. S. Allen; t. one and a quarter, right handed. Won Northern California Girls Championship, 1971; pitched in tournament play since 1969. Home: 4805 West 4805 South Kearns, Utah 84118.

NIEMANN, ARTHUR E., b. February 8, 1899. d. February 26, 1981. 1977 Member, Wisconsin HPA Hall of Fame. W. Lavanche. Salesman. S. Grodon; t. flip, right handed. Served as president, Washington Park Horseshoe Club, vice-president, state association; pitched 42 years; served as organizer and promoter. Enjoyed coin collecting. Home: 5248 North 55th Street, Milwaukee, Wisconsin 53218.

NIVEN, FRANK, New York State Champion, 1929. Known as "Hands," promoted and directed every state tournament and many county tournaments; credited with establishing state association; worked as manager, Putt Mossman Horseshoe Company, West Main Street, Rochester, N.Y.; pitched with Bob Brown, 1933 World Tournament.

NOBESS, RON, Secretary-Treasurer, Manitoba HPA, since 1968. Home: 392 Magnus Avenue, Winnipeg, Manitoba, Canada R2W 2C1.

NOE, EARL H. b. September 1, 1933. Won 42 tournament trophies. W. Phyllis Ann; child—Robert. Electric assembler. S. Allen; t. one and a quarter or one and three quarters, right handed. Won Class B championship, Ohio's Central District, 1979; pitched in four World Tournaments, Class C, Class D, Class F (won championship, 1979), and Class E (reached finals, 1980); high tournament, 62%; high game, 124 point count-all, 76% ringers; longest string of consecutive doubles: nine. Enjoys golfing, softball, pool. Home: 5809 Buenos Aires Boulevard, Westerville, Ohio 43081.

NORDLAND, O. N., 1943 North Dakota State Champion, 7-0.

NORMAN, FRANCIS, 1980 Massachusetts Doubles Champion (with William Lawson). Home: 144 Park Hill Avenue, Millbury, Massachusetts 01527.

NORWOOD, ROGERS, b. May 11, 1925. Tennessee State Champion nine times, 1962, 1966–67, 1973–76, 1978–79. W. Ann; children—Roganne, Tony, Jill, Mark. Lineman. S. Imperial, Allen or Ohio Pro; t. one and three quarters or two and a quarter, right handed. Best ringer percentage for state tournaments, 74.6% (1978); pitched longest game in state tournament, 118 shoes (with the late James Burns), 1969; won Class C World Championship, 74.4%, 1964; won Carolina Dogwood Festival, 1974; won Statesville Autumn Open, 1974–75, 1978; won dozens of Class A titles in Tennessee and in other states; pitched in championship division, World Tournament play, 9-26-69.2%, 1972. Home: Route 6, Knoxville, Tennessee 37914.

NORWOOD, TONY, 1977 Tennessee State Champion, 73.4%, dethroning his father, Rogers Norwood. Won many Class A championships.

NOYES, GEORGE, 1949 Maine State Champion. Home: Manset, Maine.

NUNAMAKER, BLAIR, d. June 28, 1944. World Champion, 1929, 1970 Member, NHPA Hall of Fame. Unmarried. S. Ohio; t. one and a quarter, right handed. Won Ohio State Championship four times, 1933–36; World Championship record: 13-1-69.5%; composite record, 246-92-59.1% with average qualifying score of 446 points; hit 60 consecutive ringers and 98 out of a consecutive 100; Cleveland address was 1238 Hayden Avenue. Records in possession of William Nunamaker, 625 Grand Central Street, Clearwater, Florida 33516.

NUNN, ROBERT, California State Champion, 1923, 1924, 1925.

O

OAKES, HAROLD, d., 1936 Washington State Champion, averaging 62.7%.

OAKEY, JOHN, 1936 Colorado State Champion, 11-4-58.6%.

O'BRIEN, KELLY, b. July 2, 1959. Washington State Women's Champion, 1977, 1978, 1979, 1980. Advertising director. S. Gordon; t. flip, right handed. 1975 Junior Girl's World Champion, 57.1% average; Washington State third vice-president, HPA; high game, 90.6%; high tournament, 72.6% (Spokane Open); finished tenth, 1978, eleventh, 1979, Women's Division, World Tournament; won 1980 Pacific Northwest Championship, 7-0-73.2%; state tournament record, 1980, 14-0-69.9%; pitched against World Champion Carl Steinfeldt, N.Y., on television show "Challenge of the Sexes." Enjoys singing, acting, dancing, guitar, and comedy. Home: 6822 North Smith, Spokane, Washington 99207.

O'BRIEN P. J., First president, Kentucky HPA, 1926. Administrator and promoter of sport of horseshoes.

O'BRIEN, RICHARD S., 1979 Massachusetts Doubles Champion, won seven out of eight games.

OCHSNER, HARVEY, Colorado State Champion, 1959, 13-1-63.2%, 1963, 11-0-59.7%, 1964, 12-2-63.2%.

O'CONNOR, JACK, b. March 19, 1930. 1979, 1980 Minnesota State Champion, all-time high percentage of 10-1-82.39%, high game 95%. W. Ester; children—Barb, Tim, Bonnie, Brian, Jeff, Erin, Rick, Jackie, Peter, Brenda. Railroad switchman. A. Allen or Imperial; t. one and a quarter, right handed. Played in championship division, World Tournament finished 24th, 10-21-67.7%, 1980; won Duluth Class A League, 1974, 70%, 1975, 71%, 1976, 73%; won Duluth 1974 Tournament championship, 75%, 1976 Hibbing, 82%, 1976 Montivideo, 76%, 1976 Canby, 79%, 1977 Eau Claire, 75%, 1979 Genola, 77%. Home: Route 8—Box 77, Brainerd, Minnesota 56401.

O'CONNOR, JACKIE, b. August 29, 1963. 1979 Minnesota Girls State Champion. Student. S. Diamond; t. one and a quarter, right handed. Championship record, 5-1-30%; finished third, state tournament, 3-2-46%, 1980; high tournament, 48%; high game, 62%; pitched in championship division, 1980 World Tournament. Home: Route 8—Box 77, Brainerd, Minnesota 56401.

O'CONNOR, PETE, b. June 14, 1967. 1979 Minnesota Boys State Champion. Student. S. Allen or Diamond; t. one and a quarter, left handed. High tournament, 68%; finished third, 3-2-56%, 1980 state tournament. Home: Route 8—Box 77, Brainerd, Minnesota 56401.

O'DELL, LEON BYRON, b. March 18, 1940. President, Bennington, Vermont Horseshoe Club, five years. W. Carol Ann; child—Susan Ellen. Batteries-Globe Union employee. S. Diamond; t. flip, right handed.

Top, left, Group picture with Glynden Moore, North Carolina State Champion in middle of second row. *Right,* Margaret Murray, Canadian National Champion. *Second row, left to right,* Esta McKee, World Champion, Dean McLaughlin, Canadian National Champion; Kelly O'Brien, World Champion. *Bottom row, left to right,* Claude Painter; Bob Pence, Hall of Fame member; Brian Neff, World Champion. *At left,* Phyllis Negaard, World Champion.

Top, left, 1961 World Championship Class. *Right,* John Passmore, at 1977 World Tournament Class B, Des Moines, Iowa. *Center row, left to right,* Dorothy Pinch, Vice President NHPA; Ed Pratt; Herb Pinch. *Bottom,* 1959 World Tournament, Murray City, Utah.

Won 1975 Middlebury tournament, 65%, finsihed second, 1977 Middlebury and South Vermont tournaments, and 1978 Bennington Turkey Shoot; finished third in ten Class A divisions; had electricity installed at Bennington Courts, 1979 and new fencing, 1978; member, NHPA, ten years. Home: Route 1A—Box 101, Shaftsbury, Vermont 05262.

OHLER, JAMES E., b. May 7, 1925. Pennsylvania State Champion, 1956–59, 1961–62. W. Margaretta. Foreman. S. Allen; t. one and three quarters and one and quarter, right handed. Finished in top ten, 1960 World Tournament; finished second, Eastern National 1955; won many local tournament titles; pitched thirty years, 12 in NHPA; high tournament, 83%; high game, 96%, 24 consecutive ringers (1961 state tournament). Home: 19 Second Avenue, Scottdale, Pennsylvania 15683.

OHMS, RAYMOND HENRY, b. November 12, 1912. d. 1963. Utah State Champion, 1946, 1948-55. W. Helen Arlene Barr; children—Darlene Larsen, Donald W., Dennis Ray. Manager, Kearns Bowling Lanes. S. Gordon; t. one and three quarters, right handed. Championship record, 65%-80%, with 98% game, 1955; won first place, Longview Park (Illinois), age 13, and 1928; pitched in World Tournament 14 years since 1948; assisted Arch Stokes in bringing World Tournament to Utah, 1947; elected president, Utah HPA; elected vice-president, National Horseshoe Pitchers Association, 1955; helped Dan Draver and others build club house, Salt Lake City, and helped organize local teams; won Annual Open tournaments, including 1956-57; composite world tournament record: 125-191-66%, 473 qualifying average; Class A championships included: First Annual American Forks Open, 1955, 1955 Salt Lake Open, 1955 Toolle Open, 1956 Payson Open, 1956 West Jordan Open, 1957 Logan Open; president, Utah State

Bowling Association; taught horseshoes and bowling.

OINAS, JEFF, 1973 Michigan Upper Peninsula Boys Champion, 3-0-25%.

OKESON, HERB, b. November 28, 1921. Washington State Secretary. W. Ida; children—Duane, Roger. Retired farmer/service station operator. S. Allen or Deadeye; t. reverse one and a quarter left handed. Pitched 46 years; served as state secretary, 1971–76, 1978; president, Fair Oaks Club (Sunnyvale Ca.), 1961–62; recipient, Stokes Memorial Trophy, 1974, for promotion of Washington Chapter to "Number One State Association"; award for outstanding contribution, 1972; inducted into Washington State Hall of Fame, 1979. Home: 27655 Northeast Ames Lake Road, Redmond, Washington 98052.

OLESEN, GAIL, b. October 26, 1965. 1979, 1980 South Dakota Junior State Champion. Student. S. Allen; t. one and a quarter, left handed. Only girl to win Junior State Crown, 34%; played in state women's division, placed fourth, 1978; earned varsity letters in track and cross country. Home: Route 2, Box 92, Arlington, South Dakota 57212.

OLFERT, LLOYD, b. March 30, 1922. Pitched 22 years. Airlines mechanic. S. Ohio; t. one and three quarters, right handed. High tournament, 61.1%, Preimesberger Arena; high game, 78%. Enjoys fishing and woodcarving. Home: 6326 Girard Avenue South, Richfield, Minnesota 55423.

OLSEN, J. ART, b. January 9, 1916, 1977 Member, Montana Hall of Fame. W. Mildred; children—Bill, Bob, Debbie. Retired, SCS. S. Allen or Gordon; t. one and a quarter, right handed. Montana State Chairman, 1959–68; president, Montana AAU, 1963; chairman, National AAU Horseshoe Pitching Committee, 1963–66; conducted National AAU Championship, Helena, 1962; coordinated all pitching and court design rules and regulations of AAU with those of NHPA, National AAU Convention, San Diego, 1963; assisted in formation of horseshoe clubs throughout Montana; wrote "Horseshoe Handbook" for Montana AAU; won National Championship gold medal AAU Doubles, with Ed Holmberg, 1961; charter member, Montana Horseshoe Hall of Fame, 1977; tied with Bob Rambo, Indiana, for National AAU Championship, lost by four points in playoff, finished second. Enjoys fishing, golf, bowling. Home: 406 South F Ruppert, Idaho 83350.

OLSEN, QUENTIN, 1948 North Dakota State Champion, 10-1.

OLSON, ALTIN, b. September 15, 1922. W. Lou; children—Sheri, Thomas, Janis. Machine Shop foreman. Imperial or Allen; t. one and three quarters, right handed. Listed in top 200 percentage pitchers in country; won several B championships and placed in Class A several times; average, 60%. Enjoys bowling, raising goats, taming wild animals. Home: 10445 Fifth Avenue, South Bloomington, Minnesota 55420.

OLSON, MYREL, b. October 26, 1913. Class A Champion, 1964 Northeastern Wisconsin Tournament. W. Lilan; children—David, Diane, Tim. Retired. S. Allen; t. one and a quarter, right handed. Pitched 40 years, 22 in tournament and league play; averages 60%; finished second, 1966–67, Wisconsin State Tournament; eight times Class A league champion; high game, 82%, 132 points in 50 shoes. Enjoys square dancing, bicycling, cutting firewood. Home: 609 Olson Avenue, Appleton, Wisconsin 54911.

OLSON, PETE, 1932 South Dakota State Champion.

ONEY, HERMAN, b. September 29, 1906.

Franklin County Champion five times, 1947–51. W. Grace. Retired. S. Ohio; t. one and a quarter reverse, right handed. Won county title, eight points, doubles with Paul Arledge, high school years 1924–26; won Central Ohio District Championship, 1949–51; won Championship Trophy, Ohio State Fair Tournament, 1950; served as district manager, Ohio Buckeye HPA; high tournament, above 60%; high games above 70%. Home: 317 Cherrinton Road, Westerville, Ohio 43081.

OPSTEEN, ANN, b. April 8, 1922. Chairman, Wisconsin Hall of Fame Committee. H. John; children—Michael, Robert, Barbara Schreiber, Thomas, James, David, Mary, Patricia. Homemaker/greenhouse worker. S. Allen; t. flip, right handed. President, Combined Locks HPA; past secretary-treasurer, Wisconsin State HPA, 1973–79; past secretary, Combined Locks Club, three years; pitched in every women's tournament in state since first one, 1969 (Combined Locks); NHPA member, 13 years; won KRA Indoor championship, 1971, 1979 Fillmore Open, 5-0-44.5%, 1980, 4-1-44%, 1980 Sheboygan Open, 4-1-43.2%, 1980 Swen's Open (Green Bay'), 5-0-44.5%; won Class B title, Eau Claire, hit 45.21%; averaged 48.3%, Mideastern Wisconsin (lost playoff). Home: 304 Williams Street, Combined Locks, Wisconsin 54113.

ORCHARD, ARTHUR, 1978 Member, Manitoba HPA Hall of Fame. Won Manitoba singles championship, 1923; held Manitoba Doubles Championship, with his father, Fred, 1917–30, won 1928 Canadian Doubles Championship (Royal Winter Fair, Toronto). Home: Miami.

O'SHEA, JAMES L., b. April 11, 1914. Massachusetts State Champion, 13 times. W. Dorothy; children—Dennis, David, Mary Ann. Prison superintendent, retired. S. Ohio; t. one and a quarter, right handed.

Among state championship records: 81.2%, undefeated in nine games, 433 ringers out of 534 shoes, 1938, 81.2%, state record average, 1940; won New England Championship seven times; finished fifth, World Tournament (Murray City, Utah), 29-6-78.4%, 1947, high game, 87.9%; high tournament, 84.7%, Massachusetts Open, hit 14 consecutive four-deads in game with Ted Allen; Member, New England HPA Hall of Fame, 1970. Enjoys bowling and golf. Home: 44 Pine Drive, RFD, Chatham, Massachusetts 02633 and 6191 Peony Road, Venice, Florida 33595.

OSTRANDER, IRENE G., b. June 15, 1923. 1973 Michigan State Champion. H. James A., d.; children—James, Roger. Secretary. S. Allen; t. one and a quarter, right handed. member, state HPA, 12 years; won 1973 Wolverine state class A championship; won a Class B State title; awarded most improved pitcher in state, 1972; high game, 68%, 1973 state tournament. Home: 5717 Hilliard Road, Lansing, Michigan 48910.

OSTRANDER, JAMES, JR., 1960 Michigan Boys State Champion. Son of James and Irene Ostrander. Home: 5717 Hilliard Road, Lansing, Michigan 48910.

OSTRANDER, JAMES, SR., b. 1918. d. September 23, 1977. W. Irene; children— James, Roger. Oldsmobile employee. Pitched 42 years; finished 26th, World Tournament, 12-23-67.5%, 1970; supporter of Wolverine State and NHPA, and Chief Okemas Sportsman's Club (Diamondale); served in World War II, China, Burma, India. Home: 5717 Hilliard Road, Lansing, Michigan 48910.

OTNES, ELMER J., b. July 14, 1926. President, Oregon State HPA, 8 yrs. W. Oneta; children—Larry, Don, Carolyn, Bill, John, Dave, Paul. Papermaker. S. Allen; t. one and a quarter, right handed. Past president, Oregon City Club; pitched 35 years, 10 in NHPA events; organized Oregon City Club, promoted 24-court facility there, 1972; high tournament, 46.9%; high game, 63%. Home: 661 Warner Parrott Road, Oregon City, Oregon 97045.

OTNES, ONETA, H. Elmer, Trains Scorekeepers, keeps statistical records; attends 20 tournaments a year; serves as social coordinator for players' wives; helps with publicity; high game, 42%; 25% average. Home: 661 Warner Parrott Road, Oregon City, Oregon 97045.

OTTO, JONAS "HAP," b. December 12, 1900., d. November 28, 1979. Member, Michigan HPA Hall of Fame. W. Meta Zill; children—Carolyn Wilson, Harlan, David. Plumber. S. Lattore and Allen; t. three quarters, right handed. President, state association, 17 years; runnerup, AAU National Championship, 1944. Enjoyed bowling, golfing. Home: 543 South First Street, Ann Arbor, Michigan 48103.

OUELLETTE, LEO J., b. February 14, 1924. First Vice-President, New York HPA. W. Helen; children—Margie, Kathy, Mark, Jenny, Meegan, Amy, Bridget, Emily. Mechanical gearman. S. Allen; t. one and three quarters, right handed. Past chairman, New York Metropolitan Horseshoe Association; club director, Brooklyn International Horseshoe Club; pitched NHPA, 13 years; high game, 60%; recipient, New York City Department of Parks Award (Mayor Beam), for design and maintenance of courts in Prospect Park; designed horseshoe bag, four types of portable courts, and four indoor courts with scoreboards (January 1979); outstanding wrestler, ice hockey player. Home: 50 Westminster Road, Brooklyn, New York 11218.

OUELLETTE, MARGE, b. February 28, 1949. President, Ringer World Emporium, Inc. Single. S. American; t. flip, right handed. Member, NHPA Promotion Committee; publicity chairperson, constitution and by-laws committee member, New York State HPA; instituted office of information officer, NHPA, 1976–78; compiled and published Directory of Horseshoe Courts and Clubs (U.S., Canada), 1977; New York State delegate, NHPA Convention, 1977–80; representative for NHPA, elected Member-at-Large, 1979 Amateur Athletic Union Convention; past secretary-treasurer, 1976–78, promotion committee, 1976–79, and other offices, Brooklyn International Horseshoe Club; entered and qualified in every NHPA World Tournament since 1976; member of local clubs, New Rochelle, Heritage Recreation Center, Middlesex, Hunterdon County, etc.; recipient, NHPA Achievement Award, 1977, New York & New Jersey Pride and Appreciation Award, 1976–77, NHPA Appreciation Award as information officer, 1979, 1979 Honor as Member-at-large, Amateur Athletic Union; her company, Ringer World Emporium, is first nationwide mail-order business for quality horseshoes and related products (60 East 42nd St., N.Y., N.Y. 10017); high game, 42% (1978 North Carolina Dogwood Festival Open Tournament); high tournament, 27% (1980 Preimesberger Arena Third Annual Fourth of July Open. Enjoys bowling. Home: 60 East 42nd St., New York, N.Y. 10017.

OVERMAN, KATHRYN, b. March 11, 1912. 1961 Ohio State Champion, 3-0-22.7%. H. Francis; children—Dean, Gordon, William, Joseph, Kenny, Lynn. Housewife. S. Gordon; t. flip, right handed. Home: 405 First Avenue, Waverly, Ohio 45690.

OVNICEK, KAREN, 1974 Washington Women's State Champion, 52.7%. Won women's title, 1974 Pacific Northwest Tournament, 6-1-61.6%. Home: North 6504 Regal, Spokane, Washington 99207.

OWEN, W.M., 1960 Virginia State Champion.

OWENS, DONALD C., b. January 21, 1916. Past President, Indiana HPA. W. Maxine; child—Connie Chesney. General Motors employee. S. Allen; t. one and a quarter, right handed. Past president, Anderson Horseshoe Club; pitched 30 years, competed 20 years; average above 70%; finished 25th, Championship division, 13-22-72.2%, World Tournament, 1964. Home: 716 Washington Street, Summittville, Indiana 46070.

OWENS, WILLIAM, First Vice-President, Washington HPA. Home: 1656 McCorquedale Road, Mt. Vernon, Washington 98273.

P

PACKHAM, EDDIE, b. 1912. W. Aeronautical engineer. S. Gordon. World Tournament record: 98-57-72.6%, average qualifying score of 506. Home: Santa Monica, California.

PADDOCK, CANDICE J., b. April 30, 1966. 1979 NCHPA Girls Champion. Student. S. Allen; t. one and a quarter, right handed. Won Shasta Open, 1979; high tournament, 40%; high game, 48%; pitched three years in NHPA competition. Home: 2361 Buttermilk Lane, Arcata, California 95521.

PADDOCK, SHARON MAE, b. March 26, 1944. 1978 California State Champion, 47%, NCHPA Tournament, 57% in state. H. Bill; children—Candice, Will. Housewife. S. Allen; t. reverse three quarter flip, right handed. Served as president and publicity chairman, local club; one of top six women pitchers in California; won Northern California Women's Championship, 1978; high game, 76%, high tournament, 65.6%, 1980 Pleasonton Tournament. Home: 2361 Buttermilk Lane, Arcata, California 95521.

PAGE, HARRY, Class B World Champion,

1952, 55.4%, and 1957, 66%. runnerup, 6-1-58.9%, Intermediate Division, World Tournament; in Senior Division, record of 14-6-65.5%. Home: Waterloo, Iowa.

PAGE, LeROY, President, NHPA, 1939–41. Home: Des Moines, Iowa.

PAGLIARINI, ANDY, b. June 21, 1912, d. January 19, 1979. Minnesota State Champion, 1962, 1964, 1966, 1968; Member, Minnesota Hall of Fame, 1969. W. Sandra. Meat cutter. S. Allen; t. three quarters, right handed. Won Minnesota Boys State Championship, 1928; won four consecutive Hibbing Opens, 1964–67, and five more in later years; won Duluth Open, 1968, Cloquet Open, 1963, 1966, Kindred, 1962–63, Sioux Falls, 1965–66, Allard Open, 1975; won Intermediate World Championship, 1975; competed 18 years in World Tournament A or B divisions; hosted open and state tournaments; promoted 1967 World Tournament, Fargo, made top class, finished with 12-23-68.8%; served as officer, Hibbing Horseshoe Club, 20 years; member, Minnesota Hall of Fame Committee. Enjoyed bowling, golf. Home: 1604 East 7th Avenue, Hibbing, Minnesota 55746.

PAINTER, CLAUDE T. "LEE," Uses one of the most unusual pitches in the game. W. Dorothy; children—Wanda Blackard, Tommy, Ellen, Michael. S. Allen; t. double flip, right handed. Played NHPA tournaments since 1966; won 69 trophies, posted high tournament, 61.3%; high game, 84.2%; class A pitcher in Virginia tournaments. Home: Route 2—Box 93, Waynesboro, Virginia 22980.

PALKA FRANK, d. 1960 Illinois State Champion, 10-1-72.9%. Competed in World Tournament play, averaging 70%.

PALMER, G. H. "GRANNY," b. July 7, 1911. Member, Board of Directors of American HPA, thirty years. W. Bea; child—Joe D. Owner/operator, Palwick Produce Co. S. Allen; t. one and three quarters, right handed. Pitched 52 years, won 533 trophies (more than 100 in Class A championships); won Indiana State Fair tournament, 15 games of 50 shoe count-all, 1929, 1930; voted "Mr. Horseshoes," AHPA; high tournament, above 80%; high league game, 88%, 188 points. Home: 1401 Weed Lane, Vincennes, Indiana 47591.

PALMER, HUGHIE, 1918 Ohio State Champion. Won Industrial Championship of the United States (sponsored by B.F. Goodrich Rubber Company), 1919, 1920; finished third, World Tournament, 1919; finished fifth, World Tournament, 1920; was one of the first to master the "open shoe" concept. Home: Akron, Ohio.

PALMER, MERLE C., b. July 8, 1907, d. January 22, 1973. Wyoming State Champion, 24 times, 1938–72. W. Ardeth; children—Rosilee Long, Robert H., Howard M. Railway postal clerk and supervisor of Sub Post Office. S. Allen; t. one and three quarters, right handed. NHPA member, 36 years; finished second, Laramie County Tournament, 1923, first in 1925, joined Cheyenne local club, finished second in first state tournament, 1937; worked with Lee Laughlin and others to construct 12 lighted courts, Holliday Park; managed Tri-State Tournament many years; competed in World Tournaments, 1947, 1949, 1950, 1951, 1952, highest finish—13th; composite record for years 1933–60: 1073-330-79,098 shoes pitched-48,885 ringers-61.9% average; won city championship, Cheyenne, 1934, 1937, 1938, 1939; won Albin, Laramie County, 1964–65, 1971; won Southwest Wyoming, 1953, 1954–55, 1957; won Wyo-braska, 1954–55; won Tri-State, 1955, 1964; high game, 90% (Tri-State, 1969); high tournament, 72.1% (1951 World Tournament).

PAQUETTE, PAT, b. April 28, 1929. 1972

Women's Champion, Michigan Upper Peninsula. H. Robert; children—Dave, Tim, Ray, Karen, Barbara. Secretary, Parish Church. S. Gordon or Allen; t. flip, right handed. Women's title record: 4-0-31.3%; won 54 of 58 league games, 1972; secretary, Ishpeming-Negaunee Women's Horseshoe League, six years; organized a six-team women's league (now 16 teams and 130 women), 1972. Enjoys golf. Home: 210 Queen Road, Negaunee, Michigan 49866.

PAQUETTE, RAY, b. January 20, 1956. 1972 Junior Champion—Michigan Upper Peninsula, 5-0-22.9%. Single. Research technician. S. Gordon; t. flip, right handed. Enjoys hunting, fishing, camping. Home: 105 Birch Street, Negaunee, Michigan 49866.

PAQUETTE, ROBERT, b. March 22, 1926. 1972 Champion—Michigan Upper Peninsula. W. Pat; children—Dave, Jim, Ray, Karen, Barbara. Sign painter. S. Imperial; t. one and a quarter, right handed. Pitched 30 years, 23 years in tournament play; championship record: 7-0-56.4%; past president, Ishpeming-Negaunee Horseshoe League; Home: 201 Queen Road, Negaunee, Michigan 49866.

PAQUIN, EDDIE, 1960 New Hampshire State Champion, 51%. Home: Pelham, New Hampshire.

PARADIS, WILLIE J., b. April 9, 1922. Connecticut State Champion, 1958, 1961, 1962 (5-0-69%). W. Daisy; children—Gary, Gail Lalonde. Chief electrician. Eagle Lock Corp. S. Ohio; t. one and three quarters, right handed. NHPA member, 33 years; won 1961 New England Championship, 14-1-64.6%; holds state record for single high game, 81.8% (1960 state tournament), eclipsed in 1962 by 93.3% game; won 60 trophies, several are city championships; performed trick pitches in exhibition games; won Massachusetts Open, 1958; won Connecticut Open, 1963; high tournament, above 80%. Enjoys pool, skiing. Home: Tower Road, Bristol, Connecticut 06010.

PARHAM, F.C., Vice President, NHPA, 1921. Home: Fort Wayne, Indiana.

PARKER, DEL, Secretary-Treasurer, Alberta HPA, Box 105, Lacombe, Alberta, Canada, TOC, ISO

PARKER, RAY, Oregon State Champion, 1946.

PARKIN, ROSE, Saskatchewan Provincial Women's Champion, 1964, 1966, 1970, 1971. Won Saskatchewan Mixed Doubles title, with Ray Parkin, 1962, with Ole Jensen, 1967.

PARSELL, PHILLIP F., b. May 20, 1964. Virginia Boys State Champion, 1977–78. Student. S. Imperial; t. one and three quarters, right handed. Championship record: 59.7%, 1977, 81.3%, 1978; won Raymond Frye Memorial, 1974, 1975, 1976, 1977; won Virginia Apple Capitol, 1977; won Virginia State Doubles, 1977; won 1978 Southeastern; high game, 92.3%. Home: 6346 Lincolnia Road, Alexandria, Virginia 22312.

PARSONS, ROGER E., Utah State Champion, 1974, 11-0-80.7%. Home: 554 Roosevelt Street, Midvale, Utah 84047.

PASONO, DANIEL RICHARD, b. March 17, 1964. 1979 New Mexico Boys State Champion. 10-0-37%. Student. S. Imperial; t. one and a quarter, right handed. Won Albuquerque City Championship, 1978–79; won Los Alton title, 1979; high tournament game; 50% three consecutive four-deads. Enjoys chess, archery. Home: 6613 Ruth Avenue Northeast, Albuquerque, New Mexico 87109.

PASSMORE, FRANCIS, b. June 26, 1919, d. 1980. Indiana state publicity director, member, Hall of Fame committee. W. Margaret; children—Janice, Jeanne, John. Salesman. S. Allen or Imperial; t. one and a quarter or one and three quarters, right handed. Wayne County Champion, 1976, 1978–79; won father and son family day title, with son John, 1974; CCC state champion, Class B Champion, Eastern Indiana Open, 1977. Home: 1011 Fairacres Road, Richmond, Indiana 47374.

PASSMORE, JANICE, b. December 12, 1957. 1972 Indiana Girls State Champion. Sales clerk. Won Class B World Championship, Class B championship of the Greenville Classic, 1972. Home: 1011 Fairacres Road, Richmond, Indiana, 47374.

PASSMORE, JOHN, b. November 5, 1958. Indiana Boys State Champion, 1971–74. W. Kimberly. United States Army, Feb. 1979–1983. S. Allen; t. one and a quarter, right handed. Averaged 89.5% ringers, 1975 World Tournament, Junior Boys class, seven games, holds world record for all divisions; high game, 96.4%; recipient, NHPA Acheivement Award, and Indiana HPA Junior Achievement Award; holds or shares 13 junior world records; finished fourth, 1972, 1975 World Tournament; won Wayne County Championships, 72% average, 1974–76 (men's division); finished 35th, 68%, championship division, 1977 World Tournament; high game (men's), 90%; high tournament, 75.3% (Wayne County, 1977); finished fifth, Indiana State Tournament, 71.8%, 1976. Home: 1011 Fairacres Road, Richmond, Indiana 47374.

PATENAUDE, ANITA, b. July 10, 1937. Secretary, Maine HPA, 1966 State Champion. H. Wesley; children—Michael, Linda. Registered Nurse. S. Allen; t. flip, left handed. Home: Route 1, Box 326, South Paris, Maine 04281.

PATENAUDE, LINDA, b. March 8, 1963. Junior World Champion, 1978–79, 11-0-53.2%. Student. S. Reno; t. flip, right handed. Averaged 69.8%, new record for girls, along with high game, 78.6%, 1979

World Tournament (both records broken in other tournaments, 74.6% ringers, 1978 Keene Open, and game, 84%, 1979 Maine Open); won Maine State Championship, 1975–79; debuted in women's division, 1980, won with 6-1-73.6%, Women's State Championship. Home: Route 1, Box 326, South Paris, Maine 04281.

PATENAUDE, MIKE, 1980 Main State Champion, 5-0-67.1%. Home: Route 1, Box 213, Oxford, Maine 04270.

PATENAUDE, WESLEY, b. August 31, 1938. President, Maine HPA. W. Anita; children—Michael, Linda. Mechanic. S. Allen; t. one and a quarter, right handed. President, Oxford Hills Horseshoe Club; pitched 13 years in NHPA; high tournament, 44%; high game, 60%. Home: Route 1, Box 326, South Paris, Maine 04281.

PATTERSON, Calvin, b. September 26, 1922. Marietta City Championship, 1939. W. Dorothy; children—Brenda, Robert, Dale. Building superintendent, Channel 6-TV Columbus. S. Gordon; t. one and a quarter, right handed. Pitched in 50% bracket. Home: Columbus, Ohio.

PATTERSON, E.B., Past President, Kentucky HPA, 12 years. Home: 1050 South Seventh Street, Louisville, Kentucky.

PATTON, SHELL, Wyoming State champion, 1939, 9-2-60.1%, 1946, 12-2-57.2%, 1958, 7-0-60%, 1962, 9-1-62.6%.

PAUL, RICHARD E., b. May 31, 1938. Regional Director, Montana/Wyoming, NHPA. W. Sharon; children—Dawn Maree, Shelbi Lynn, Richard Lee, Danita Jo. Supervisory supply techinican. S. Ohio; t. flip, right handed. Secretary-treasurer, Western Montana HPA; past offices—vice-president, WMHPA, president and secretary, Great Falls Horseshoe Club; pitched 30 years; voted "Mr. Horseshoes" by Montana Association, 1979; high tournament, 52.4%; high game, 69.7%. Home: 2223 3rd Avenue North, Great Falls, Montana 59401.

PAULSON, GEORGE, b. 1909, d. September 4, 1979. South Dakota Regional Director, 1937 State Champion. W. Lucella; children—Glenn, Beverly, Loren. Operator, Power and Light Company. S. Gordon or Allen; t. one and a quarter, right handed. High tournament, 61.5% (Ortonville, Minnesota), 1974; high game, 74%, 1971 state tournament; held offices of president, vice-president, secretary-treasurer, local clubs, president and secretary-treasurer, 4 years, state association.

PAULSON, KENNETH G., b. February 15, 1928. Chairmen, 1981 World Tournament Advertising Committee. W. Alice: children—Debbie, Marc, Gail. County engineer (Morrison County). S. Allen; t. three quarters and flip, right handed. Won class title, Minnesota state meet, 1979, and high ringer percentage in his clients class. Home: Route 1, Pierz, Minnesota 56364.

PAXTON, JOHN. 1982 Member NHPA Hall of Fame. Senior World Champion five times, 1966, 69.4%, 1967, 67.2%, 1968, 65.4%, 1969, 68.5%, 1970, 66.2% (Record for men over 65); ten-year record: 62-15-69.4%; composite record in World Tournament championship division: 111-146-66.6%, average qualifying score, 476, charter member, Iowa Hawkeye HPA Hall of Fame. Home: Route 5, Ottumwa, Iowa 52501.

PAYNE, HOLLAND I., b. September 29, 1918. Secretary-Treasurer, Northern California HPA. W. Vida M.; children—John H., Steven W., Karl I., Keith B. Director of Education Research, Sacramento City Unified School District. S. Allen or Deadeye; t. three quarters and one and a quarter, right handed. Holds PhD, Oaklahoma State University; pitched 45 years, three in tournament play; president, Sac-

ramento Horseshoe Club since 1978; was boys champion in his area, 1931 33; won Bremerton Navy Base Championship, 1945; high tournament, 56.4%; high game, 74%; runnerup to Monte Latino, Sacramento City Tournament, 1964; won Class B Title, Sacramento, 1979; finished 20th, California State Tournament; finished second, NCHPA Class B. 1980. Enjoys coin-collecting, Christmas-tree farming. Home: 4985 Helen Way, Sacramento, California 95822.

PEAKE, MILLARD, 1929–30 Maryland State Champion.

PEARCE, EARL, President, Kansas HPA. Home: 107 Hamilene, Garden City, Kansas 67846.

PEARCE, EMALINE, 1978 Kansas Women's State Champion, 43.8%. Home: 1107 Hamilene, Garden City, Kansas 67846.

PEARCE, TOM, b. May 31, 1914. Mel Montgomery Memorial Championship, 1980. W. Esther Hutson; children—William, James, Robert, Farmer, S. Ohio O; t. one and a quarter, right handed. Graduate, Columbus Art School, 1937; won Ox Roast Tournament (London, Ohio), three times, best record set in 1961, 9-0-65.8%; won Central Ohio AAU Title, 1955, 1960; high tournament, 67.9%, high game (against Mel Montgomery). 83.2%; qualified for World Tournament with 73% ringers, Class B, finished fifth, 6-5-59.8% (against Ted Allen); ten-year average in ten Ohio State Tournaments: 55.6%, 82nd on the Ohio all-time list; won Class C, 1958, Class D, 1973, 5-0-58.9%, and Class D, 1978, 5-0-61.9%; president and corresponding secretary, New Rome Horseshoe Club; served as tournament director or assistant, 40 tournaments; designed backdrop for New Rome Club indoor courts. Home: 5860 State Route 142 Southeast, West Jefferson, Ohio 43162.

PEARMAN, GARY A., b. November 6, 1953. In Top 100 Percentage NHPA Pitchers List. Divorced; child—Penny. Finishing-recovery operator, Hercules, Inc. S. Allen; t. one and a quarter, right handed. High tournament, 67.8%, Flagtown USA Open Mellot, Indiana, 1980, finished second, Class A. Home: Trailer Lot #3, Newport, Indiana 47966.

PEARSON, ROY, New England Champion, 1953–54; Rhode Island Champion, 1950–51, 1953, ringer percentages of 64.2%, 66.3%, 65%.

PELL, HILLMER, d. Oregon State Championship, 1933, 61%, 1938, and 1939, 59.6%.

PELTON, RICHARD, b. February 2, 1927. President, Michigan Wolverine State HPA. W. Charlotte; children—Don, Ron, Mike, Chris, Todd. Auto mechanic. S. Allen; t. one and a quarter, right handed. Pitched 30 years, 11 in tournament play; won Class B-2 championship, Michigan, 1973; won Jackson County Tournament of Champions; finished fifth, state tournament, championship division; finished fifth, Class C, World Tournament, 1980; high game, 86.5% (1976 World Tournament); inducted into WSHPA Hall of Fame, 1980. Home: 107 Moscow Road, Horton, Michigan 49246.

PENCE, HAROLD, 1931 Wyoming State Champion.

PENCE, ROBERT G., b. December 7, 1909. Member, NHPA Hall of Fame, 1969. W. Lois; children—Janet, Judy, Jerry. Steel worker. S. Allen and Ohio O; t. one and a quarter and one and three quarters, right handed. Won 1926 Fort Wayne Club championship; won Columbia City tournament, 1927; pitched 55 years; joined NHPA, 1929; secretary-treasurer, Indiana HPA, 1955+, built state chapter to largest in the country, gained national reputation as administrator and office of National Secretary-Treasurer, 1958, 1958–72; under Pence's office, rotation of World Tournament sites, addition of Classes C and D for men, B and C for women, B, C, and D for boys, a Senior Division, and an Intermediate Divison (for men between 60–65), a girls division, sale of game-related items for raising revenue, issuing championship patches, establishment of National Hall of Fame, 1965, printing and distributing of NHPA "How To Do It" booklet, establishing NHPA recognition awards; tournament director for 15 World Tournaments; best game, against Wilbur Kabel, more than 85%, 1959 Eastern National; ten consecutive four-deads, against Clayton Henson, 1936, 38 consecutive ringers, 1936, and a 51-48 loss to Guy Binkley; recipient, Stokes Award, 1961. Home: 1325 South 24th Street, Lafayette, Indiana 47905.

PENTTILA, WILLIAM W., b. January 18, 1916. 1939 Pennsylvania State Champion, 11-0-76.9%. W. Laura; child—William Lee. Steelworker. S. Ohio O; t. one and a quarter, right handed. Finished second, 1962 Ohio State Tournament, 80% average; runnerup, Michigan Water Wonderland, average 72.1%; averaged 78.6%, Lakeside Open; high game, 87.5%, Ohio State meet; reached championship division, 1962 World Tournament, finished 14th, 21-14-75.7%; served as secretary-treasurer, Lorain County Horseshoe Club. Home: 141 Ridgeland Drive, Amherst, Ohio 44001.

PENWELL, DAVE, b. May 22, 1944. Texas State Secretary. W. Carolyn. Department manager, Skaggs Alpha-Beta Food Stores. S. American; t. single flip, right handed. Editor, Texas State HPA, 1979; secretary-treasurer, Arlington Iron Benders, 1978; won several class championships, second place and league trophies; high tournament, 34.5%; high game, 52%. Home: 6700 Vivian Court, Tyler, Texas 75703.

PEPIN, MARC, 1969 Boys Maine State Champion, 6-0-50.9%. Finished third, 1968, state tournament.

PEPPLE, PERL, b. May 1, 1892. Member, Kansas State Hall of Fame, 1977. W. Etta Mae (dec.); children—Nona Lee Dresner, Jack L. Elliott. Retired, U.S. Department of Labor. S. Allen, Gordon, Ohio; t. one and three quarters, right handed. Award, 1974, for outstanding contributions to horseshoe pitching; known for ornamental Spencerian penmanship; boxed professionally (the last a draw against Earl Shaner, 1926); pitched baseball; became official timekeeper in Topeka, counted for knockdowns from 1926 until TV intervened in the boxing profession. Began pitching horseshoes at age 51; promoted and conducted first State American Legion Championship Tournament (Topeka) 1948; won Class B Championship, 1948–50, State American Legion Tournament; joined Kansas State HPA, 1948; served as player, organizer, promoter, publicity director, tournament director in all state tournaments for many years; regional director, West Central States, 1957–58; charter member, Topeka Horseshoe Association, 1948; served as president, Kansas Association, 1952–53; chairman, Horseshoe Committee of American Legion, 1948–68; high game, 80%; high tournament, 70%; lifetime member, Kansas Association, member of Hall of Fame Committee. Home: 5260 South West 22nd Street, Plaza West Apartments, No. 212, Topeka, Kansas.

PERGAL, HENRY, 1931 Indiana State Champion. Lost to Guy Zimmerman, 51-0, World Tournament, 1948. Zimmerman's game was the first perfect game in World Tournament play, 44 ringers out of 44 for Zimmerman, and 27 out of 44 for Pergal.

PERKINS, HAROLD, Massachusetts Hall of Fame, 1978, organizer. Home: Springfield, Massachusetts.

PERRIN, DEBORAH TRAQUAIR, b. February 5, 1958. 1974 New Hampshire Girls State Champion, H. Christopher J. Purchasing Clerk, Brookstone Company. S. Ohio; t. one and a quarter, right handed. Pitched four years, NHPA; won the Tournament of Champions, Sutton, Mass., averaged 40.4%; won Northeast Girls title, 5-1-33.2% Home: Route 1, Box 393, Peterborough, New Hampshire 03458.

PERRY, ALBERT, b. December 27, 1927. President, Colorado State HPA, 1978–79. W. Louise; four children. Retired, Navy. S. Ohio Pro; t. one and three quarters, right handed. Won Colorado State Class C title, 1974, Class B, 1977; elected vice-president, Colorado Association, 1977; high tournament, 50%; high game, 66%. Home: 3645 Miller Street, Wheatridge, Colorado 80033.

PERRY, ALLEN, b. September 11, 1941. 1976 Virginia State Doubles Champion (with twin brother, Alvin); W. Patsy; children—Tammy, Keith. Machinist. S. Allen; t. one and a quarter, right handed. High tournament, 69%; high game, 86.6%. Home: 10,000, P.O. Box 101, Midlothian Turnpike, Richmond, Virginia 23235.

PERRY, ALVIN, b. September 11, 1941. 1980 Virginia State Champion, 11-0-78.8%. W. Harriet; children—Ross, Shannon, Mary Nichols. Machinist. S. Allen; t. one and quarter, right handed. Won 1976 Virginia State Doubles Championship, with twin brother Allen; was runnerup for Virginia State Champion, 1975–79; runnerup, Class B, World Tournament, 1979; averaged 80.4%, Frye Memorial, 1980; high game, 89%. Home: Route 1, Box 123-3A, Hanover, Virginia 23069.

PERRY, ROSS, b. February 7, 1965. 1975, 1979–80 Virginia Boys State Champion. Student. S. Allen; t. one and quarter, left handed. Defeated World Champion Mark Dyson, championship division, 1979 Frye

Memorial; third vice-president, local club; won Hill City Open, 1976, 1978–79, the Southeastern, 1976–77, Virginia State Doubles, 1976, Elmont Fall Open, 1975, 1977, Virginia State Cash Tournament, 1978, Elmont Spring Warmup, 1976, Virginia State Fair, 1979; finished fifth, 1979 World Tournament; high tournament, 80.3%; high game, 88.6%; hit perfect game, 100%, against Frank Haines, average 88%, 1980 Winchester Tournament; 1980 Virginia State tournament, 6-0-77.6%. Home: Route 1, Box 123-A, Hanover, Virginia 23069.

PERTICONE, JUSTIN, b. June 25, 1928. Class C. Michigan State Championship, 1975. W. Marilyn Jean; children—Tony, Julie, Janet, Anne, Steve, Mike, Joe. Teacher/coach. S. Allen; t. one and a quarter, right handed. Finished third, Class A, 1978, fourth in Class A, 1979, third in Class A, 1980, state tournaments; high game, 86%; listed in top 200 percentage pitchers in country. Enjoys gardening. Home: 2437 Smiley Way, Jackson, Michigan 49203.

PETERS, H. D., North Dakota State Champion, 1922–24.

PETERSON, GAYLORD, b. October 7, 1908. Illinois State Champion, 1928, 1934. W. Evelyn, d.; children—Donna, William, Bethane. Owner/operator, bowling lane, retired. S. Ohio, Gordon, Allen; t. one and three quarters, right handed. Competed in tournaments, 1926–56; World Tournaments, 1937 qualifying score of 464, 1929 W, 7-8-59.2, tenth place, 1935, 4-19-56.2%, 23rd place; state secretary, Illinois, 1927–38; inducted into Illinois HPA Hall of Fame, 1978. Enjoys bowling. Home: 502 Adams Street, Varna, Illinois 61375.

PETERSON, GUSTAV "GUS," b. August 16, 1942. Director, annual tournament for youth, Frazeysburg, Ohio. W. Donna; children—Gustav, Jr., Valerie. Group Home director (The Navigator House), Muskingum,

County Juvenile Court and soccer coach, Mt. Vernon Nazarene College. S. Allen; t. one and three quarters, right handed. Worked for Ohio Youth Commission as guidance counselor, 3 years; member of pro soccer team, Chicago Sting; selected for 1968 U. S. Olympic Soccer Team; U.S. Navy veteran, 1960–64; participated in basketball, and track, winning many distinctions; high tournament, 50%, (Marietta); high game, 64% (Crestline); hit seven consecutive doubles, (St. Louisville). Home: P.O. Box 311, Navigator House, Frazeysburg, Ohio 43822.

PETERSON, GUSTAV "GUS," JR., b. May 10, 1972. Class C Champion, Ringer Classic, Greenville, Ohio, 1980. Son of Gustav and Donna Peterson. S. Allen; t. one and a quarter, right handed. Won state pool championship, Ohio Association, age 7. Enjoys soccer and baseball. Home: P.O. Box 311, Navigator House, Frazeysburg, Ohio 43822.

PETERSON, HARVEY, North Dakota State Champion, 1973, 7-0-61%, 1977, 63.4%. Home: Havana, North Dakota 58043.

PETERSON, HOWARD, Oregon HPA Hall of Fame, 1974.

PETERSON, JAMES C., b. February 24, 1921. President, Florida HPA. W. Mildred; children—James, Susan, John. Offset printer. S. Imperial; t. one and a quarter, right handed. President, Orlando Horseshoe Club; pitched 30 years; voted Outstanding Member, Florida HPA, 1977; high tournament, 61.7%; high game, 78%. Home: 220 Maynard Avenue, Orlando, Florida 32803.

PETERSON, LAVERNE, Peace Country Champion, 1976–78.

PETERSON, NELS, b. June 29, 1900. Minnesota State Champion, 1947, 10-2-61.6%, 1952, 15-0-62.6%. W. d.; children—June Houland, Della Johnson, Elnora Schmidt,

Nels, Jr. Retired. S. Allen; t. one and a quarter, right handed. Pitched five times, championship division, World Tournament (hit 12 four-deads with Dean Brown in one game); served as president, Minnesota HPA. Enjoys collecting antique musical instruments and phonographs. Home: 205 Third Street, Northwest Rochester, Minnesota 55901.

PFEFFER, CARL, 1956 Wisconsin State Champion. Home: 2470 West Concordia, Milwaukee, Wisconsin 53200.

PHELPS, CECIL W., b. November 16, 1945. Past President, Virginia State HPA, 1977–78. W. Juanita; children—Wendy, Wayne. Machinist. S. Allen; t. one and a quarter, right handed. Past vice-president, Virginia HPA, 1976; vice-president, Elmont Club; won Elmont Club League Championship, 13-2-53%; high tournament, 57%; high game, 68%. Home: 319 Colonial Estates Drive, Glen Allen, Virginia 23060.

PHELPS, JUANITA, b. September 19, 1945. Virginia State Champion, 1976, 7-0-54.5%, 1977, 4-0-67.4%, 1979, 4-0-65.8%, 1980, 2-0-70.3%. H. Cecil; children—Wendy, Wayne. Secretary. S. Allen; t. flip, right handed. Won Class B title, World Tournament (Huntsville, Alabama), 6-1-68.5%, 1980; won many Class A championships, including Raymond Frye Memorial, 1976, 1978, and Virginia Cash, 1979; won state doubles championship 1976–80; high tournament, 73.6%, 1978 Russel Robey Open; high game, 92%, against Cindy Dean, Frye Memorial; holds state record for qualifying, 80%, 253 points, 1977; secretary-treasurer, Elmont Club. Home: 319 Colonial Estates Drive, Glen Allen, Virginia 23060.

PHILLIPS, FRANCES, Oregon Women's State Championship, 1976, 5-1, 1977, 7-1, 1978, 5-0-57%. H. Les; children—Leslie, Joanne Johnson, Carol Jones. Cannery, food processing employee. S. Allen; t. flip,

right handed. Won Portland Rose Festival, 1972–76, Seattle Memorial, 1975, Strawberry Festival, 1973–79; member, Salem-Dallas Club; high game, 83.3%, 1978 state tournament; high tournament, 59.7%. Home: 1324 S.W. 8th Street, Dallas, Oregon 97338.

PHILLIPS, FRANK, Kansas State Champion, 1933, 6-1-63%, 1936, 20-3-63%. Home: Topeka, Kansas.

PHILLIPS, RAYMOND L., b. June 4, 1920. Illinois State Champion, 1980, 9-2-67.6%. W. Lois; children—Tom, John, Linda, Judy, Lisa. Farmer. S. Allen; t. one and a quarter, right handed. Pitched 50 years, 20 in tournaments play. Home: Magnolia, Illinois 61336.

PHOENIX, NORMAN, b. June 10, 1921. Secretary-treasurer, Preeceville Horseshoe Club. Single. Farmer. S. Ohio; t. no preference, right handed. Secretary-treasurer, Saskatchewan Provincial Horseshoe Club, 1975–80; recipient, plaque, Saskatchewan association, for years of secretarial work; defeated Saskatchewan doubles champions, with Hilding Rosaasen, 50-4 and 50-3, c. 1950. Enjoys geneology and local history. Home: Box 211, Preeceville, Saskatchewan, Canada SOA 3BO.

PICKERING, DON, b. September 7, 1930. New Hampshire State Champion, 1964, 7-0-60.5%, 1965, 8-1-61.4%, 1966, 10-0-66.6%. W. Jeanette; children—Michael, Debra, Brian. Machine assembly, Kingsbury Machine Tool. S. Allen; t. one and a quarter, right handed. Won Keene Warmup, three times; secretary, past president, tournament director, Keene Horseshoe Club. Enjoys bowling, golf. Home: P.O. Box 208, Keene, New Hampshire 03431.

PICKERING, MICHAEL A., b. December 25, 1953. New Hampshire Boys State Champion, 1966, 5-0-33.4%, 1968, 1969, 5-0-42.3%. W. Diane. Department manager,

Frito-Lay, Inc. S. Allen; t. one and a quarter, right handed. Won New England Junior Championship, 1967, 1969; won many junior championships in New England states, undefeated in his last year as a junior. Home: 2438 Twisted Oak Drive, Jackson, Mississippi 39212.

PIKE, ROBERT, b. February 27, 1969. New York Boys State Champion, 1980, 7-1-56.4%, with 65.7% play-off against Bob Deuster (high game). Student. S. Deadeye; t. one and a quarter, right handed. Won Canton Junior League Championship, 1979 (his first Class A title), 1980, recipient of League's Silver Shoe Trophy for outstanding accomplishment; won Northern Open, 6-1-37.1%; won Pine Grove Open, 5-0-48.6%; high tournament, 56.4%. Home: Route 2, Canton, New York 13617.

PILETZ, WALTER A., JR., b. December 26, 1946. New Hampshire State Runnerup, 1973 (lost to his father, 50-48). W. Debra; children—Jessica, Meredith, Damon. S. Imperial; t. one and three quarters, ambidextrous. Enjoys bowling, basketball, hunting, fishing, music. Home: Willard Street, Box 803, Charlestown, New Hampshire 03603.

PILETZ, WALTER A., SR., b. October 2, 1910. New Hampshire State Champion, 1969, 8-1-66.1%, 1970, 9-0-68.9%, 1971, 8-1-57.2%, 1973, 7-2-61.4%. W. Barbara; children—Carole Curtis, Walter A., Jr. Time study engineer, retired. S. Allen; t. one and a quarter, right handed. Only player to receive trophy from Governor of New Hampshire; in Franklin, N.H., game, went from a 49-25 deficit to win 50-49. Enjoys singing, yodeling, accordian, violin, banjo. Home: Box 235, Charlestown, New Hampshire 03603.

PILON, HARVEY, 1980 Senior Canadian Champion, 7-1-57.4% (winning in a three-way tie with Ken Drury and Roy Hore). Home: Ottawa, Ontario, Canada.

PINCH, DOROTHY, b. January 25, 1920. Fourth Vice-President, NHPA, six years. H. Herb; children—Barbara Meyer, Marilou Zampedro, Robert, John. Office worker, Westinghouse Electric. NHPA member since 1972 (does not pitch); handles purchase and sale of game-related items; worked with tournament officials in scorekeeping, scheduling, correspondence, etc. Home: 592 Hull Street, Charon, Pennsylvania 16146.

PINCH, HERB, b. July 18, 1916. Member, Pennsylvania HPA Hall of Fame, 1978. W. Dorothy; children—Barbara Mayer, Marilou Zampedro, Robert, John. Steelworker, Sharon Steel Corp. S. Ohio; t. one and a quarter, right handed. NHPA regional director for Pennsylvania and New York; recipient, Sportsman Award, Pa. State HPA, 1960, special service award, 1969; inducted into Mercer County All-Sports Hall of Fame, 1980; past secretary and delegate of state association; brought exhibition games to Sharon, Pa., with Ted Allen, Jimmy Risk, Raymond Frye; tournament average, 70% or better, 1960–68; finished 15th, 72.7% with 524 qualifying points, World Tournament, 1961, finished 25th, 1962, finished 19th, 1964, finished 26th, 1965; won New Brighton (Class A) Championship, 69.3%, 1962; won AAU (Meadville), 1963; won New Castle championship, 67.7%, 1967; worked as promoter and organizer of tournaments; works as professional clown; stricken with myastenia gravis. Home: 592 Hull Street, Sharon, Pennsylvania 16146.

PINION, LILLARD, 1970 Missouri State Champion, 11-0-66.8%.

PINTOR, RICHARD, 1978 Colorado Boys State Champion.

PITTMAN, BUDDY, 1976 Canadian Junior Boys Champion, 4-0-71.9%.

PIZZINI, JOE, 1975 Texas Boys State Champion.

PLOGMAN, E. K., finished fifth, 1922 World Tournament (Des Moines), 10-5. Home: Conroy, Iowa.

PLOTT, OTIS SIDNEY, b. August 13, 1906. Louisiana State Champion, 1929–74. W. Leona Ellis; children—Robert, Grace Ellen, Mary Oles. Telegraph operator for Kansas City Southern Railroad. S. Gordon; t. one and three quarters, right handed. Attended 1927 World Tournament (Duluth), achieved place in 36-man championship class, 11-23, finished 25th; won Class B World Championship, (Murray City, Utah), 1959; won Neosho Open, 1923; in Missouri state tournaments, finished 9th, 1934, 6th, 1936 (60%), 6th, 1937 (60%), 8th, 1938 (60%); defeated C. C. Davis in tournament game; high tournament, 66.5% (Tournament of Champions, Springfield, Mo., 1960); averaged 77% for four games, exhibition against John Elkins, with high game, 84%; hit eleven consecutive doubles, Springfield tournament, to win over Marines Tamboer. Home: 2728 Rosemont Street, Shreveport, Louisiana 71108.

PLUMB, FLOYD, b. June 23, 1908. Intermediate Class B World Champion, 1973. W. Mildred; children—Forrest, Paul, James, Josephine Swiatecki, Caroline Franklin. Retired DuPont chemical worker/minister, Fundamental Ministers and Churches of Kansas City, Mo. S. Allen; t. one and three quarters, right handed. Pitched 63 years, 45 in organized competition; high game, 88% (1978 Toledo City League); high tournament, 72% (1974 Toledo Recreation Tournament); finished second, 1974 Senior World Tournament Championships, high qualifier, third place, 1975, 1976; won three Fulton County Fair titles, eleven Toledo Area championships, three Fulton County Old Timers Open, two Hillsdale Fair titles, two Lenawee Fairs, and the Sturgis Open. Boxed in several shows; played semi-pro football.

Home: 3838 Wrenwood Road, Toledo, Ohio 43623.

PLUTE, DAN, Missouri Boys State Champion, 1969, 5-0-25.8%, 1970, 5-0-34.9%, 1972, 5-0-40%, 1973, 5-0-59.3%. Home: 810 South Maguire, Warrensburg, Missouri 64093.

POOLE, LINDA, b. June 26, 1945. Idaho Women's State Champion, 1979. H. Jack; children—Mark, Mike, Brent. Homemaker. S. Gordon; t. single flip, right handed. Treasurer, Kootenai HPA, two years; high game, 56% (1979 state tournament), shared run of three four-deads with Ruth Welsh. Enjoys Christian Women's Club, swimming, oil painting, sewing. Home: 3705 Sherwood Drive, Coeur D'Alene, Idaho 83814.

POOLE, MIKE J., b. November 2, 1964. Idaho Boys State Champion, 1978, 30%, 1979, 56.4%, 1980, 34%. Student. S. Allen; t. one and a quarter, right handed. Finished second, Yakima regionals, hit four consecutive doubles against Peter Clark, averaged 58.03%, hit high game, 75%. Enjoys basketball, football, hunting, fishing, water skiing, baseball, bowling. Home: 3705 Sherwood Drive, Coeur D'Alene, Idaho 83814.

PORTER, BILL, b. January 11, 1916. Winner, Class A Championships, New Jersey, Pennsylvania. W. Laura. Steelworker. S. Imperial, Gordon, Allen; t. one and a quarter, right handed. Pitched 50 years, active in tournaments 1959–76, including world tournaments; averages 70-75%. Enjoys bowling, teaching youngsters to box, play baseball and softball. Home: 11 Butterfly Lane, Levittown, Pennsylvania 19054.

PORTER, HAL, 1977 Member, Florida HPA Hall of Fame. Horseshoe editor, The Bradenton Herald—wrote column to promote horseshoes. Home: Bradenton, Florida 33507.

PORTT, GLEN A., b. February 23, 1914. Georgia State Champion, 1974, 8-0-61.6%, 1977, 10-1-64.8%, 1978, 7-0-72.4%, 1979, 9-0-70.6%. W. Jane; children—James, Virginia Cannon. Retired Air Force colonel, associate realtor/management consultant. S. Imperial; t. one and three quarters, right handed. Won Opelika, Ala., Open, 6-0-67.5%, 1979, 7-0-68.8%, 1980; high tournament, 73.6% (1980 Strawberry Festival, Fla.); high game, 92% (Panama City, Fla., 1977); recipient, 3 National Honors, NHPA: second highest count-all average, 117.85, second highest ringer average, 72.1%, fourth highest ringer percentage for one game, 84%; president, Albany Club; publicity director, Georgia State HPA; toured with Jimmy Risk in Michigan as fall guy for trick shots. Home: 2803 Newcomb Road, Albany, Georgia 31705.

POSEY, CHARLES, b. December 23, 1931. Texas State Champion, 1978, 54.4%, 1979, 6-1-60.8%. W. Leah; children—Brenda, Jeanne, Eddie. Accountant. S. Allen; t. one and a quarter, right handed. Voted Most Improved Pitcher, Texas HPA, 1977; state secretary, 1977, state treasurer, 1978–79; treasurer, Arlington Ironbenders Horseshoe Club, 1976–77, president, 1978. Enjoys ranching, hunting, fishing. Home: 2026 Rockcreek Court, Arlington, Texas 76010.

POSEY, EDDIE, b. August 19, 1964. Texas Junior State Champion, 1976, 1977, 32.5%, 1979, 6-0-36.1%. Student. S. Ohio Pro; t. one and a quarter, right handed. Enjoys mechanics. Home: 2026 Rockcreek Court, Arlington, Texas 76010.

POTTER, LLOYD L., b. January 25, 1918. Member, Northern California Hall of Fame, 1975. W. Virginia; child—Sandra Ostendorf. Operating engineer. S. Gordon; t. one and a quarter, right handed. President, Sallisaw Horseshoe Club; past-president, 11 years, Northern California HPA; past president, 12 years, San Jose Golden Eagles Club; pitched tournament horseshoes 54 years; won San Francisco Memorial Open, and Santa Rosa Open; won Northern California title, age 15, 75% ringers; promoter of horseshoes. Enjoys raising Polled Herefords, square dancing. Home: Route 2, Box 152, Sallisaw, Oklahoma 74955.

POTTS, MERLIN, b. February 15, 1927. Kansas State Champion, 14 times. W. Marlaine; children—Diane, Roger. Farmer. S. Imperial; t. one and a quarter, right handed. Holds state record for most championships won, for nine consecutive titles won, and for 78.9% ringers for an entire tournament; won numerous local and regional tournaments; high game, 96%; high world tournament, 79.1%-80%; member, Kansas State Hall of Fame; recipient, 1966 Outstanding First-Year Pitcher in World Tournament award; vice-president, Kansas State Association; pitched 40 years. Home: Route 1, Box 122, Leonardville, Kansas 66449.

POTTS, ROGER, 1973 Kansas Boys State Champion, 5-0. Won 1980 Donut Open, 5-0-54%. Home: Route 1, Leonardville, Kansas 66449.

POUTANEN, ROGER A., b. October 12, 1951. Won ten individual championships, 6 in Class A, 4, Class B. W. Barbara J. Actuarial analyst, Wausau Insurance Companies. S. Deadeye, Allen; t. one and three quarters, right handed. Member, 1968 league championship team, Ishpeming, Michigan; high game, 80%; high tournament, 66.7%; 20 consecutive ringers. Enjoys many sports, reading, music. Home: 525½ Fulton Street, Wausau, Wisconsin 54401.

POWELL, TARI CARPENTER, b. November 29, 1959. Illinois Women's State Champion, 1978, Girls World Champion, 1976, 7-0-59.7%. H. Thomas A.; child—Jennifer R. Housewife. S. Diamond; t. three quarters, right handed. Runnerup, women's division, Illinois State Tournament, 1977; set or tied twelve world records for girls in a seven-game World Tournament, Bristol, Pa., 1976; high tournament, 71%; hit 20 consecutive ringers; played against Ray Martin, Karl Van Sant, in Illinois tournaments. Enjoys volleyball, softball, Home: Route 1, Rankin, Illinois 60960.

POWERS, GRANT M., b. March 4, 1920. Maryland State Champion, 1974, 1975, 1978, 1979, 5-0-69.3%, 1980, 5-0-70%. W. Blanche; children—Allen, John, Robert, Sharon, Janet. Retired. S. Imperial; t. one and three quarters, right handed. Pitched 50 years, 10 in tournament play. Home: 8702 Emge Road, Parkville, Maryland 21234.

POWERS, TERRY, 1973 New York Boys State Champion, 3-0-53.1%. Home: Route 1, Fulton, New York, 13069.

PRANGE, NORMAN "BUD," b. January 24, 1935. President, Ontario HPA. W. Patricia; children—Dawn, William, Heidi, Plumber. S. Any pro shoe; t. one and three quarters, right handed. Pitched 30 years, 20 in organized competition; president, North Waterloo Horseshoe League. Enjoys directorship, Ventures Drum and Bugle Corps; past president Twin Cities Waterloo Region Optimist Club. Home: 11 Nelson Street, Kitchener, Ontario, Canada N2K 1C7.

PRANGE, WILLI, b. December 4, 1963. 1979 Canadian Junior Champion, 7-0-63.4%. Student. S. Ohio Pro, Imperial; t. one and a quarter reverse, one and three quarters reverse, right handed. Won 1979 Hamilton Open, 6-0-58.7%, 1980, 7-0-69%; won Greenville Classic, 1980, set highs of 87.5% game, 79.8% tournament average; pitched in NHPA events since 1977. Home: 11 Nelson Street, Kitchener, Ontario Canada N2K 1C7.

PRATT, ARCHIE, d. Member, West Vir-

ginia HPA Hall of Fame. Was dedicated organizer and pitcher, Wood County Horseshoe Club. Home: 3106 Liberty Avenue, Parkersburg, West Virginia 26101.

PRATT, EDWARD J., b. May 30, 1923. Won 50 trophies. W. Pauline. Retired. S. Ohio; t. unusual unidentified turn, right handed. Played in Class D, 1979 World Tournament, Class E, 1980. Home: 6257 Sharon Woods Boulevard, Columbus, Ohio 43229.

PRATT, JOHN N., b. January 12, 1916. d. June 22, 1980. Pitched in Class A division, World Tournament, 1970, 4-31-63.4%, 1973, 2-33-61.9%, 1978, 8-27-60.2%. W. Charlotte L.; children—Stephanie, Thomas W., Betty Jean O'Neill. Indian Health Services, H.E.W. S. Allen; t. one and a quarter, right handed. Won 1980 Laurelhurst tournament, high average 74%; high game, 81%; won Pleasanton Open, 63.8%, 1969; president, 12 years, Sacramento Horseshoe Club; won Feather River Open, 1973, Arroyo Viejo Park, 1963, Gold Country Open, 1972, 1974, Mosswood Open, 1969, Grass Valley, 1968, San Jose, 1968, Turlock Open, 1969, Golden Gate Classic, 1970.

PRATT, ONA, Women's State Champion, Maine, 1970, 7-1-40.8%, 1971, 5-0-45.1%, 1972, 5-0-51.1%. Home: Oakfield, Maine.

PREIMESBERGER, HENRY, b. March 5, 1923. Operator, Preimesberger Arena. W. Delores; children—Nora, Lois, Joan, Zeno, Tom, Iris, Joe, Mary, June, John, Daniel, Jason. Self-employed, lumber business, S. Allen; t. three quarter flip, right handed. Recipient, 1979 Minnesota Tourism Award; 1981 World Tournament held at Arena, as well as many state and league tournaments; designed the 18-court arena on campsite; won 1974 league title; high tournament, 53%; high game, 70%. Home: Route 2 (Genola), Pierz, Minnesota 56364.

Top, left, 1980 World Tournament for Women, Huntsville, Alabama. *Right,* Willie Prange, Canadian Junior Champion. *Center row, left to right,* John Pratt; Dolores and Henry Preimesberger, owners of indoor arena, right, which was scene of 1981 World Tournament. *Bottom, left,* John Rademacher. *Right,* Five world champions, Fernando Isais, Paul Focht, Ted Allen, Harold Reno, Don Titcomb.

Top, left to right, Audrey Reno, World Champion; Jennifer Reno, World Champion; Ottie Reno with Alabama Governor George Wallace. *Second row, left to right,* Glen Riffle, National AAU Champion; Gary Roberts, World Champion; Jerry Schneider. *At left,* Hazel Russell, World Champion.

PRESCOTT, PHIL, Montana State Champion, 1962, 7-0-53.3%, 1963, 7-0-58.7%, 1967, 7-1-53.5%, 1969, 7-0-60%. Won North ₋kota state championship, 14-1, 1941.

PRESSLER, DAVE, Vice-president, Nevada HPA. Home: 1580 Van Petten, Reno, Nevada 89503.

PRICE, ALBERT J., Publicity service for 1971 World Tournament, Middlesex, N.J. Vice-president, Ringer World Emporium, supplier of game-related items. Home: 291 LaGrande Avenue, Fanwood, New Jersey 07023.

PRICE, BONITA SEIBOLD, b. April 11, 1952. Junior Girls World Champion, 1967, 29.1%. H. Byron; child—Adam. Teacher. S. Ohio; t. one and a quarter, right handed. Won 1967 Indiana State Girls Championship. Home: 631 McGahn, Huntington, Indiana 46750.

PRICE, CHARLES L., b. May 18, 1926. 1969 Virginia State Champion, 13-0-70.4%. W. Hilda Mae; child—Timmy Lee. Sheet metal mechanic. S. Imperial; t. one and three quarters, right handed. Pitched 23 years, 15 in league and tournament play; won Virginia State Doubles championship, with Paul Good, 1972, with Bob Dean, 1977, with Cecil Monday, 1980; set records: most shoes pitched in one tournament, 1054, and most ringers for one tournament, 760, 1969 Virginia tournament. Enjoys bowling, rabbit hunting, fishing. Home: Route 1, Box 301, Stanley, Virginia 22851.

PRICE, MARION, b. November 2, 1933. Past President, Alabama State HPA, 1978–79. W. Peggy; children—Patty, Jayne, Mike, Tina. Engineering assistant, Thiokol Chemical Corp. S. Ohio Pro; t. three quarters, right handed. Past president, secretary, Huntsville City Club; finished second, Alabama State Tournament, 1977; won Madison County Championship, 1976, 1978; hit 50.2%, Class C, 1980 World Tournament; high game, 60% or better; high tournament, 50% or better. Home: 217 Bierne Avenue Northwest, Huntsville, Alabama 35801.

PRITZLAFF, BRET, b. September 22, 1967. Wisconsin Boys State Champion, 1976, 40.5%, 1977, 64%, 1978, 66.1%, 1979, 61.4%. Student. S. Allen; t. one and a quarter, right handed. Averaged 80%, high game, 90%, Germantown tournament, 1979; finished second, Class B, 1979 World Tournament; interviewed by Nashville Radio, has pitched and been interviewed on Germantown TV, 1980. Home: W 204 N 11912 Goldendale Road, Germantown, Wisconsin 53022.

PRITZLAFF, RICK, b. November 20, 1957. 1977 Wisconsin State Champion, 64.4%. Lead man, Dry Mix Dept., P. H. Orth Co. S. Allen; t. one and a quarter, right handed. President, Wisconsin State Association since 1978; high tournament, 67.6%, LaCrosse, 1974; high game, 86%, Newport, Indiana, 1974. Home: W 204 N 11912 Goldendale Road, Germantown, Wisconsin 53022.

PRITZLAFF, RUSTY, b. October 1, 1964. Finished second, 1979 Wisconsin State Tournament, 64%. Student. S. Ohio O; t. three quarters, right handed. Played in World Tournaments since 1977, from Class D to Class B; won (Class A) Fond du Lac, 1975, Germantown Bicentennial Open, 1976, Goldendale Opens, 1979; high game, 84% (Goldendale Open); high tournament, 69%, 16 consecutive ringers; subject of 1979 Grit Magazine article; has pitched and been interviewed, Germantown TV, 1980. Home: West 204 North 11912 Goldendale Road, Germantown, Wisconsin 53022.

PROGEN, ROBERT, Massachusetts Boys State Champion, 1969, 3-0-35%, 1970, 1971, 1972, 5-0-50.4%.

PROUDMAN, LARRY, b. April 7, 1920. 1975 Member, New York State HPA Hall of Fame. W. Anne; children—Brenda, Stephanie, Laurie, Brent, Amy, Charles. Retired. S. Allen; t. one and a quarter, right handed. Pitched 25 years, 20 in tournament play; won city and county championships; finished third, New York State Tournament, more than once; served as president, Falconer Horseshoe Club; served two terms as president, New York State HPA, and two terms as regional director, NHPA; Falconer Park horseshoe courts known as "The Larry Proudman Horseshoe Park . . . Home: 122 Denver Street, Rochester, New York 14609.

PROUTY, LEWIS E. "PETE," b. September 9, 1934. Vermont State Champion, 1967–68, 1972–74, 1977. W. Joanne Marie; children—Mark, Beth, Lynn, Dawn. Graphic artist, Brattleboro Reformer. S. Allen; t. one and a quarter, one and three quarters, right handed. High tournament, 72%; high game, 88%; longest string of consecutive ringers, 28; won second place, 1973 New England Championship, Keene, N.H., 71.2%. Home: 54 Clark Street, Brattleboro, Vermont 05301.

PRUIKSMA, WALTER N., b. July 26, 1923. New Jersey State Champion, 1976–77, 7-2-57.1%, 7-2-58.7%. W. Claire; children—Walter, Ronald, Richard. Textile salesman. S. Allen; t. one and three quarters, right handed. Tied with Sol Berman, New Jersey State Tournament, 1978, lawsuit filed by Pruiksma, court awarded title to Berman; high tournament (Middlesex Memorial, 1978), 7-0-64.3%, first place; won Mid-Atlantic Open, 7-0-60.2%, 1978; awarded "Outstanding Service in Promoting Horseshoes," New Jersey HPA, 1975; past president, Clifton Inter-city Horseshoe Club; past first vice-president, New Jersey HPA; pitched for 15 years, in NHPA since 1971. Home: 84 Greendale Road, Clifton, New Jersey 07013.

PUGLISE, JOSEPH, b. June 6, 1911. New Jersey State Champion, 1933, 9-0-36.9%, 1973 Member, New Jersey Hall of Fame. W. Antoinette; children—Joseph, Rosemary. Carpenter foreman. S. Lattore; t. one and three quarters, right handed. Past secretary, New Jersey HPA; high game, 88.3%, Hudson County Tournament, 1935. Enjoys photography. Home: 63 Butler Street, Paterson, New Jersey 07524.

PUGLISE, PAUL, 1971 Member, New Jersey Hall of Fame (first and only charter member), known as "Father of New Jersey Horseshoes." Brother of Joseph. With Santoro Brothers of Perth Amboy, founded New Jersey HPA, 1933, inducted sixty new members, conducted state tournament; with Lee Davis, formed New Jersey Horseshoe League, introducing 50-shoe game, 1937; elected state president (with Lee Davis, vice-president), NJHPA, 1946, and added handicap system to increase interest in state play; worked to strengthen New Jersey clubs, e.g., Middlesex Club, which hosted 1971 World Tournament; served continuously as vice-president or tournament director for more than 30 years; served in Navy Sea Bees, 1943–46. Home: Paterson, New Jersey.

PULLIAM, EDDIE, 1978 New Mexico Boys State Champion, 29% ringer average. Home: Route 5, Box 261-B, Santa Fe, New Mexico 87501.

PULLINS, S. N., 1926 Arizona State Champion.

PURSE, CHARLES, b. September 17, 1903. 1978 Member, Saskatchewan Hall of Fame. Won Senior Men's Championship, 50.5%, at age 74. Home: Regina, Saskatchewan, Canada.

Q

QUANTRILLE, HUBBARD, 1932 Washington, D.C., Champion.

R

RADCLIFF, ROY, 1965 Colorado State Champion, 13-1-61.7%.

RADEMACHER, GENE, Florida State Doubles Champion (with Joe Thonert), 5-0, 1965. W. Kim. Crew supervisor, Dredge Co., college student. S. Allen; t. one and three quarters, right handed. Finished second, Florida State Tournament, several times; won Class A Championship, Western Week Celebration, Bradenton, 4-1-73%, 1968; won Midland Open, St. Joseph, Mo., undefeated, and the Plattsburg Fall Festival, 1970; won Class A Championship, Florida State Open, and Strawberry Festival, 1975; won Fun-N-Sun Festival, Clearwater, 7-0-70.5%, 1976; high tournament, 73.5%; high game, 85.7%; best qualifying round, 89 ringers out of 100 shoes. Home: 1853 Kim Acres Lane, Dover, Florida 33527.

RADEMACHER, JOHN, b. June 21, 1920. Florida State Champion, ten times since 1963, NHPA Second Vice-President. W. Laura; children—Gene, Joyce, John. Insulation manufacturer and contractor. S. Allen or Ohio Pro; t. one and a quarter, right handed. Won 180 trophies; major tournament titles include: Statesville, North Carolina Dogwood Festival, Los Altos, Albuquerque; hit 80.1% ringers for 35 games, World Tournament, Keene, N.H., 1968; finished fifth, 90% single game, World Tournament, Eureka, Ca., 1973; holds world record for most shoes pitched in world tournament, 3386; received Most Improved Player award; won National A.A.U. Championship, Texas, 1972; served as secretary-treasurer, Florida State HPA, 10 years; second vice-president, NHPA, since 1973; secretary-treasurer, Plant City Club; career record in world tournament play: 147-168-73.9%, 512 qualifying points. Home: 408 North Pevetty Drive, Plant City, Florida 33566.

RAINBOW, JACK, b. September 21, 1918. 1971 Class C World Champion. W. Betty; children—Marsha, Nancy. Employee, Jones & Laughlin Steel Corp., Electrical Repair Shop. S. Imperial; t. one and a quarter, right handed. Pitched 48 years, 18 in tournament play; served as State Advisory Board Committee member, Pennsylvania HPA; high game, 85%; high tournament, 75%. Home: 106 Newgate Drive, Monaca, Pennsylvania 15061.

RAMQUIST, EARL, 1955 Wisconsin State Champion. Home: 1162 Townline Avenue, Beloit, Wisconsin 53511.

RAMSHAW, ED, 1930 Utah State Champion.

RANDALL, GEORGE, 1925 Indiana State Champion.

RANDALL, RALPH E., b. November 30, 1911. 1973 Intermediate World Champion, 6-1-72.4%. W. Josephine; child—Mike. Offset pressman, retired. S. Allen; t. one and a quarter, right handed. Pitched 60 years, 41 in NHPA; secretary-treasurer, Barstow Horseshoe Club, 20 years; president, Oklahoma Association, 1939–45, secretary-treasurer, 1946–50; set world records: hit 76 ringers in one game against Jim Johnson, and hit (with Art Kamman) combined average of 75%; won San Bernadino County title, eleven times (49-0 for last seven years); won Southern California Oxnard Open "AA," 6-1-67.4%, 1966; won Pacific Coast Open, 6-1-66.5%, 1966; high tournament, 5-0-78.5%; high game, 84.8% (1973 World Tournament); "Ralph Randall Open" held annually in Barstow; engineered a six-court layout for third annual Calico Tournament. Home: 408 Highland Avenue, Barstow, California 92311.

RANSDELL, R.M., d., 1922-23 Minnesota State Champion. Right handed.

RASMUSSEN, RALPH, Minnesota Boys State Champion, 1923–25.

RASMUSSEN, SIFTON, b. 1898; d., September 15, 1979. 1979 Manitoba Hall of Fame member. Won Manitoba Provincial Championship, 1962; served as promoter in Southern Manitoba.

RAY, ELZIE, Finished 10th, 1922 World Tournament, Des Moines, 7–8. Home: Shenandoah, Iowa.

RAYMOND, GARY, 1974 Wyoming Boys State Champion. Home: Ferris Mountain Ranch, Lander Route, Rawlins, Wyoming 82301.

RAYMOND, JACK, b. August 16, 1925. President, Utah HPA, 1979. W. Mary Lou; children—Tom, Linda, David, Pat, Tina, Cindy. U.S. letter carrier/U.S. Navy (20 Years). S. Allen; t. one and a quarter, right handed. Won Class A title, 1976 Pop Wahlin Memorial, 5-0-60%; won Class B title, 1977, finished third, 1979, Utah State Championship division; high game, 82%; past vice-president, Utah HPA, 1976–77. Home: 8071 South 535 East, Sandy, Utah 84070.

RAYMOND, KENNETH, b. December 11, 1922. Wyming State Champion, 1976, 1978–80. W. Ruth; children—Donna, Cheryl, Sandy, Gary. Rancher. S. Allen; t. three quarters, right handed. Pitched since 1972, 8 years in NHPA competition; won Wyoming State Winter Fair, 1977–78, 1980, Medicine Bow, 1976, Cowboy Open, 1975, North Weld Fall Festival, 1979, averaging 55%; high tournament, 63%; high game, 79.03%; 1980 state winning record, 8-1-45.9%; fourth vice-president, Wyoming State HPA; secretary-treasurer, local club (also past president and vice-president). Home: Ferris Mountain Ranch, Lander Route, Rawlins, Wyoming 82301.

REBMAN, RICK, b. April 10, 1938. Host, Annual Oregon Open Horseshoe Tournaments, Hermiston. W. Pat; children—Don, Scott, Tami. Owner, manager, Recreational Vehicles Sales Lot. S. Allen; t. one and a quarter, right handed. Won LaGrande, Oregon, Open, 49.1%, 1980; high game, 64.5%; recipient, Outstanding Jaycee of the Year, Jaycee Spark Plug Award (twice), Businessman of the Year, Outstanding Young Man of the Year; president, Hermiston Chamber of Commerce. Enjoys hunting, fishing. Home: Route 3, Box 3150-B, Hermiston, Oregon 97838.

REDDON, LIL, Manitoba Women's Champion, 1975–76, 1978–79. Won Doubles Championship, with Minnie Oliver, 1975, 1976, 1978; finished third, 4-3-53%, Canadian National Championship, 1979.

REED, LYNN A., b. August 16, 1937. President, West Virginia HPA. W. Joann; children—Susan, Beth, Thomas. Insurance agency manager. S. Ohio; t. one and three quarters, right handed. President, Lewis County HPA; won State Class E title, 20.1%, 1974, Class C Champion, 49.7%, 1976, Class B title, 59.3%; pitched ten years, four in NHPA. Home: 107 Montgomery Road, Weston, West Virginia 26452.

REEL, CHET, b. November 16, 1935. Indiana Class B. State Championship, 1961. W. Carolyn; children—Lynn, Lori, Susan, Patrick. Beauty supply salesman. S. Allen; t. one and a quarter. Pitched 30 years, in tournaments since 1959; high tournament, 81%; finished second, Indiana State Tournament, 1964; reached championship division, World Tournament play, qualified at 505, finished 25th, 1972, qualified at 514, finished 25th, 1975; past secretary-treasurer, Kokomo Horseshoe Club; went 5-0-82.8%, 1975 Mid-Winter Indoor Invitational, Pinecrest Courts, Elwood, Ind. Home: 3314 Normandy Boulevard, Holiday, Florida 33590.

REEVES, JOHN P., South Carolina State Champion, 1974, 7-0-52.8%, 1975, 5-1-

67.7%. Home: 750 Norwood Avenue, Rock Hill, South Carolina 29730.

REEVES, JOYCE K., b. March 4, 1949. Champion, 1980, Illinois Women's, Adams County Fair, the Quincy City League, and the Loraine Open. H. Jim V.; children— Angie, Teresa, Stacy, Debbie Joe. House- wife. S. Ohio; t. flip, right handed. Presi- dent, Quincy Women's Horseshoe League; top game, state tournament, hit 18 of 22 for 81.8%; won Illinois State Championship with record of 6-1-41.1%. Home: 2906 Ver- mont, Quincy, Illinois 62301.

REHARD, ALICE M., b. August 29, 1920. Washington State Champion, 1964, 1965, 1967; Northwest Open Champion, 1967. H. John (Wally); children—Beverly Jeanne, Sylvia Norene, Kathleen Louise. Proprietor, Arts and Crafts Shop. S. Imperial; t. modified three quarter flip, right handed. Third Vice-President, Washington State HPA; State tournament play 1964, 5-0-25%; 1967, 4-1-42%; high tournament, 52%; high game, 65%. Home: 4203 North Locust, Spokane, Washington 99206.

REHARD, WALLY, b. January 25, 1914. Washington State Statistician. W. Alice; chil- dren—Beverly, Sylvia, Kathy. S. Imperial; t. one and a quarter, right handed. Organized the Pasadena Park Horseshoe Club; fifth place, Washington State Tournament; high game, 86%; high tournament, 69.5%; estab- lished Spokane HPA. Home: 4203 North Locust, Spokane, Washington 99206.

REHEIS, BERYLDEAN "DEANIE", b. November 17, 1937. 1977 Kansas State Champion, 37.2% ringers. H. Marvin; chil- dren—Terri, Tommy. Secretary and electri- cal draftsman. S. Gordon; t. flip, right handed. Secretary, Air Capital Horseshoe Club, Wichita. Home: 2173 Wallace, Wichita, Kansas 67218.

REHEIS, MARVIN, b. February 9, 1918.

1963 Kansas State Champion with 13-2- 68.4% and 12 consecutive double ringers. W. Berlydean; children—Sandra, Gary, Linda, Roger, Steve. Retired. S. American or Gordon; t. one and three quarters, right handed. Three times Kansas Class B Cham- pion; High game, 81% against Earl Winston. N/C programmer for tape milling machines. Home: 2173 Wallace, Wichita, Kansas 67218 and 900 North San Marcos, Lot #91, Apache Junction, Arizona 85220.

REID, ROBERT L., b. February 12, 1917. State Secretary, Indiana HPA. W. Viola; child—Robert D. Rural mail carrier, retired. S. Allen; t. three quarter, right handed. High game, 57%; high tournament, 50%; staged tournaments, Scott County Fairgrounds. Home: 34 North Beechwood Avenue, Scottsburg, Indiana 47170.

REID, VIOLA M., b. January 26, 1923. NHPA member. H. Robert L.; child— Robert D.. Owner, "Specials By Viola". As- sists husband—State secretary—in schedul- ing and tournament details. Home: 34 North Beechwood Avenue, Scottsburg, Indiana 47170.

REIGHARD, LES. Idaho State Champion 1966, 7-0-57.7 and 1967, 6-1-55.1.

RENO, AUDREY, b. January 4, 1963. Junior Girls' World Champion, 1977, 5-0- 59.75%. Single. Student. S. American; t. flip, right handed. Ohio Girls' Champion, 1977 and 1978 with two games of 79.2% ringers; Runnerup to Junior Girls' World Champion, Linda Patenaude, 1978 with a 10-1 record and high tournament average of 62.8%; high game of 83.3% against Grace Duncan in 1976; 1980 Greenville Classic, set her tournament high at 67.5%, qualifying in Class A of the Women's division and finished fourth; hit six consecutive four- deads against her mother, World Champion, Opal Reno, to tie state record. Home: 2593 Camp Creek Road, Lucasville, Ohio 45648.

RENO, BRENDA, b. November 2, 1968. 1979 Ohio Girls' State Champion, 4-0-31.6%; Champion, Girls' B Division, World Tournament, Statesville, North Carolina, 1979; made Girls' Championship Division, Des Moines, Iowa, World Tournament, 1978. S. Reno; t. flip, right handed.

RENO, CHARLES, b. February 27, 1887, d. April 14, 1973. Ohio Seniors Champion, 1954. W. Alma Aills; children—Mary Imogene Hale, Harold, Dorothy Hesse, John Franklin, Mae Harris, Faye. Farmer and McPherson-Huff Tool Company employee. S. Ohio; t. one and three quarters, right handed. Averaged 65-75% ringers for many years. Home: Sabina, Ohio.

RENO, ELI, b. August 20, 1893, d. July 13, 1966. Member 1961 Ohio League Champions. W. Banna; children—Ruth Kirk, Wade, Marjorie Roosa, Ottie, Jessie Scaggs, Gene. Farmer. S. Ohio; t. one and three quarters, right handed. In his four best seasons, hit 70% ringers; highest count-all 50-shoe game, 86%, 134, in 1948, averaging 108 points per game.

RENO, GENE, b. July 30, 1934. Qualified, Championship Division, 1979 World Tournament with 512 score. W. Opal; children—Audrey, Brenda, Dempsey, Dorothy, Eleanor. Sawmill operator. S. Ohio; t. one and a quarter or one and three quarters, right handed. Qualified, 1972 World Tournament; highest tournament average, 74.2%, Dayton, Kentucky; highest sanctioned cancellation game, 90.4%; highest count-all, 90% 139 point game; won several Pike County Championships and Southeastern Ohio Class A titles and league championships.

RENO, HAROLD, b. February 16, 1915. World Champion, 1961, 34-1-83.8%, and 1964, 32-3-84.1%. W. Wenonah; children—Ann and Karen Smith. Farmer. S. Ohio O; t. reverse one and a quarter, right handed. 1974 Member NHPA Hall of Fame; Ohio State Champion—1954, 14-1-74.6, 1956, 14-1-77.6, 1957, 15-0-76.1, 1958, 12-1-77.8, 1959, 13-0-81.1, 1960, 13-0-80.7, 1961, 11-0-84.7, 1964, 11-0-88.6, 1966, 10-1-83.2, 1967, 9-2-80.9, 1969, 10-1-81.0. From 1959–1972, had a composite ringer percentage over 80% and dozens of games above 90%; Other World Tournament play: 1957, 9th, 17-13-79.1, 1959, 2nd, 33-2-81.6, 1960, 8th, 28-7-79.6, 1962, 4th, 30-5-81.7, 1963, 4th, 29-6-78.9, 1965, 8th, 27-8-83.2, 1966, 9th, 17-11-78.9, 1967, 7th, 25-10-75.5, 1968, 7th, 25-10-81.1, 1971, 6th, 27-8-78.3, 1972, 8th, 25-10-79.6; Won 1961 World Tournament Sportsmanship Award.; Won Clinton County League 24 times between 1947 and 1976; Southwestern Ohio District 1951, 1955, 1960, 1967, 1970; the Southeastern 1966, 1968, 1969, 1971, 1972; Winston-Salem 1960; Ohio State Fair 1954-1956; Lakeside Open 1958, 1961, 1963; Corn Belt Open 1959, 1961, 1962, 1967, 1969, 1970; Ohio—Indiana 1966, 1970; Ann Arbor 1955, 1958, 1963; Eastern National, Warren County Fair 1960, 1962; Bremen 1966, 1967; Leo McGrath Award 1960, 1961, 1964; 1963 West Virginia Centennial; 1964 Wilmington Open; 1965 West Virginia Open; 1968 Greenfield Open. Home: 2121 Haley Road, Sabina, Ohio 45164.

RENO, JANET, b. November 9, 1931. 1977 Alabama State Champion. H. Ottie; children—Ottie Wayne II, Jennifer, Lorna. Legal secretary. S. Gordon; t. three quarter flip, right handed. In 1977, won the Hamilton Open, the Lancaster Silver Open, Pike County Open with 71.1%; 1977 World Tournament Class A, 6th with 65%; member of first American team to play against South African team, 1972. Home: 148 Reno Road, Lucasville, Ohio 45648.

RENO, JENNIFER, b. September 2, 1955. Junior Girls' World Champion 1971 and 1972. Single. Court reporter. S. Reno; t. flip, right handed. 1970, 2nd place, Junior Girls'

Champion; Held or shared seven world records—highest percentage, one game, 71.9%; highest percentage, one tournament, 59.8%; most double ringers, one tournament, 46; most double ringers, one game, 13; most consecutive ringers, 10; highest percentage game for both players, 59.5% with Mary Sin Lee; most cancelled ringers in one game by both players, 46 with Mary Sin Lee: Won 15 tournaments including 1971 Ohio Girls' Championship and three Greenville Classic titles. Home: 148 Reno Road, Lucasville, Ohio 45648.

RENO, JOHN FRANKLIN. World Tournament Judge. Dayton Power and Light employee. S. Ohio; t. one and three quarters, right handed. Won many class titles; averages in mid-sixties. Home: Box 28 Reesville, Ohio 45166.

RENO, LORNA, b. June 1, 1966. 1980 Ohio State Girls' Champion with her highest average, 5-0-48.4%. Single. Student. S. Reno; t. flip, right handed. Won 22 Class A championships including the 1977 Alabama Girls' State, the 1979 Ohio Indoor State, the 1980 Ohio Outdoor State, the Greenville Ringer Classic, the Carolina Dogwood Festival, and the Midwest Ringer Roundup championships; highest game, 72% and 115 points; Girls' Division World Tournament play, five times Class A and once Class B. Home: 148 Reno Road, Lucasville, Ohio 45648.

RENO, OPAL, b. November 13, 1943, Women's World Champion, with a world record 82.8% ringers, 1978, and with 78.8%, 11-0, 1980. H. Gene; children—Audrey, Dempsey, Brenda, Dorothy and Eleanor. Housewife. S. Ohio "O"; t. flip, right handed. Set records at the Ohio 1978 Outdoor Championship, with 84.5% ringers, and the 1978 Ohio Indoor Championship, with 88.1%, and a single game record of 97.1%, 33 out of 34 shoes;

Hit 87.1% at the 1980 Ohio State Indoor Tournament, including a perfect game, 20 out of 20; won Ohio Outdoor State title in 1972, 1973, 1977–1980 and three Ohio Indoor State titles; hit a second perfect game in a 1980 NHPA Sanctioned League game, 30 out of 30 on the Roberts Indoor Courts; in other World Tournament play: 1972, 3rd, 5-2-64.3; 1973, 3rd, 5-2-74.7; 1977, 5th, 4-3-69.1; 1979, 2nd, 9-2-76.1.

RENO, OTTIE W., SR., b. April 7, 1929. Fifteen times Alabama State Champion, 1963–1977; legal representative, NHPA, 1959–1976. W. Janet; children—Ottie Wayne II, Jennifer, Lorna. Common Pleas Judge and Attorney-at-Law. Designer and manufacturer of the Reno brand pitching shoe. S. Ohio; t. one and a quarter, right handed. Statutory Agent, NHPA; Chairman, Constitution and By-Laws Committee, NHPA, 1966; Author of: *The Story of Horseshoes*, 1963, Vantage Press, New York; *Pitching Championship Horseshoes*, 1971, and second revised edition, 1975, A. S. Barnes & Co., Inc., Cranbury, New Jersey; 1964 Arch Stokes Memorial Award; contributed thirty articles to the Horseshoe Pitchers News Digest; participated in the formation of the Alabama chapter of the NHPA, 1963–1964, organized and incorported the Ohio, Pike County, Horseshoe Club, serving as President, 1956–1963, and secretary, 1963–1981; Third Vice-President, Ohio Buckeye HPA; Third Vice-President NHPA, 1959; NHPA Regional Director, East Central States; President, Vice-President, or Secretary from 1964–1980; set State record, Alabama, 1972, 27 of 30 for 90%; Member Pike County, Alabama State, Ohio State and NHPA Halls of Fame; Alabama State play: 1963, 7-0-56.7, 1964, 6-0-62.7, 1965, 5-0-52.2, 1966, 3-0-48.5, 1967, 7-0-55.7, 1968, 5-0-53.2, 1969, 5-0-55.8, 1970, 8-1-61.6, 1971, 5-0-66.7, 1972, 7-0-60.2, 1973, 7-0-58.9, 1974, 10-0-60.2, 1975, 5-0-62.8, 1976,

15-1-45.6, 1977, 8-2-47.7, 1978, 6-1-52.0, 1979, 7-2-47.1, 1980, 7-2-53.9; Alabama State records: 100 shoe qualifying records, 74 ringers, 27 doubles, and 246 points, 1971; most consecutive titles, 15; most consecutive ringers, 22 in 1971; highest single game, 27 out of 30, 90%, 1972; most consecutive games won, 50; highest ringer percentage for entire tournament, 66.7%, 1971. Home: 148 Reno Road, Lucasville, Ohio 45648.

RENO, OTTIE W. II, b. January 12, 1954. President of Reno Horseshoe Co., 1970 Pike County Junior Boys Champion. W. Robin; children—Kane and Hannah. Goodyear Atomic Corporation employee. S. Reno; t. one and a quarter, right handed. Home: 670 Reno Road, Lucasville, Ohio, 45648.

RICE, BARBARA LOWERY, b. April 20, 1935. 1962 Ohio State Champion with a state record of 8-1-52.8%. H. Charles; children—Mary, Eddie, Roy. Police Planner, Special Deputy. S. Gordon; t. one and a quarter, right handed. Second highest qualifier in 1962 World Tournament, and finished in eighth place. Home: 1525 Jackson Avenue, Portsmouth, Ohio 45662.

RICHARDSON, CHARLES E., b. November 27, 1920. 1979 Massachusetts State Champion with 10-1-72.1%. W. Edna; children—Ann, Charles, Jr., Donald, Herbert, Linda, Gary. Mechanical Engineer. S. Imperial, Deadeye or Allen; t. one and a quarter, right handed. Highest tournament average, 75%; highest game, 90%; finished 3rd place, 1961 and 1962, New England Championship. Enjoys hunting. Home: 90 Ward Road, Orange, Massachusetts 01364.

RICHEY, BOB. Chief organizer of horseshoes for Halifax region. Member, Board of Directors, for both Nova Scotia and Maritime Provinces Horseshoe Associations. Coordinator, 1979 Nova Scotia championships. Home: Halifax, Nova Scotia.

RICHMOND, MARVIN. 1977 Seniors World Champion, with 71.1% ringers, setting two world records for seniors, when he and Floyd Plumb hit six consecutive four-deads and when he hit 127 double ringers in a seven game tournament. S. Allen; t. one and a quarter turn, left handed. Won Class A titles in Florida, Minnesota, Alabama. Tied for Minnesota State championship but lost a play-off. Home: Route 2, Pequot Lakes, Minnesota 56472.

RIEDL, MICHAEL, b. November 26, 1897. President, Dormont Horseshoe Club. W. Caroline, deceased; children—William, Leona, Harold, Alice, Melvin. Retired, employee, Jones & Laughlin Steel Corporation. S. Imperial; t. one and a quarter, right handed. Booked exhibitions for Ted Allen; High tournament average, 67%. Played professional minor league baseball, Pittsburg Pirates, Michigan-Ontario league. Home: 2631 Broadway Avenue, Dormont, Pittsburg, Pennsylvania 15216.

RIETVELD, JOHN, b. January 10, 1931. President Wisconsin HPA, 1976 and 1977. W. Harriet; children—Mike, Dan, Sally. Instrument technician—paper mill. S. Allen; t. flip, right handed. Tournament director, Combined Locks, mid-eastern Wisconsin, Wisconsin State Tournaments. Enjoys golf, bowling, fishing; choir member; Red Cross first aid instructor. Home: 212 Williams Street, Combined Locks, Wisconsin 54113.

RIFFLE, DENNIS, b. December 25, 1952. Ohio Junior State Champion, 1964, 1965, 1966, 1967, 1968—the only junior to win five state championships. W. Paulette; child—Pelee. Employee, Scheduler—Frigidaire. S. Allen; t. one and a quarter, right handed. 1966 State Tournament, averaged 72.7%; World Tournament play, runnerup, 1964. He and father, Glenn, became in 1965 the only father-son combination in Ohio history to win state championships. Home: 751 Talbott Drive, Kettering, Ohio 45429.

RIFFLE, DOUG, b. February 1, 1958. 1971, 1972, 1974 Ohio State Junior State Champion. W. Tonia; child—Brandon. Tool and die maker. S. Allen, t. one and a quarter, right handed. 1980 won Champion of Champions Tournament, Union, Ohio. 1971, 1972, 1974 Ohio Boys State Champion. Home: 44 Filmore Street, Dayton, Ohio 45410.

RIFFLE, GLENN, b. February 7, 1917. National AAU Champion 1955, 1958, 1959, 1960. Ohio NHPA State Champion in 1965, 10-1-77%, and in 1975, 12-1-75.9%. W. Marie; children—Steve, Dennis, Doug. Machine operator—Delco Air. S. Ohio Pro; t. one and three quarters, right handed. 1964 World Tournament, Most Improved Player Award, with 21-14-75.5%; best finish, World Tournament competition, 1970, ninth place, 24-11-73.8%.; highest game, 87.5%; World Tournament play, won 176, lost 179, averaged 72.3%; Intermediate Division, won 6, lost 1, hit 76.3%. Home: 2606 Marigold Drive, Dayton, Ohio 45449.

RILEY, P. D., b. February 12, 1912. New Mexico State Champion, 1959, 4-0-62.9, 1960, 4-0-63, 1961, 9-0-61, 1963, 9-0-60.2, 1965, 5-0-58.2, 1971, 8-0-64.2, 1972, 7-0-60.6, 1974, 9-0-60.1, 1975, 7-0-57.1, 1977, 7-0-64.9; Texas State Champion 1958, 9-1-51.9. W. Frances; child—Kathleen. Retired supervisor and investigator, United States Department of Labor. S. Allen; t. one and a quarter, right handed. Highest game, 91.8%; highest tournament, 71.6%; Regional Director New Mexico Horseshoe Association. Past president and vice-president, New Mexico State Association and the Albuquerque Club; directed a 1977 New Mexico State Wheelchair Horseshoe Pitchers Tournament. Home: 2736 Rhode Island, N.E. Albuquerque, New Mexico 87110.

RILEY, WILLIAM, b. October 16, 1925. 1971 Florida State Champion, 6-0-63%.

Children—Janet, Bruce, James, Brenda, Margaret, Karen. Painter. S. Ohio; t. one and three quarters, right handed. Highest game, 92%; highest tournament, 74%—Parkersburg, West Virginia. Home: 3618 17th Street West, Bradenton, Florida 33505.

RIORDAN, MARY ELLEN. Massachusetts Girls' State Champion, 1973, 3-0-22.0%, and 1974, 7-0-25.4%.

RIOUX, NORMAN, b. October 24, 1938. Connecticut State Champion, 1970, 1971, 1973, 1974, 1975, 1977, 1978, 1980. W. Bernice; children—Lawrence, Nadene, Carol, Lisa, Norman. Route Salesman. S. Allen; t. one and a quarter, right handed. Treasurer and past president, New London County Horseshoe League; Vice-president, Connecticut HPA; won New England Championship, 1972, 1973, 1974, 1976, 1977; highest tournament average, 81%, highest game, 94%; 1973 World Tournament, championship division, Rookie of the Year, finished ninth place, 22-13-75.7%; 1974 World Tournament, eleventh place; New England Horseshoe Pitchers Hall of Fame, 1978. Home: 31 Bridge Street, Montville, Connecticut 06353.

RISK, JIMMY, b. 1913. d. c.1970s Indiana State Champion, 1927, 1928, 1930, 1932, 1933, 1935, 1939. 1927 NHPA World Championship, 2nd place with 53-5. W. Norma, deceased. t. one and three quarters, right handed. NHPA Hall of Fame, 1971; 98 ringers out of 100 shoes and 45 consecutive ringers; known as Montpelier's "Boy Wonder" who gave exhibitions at the White House to President Truman and throughout the world to troops during World War II and the Korean War; toured fairs, schools, clubs throughout the United States and Canada as a great ambassador of the sport, giving exhibitions of play and trick shooting with wife Norma.

RISLOV, WALLY S., b. October 8, 1924.

1966 North Dakota State Champion, with 9-1-52.5%. W. Mildred; children—Larry, Mark, Kay, Dave. Grain Elevator Manager. S. Allen or Imperial; t. one and three quarters, right handed. Won the Allard Open, 1980 with 60% ringers; highest tournament average, 69.4%; top tournament game, 82%; past president, North Dakota State Association, for two years; past president, Hannaford Horseshoe Club, for six years; director and secretary of the local club. Enjoys fishing, bowling, golf and watching pro football and baseball. Home: P.O. Box 26, Route 2 Cooperstown, North Dakota 58425.

RISTAU, MARION. Wisconsin Women's State Champion, 1970, 5-1-21.4%, and 1971, 5-0-42.6%. Home: 218 Williams, Combined Locks, Wisconsin 54113.

RIVERA, RHONDA MOON, b. October 4, 1962. 1976 California Girls' State Champion. H. Mike; child—Terra. Insurance Supervisor. S. Gordon; t. one and a quarter, right handed. 1975 Northern California Girls' Championship; 1976 NCHPA runnerup; won the Auburn, Southern California championships; 1977 runnerup, California State championship and the San Jose Open and won the Shasta Open; Miss Congeniality, 1978. Home: 2791 Twin Oaks Lane, San Jose, California 95127.

ROACH, ARCHIBALD WILSON KILBOURNE, b. September 15, 1920. President, Texas HPA. W. Leta Allis; children—Leta Allis, John W. Professor of Botany, North Texas State University. S. Ohio; T. one and three quarters, right handed. Region director, NHPA; High game, 78% (Arlington League); high tournament, 66.7% (1980 tournament, Harrison, Michigan). Enjoys sculpture, oil painting. Home: 2319 Fowler, Denton, Texas 76201.

ROBERTS, DONNIE, b. July 8, 1943. Secretary-Treasurer, NHPA. W. Helen; children—Sheila, Susan, Donnie. Superintendent, Pike Country School of Child Advancement. S. Ohio; t. one and a quarter, right handed. Won Stokes Memorial Trophy, 1978; statistician, Pike County Club, 1956–64, president, 1965–present; vice-president, Ohio Buckeye Association; chairman, Ohio Hall of Fame Committee and By-Laws Committee; member, national Hall of Fame Committee, prepared Regional Directors' Guidelines; operates own four-court indoor facility; won Ohio and World Championships as Junior (1959); with brother Gary, was instrumental in formation of junior rules in competition; won Ohio State Championship, 1972, 81.5%, qualified 82%; hit perfect NHPA-sanctioned game, 38 ringers out of 38 shoes against Ernie Danielson, Iowa, Day-Bell Winter Classic Ky.; won 19 Class A tournament; pitched qualifying rounds of 88%, Va., 92%, N.C., 91%, Ohio, 86%, Ohio; posted tournament averages of 86.6%, Ky., 85.8%, N.C., 86.9%, Ohio; Hit 30 games above 85%, nine above 90%; averaged above 80% in nine tournaments; pitched exhibition games. Enjoys basketball, softball, operating a farm, operating trophy and engraving business, public speaking. Home: 9439 Camp Creek Road, Lucasville, Ohio 45648.

ROBERTS, GARY, b. August 5, 1947. Junior Boys World Champion, 1961–64. Single. Director, Pike County Children's Service. S. Allen; t. one and a quarter, right handed. Tied with Hal Brown for World Title, lost play-off, 1960; won Pike County championship, 1974, Pike County Open, 5-0-73.5%, 1964 New Rome Indoor, 5-0-72.9%, 1977 Bainbridge Festival of Leaves, 5-0-76.5%, 1977 Pike County Indoor Open, 5-0-67.8%, 1978 Eli Reno Memorial, 5-0-72.3%; won Ohio Indoor State Championship, 5-0-77.8%; high tournament, 1980 Moundsville Open, 79.9%; won 1980 Kenia Open, 7-0-75.3%, 1980 Hamilton Open, 6-1-77.8%, Hebron, 6-1-78.9%; high game,

94.4%, against Ancil Copeland, 1980 Lancaster Silver Dollar; finished ninth, 1980 World Tournament, 18-13-73.8%; currently in charge of the Southeast Ohio District Tournament; pitched from 40 feet at age ten; won Men's Southeastern District, av. 60%, at age eleven; lost 50-49 to Sue Gillespie Kuchinski, 1964, pitched exhibitions and appeared on TV (W. Va), defeated Mark Seibold, 1974 World Tournament. Home: 9304 Camp Creek Road, Lucasville, Ohio 45648.

ROBERTS, HELEN, b. September 27, 1942. Ohio State Champion, 1974–75. H. Donnie; children—Sheila, Susan, Donnie. Teacher's aide/housewife. S. Gordon; t. flip, right handed. Played in World Tournaments since 1972; finished second, World Tournament, 50-44 to Vicki Winston, 1975; high tournament, 88%; set two world records (with Ruth Hangen): six consecutive four-deads and highest ringer percentage for both players combined, 1974 World Tournament. Home: 9439 Camp Creek Road, Lucasville, Ohio 45648.

ROBERTS, PAUL W., b. November 21, 1961. Iowa Boys State Champion, 1973, 1976, 1977–78. Single. Electrical apprentice. S. Allen; t. one and a quarter, right handed. Set state records: highest percentage for entire tournament, 68.7% (1978), highest game, 81.8% (1976); averaged 67.3%, 1977 tournament; tied national record for qualifying points (143) in 50 shoes, and out of 25 pitches in that round, hit 23 doubles, a four and a one, for 94% ringers; finished sixth, championship division, World Tournament, 1977; finished second to Steve Hohl, World Tournament, 1978; Home: Route 1, Hartford, Iowa 50118.

ROBERTS, SUSAN, b. September 12, 1968. 1980 Ohio Indoor State Girls Champion, 3-0-41.2%. Student. S. Allen; t. one and a quarter, right handed.

ROBERTS, WENDELL, b. November 12, 1913. President, Eastern Montana HPA. W. Doris; Three children. Retired bookkeeper. S. Gordon; t. flip, right handed. Secretary-treasurer, Fairview Horseshoe Club; pitched NHPA since 1968. Home: Box 42, Fairview, Montana 59221.

ROBERTSON, JOE, 1968 New Mexico State Champion, 5-1-56.4%. Home: 1731 Sheldon, Clovis, New Mexico 88101.

ROBERTSON, TOM, Served as State Secretary, Rhode Island HPA. Home: 10 East Avenue, Lincoln, Rhode Island 02865.

ROBINSON, FRANK M. (DR.), 1919 Vice-President, NHPA. Runnerup for World Title, 47-7, 1919 World Tournament (St. Petersburg, Fla.).

ROBINSON, HOWARD, Nebraska State Champion, 1954, 8-0-72%, 1955, 7-1-72%, 1956, 8-0-72%, 1958, 7-0-73.6%, 1929, and 1932. Qualified for championship division, 1962, withdrew from tournament; played championship division 1959, Murray City.

ROBINSON, LAWRENCE, 1930 Missouri State Champion.

ROBINSON, RALPH "DOC," Maine State Champion, 1933, 1934, 1937 (60.3%). Home: South Paris, Maine.

RODOCKER, TAMMIE E., b. December 13, 1962. 1978–79 California Girls State Champion. Single. Waitress. S. Gordon; t. flip, right handed. Won title at Calico Days 1979 Celebration. Home: 7526 Victoria Avenue, Highland, California 92346.

ROE, DON, 1961 Washington State Boys Champion, 23.6%.

ROEDER, PAUL, 1979 Ontario Junior Boys Champion, 67.5%.

ROGERS, FRANCIS, 1960 Iowa State Champion, 13-2-73.6%.

ROGERS, GEORGE H., b. May 10, 1925. Past President, Colorado HPA. W. Lois Marie; Children—Cathy, Jerry, Elaine. Insurance and Investment Broker. S. Ohio Pro; t. one and three quarters, right handed. Past secretary and president, Denver Metro Horseshoe Club; played 25-point cancellation game (with Dick Wetherbee) and shutout Ted Allen and Leo Huls 25-0, doubles match; promoter of Speakeasy Tournament, Rocky Mountain area, president and Founder of Speakeasy, Inc., aff. American Cancer Society; underwent Laryngectomy. Home: 3160 Wright Street, Denver, Colorado 80215.

ROGERS, HUGH, d. Set Class B World Record, 1969, averaged 79.8%, won Class B Championship. Pitched in World Tournaments, composite record: 85-144-69.3%, qualifying 488. Home: Cedar Falls, Iowa.

ROLAND, ERNOLFO. "RED," B. October 5, 1916. d. December 10, 1979. 1933 North Dakota State Champion. W. Clarice; child—Virginia. Accountant. S. Allen; t. one and a quarter, one and three quarters, right handed. Pitched exhibitions with Guy Zimmerman; served on 1967 World Tournament Committee (hosted Fargo tournament); played basketball, Gonzaga Univ., worked many years in Legion baseball, Billings, Montana, was all-state basketball player, high school; headed numerous civic, fraternal, church, business organizations; did play-by-play broadcasting (sports). Home: Montana.

ROLLICK, LEE. 1943 Utah State Champion.

ROME, WILMA VAN EGDOM., b. October 23, 1951. Washington Girls State Champion, 1966, 1967, 1968. Also Girl Athlete of the Year for those years. H. Russell; children—Krista, Kelli. Housewife. S. Gordon; t. flip, right handed. Home: 2269 Yew Street Road, Bellingham, Washington 98225.

ROMERO, BETTY. x 1973 New Mexico Women's Champion, 4-1-23.2%. Home: 720 57th Street Northwest, Albuquerque, New Mexico 87105.

RONCHETTI, TOM. 1966 Minnesota Boys State Champion.

RONEY, JESSIE. 1975 and 1976, 7-0-42.7% Colorado Junior State Champion. Class C, Colorado State Champion, men's division, 1977. Home: 839 East Kiowa, Colorado Springs, Colorado 80903.

RONEY, MIKE. 1971 Colorado Boys State Champion, 6-1-40.9%. Home: 839 East Kiowa, Colorado Springs, Colorado 80903.

ROSE, DAVE, b. June 20, 1947. Class A Champion, 1980, Whetstone Summer League, with a high game of 80% and named player of the year. W. Barbara; children—Dave, Danny. Contractor. S. Reno; t. one and three quarters, right handed. Ohio State Champion, Class K, 1974, Class l, 1975, Class G, 1978, Class D 1979, Class C, 1980. Central District, Class F, 1973, Class D, 1977, Class B, 1978 and 1980. Enjoys hunting, fishing, camping, softball. Home: 1729 West Wind Lane, Columbus, Ohio 43223.

ROSE, LESTER, b. March 29, 1919. Secretary-treasurer New Rome Horseshoe Club. W. Lucille; children—Carolyn, Judy, David, Allen. Storekeeper. S. Allen; t. one and three quarters, right handed. High tournament, 69.8%; high game, 90%. 16 consecutive doubles. Pitched for 50 years. Won tournaments, Class A to E. Home: 891 South Harris Avenue, Columbus, Ohio 43204.

ROSEBERRY, MAX, b. January 15, 1921. Vice-President, Ohio Buckeye HPA. W. Maxine; children—Dan, Vicki Wright, Colleen. Railroader (Erie-Lackawanna). S. Allen; t. one and three quarters, right handed. Won Class A championships including Lancaster District, Frazeysburg, Ross County

Open, Toledo Open; played Championship Division, World Tournament, 1975, 1976, 506 qualifying score, won 12 games; high tournament, 72%, Lancaster District; high game, 92% against A. J. Nave, Statesville, N.C.; served as tournament director, Marion Open, 12 years; fifth vice-president, Ohio Buckeye HPA. Serves as assistant basketball coach, Capital University, Columbus. Home: 267 Thew Avenue, Marion, Ohio 43302.

ROSENBOHM, ALBERT, past State Secretary, Nebraska HPA. Home: 7530 Starr, Lincoln, Nebraska 68505.

ROSENTHAL, MARK, 1972–73 Minnesota Boys State Champion: 7-0-60%, 4-1-67.5%. Home: Cloquet, Minnesota.

ROSS, AL, b. May 1, 1927. 1979 Saskatchewan Champion. W. Kelly; children—Calvin, Sheila Wichert, Glen, Janice. Trucker, Prairie Transport, Ltd. S. Hohl; t. one and three quarters, right handed. High tournament, 58.6%; high game, 75%; won 1973 doubles competition, Prince Albert, with his father, Basil Ross; won doubles titles, 1978, 1979, with Dave Stumph (Saskatchewan), with Stu Caing, 1970–72; won Regina singles championship, 1973; competed in 1980 World Tournament, Huntsville, Ala.; organized and served as president, Regina Horseshoe Club, 1978–79. Home: 708 Grey Street, Regina, Saskatchewan, Canada S4T 5G3.

ROSS, CHARLIE, Member, Utah HPA Hall of Fame.

ROSS, JANICE, b. January 7, 1967. 1980 Canadian Girls Champion. Student. S. Ohio O; t. flip, right handed. Won junior tournament, North Battleford, 56%. Home: 708 Grey Street, Regina, Saskatchewan, Canada S4T 5G3.

ROSS, LOY, Oklahoma State Champion: 1948, 7-0-53.3%; 1951, 7-0-67.2%; 1952, 7-0-62.5%; 1953, 8-1-61.5%; 1954, 11-0-64.3%; 1955, 11-0-67%.

ROSSEAU, DEBBIE, 1975 New Hampshire Girls State Champion. Home: 57 Merrimack Street, Penacook, New Hampshire 03301.

ROSSELET, JOHN, d. during World War II. 2nd Vice-President, NHPA, 1942. Joined New Jersey State Association, 1937, served as executive board member, secretary-treasurer, 1940; the only NHPA officer to die in service; annual tournament played in his honor, John Rosselet Memorial, N.J.

ROTH, FRAN, b. June 14, 1919. Colorado State Champion, 1976–79, 7-0-37%, 4-2-29%, 6-0-33%, 7-0-38%, respectively. H. deceased; children—Donald, Ed, Charlotte Britton, Carol Stepanich. Denver school bus driver. S. Gordon; t. one full, right handed. Won Denver Speakeasy Open titles three times, high tournament, 49% (1979), high game, 69%; treasurer, Colorado State HPA; president, Denver Metro Club, 3 years; pitched 30 years. Enjoys softball, bowling. Home: 6705 South Santa Fe, #91, Littleton, Colorado 80120.

ROUX, LARRY H., b. September 30, 1953. Maine Boys State Champion, 4-1-58%, 1968, 6-0-56.4%, 1966, 3-0-44.8%, 1967. W. Rachel; children—Sandra, Shelly. Carpet cleaner. S. Allen; t. one and a quarter (three quarter as junior), right handed. Won New England championship, 50.5%, 1968; played in 10 tournaments, 1966–68, 44-7; high game, 75%. Home: P.O. Box 65, Alfred, Maine 04002.

ROWAN, JAMES, Tied for third place, 1920 World Tournament, St. Petersburg, Fla. Home: Akron, Ohio.

ROWE, LEROY, b. April 18, 1914. Won 45 trophies, Class A Championships. W. Marion; children—Barbara, Karen, Rita, Martin. General contractor, farmer, journeyman toolmaker. S. Allen; t. one and a quarter, right handed. Finished third, Indiana, 1980; finished 27th, World Tournament, 1980; pitched 47 years. Enjoys baseball, photography, trapping, hunting, fishing. Home: Route 2, Angola, Indiana 46703.

ROWE, NANCY HENSON, b. March 11, 1952. New Mexico Women's State Champion, 6-0-26.8%, 1968, 5-0-31.6%, 1969, 5-0-43.6%, 1972, 45%, 1977, 37.8%, 1978, 7-2-42.2%, 1980. H. Randall H.; children—Ishmael Nathan, Veronica Heather, Isaac Randall. Teacher. S. Allen; t. three quarters, right handed. Home: 222 Mexcal Circle Northwest, Albuquerque, New Mexico 87105.

RUGG, RAYMOND P., b. July 3, 1946. President, Fayette County HPA. Farmer/machine operator. S. Allen; t. one and a quarter, right handed. Won Weston, West Virginia Class A championship, 6-1-60%, 1980; won Fayette County Sanctioned, 4-1-60%, 1980; finished second, Class B, 63.3%, Pennsylvania State Tournament; chairman, Horseshoes Committee, Dogwood Acres C. B. & Horseshoe Club; high tournament, 65.4% (1979 Frye Memorial, Winchester, Va.), high game, 69.4%. Home: Route 1—Box 19, Mill Run, Pennsylvania 15464.

RUNNING, EDWIN, b. January 27, 1912. Vice-President, South Dakota HPA. W. Mary; children—Leonard, Norman, Phyllis. Employee, South Dakota Highway Department & Custer Lumber Company. S. Gordon; t. one and three quarters. Pitched 60 years, 13 in organized competition; finished second, state tournament, 1967; finished fifth, state championship division, 1977, 1978. Home: 230 North 11th Street, Custer, South Dakota 57730.

RUPNOW, ARNIE W., b. August 24, 1908. 1980 member Wisconsin HPA Hall of Fame. W. Viola; children—Barbara, Allen, Ethel, David, Thomas. Retired dairy farmer.

S. Ohio; t. three quarters, right handed. Charter member and former secretary of the Inter-County League, 1933, renamed Land-O-Lakes League in 1936, the LaBelle League in 1940, and the Tri-County League in 1954; Class A and B, state tournaments, averaging 60% ringers. Enjoys bowling, gardening, and fishing. Home: 39488 Lang Road, Oconomowoc, Wisconsin 53066.

RUSHING, HERBERT RAY, b. March 29, 1915. Past vice-president, North—California HPA. Past president, Livermore Valley Club. W. Ruby; children—Gary Lee, Lois Rae. Carpenter. S. Imperial; t. one and three quarters, right handed. Member, Nevada City Gold Country Horseshoe Club; Class E champion, N.C. HPA; Class C champion, second in B and in A tournament play; high game, 78%, Stockton; 61.7% average, finished second to Monty Latino, California Seniors. Home: 14338 State Highway 49—Space 76, Grass Valley, California 95945.

RUSSELL, HAZEL LORRAIN HARRIS, b. November 12, 1923. 1955 Women's World Champion, 5-0-47.7%. H. Harry E.; children—Douglas Mark, Ronald Russell, Marlene Bowen. Housewife. S. Gordon; t. one and a quarter, right handed. Competed in 1956 World Tournament, lost title to Vicki Chapelle, 5-2. Enjoys golf, bowling, needlework, tennis, and skiing. Home: 9340 West 74th Avenue, Arvada, Colorado 80005.

RUTZ, JOHN, 1947 Wyoming State Champion, 11-2-56.7%.

RYAN, CLYDE K., b. July 23, 1921. Pitched exhibition games with Blair Nunamaker and Frank and Hansford Jackson, 1935, 1936 (Sportsman's Show, Cleveland). W. Harriett; children—David, Susan, Bruce, Barry, Ellen. Employee, Tool Crib—Ohio Screw Production. S. American; t. one and three quarters, right handed. Pitched since 1933; won Cleveland City Championship twice; won Elyria City Championship;

high game, 87.5%, 13 consecutive doubles; led all pitchers in Greater Cleveland League, 93-3, 1935. Home: 290 16th Street, Elyria, Ohio 44035.

RYLANDS, RAY, 1973 Rhode Island State Champion, 7-0-52.6%.

S

SAARI, JAMES E., b. August 1, 1941. d. November 30, 1980. 1957 Washington Boys State Champion. Children—Scott, Sheri. Teacher. S. Ohio; t. one and three quarters, left handed. Won many division titles; pitched 20 years in tournament and league play; served as promoter, Northwest Regional director, NHPA; as secretary, Washington HPA. Graduate, Central Washington University, 1964. Home: Vancouver, Washington.

SAASVILLE, TED, 1949 Vermont State Champion, 10-1-54%.

SAEGER, WALLY, b. June 29, 1920. d. July 10, 1979. 1964 Wisconsin State Champion, Member, 1980 Wisconsin Hall of Fame. W. Delores; two children. Employee, Jefferson County Highway Department/ Member, Ixenia Fire Department, Park and Recreation Board/Town constable. Established courts in Ixenia Park (now called Saeger Horseshoe Court), maintained them 30 years; held exhibitions with Casey Jones; appeared on "Pitching Horseshoes", WTMJ, 1955; president, Tri-County League, more than 30 years; member, state and national HPA, served on board for Milwaukee tournaments; won Jefferson County, Tri-County championships many times. Veteran, World War II. Enjoyed softball, bowling. Was founding father of Oconomowoc Memorial Hospital. Home Ixenia, Wisconsin.

SALES, GEORGE L., b. October 7, 1922. Listed twice in top 100-percentage pitchers,

Horseshoe Pitchers News Digest, 1975. W. Patricia; children—William, Dan, Lina Rogan, Marsha Clift. Social worker. S. Gordon; t. one and three quarters, right handed. Played 37 NHPA tournaments, 1973–78, won 15, finished second eight times, third, four times, averaged 66% for 27 tournaments; high tournament, 75.7%, 1975 Sheppard Open; high game, 86%, 1975 Eastern Indiana. Home: Route 2, Box 95, New Castle, Indiana 47362.

SALES, MARY, b. October 24, 1910. 1934 District of Columbia Women's Champion. H. Curtis; children—Curtis, Jr., Mary. Housewife. S. Gordon; t. three quarters, right handed. Enjoys bowling. Home: 4810 Edmonston Avenue, Hyattsville, Maryland 20781.

SAMMONS, WILLARD P., b. June 20, 1919. Secretary-treasurer, Delaware HPA. W. Irene; children—Kelvin, Randy. Carpenter. S. Ohio, Deadeye; t. three quarters, one and a quarter, right handed. Pitched 50 years, 25 in organized play, 12 years, NHPA; president, Wicomico Horseshoe Club; assistant NHPA director for Delaware, Maryland, N.J.; served as judge in three world tournaments; won lower class championship, 1976 Bristol Township, Pa., tournament; high tournament, 55%: Home: 1713 Laurel Highway, Seaford, Delaware 19973.

SAMUELSON, HAROLD, Past State Secretary, Alaska Horseshoe Pitchers Association. Home: 300 Glacier Avenue, Fairbanks, Alaska 99701.

SANCHEZ, SADIE, 1980 Rocky Mountain Open Champion, 6-0-40%. Home: Box 72, Hochne, Colorado 81046.

SANDERS, ROSS ALLEN, b. November 20, 1947. President, Kentucky HPA, 1978–79. W. Annetta Sue; children—Erik, Brandon. State worker/photolithographer. S. Allen; t. double flip, left handed. Won Class B state championship, 1974; qualified twice, Class A, Kentucky State Tournament; won doubles league 10 times with his father; elected State President, 1977–79; regional representative, 1975–76; high tournament, 53.2%; high game, 77%. Home: Route 3—Hilltop Meadows, Frankfort, Kentucky 40601.

SANDQUIST, ALDEN, b. October 6, 1961. 1974, 1977 Minnesota Boys State Champion, 50-0-65%, 62.4% respectively. Single. Student. S. Imperial; t. one and a quarter, right handed. Competed in nine tournaments, won eight, 1974; high tournament, 72%; participated in 1972 World Tournament. Enjoys fishing, hunting, basketball. Home: RRI, Watertown, Minnesota 55388.

SANTEE, GLENDEN, b. May 11, 1940. President, Washington County Horseshoe Club. W. Rose; child—Jennifer. Carpenter/Vice-president, Green River Builders. S. Ohio; t. flip, right handed. Holds Class A championships: Marietta Open, 5-0-63.5%, Lewis County Open, 7-0-62.3%, Washington County Open, 5-2-69%; recipient, Sportsmanship Award, Washington County Horseshoe Club, 1974; averaged 70.4%, Ohio Indoor State Tournament, 1979; high game, 93.2%. Home: 1001 Gilman Street, Marietta, Ohio 45750.

SARFF, BLAKE, Oregon Boys State Championship, 1970, 23.8%, 1971, 17.6%. Home: 377 Northwest Douglas, Dallas, Oregon 97388.

SAUCO, JOE, 1931 South Dakota State Champion.

SAUNDERS, ALBERT WILLIAM, b. September 21, 1917. 1974 New Hampshire State Champion, 64.7%. W. Mary Lou; child—Janet. Oil burner serviceman/Transportation foreman, Merrimack School District. S.

American; t. two and a quarter, right handed. Won Class B State Championship, 58%, 1973; high tournament, 71.1%, Heritage House, Sutton, Mass. Was professional lightweight boxer; ran in Boston Marathon, Washington Star Marathon. Enjoys golf, fishing. Home: 87 Chandler Street, Penacook, New Hampshire, 03303.

SAUNDERS, HARRY, District of Columbia Champion, 1930, 1933, 1934, 1937.

SAURO, ANTHONY, b. February 7, 1913. Member, New York Horseshoe Pitchers Association Hall of Fame Committee. W. Helen; children—Michelina, Joseph, Thomas, Patricia Ann, John. General factory worker. S. Allen; t. one and a quarter, right handed. Won Syracuse City Championship 21 times; won Onondega County championship 16 times; finished one game, New York State Tournament, with 32 consecutive ringers; president, Municipal Horseshoe League; pitched 53 years, 46 in NHPA. Home: 1021 Avery Avenue, Syracuse, New York 13204.

SAVAGE, WENDELL, b. October 1, 1910. 1980 Illinois Senior State Champion. W. Lucille; children—Joyce Ann, Carol Jean. Office manager, The House of Sunshine. S. Allen; t. one and three quarters, right handed. Won more than 90 trophies, Class A to Class F; averages 60%, high average, 85%; director, annual Litchfield Tournament, Lake Lou Yaeger. Enjoys checkers (Illinois Class B checker champion twice). Home: 607 North Jefferson Street, Litchfield, Illinois 62056.

SAXTON, EARL "CURLEY," First Vice-President, New Mexico HPA. Home: 10412 Stovall Northeast, Albuquerque, New Mexico 87112.

SAYRE, FLOYD W., b. October 1, 1892. First recognized Washington State Champion, 1925, 21-2-51.3%. W. Myrtle; chil-

Top, left, 1978 Carolina Dogwood Festival championship division, won by Carl Steinfeldt, fourth from left in top row. Max Roseberry is second from left in top row. *Right,* Wally Shipley, NHPA President and Hall of Fame member. *Second row, left,* Jimmy Risk, John Rademacher, Sarg Cook. *Right,* Bonnie Seibold. *At right side, second row up,* Mark Seibold, World Champion. *Bottom, left,* Jim Solomon. *Right,* Peter Shepard.

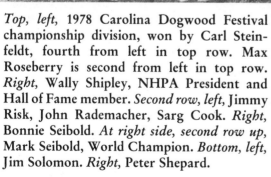

Top, left, 1978 Iowa HPA, Des Moines. Bill Vandegriff, M. W. "Woody" Wilson, Danny Sease. *Right,* Bert Snart, Hall of Fame member. *Second row,* 1980 Boys World Tournament. Tracy Sperline is at left in front row. World Champion Mark Dyson and Jim Kuchcinski are at right in top row. *Bottom row, left,* Jack Springer and Carl Steinfeldt. *Right,* Huntsville, Alabama, courts (site of 1980 and 1982 World Tournaments. *At right,* Wiley Stapp.

dren—Hazel D. Stovall, Verne W. Mechanic, Standard Oil of California, to 1957. S. Mossman and Gordon; t. three quarters, one and a quarter, right handed. Won state championship, 62%, 1926, 64%, 1927, 1931, 15-0-69%, 1932, 14-1-67.8%. Home: 8311 South "I" Street, Tacoma, Washington 98408.

SCHAFERS, DALE, 1974 Canadian National Boys Champion, 53.3%. Won Alberta Men's title, 1974, 1976. Home: Calahoo, Alberta, Canada.

SCHAMP, BURDETTE "BUS," b. January 8, 1914. Operates three leagues, 15 courts. W. Evelyn; children—Deborah, Bradley, Bill. Salesman. S. Gordon, Diamond; t. one and a quarter, right handed. Pitched 30 years, 16 in tournament play; won more than 80 trophies; finished second, Class B, Ohio State Tournament, 22 consecutive ringers, 1975; pitched Class A twice, qualifying with 251 and 257 for 100 shoes. Enjoys music. Home: 919 Williams Street, St. Marys, Ohio 45881.

SCHAUMBERG, IRVING, 1949 Oregon State Champion.

SCHAUNAMAN, DONALD A., b. July 15, 1928. 1978 South Dakota State Champion, 7-0-61.4% (defeated player who had won state title 27 times). W. Hazel; children—Mark, Kristie, Craig, Kirk. Farmer. S. Allen; t. one and a quarter, right handed. NHPA member, 18 years; past president, vice-president, South Dakota HPA; won Brown County Tournament, 1964; won 1965 Quint Cities Open, 8-0, 1978 Swarthout Open, 1979 Brooklings Art Festival, 7-0-61.7%; high tournament, 67.7%; high game, 78%. Home: 3550 South 40th Street, Aberdeen, South Dakota 57401.

SCHAUNAMAN, HENRY R., b. June 3, 1896. 1970 Member, South Dakota HPA Hall of Fame. W. Cecilia, d.; thirteen children. Farmer. S. Allen; t. one and a quarter, right handed. President, county association and South Dakota State Association; won 1934 Tri-State Championship; won 1967 Class C championship, Senior Division, World Tournament; pitched for more than 50 years. Home: Route 2, Aberdeen, South Dakota 57401.

SCHAUNAMAN, KIRK, b. January 6, 1961. 1973, 1974 South Dakota Boys State Champion, 3-0, 5-0-28.5% respectively. Single. Student. S. Allen; t. one and a quarter, right handed. Won 1973 Quint City champion; high game, 38%. Home: 3550 South 40th Street, Aberdeen, South Dakota 57401.

SCHEUB, PAUL, b. June 25, 1917. President, Florida HPA. W. Dolores; children—Bonnie, Patricia, Nancy. S. Diamond; t. flip, right handed. Past vice-president, Florida State HPA, and Sarasota Horseshoe Club. Home: 2139 Piazza Drive, Sarasota, Florida 33581.

SCHEETS, HAROLD, Wisconsin State Champion, 1932, 1933, 1973, 1975, 1976.

SCHIMEK, EDWARD J., b. July 25, 1911. Wisconsin State Champion, 1960, 9-2-60%, 1962, 11-0-58.7%, 1963, 9-2-61.3%. W. Katherine; children—Margaret, Katherine. Cost accountant. S. Ohio; t. one and a quarter, right handed. Pitched 50 years, 21 in NHPA play; won Milwaukee City Tournament, 7-0, 1931, 1948, 5-0; won Mid-East, 5-2, 1966; high tournament, 67.8%; high game, 89.2%; past president, local horseshoe club; past director, Wisconsin State HPA. Home: 6636 West Chambers Street, Milwaukee, Wisconsin 53210.

SCHLIEMANN, MALCOLM W., b. October 12, 1916. 1980 Member, South Dakota Hall of Fame. W. Myrline; children—Donald, Malvia, Milford. Computer operator. S. Allen; t. three quarters, right handed. Pitched 50 years, 24 in local leagues, 15 in NHPA; high tournament, 44.3%; high game, 69.5%; served as tournament director, 10 years, president, 9 years, league secretary, 12 years, State Committeeman, 10 years, presently state secretary. Home: 405 South Jessica Avenue, Sioux Falls, South Dakota 57103.

SCHLIEMANN, MYRLINE, b. February 11, 1917. Women's State Champion of South Dakota, nine times, Member, South Dakota HPA Hall of Fame. H. Malcolm; children—Donald, Malvia, Milford. Housewife. S. Allen, Imperial; t. three quarters, right handed. High tournament, 55.4%, state tournament, 1978; competed in World Tournaments, Class B, 1969 (three times), Class A (twice); high tournament, 57.5% in Class D, 1977 World Tournament; high game, 69.2%; league secretary, 12 years; member, state committee, 6 years, state treasurer, 1975, state secretary, 1980. Home: 405 South Jessica Avenue, Sioux Falls, South Dakota 57103.

SCHLISKE, ARTHUR, b. August 22, 1922. Secretary-treasurer, Wyoming State HPA. W. Doris; children—Larry, Patricia. Rancher. S. Allen; t. one and a quarter, right handed. President, Cheyenne Horseshoe Club. Played for 45 years. Won 1976 Crested Butte Classic; 1977 Class B titles and Western Nebraska Open, Scott's Bluff and Wyoming State; in 1978, the Cowboy Open at Rawlins; in 1979 in the Rawlins Cowboy Open, the Rocky Mountain Open at Boulder, Colorado and the Crested Butte Classic. Enjoys bowling with a 196 average and a high series of 727. Home: 819 Evergreen, Cheyenne, Wyoming 82001.

SCHLOSSER, DAN L., b. July 29, 1942. Chairman, 1977 World Tournament committee. W. Joyce; child—Todd D. Owner of Retail Gift Business; manager of Regional Trade Organization. S. Ohio Pro; t. any, left handed. Helped run Ohio State Tournament since 1971 as well as Greenville Ringer Classic. 1972 Chairman World Tournament Publicity Committee. Past Secretary, Darke County Horseshoe Club; Trustee of local club. 30–35% average; won about 30 trophies in lower classes. Home: 6370 Daly Road, Greenville, Ohio 45331.

SCHMIDT, HARRY C., b. September 5, 1912. 1977 Member New Jersey Hall of Fame. Retired Air Force and Technical Writer. S. All brands; t. one and three quarters, right handed. 50 years of service to the game. Past tournament director and secretary, Hudson County Horseshoe Club. 1979 NHPA and 1974 N.J. Achievement Award as promoter. High game, 70.5%; high tournament, 52.5%; average 40% Home: 20 Linden Avenue, Jersey City, N.J. 07305.

SCHNEIDER, CAROLYN L., b. March 9, 1943. 1973, 1975 Nebraska State Champion. H. Lloyd; children—Dwaine, Karen, Gail, Darrell. Farm and ranch wife and mother. S. Diamond Super Ringer or Tournament; t. flip, right handed. Only woman to be two-time Nebraska state champion. 1977 Vice-president Nebraska HPA. Averages 50%. Home: South Route Cody, Nebraska 69211.

SCHNEIDER, GERALD F., b. March 21, 1925. California State Champion 1963, 1966, 1968, 1972 and 1973. W. Herma; children—Gary, Traci, Heidi. Letter carrier. S. Gordon; t. one and three quarters, right handed. 8th Place 1968 World Tournament, 24-11-80.9%. High tournament average, 86.9%; high game, 94.4% (34 out of 36). Won Valley of the Sun, Western States Open, Santa Barbara Open, Elmer Beller Open, San Diego Open. Second vice-president NHPA, 1969–1970. Served two two-year terms as president and four two-year terms as vice-president of the Southern California HPA and four years as Secretary-Treasurer of the Orange Club. World tournament play: 134-

149-73.9%. Technical director for television shows: "Petticoat Junction" and "the Doris Day Show." Home: 3144 West Paso Robles Drive, Anaheim, California 92804.

SCHNEIDER KAREN M. b. June 18, 1964. 1979 Nebraska State Girls Champion. Student. S. Gordon; t. flip, right handed. State tournament play: 1977-6.8%; 1978-11.5%; 1979-23.4%. Active in 4-H, school bank, National Honor Society, Society of Distinguished High School Students and Junior American Maine-Anjou Association. Home: South Route, Cody, Nebraska 69211.

SCHNEIDER, PETER. 1978 Treasurer, British Columbia HPA. Box 80834, Burnaby, British Columbia, Canada V5H 3Y1.

SCHOMMER, TIMOTHY R., b. October 29, 1961. 1975 Wisconsin Boys State Champion. Single. Student. S. Allen; t. one and three quarters, right handed. 1976 Champion, Boys Division, Mountain Open. 1976 Second Place, Winnebagoland Open. Enjoys soccer. Home: 202 Elm Street, Combined Locks, Wisconsin 54113.

SCHRUM, CHARLES. Oklahoma State Champion 1959 (5-0-58.1%); 1960 (4-1-56.8%); 1968 (4-1-62.2%).

SCHULTZ, CHARLOTTE. World Tournament runnerup, 1933 and 1934. 2-year record: 10-2-67.4%. Performed exhibitions with sisters Caroline and Helen, the Schultz Sisters. Home: Chicago.

SCHULTZ, JOSEPH F. b. 1930. 1978 New York State Champion with 75.5% ringers. New York HPA Hall of Fame, 1979. W. Alice; children—John, Linda, Paul. Mail carrier. S. Allen; t. one and a quarter, right handed. 1980, won Raymond Frye Memorial, Winchester, Virginia World tournament play—99-91-74%; 1980 World Tournament-15 place, 17-14-69.2%. Home: 11 Gull Lane, Brentwood, New York 11717.

SCHULTZ, MILLIE, b. August 30, 1925. 1974 Second Vice-president NHPA. Income tax return preparer. H. Joe; child—Wayne. S. Gordon; right handed. Secretary-treasurer Northern California HPA 1975-1976; secretary-treasurer, Stockton Club, 1973-present; with husband, Joe, NHPA Pacific Coast Director, 1975-1976. Home: 1425 West Harding Way, Stockton, California 95203.

SCHULTZ, PAUL, b. 1959. 1974-1975 New York Boys State Champion; averaged 73.5%, 3rd Place Class B, Junior World Tournament.

SCHUMMER, GEORGE. 1965 Florida State Champion. Runnerup, Canadian Championship. Won Florida Championship with 8-1-58.4%. Promoter, Schummer System—equipment and play. Retired poultry farmer. Home: 5754 Yonge Street, Suite 1106, Willowdale, Ontario, Canada or Gulf Stream Hotel, Lake Worth, Florida.

SCHUSTER, GEORGE LAWRENCE. b. September 7, 1960. 1973 Oregon Boys State Champion. Single. Cement finisher. S. Allen; t. one and three quarters, right handed. 2nd Place Oregon State, Junior Division, 1974, 1975, 1976. Best tournament average, 64%; best game, 83%. Home: 375 East Cherry Street, Hermiston, Oregon 97838.

SCHWARTZ, FRED W. b. July 31, 1912. 1980 National Chairman A.A.U. Horseshoe Pitching Committee. W. Geneva Potts; child—Judith Davis. Insurance business. Indiana Association A.A.U. vice-president; 1963 Outstanding Indiana Sportsman; 1974 Silver Shoe Award. Home: P.O. Box 187, Terre Haute, Indiana 47808.

SCOLARI, ARTHUR, d. 1975. 1936 New Jersey Junior State Champion, with 75% ringers. New Jersey State Champion, 1942, 9-0-70.6%. Attorney.

SCOTT, ELWOOD M., b. July 12, 1915. 1971 Utah State Champion. W. Sylvia; children—Gordon, Darla, Larry, Dena. Rail-roader for U.P.R.R. S. Allen; t. one and a quarter, right handed. 1936 Logan Title; 1948 Ogden Title; 2nd Place, Utah State Title; 1971 Championship record, 11-1-55.9%. 1948 President, Utah State HPA. Home: 1520 Grant Avenue, Ogden, Utah 84404.

SCOTTEN, JAMES O., b. December 18, 1920. 1967 North Carolina State Champion. W.; 4 children. s. Allen; t. one and a quarter, right handed. Won 1957 and 1965 AAU North Carolina State Titles. Home: Route 1, Box 654, Thomasville, North Carolina 27360.

SCRIBNER, WILLARD W., b. March 4, 1906. 1977 Member Maine HPA Hall of Fame. W. Sadie; 8 children. Retired. S. Ohio Pro; t. one and three quarters, right handed. 1970 Southern Maine Title with 52%. Introduced Special Awards to Maine and served as State Chairman of Special Awards Committee. Past Secretary, Southern Maine Horseshoe Club, Vice President Maine HPA and member, Maine HPA Executive Committee. 1971, named Mr. Sportsman by Southern Maine Horseshoe Club. Enjoys wood working; collects pocket knives; boxing fan. Home: 1207 Highland Avenue, Portland, Maine 04106.

SEALS, FRANK. Won 1926 Michigan State Championship. Home: Cassopolis, Michigan.

STRODE, B. E. 1923 and 1924 Texas State Champion; first recognized State Champion.

SEAMAN, HAROLD. 1933 New York State Champion, with record-setting, 64.8%.

SEAS, W. J., NHPA Treasurer, 1923–1933. Honored by Florida Hall of Fame. Deceased.

SEASE, DANNIE D., b. April 28, 1939. Iowa State Secretary-Treasurer for seven years. 1978 Chairman, World Tournament Committee, Des Moines, Iowa. W.; 4 children. Letter carrier. S. Imperial; t. one and a quarter, right handed. Co-chairman, State Fair competition for 6 years. Home: 1229 Southwest Evans, Des Moines, Iowa 50315.

SEASE, JERRY LAVERN. b. April 24, 1961. 1974 and 1975 Iowa State Boys State Champion. W. Lori. Maintenance worker. S. Allen; t. one and a quarter, right handed. 1977 Class G Champion, Boys' Division, World Tournament. Enjoys bowling and baseball. Home: 109 Twelvth St. Southeast, Altoona, Iowa 50009.

SEBEK, JOHNNY. 1946 Ohio State Champion, 15-0-80.1%, 601 out of 750 shoes. 1948 Vice-president, NHPA. Deceased.

SEBRING, GLEN H., b. July 4, 1920. 1952 Pennsylvania State Champion, 3-0-72.4%. 1977 Member, Pennsylvania HPA Hall of Fame. W. Arlene; children—David, Rebecca, Barbara. Powder Metallurgical Engineer. S. Imperial or Ohio; t. one and a quarter or one and three quarters, right handed. 1962 Vice President, NHPA; past president Pennsylvania State HPA; Secretary PHPA; president of Erie County and President, Croawford County Horseshoe Clubs. Present Secretary Erie Horseshoe Club and Director, Pennsylvania State HPA. Member NPHA for 35 years. Won 1941 McKean County Championship; 1948–1955, Crawford County Championship; and 1950–1955 Northern Pennsylvania Championship. xxx, 1964, broke state qualifying record, 87%, 271 points. Eight-year champion, Erie County. 1971, Elk County Champion, Highest tournament, 81.5%. Highest game, 100%, 34 out of 34. Home: 3304 Harvard Road, Erie Pennsylvania 16508.

SECORD, JEFF, b. October 18, 1968. Youngest competitor, 1977 World Tournament. 2nd Place, Class D, 49.5%, 1980 World Tournament. Single. Student. S. Allen; t. one and a quarter, right handed. Class B championships: Green Bay, Fond du Lac, Goldendale. 3rd Place, Class A, 1979 Preimesberger Holloween. 1978 subject of article in Second Grade Weekly Reader, Articles in Milwaukee Journal and Milwaukee Sentienal. Home: 2123 Brown Road, Fond du Lac, Wisconsin 54935.

SECORD, JOHN, b. February 7, 1941. Wisconsin State HPA Secretary-treasurer and Tournament Director. W. Sandy; children—J.D., Kim, Jeff. Auto Service Manager. S. Allen; t. one and three quarters, right handed. 1980 Wisconsin First Vice-President; 1976–1978, President, Fond du Lac Club, 1973–1976, First Vice-President. High tournament, 52.4%; highest game, 62%. Won Class C 1979 Fond du Lac tournament, 6-1-40% and Class D 1980 Combined Locks, 5-2-51.4%. Home: 2123 Brown Road, Fond Du Lac, Wisconsin 54935.

SECORD, J. D., b. September 3, 1964. Five Class A Championships, 1978 and 1979 Mountain Opens, the 1979 and 1980 Preimesberger St. Patrick's Day Opens and the 1979 Eau Claire Open. Single. Student. S. Ohio O; t. one and a quarter, right handed. Highest game, 86%; best tournament average, 67%. World tournament play, 1977, 1978, 1979 and 1980, averaging in Class B competition 59%. 2nd Place, State Tournament. Home: 2123 Brown Road, Fond du Lac, Wisconsin 54935.

SEHN, JACKIE. Women's Canadian National Champion, 1972, 28.1%, and again in 1973, 42.1%.

SEIBOLD, BONNIE, b. September 22, 1934. 12 Times Indiana State Champion, 4th Vice-president, NHPA. H. Wilbert; children—Bonita, Mark, Paris. Elementary School Secretary. S. Ohio O; t. one and a quarter, right handed. Past secretary, Indiana HPA. 1976 Indiana Hall of Fame

Member. Highest Tournament, 75.7%; highest game, 81%. Indiana State Tournament play; 1961, 3rd; 1962, 4th; 1963, 4th; 1964, 2nd; 1965, 2nd; 1966, 1st-64.6%; 1967, 2nd; 1968, 1st; 1969, 1st, 58.5%; 1970, 1st; 1971, 2nd; 1972, 1st; 1973, 1st, 62.5%; 1974, 1st, 60.4%; 1975, 1st, 67.3%; 1976, 1st; 1977, 2nd; 1978, 1st, 71.4%; 1979, 1st, 68%; 1980, 1st, 72.9%. World Tournament play: A class: 1964, 6th, 56.1%; 1965, 7th, 49.6%; 1966, 4th, 62.7%; 1967, 6th, 50%; 1968, 7th, 53.1%; 1969, 5th; 1970, 4th; 1971, 5th, 54.4%; 1972, 7th, 54.9%; 1973, 5th, 63.8%; 1974, 6th, 62.6%; 1975, 6th, 57.3%; 1977, 7th, 67%; 1978, 4th, 69%; 1979, 7th, 66.8%; 1980, 2nd, 75.7%. B class: 1962, 1st; 1976, 2nd. Home: 1043 Grayson Avenue, Huntington, Indiana 46750.

SEIBOLD, MARK, b. January 16, 1954. 1979 World Champion. W. Renee. Dana Corporation, Ft. Wayne. S. Ohio; t. one and a quarter, left handed. Indiana Boys' State Champion: 1965–1970. Boys' World Champion: 1966, 7-0-75.5% and 1969, 7-0-83.5%., breaking all junior world records. Indiana State Champion, 1973, 1976, 1978, 1979 and 1980, 10-1-77.5% World Tournament Play: 1971, 4th, 28-7-78.9%; 1972, 3rd, 32-3-81.8%; 1973, 2nd, 32-3-80.9; 1974, 5th, 29-6-79.3%; 1975, 3rd, 29-6-81.1%; 1976, 3rd, 31-4-84.9%; 1977, 5th, 21-5-82.8%; 1978, 2nd, 29-6-80.9%; 1979, 1st, 27-4-82.6%; 1980, 5th, 26-5-76.3%. Home: 1890 Sabine Street., Huntington, Indiana 46750.

SEIBOLD, WILBERT CURLEY, b. December 26, 1923. Past president, Indiana State HPA. W. Bonnie; children—Bonita, Mark, Paris. S. Allen; t. one and a quarter, right handed. Past treasurer, Indiana Chapter NHPA and Vice President, Northern Indiana. Best World tournament play, 1975, 72%. Home: 1043 Grayson Avenue, Huntington, Indiana 46750.

SEMANS, CHARLES M., b. September 20, 1913. Class A City Champion of Pittsburg, 64%. Vice-president, Dormont Horseshoe Club. W. Rita; children: Nancy, Holly, Thomas. Retired. S. Imperial; t. one and a quarter, right handed. 35 Class B championships. Allegheny Championship, 63.5%; Fayette County Champion. Class B Eastern National Champion. High game, 80.1%, Three Rivers Tournament, with 7 consecutive four deads. Home: 16 East Sycamore Terrace, Pittsburg, Pennsylvania 15211.

SEMINGTON, TIM, 1974 Wisconsin Boys' State Champion.

SEVERS, T. EDWARD, b. January 24, 1933. Tied for New Jersey Class A Championship., losing in play-off, W. Pat; children: Tom, Vicky, Wayne, Cindy. Taxi cab owner. S. Allen; t. one and three quarters, right handed. NHPA Assistant Regional Director; 4th Vice-president New Jersey HPA. High tournament average, 68.8%; high game, 90%. Class A Middlesex Open champion, 67.5% and Flemington Open, 62.5%. Home: 72 Evelyn Avenue, Vineland, New Jersey 08360.

SEVERSON, TAL. 1979 British Columbia Provincial Champion, 65.8%. Canadian National Championship finalist, 6th in 1976, and 8th in 1977. Finalist, 1978 summer games. Home: Peachland.

SEVIGNY, ALTHEA. 1978 and 1979 Women's New Hampshire State Champion, in 1978 with 5-0-40.6%.

SHARFF, LEE H. North Dakota State Champion, 1969 and 1970. In 1969, 8-1-56%, and in 1970, 8-1-58.8%. Highest tournament average, 69.7%, and highest game, 83.6%. Won North Dakota Jaycee Open, 1968. Won Capitol City Open, Bismark, 1968–1974. Enjoys bowling and golf.

SHARKEY, DOMINICK P., b. June 8, 1888. d. April 7, 1971. Namesake of Sharkey Park, New Rochelle, Fort Slocum Park. Park hosted 1978 New York State Championship and scene of Annual Dominick Sharkey Memorial Tournament. W. Susan; children—Margaret, Terrence, Thomas, Edward, James, John, Joseph, Vincent. Retired lineman New Haven and Hartford Railroad. S. Gordon; t. one full turn in 1920s and one and a quarter thereafter, right handed. 1936 New Rochelle Champion. Home: New Rochelle, New York.

SHARKEY, JAMES F., b. July 17, 1916. Past president, Westchester County HPA and New Rochelle HPA. W. Eleanor; children—Kathleen, Susan, Edward, Timothy. Superintendent of Painting Bridges for Greater New York Area. S. Deadeye; t. one and a quarter, right handed. Westchester County Champion; won New Rochelle City Title Highest tournament average, 66%; Best game, 72%. Won 1974 singles Title, Westchester-Putnam. Captain, winning team in 1965 Greater-Connecticut-Westchester Horseshoe League. Home: 8 Peach Lake Drive, P.O. Box 221, North Salem, New York 10560.

SHARP, EDWARD A., b. June 23, 1908, d. September 17, 1980. 1958 Indiana State Champion, 9-2-75%. W. Louise Maxine; children—Arthur (deceased), Avonell, Maurice, Yvonne, Jack, Paul, Tom, Bonita, Kimberly. Inspector for Ingram-Richardson. s. Allen; t. one and a quarter or one and three quarters, right handed. 2nd Place in eight other years in Indiana State Championship. Home: Route 1, Rossville, Indiana 46065.

SHAVER, NED. Class A pitcher, 13th place, 1963 World Tournament, 8-27-68.8%. Home: 8149 California, Whittier, California 90602.

SHAW, HAROLD R., b. March 16, 1908. Iowa State Champion, 1947, 1948, 1949, and 1951. W. Blanche. S. Allen or deadeye; t. one and three quarters, right handed. Pitched for 56 years, 51 tournament play. 5-time participant in championship world tournament play, best finish, 11th place in 1955. Past president, Iowa Hawkeye HPA. Home: 5120 14th Street, West Cottage, Bradenton, Florida 50268.

SHAWL, SARAH. 1979 Virginia Girls' State Champion. Home: 412 Bermuda Road, Chester, Virginia 23831.

SHEAR, DOUGLAS G., b. September 14, 1943. 1980 President, North Carolina HPA. W. Cynthia. Teacher. S. Ohio Pro or Diamond; t. one and three quarters, right handed. 1977, 3rd, State Tournament and 1978, 4th. Singles and doubles champion, 1975, Moore County. Promoter, supervising construction of local courts. Highest tournament, 62%; highest game, 74%. 1979 First Vice-president, North Carolina HPA. Home: P.O. Box 892, Southern Pines, North Carolina 28387.

SHELLEY, LARRY. Florida State Boys' Champion, 1968, 9-0, and 1970, 3-0.

SHEPARD, GARY. 1977 Colorado Boys State Champion, 6-0-25.2%. Home: 5555 West Ohio, Lakewood, Colorado 80226.

SHEPARD, PETER H. JR., b. February 3, 1923. General Manager, St. Pierre Manufacturing Corp., the world's largest manufacturer of pitching horseshoes, including a new shoe called the "Budweiser." S. American; t. one and three quarters, right handed. Chairman, NHPA Manufacturers Committee. Past President, Massachusetts Transportation Committee; one of the first employers to support the Work Release Rehabilitation Program; Worchester County Jail and House of Correction; active fund raiser, Greater Transportation Road Race for the Handicap and Scholarship Fund. Home: 317 East Mountain Street, Worchester, Massachusetts 01606.

SHEPARD, RICHARD C., b. December 10, 1934. Vice-president, Massachusetts HPA. W. Camille; children—Caroline, Richard C., Jr. Service manager. S. Imperial; t. one and three quarters, right handed. Home: 36 Oxford Street N, Auburn, Massachusetts 01501.

SHEPPARD, ROBERT, b. February 3, 1933. Builder of the Rush Indoor Courts at Rushville. W. Ruby; children—Stuart and Brent. T.V. repairman. S. Deadeye; t. one and a quarter, left handed. Three term vice-president, IHPA; Secretary-treasurer, Rushville club; Received plaque in appreciation for his contributions from IHPA. High tournament average, 67%; high game, 85%. Two time Champion, Ben Shores Memorial, 1972 (6-1-62%) and 1973 (6-1-59%). Won Al Bills Indoor Open (6-1-63.8%). Home: Route 1, Box 46, Rushville, Indiana 46173.

SHIPLEY, WALLY, b. April 2, 1923. President, NHPA; 1979 Member, NHPA Hall of Fame. W. Sally; children—Beverly, Bob, Barbara, Bonnie. Manager, Pacific Telephone. S. Budweiser; t. one and three quarters, right handed. President NHPA, 1973–1981. NHPA, Second Vice-president. President, Southern California HPA, seven years. Received, Stokes Award; member, Southern California Hall of Fame. 1960 Class A Championship, Western Open. Highest tournament, 70.9%; highest game, 82.8%. Home: 500 South La Veta Park Circle, Apt. 42, Orange, California 92668.

SHORT, JERRY. 1976 Idaho State Women's Division Champion.

SHRIVER, HOWARD, b. August 12, 1914. D. August 11, 1973. 1968 and 1969 West Virginia State Champion. W. Wilma; child—Howard Arnette. Farmer and school bus driver. S. Imperial; t. one and a quarter, right handed. 1940 City Championship, Mt. Pleasant. President, Red Mill Horseshoe Club, Washington, Penna. Won Winchester, Virginia Open, 80.2%, qualifying at 94%, high game, 90.7%. 1974 West Virginia Hall of Fame, election posthumously. Home: General Delivery Wadestown, West Virginia 26589.

SHUCK, JOHN N., b. January 2, 1923. 1977 World Tournament, 3rd Place, Class D., 68%. W. Hazel L.; children—Roger, Patricia, Justin, Keith, Laura, Harry. Machinist. S. Allen; t. reverse one and a quarter, left handed. Class A championships: Indiana Left Handers 1963, 1964, 1965; 1964 Kokomo League, 1960 Steelite-Kokomo League, 1975 Tipton League, 1972 Tipton County Tournament; 1976 Marion Open; 1976 Central Indiana. Home: Route 1 Box 202, Sharpsville, Indiana 46068.

SIBERT, HARRY, b. July 18, 1913. Class A competitor. Has hit 92 ringers out of 100 shoes. 75% average. Pitched for 52 years. S. Imperial; t. one and three quarters, right handed. Home: 226 Heikes Avenue, Dayton, Ohio 45405.

SILVA, LEO, b. July 20, 1933. Founder, Nevada HPA, 1968. W. Charlene; child—Bonnie. Grounds Supervisor, University of Nevada. S. Ohio O; t. three-quarter flip, right handed. High game, 65%; high tournament, 50%. Received Outstanding Service Award, NHPA, 1970, presented at World Tournament. Staged first Nevada State Open and State Closed Tournaments. First State Secretary, Nevada, 1968–1970; State Vice-president, 1979. Home: 11430 Andes, Reno, Nevada 89506.

SIMMET, DAVE, b. January 20, 1965. Michigan State Boys Champion, 1975, 5-0-46.8%, 1977, 5-0-68.6%, 1978, 5-1-63.7%, 1979, 5-0-75%. Student. S. Allen; t. one and a quarter, right handed. High tournament, 75%, high game, 86.4%, both at 1979 World Tournament; 3-8-70.3%, 1978 World Tournament; 7-4-73.3%, 1979 World Tournament. Home: 970 Gremel Road, Sebewaing, Michigan 48759.

SIMMET, PAT, b. February 28, 1964. Student. s. Allen; t. One and a quarter, right handed. High tournament 65%, high game 78%. Fourth in Class A Boys Division World Tournament 1979. Home: 970 Gremel Road, Sebewaing, Michigan, 48759.

SIMMONS, BRIAN KEITH, b. January 30, 1961. Maine Boys State Champion, 1977–78. Single. Machine Operator. S. Imperial; t. one and a quarter, right handed. Won Class A titles: New Hampshire Open, Maine Open, Franklin Open, Massachusetts Open, 1969; won New England title, 1976–77; won Class C Championship, World Tournament, 1974, Class B Championship, 1975; won Class A Championship, Oxford Hills Invitational; high tournament, 85%; high game, 94%; hit 20 consecutive doubles. Enjoys softball, basketball, cars, machines. Home: Haley Road, Kittery Point, Maine 03905.

SIMMONS, RONNIE, b. November 11, 1938. 1974 California State Champion. W. Verbena; children—Bobby, Kelly, Greg. Checker, Ford Motor Company. S. Deadeye; t. one and a quarter, right handed. Inducted, California HPA Hall of Fame, 1979; high tournament, 79.9%, 1980 California State Tournament; high game, 88.9%, World Tournament play; World Tournament record, championship division: 136-171-72.2%, 511 qualifying points. Enjoys fishing, baseball. Home: 9559 Olive Street, Bellflower, California 90706.

SIMON, RALPH, b. December 2, 1918. 1980 Iowa State Champion, 6-1-74.9%. W. Cecilia; children—Michael, Susan, Patrick, MaryLou, Thomas, Timothy. Avey drill operator. S. Allen; t. one and a quarter, left handed. Pitched 45 years; won first place in 91 out of 100 tournaments in Iowa, Minnesota, Illinois; World tournament play— 1978, 10th Place; 1979, highest qualifier, 180 ringers out of 200, and finished in 3rd Place;

1980, 4th Place, 26-5-77.7%. Highest sanctioned game, 94%, 1979 Rapidan Open; highest tournament, 82.5%, 1980 DuLuth Open. Won Preimesberger Halloween Open, 1980.

SINGHASS, LESTER P., b. August 27, 1923. Virginia HPA Secretary-Treasurer. W. Louise; children—Susan, Scott. Superintendent of Parks. Motivating force in Apple Capitol Open and the Frye Memorial. Formed the Winchester HPA. Aided in staging the 1979 World Tournament, Statesville, North Carolina. Home: 1607 Valley Avenue, Winchester, Virginia 22601.

SIPPLE, B. E. 1944 Texas State Champion.

SIROIS, RENE J., b. March 9, 1950. 1967 Maine State Champion, 7-0-62.2%. W. Christine. Postal clerk. S. Gordon; t. one and a quarter, right handed. 1966 New England Class A Junior Title. Highest tournament average, 64.8%; highest game, 86%. 1975 Member Maine Hall of Fame. Enjoys bowling, golf, skiing. Home: 52 Ipswich Street, Auburn, Maine 04210.

SJOHOLM, CARL E. Secretary and Statistician, Ishpeming-Negaunee League. W. Ruth. S. Allen; three quarters, right handed. Home: Route 3, Box 1046, National Mine, Michigan 49865.

SJURSET, CLINTON R., b. May 3, 1925. President, Northern Illinois Horseshoe League. W. Dorothy; children—Linda, Craig, Melody, Gary. Plumber. S. Imperial; t. one and a quarter, right handed. Won 28 Class A championships. Ten-time winner, Northern Illinois Horseshoe League. Won Goldendale Open in Wisconsin, 1973, 1974, 1976, 1977, 1978. Won Big Rock, 1968, 1969, 1974; Galesburg, 1977; Heart of Illinois, 1974; Joliet, 1971; Aurora, 1976, 1977; Gem Open, 1975, 1976, 1978, 1980; Morris, 1971, 1972, 1976; Illinois State Fair, 1980; Walnut Open, 1979; Len's and Don's

Open, 1980; Illinois State Tournament, 1973 3rd Place; Jannesville, Wisconsin, 1980; Ron's Open, 1972; Forkfest, 1979; Eagle Open, 1980; Sussex Open, 1978. Home: 221 North Melrose, Elgin, Illinois 60120.

SKINNER, JIM. 1935 Michigan State Champion. Runnerup, Michigan State Championship, 1931. Home: Athens, Michigan.

SLAGG, HAROLD. Took part in record-breaking 120 hour marathon staged by the California HPA for the benefit of the Arthritis Foundation, 1977. Class A pitcher and promoter. Home: 10805 Rose Avenue, Ontario, California 91762.

SLOCUM, RAY., b. September 28, 1910. President, Horseshoe Pitchers of America, 1962–1971. W. Gertrude; children—Fred, Barbara, B. F. Goodrich Worker. S. Imperial; t. one and a quarter, right handed. Pitched for sixty years. President, B. F. Goodrich Club. Highest tournament average, 71%. 1971 Class C Champion, NHPA, 11-0-63%. HPAA Tournaments, champion, Class A, 1965, Class AA, 1977, 1978. Home: 131 Middlebury Avenue, Akron, Ohio 44305.

SMITH, ADA, 1967 Maine Women's State Champion, 3-0-37%. Runnerup, state tournament, 1966, 1968. Home: Florida.

SMITH, ALLEN, b. September 29, 1946. United States Marshall, Southern District of Ohio. W. Janet; children—Eric, Lee. United States Marshall. S. Ohio; t. one and a quarter, right handed. Member, National Championship Jukskei team; B.S., Ohio University, 1971, M.S., criminal justice and police administration, Eastern Kentucky University; served in Viet Nam, U.S. Marine Corps; as Pike County Deputy Sheriff; guard, Chillicothe Correctional Institute; adult parole officer, Ohio Dept. of Corrections; chief probation officer, Pike County

Juvenile Court; member, F & AM Orient Lodge #321, Waverly, Ohio, York Rite Bodies, Chillicothe, Ohio, O.E.S. Chapter #99, Waverly, Ohio; was All-Conference tackle, Piketon High School. Home: 146 Lakeview Drive, Waverly, Ohio 45690.

SMITH, BRIAN, b. April 15, 1962. 1979 New Hampshire Boys State Champion, 6-0-64.8%. Single. Student/employee, Pneumo Precision Machine Shop. S. Deadeye; t. one and a quarter, right handed. Most Improved Junior Player award, 1978; finished tenth, World Tournament, 3-8-64%; high tournament, 71.1%, New Hampshire Warmup; high game, 81.5%. Enjoys bowling, woodworking. Home: 664 Maine Street, Keene, New Hampshire 03431.

SMITH, CARL, b. September 14, 1963. 1971, 1980 Michigan Boys State Champion 6-1-65.8%. Single. Student. S. Allen; t. one and a quarter, right handed. High tournament, 64.1%, 1979 state tournament. Home: 513 Alva Street, Muskegon, Michigan 49442.

SMITH, DOROTHY, b. August 10, 1926. 1963, 1968 Michigan Womens State Champion. H. Roy; children—Tom, Barbara, Linda, Peggy, Jim, Carl. Housewife. S. Allen; t. one and a quarter, right handed. Won Class B World Championship, Southgate, 1970; played in M-46 Handicap League, World Tournaments in Keene, New Hampshire, Salt Lake City, Utah, Southgate, California, Erie, Pennsylvania. Home: 513 Alva Street, Muskegon, Michigan 49442.

SMITH, DWIGHT, Connecticut State Champion, 1950, 11-0-57.8%, 1951, 9-2-63%, 1954, 10-1-60.9%.

SMITH, EVELYN, b. June 10, 1934. Wyoming State Champion, 1976–1980. H. Wayne; children—Dana, Denis, Kurt, Vicki. Administrative secretary. S. Diamond or Gordon; t. flip, right handed. Championship record, 8-1-43.5%, 1980; high tournament,

63.8%, 1979 Cheyenne Open. Enjoys all sports, bowling. Home: 920 "W" Hill Road, Laramie, Wyoming 82070.

SMITH, FRED L., SR., b. September 30, 1935. Past President, Michigan Wolverine HPA, four years. W. Roseanne M.; children—Fred, Jr., Norman, David, William. United Auto Workers bargaining chairman. S. Allen or Ohio; t. one and a quarter, right handed. Past president, Diamondale Club, two years; pitched tournament play, 1962–77; high tournament, 52%; high game, 72%. Home: 150 Pine Street, Box 37, Diamondale, Michigan 48821.

SMITH, FREDERICK L., JR., b. November 25, 1953. Michigan Boy's State Champion, 1966, 5-0-37.6%, 1967, 5-0-62%, 1968, 5-0-72%, 1969, 4-1-81.1%. Single, Student. S. Ohio Pro; t. one and a quarter, right handed. Won Boys Division, Midwest Ringer Roundup, 1968; finished fourth, World Tournament, 1968; won Class B Michigan State Championship, Mens Division, 1971; high tournament, 81.1%; high game, 87.5%. Home: 3955 #4 Hunters Ridge Drive, Lansing, Michigan 48910.

SMITH, JIM, b. May 27, 1959. Michigan Boys State Champion, 1972–73. Single. Printer. S. Allen; t. reverse one and three quarters. Won Class B World Championship, 6-1-64.5%, high tournament, 1972; high game, 78%, 23 consecutive ringers. Home: 513 Alva Street, Muskegon, Michigan 49442.

SMITH, JASON, 1980 Oklahoma Boys State Champion. Home: Route 1, Marshall, Oklahoma 73056.

SMITH, JOHN V., b. November 5, 1929. President, Kansas State HPA. W. Jeanne M.; children—Mike, David, Paul, Janis, Sheila. Owner, John V. Smith Insurance Agency. S. Deadeye; t. one and a quarter, left handed. Won many Class A championships, Kansas and Missouri tournaments: St. Joseph, 69%, Midland Open, 71%, Atchison, 71%, Leavenworth (twice), 65%, 72%, Kansas City, 75%, Horton Open, 66%; finished third, Class B, World Tournament, 1978; finished 22nd, championship division, World Tournament, 11-20-65.7%, 1980; holds state record for high game, 96.1%, 1978 Kansas State tournament; ranked second, Kansas, four years. Enjoys photography, was past master, Master Lodge #5, Atchison, Kansas, 1969–70. Home: 1011 Kansas Avenue, Atchison, Kansas 66002.

SMITH, KEN, Runnerup to Elmer Hohl, Canadian National Championship, 7-1-61.3%, 1972. Home: Moncton, Ontario, Canada.

SMITH, NORMAN E., b. January 18, 1955. 1970 Michigan Boys State Champion. Single. Employee, Oldsmobile S. Allen; t. three quarters, right handed. Won 1967 Class E Championship, World Tournament, Fargo, N.D.; won Class C Championship, World Tournament, Keene, N.H., 1968, and Class D Championship, Erie, Pa., 1968; high tournament, 67.6%; high game, 80%; runnerup, Michigan state tournament, 1967–69. Home: 150 Pine Street, Diamondale, Michigan 48821.

SMITH, PEGGY ANN, b. February 2, 1955. 1970 Girls World Champion, 5-2-32%; 1969, 1970 Michigan Girls State Champion. Single. Music teacher. S. Detroit Flyer; t. reverse three quarter, right handed. Won Class B Girls title, World Tournament, 1967; high tournament, 46.8%; high game, 54.9%. Home: 513 Alva Street, Muskegon, Michigan 49442.

SMITH, ROY, b. March 8, 1922. Michigan State Champion, 12 times. W. Dorothy; children—Tom, Barbara, Linda, Peggy, Jim, Carl. Inspector. S. Imperial; t. one and three quarters, right handed. Won Class B World Championship, twice; won Michigan Water

Wonderland, four times; won Muskegon City Championship, 15 times; finished fifth, World Tournament, Erie, Pa.; high tournament, 84%; high game, 94%; member, Michigan State Hall of Fame; president, Michigan Wolverine State HPA; past regional director, secretary-treasurer, M-46 Handicap State Association; pitched 45 years, 27 in organized play, 15 in NHPA. Home 513 Alva Street, Muskegon, Michigan 49442.

SMITH, ROY W. Deceased. Author of *Science at the Stake*, tracing the history of the game and providing instruction. t. one and a quarter, left handed. Records: 87 ringers out of 100 shoes; 46 out of 50; 16 consecutive double ringers. Home: California.

SMITH, STAN, b. May 22, 1936. President, Texas HPA. W. Shirley; children—Bruce, Richard. Aircraft pilot, U.S. Border Patrol. S. Ohio; t. three quarters, right handed. Secretary, Del Rio HPA. Past vice-president and assistant regional director, Texas HPA. Pitched for 35 years. High game, 68%; high tournament, 50.3%. Winner, Del Rio Open in 1980, 4-1-45.6%. 1979 recipient, Mose Sanderson Sportsmanship Award. Home: P.O. Box 1018, Del Rio Texas 78840.

SMITH, THOMAS, b. June 9, 1948. Michigan State Boys Champion, 1963, 1964, 1968. W. Kathy. Construction worker. S. Ohio; t. one and three quarters, left handed. 1968 Class D Champion, men's division. Highest tournament, 58.6%; best game, 72.4%. Home: 433 Langley Street, Muskegon, Michigan 49442.

SMITH, WILLIAM ALFRED. 8-time Provincial Champion, Manitoba. 1972 Saskatchewan Open Champion. 1975 Canadian Intermediate Champion.

SMITH, WILLIAM G., b. September 13, 1958. 1970 Water Wonderland Boys Champion. Oldsmobile GM Plant Employee. S.

Ohio; t. flip, right handed. Best tournament, 45.3%; best game, 54%. 1972 Runnerup, Michigan Boys' State Championship and 3rd place, 1968, 1969, 1970, 1971. Home: 5823 Benton Road, Charlotte, Michigan 48813.

SNART, BERT, b. March 31, 1912. 1976 NHPA Hall of Fame Member. W. Doreen; children—Elaine, Allen, Fern. Retired, inspector. S. Diamond Tournament; t. one and a quarter, right handed. Received Her Majesty the Queen's Silver Medal. Won the Canada-Centennial Pan-Am Championship. High tournament, 86%; high game, 90.0%. Played for 55 years. President, Manitoba HPA, 1948–78. President, Dauphin Horseshoe Club 32 years. Member, Executive Council for 20 years. Instructor of Horseshoes in Manitoba schools as an extracurricular activity. Runs a junior summer school. He and his wife have organized more than 500 tournaments. Pitched television demonstrations; made a 1970 film called "Trick Pitching." Known as Manitoba's "Mr. Horseshoes." Manitoba Champion, 1938, 1939, 1943, 1945, 1946, 1947, 1949, 1951, 1952, 1954, 1955, 1956, 1957, 1964, 1965. Manitoba Ringerama Champion, 1969, 1970, 1971, 1972. Home: 231 Third Avenue Northeast, Dauphin, Manitoba, Canada R7N Oy9.

SNART, FERN. b. April 11, 1951. Manitoba Provincial Champion, 1968, 1969, 1972. Doctor of Psychology. S. Diamond; t. one and a quarter, right handed. High tournament, 67%; high game, 72%. Home: 9708 64th Avenue, Edmonton, Albert, Canada T6E OJ4.

SNIVELY, LOUIS D., Past Secretary Oklahoma Horseshoe Pitchers Association. W. Virginia June; children—Dee, Dean, Mark, Tim and Joel. Illustrator, Designer and Sign Writer. S. Deadeye; t. one and three quarters, right handed. Fort Bliss Champion, 1950 and 1951. High game 78%. Director, Cleveland County tournaments, worked

with senior citizens, built an active junior division and helped construct twelve courts in Noble's Horseshoe Park. Home: Box 176, Noble, Oklahoma, 73068.

SNYDER, G. E. 1922 New York State Champion.

SOETE, W. P. 1924 Kentucky State Champion.

SOLESBEE, DAVID, b. September 21, 1935. South Carolina State Secretary. Security Guard. S. Imperial; t. one and a quarter, right handed. Averages 50%. Home: 1201 West Poinsett, Greer, South Carolina 29651.

SOLESBEE, JOHNNY, b. June 11, 1941. Runnerup, South Carolina State Championship. W. Nancy; children—2 sons, 2 daughters. Textile worker. S. Imperial; t. two and a quarter, right handed. Averages 65%. Home: 1201 West Poinsett, Greer, South Carolina 29651.

SOLLAR, BILL, b. July 16, 1914. 24th Place, World Tournament, Championship Division 1961 (13-22-69.6%) W. Mamie; children—Sheila, Herbert. National Cash Register employee. S. Ohio; t. one and a quarter, right handed. 4-time champion, Warren County, Brown County Fair Champion, twice; Lynchburg Open champion. Home: 101 Farview Avenue, Lebanon, Ohio 45036.

SOLOMON, JAMES F., b. July 22, 1929. Pennsylvania State Champion 1964 (15-0-81.2%); 1977; 1978 (81.5%); 1979 (15-0-81.9%). W. Nancy; children—Deborah, Terry. Public Accountant. S. Imperial; t. one and three quarters, right handed. High game, 97.8%. Two-time winner, Frye Memorial. World tournament play, composite record, 206-229-75.4%. National auditor, NHPA. President, Fayette County HPA. Home: 95 Dawson Avenue, Uniontown, Pennsylvania 15401.

SOMERHALDER, SAM, b. 1915. 4-time Nebraska State Champion, 1931, 1934, 1935, 1936. Hit 92 ringers out of 100 shoes and 18 consecutive doubles. Vice-president, NHPA, 1939. 1956, Class B World Champion, 63%.

SORENSON, CLIFFORD A., b. January 9, 1925. 1980 South Dakota State Champion. W. Lois; children—Diane, Donna. Salesman. S. Deadeye; t. one and a quarter, left handed. High game, 80%; high tournament average, 70%. State Director, South Dakota HPA. Home: 318 State Avenue, Brookings, South Dakota 57006.

SORNBERGER, ROSS, b. July 15, 1912. Class B State Champion. W. Helen; children—Joan, Carolyn, Ronnie, Peggy. Pressman, Galesburg Register-Mail. S. Allen; t. one and three quarters and one and a quarter, left handed. President, 5 years, treasurer, 25 years, local club. Galesburg Board of Directors. High tournament, 71%; high game, 84%. 1978 Illinois Senior Championship, 2nd place. Home: 1904 Baird Avenue, Galesburg, Illinois 61401.

SPENCER, RALPH KELLEY, 1930 Oklahoma State Champion. 1922 World Tournament, 4th Place, 11-4 in finals. World tournament play, 183-76-52.5%.

SPERBER, ARTHUR R., May 28, 1929. Washington State HPA Secretary, 1977–1978. W. Carol J.; children—Mary, Ann, Robert. Elementary School Principal. S. Allen; t. one and three quarters, right handed. Member, Washington State Board of Directors. 1979, 5th Place, Washington State Tournament. 3rd Place, Class C, 1979 World Tournament. Best tournament, 69.1%; high game, 86.4%. Home: 6923 Chico Way, N.W., Bremerton, Washington 98310.

SPERLINE, TRACY, b. February 13, 1965. 1979, 75%, and 1980, 6-0-80.8%, Kansas State Boys' Champion. 4-time Topeka Open Champion. High game, 91%. 3rd Place, Class D, 1978 World Tournament. 1980, qualified championship division, 228-71%. S. Allen; t. three quarters right handed. Home: Box 75, Morrill, Kansas 66515.

SPRINGER, JACK. Secretary-Treasurer, North Carolina, HPA. Recreation Director, Statesville, North Carolina Recreation Department for nearly 30 years. Director, Carolina Dogwood Festival Horseshoe Tournament.

SPRINGFIELD, H. WAYNE, b. September 24, 1920. New Mexico State Champion, 1942, 75%, and 1973, 6-1-55.1%. W. Cordelia. Range ecologist. S. Allen; t. three quarters, right handed. Class B State Champion twice; runnerup, State Champion, Class A twice. Home: 13822—108th Drive, Sun City, Arizona 85351.

SQUIRES, BRENDA. 1980 Vermont Girls' State Champion, 3-1-23.5%.

STAFFORD, EDITH. 1967 Oregon Women's State Champion, 19.6%.

STAKER, LARRY. 1969 Illinois Boys' State Champion, 7-0-41.1%.

STAKER, RUSSELL. 1968 Illinois Boys' State Champion, 7-0.

STALEY, GERALD LEE, b. August 21, 1920. Class B Runnerup, Washington State Title. W. Shirley; children—Brian, Kathleen. Major League baseball pitcher. S. Allen and Imperial; t. one and a quarter, right handed. 1980, won Class C, Pacific Northwest Tournament, 6-1-56.3%. averages 56%. High game, 75%. Home: 2600 Northeast 99th Street, Vancouver, Washington 98665.

STALLINGS, DEXTER. b. October 15, 1927. Secretary-treasurer, Tennessee State HPA for 14 years. W. Lois Faye; children—Melba, Charles. Carpenter. S. Ohio pro; t. one and a quarter, right handed. NHPA Regional Director for Tennessee, Alabama, Georgia, Mississippi. Playing for 30 years. 2nd Place, Tennessee State Tournament. Averages 70%. Class B competitor, 1980 World Tournament. Home: Route 6, Reed Drive, Powell, Tennessee 37849.

STANDARD, HEMAN W., b. June 17, 1913. California Seniors State Champion, 1979, qualifying 78 ringers out of 100 shoes, and 1980, 68.8%. Child—Howard. Educator. S. Deadeye; t. one and three quarters, right handed. President, Orange Horseshoe Club. 1980, First Vice-president, Southern California HPA. 1980, placed 7th, seniors championship division, World Tournament. 1980 Class A Southern California Championship, 6-0-71.1%. Home: 612 South Orange Street, Orange, California 92666.

STANDARD, TRUMAN, b. May 8, 1917. Illinois State Champion, 1953, 1954, 1956 (678 ringers out of 860 shoes, 10-1-78.8%). W. Loretta; children—Marilyn DeLeon, Mark, Steve, Mike Calvert, Terry Calvert, Jeanine Bloyd, Pat Mclouth. Farmer and Bulldozer Operator. S. Allen; t. one and a quarter, right handed. World tournament play, 4000 out of 5000 shoes were ringers for an average of 80%. Won the 1949 Moline and Heart of Illinois Tournaments. 5th Place, 1952 World Tournament; 1956 World Tournament, 5th Place, with an 87.5% game. Won 3 gold-plated horseshoes on the T.V. show, "Championship Horseshoes Show" and also pitched on the "Tonight Show" hosted by Jack Paar. Played for more than 57 years. Member of the NHPA for 40 years. Entertains guests with spontaneous chalk sketches. Home: Route 2, Canton, Illinois 61520.

STAPP, WILEY, b. August 16, 1963. 1979 California Boys' State Champion, 73.9%. Student. S. Allen; t. three quarters, left handed. Junior Boys' Champion, Rio-Del

Open, the Shasta Open. Home: 4416 Campton Road, Eureka, California 95501.

STATZER, FRANK. Florida State Champion, 1966, 5-0, 1967, 8-0, 1969, 6-0.

STEARNS, REV. WALTER B. b. December 3, 1903. Arizona State Secretary for 19 years. W. Gladys; child—Bonnie Jean. Retired minister; past pastor, Apostolic Christian Church and President, Mesa Association of Churches. S. Allen; t. one and a quarter, right handed. Won the Arizona Class B State Championship in 1970. High game, 72.8%. Started the Valley of the Sun Open and directed it from 1958 through 1976. Home: 332 West 9th Street, Mesa, Arizona 85201.

STEEVES, SHELDON ANDREW, b. May 22, 1969. 1980 Massachusetts Boys' State Champion, 5-0-45.7%. Student. S. American; t. flip, right handed. In 1980, won the Keene, the New Hampshire Open, and the New England Class B Championship. Plays baseball and hockey, collects coins and is an active boy scout. Home: 138 Farmington Circle, Marlboro, Massachusetts 01752.

STEINFELDT, BETTY, b. September 17, 1947. Vice-president, New York NPA. Secretary. S. American; t. flip, right handed. 1979 World Tournament, one of top twelve. Won 1979 Heritage Recreation Club Championship, 6-0. High tournament average, 64%; high game, 75%. Secretary-treasurer New York NPA, for 4 years. Home: 44 Ridgecrest Road, Rochester, New York 14626.

STEINFELDT, CARL, b. September 20, 1917. 1976 World Tournament Champion, 1st Place, 33-2-82.6%, 1976, Intermediate World Champion. New York State Champion 22 times. Eastern National Champion, 8 times. Member New York State Hall of Fame. Member National Hall of Fame. 1971 Winner Hickock Award, amateur athlete of the year. Holds world record, with Elmer

Hohl, 15 consecutive four-deads. 1980 Florida State Champion, 6-0-81.7% with a 93.3% game. W. Beatrice; children—Carl, Betty. Retired, General Motors. S. American; t. one and a quarter, left handed. Has posted an 89.5% tournament and hit two 100% games, one in 1979 and one in 1980. On the T.V. show, "Challenge of the Sexes," hit 17 ringers out of 18 shoes. 8th on all-time list of winners with 375 wins in World Tournament play. Career of more than 50 years. Other World Tournament play: 1953, 8th place, 23-12-71.1%; 1954, 5th Place, 11-6-80.2%; 1955, 5th place, 27-8-77.5%; 1960, 4th Place, 28-7-81.9%; 1962, 11th Place, 22-13-79.4%; 1963, 3rd Place, 29-6-79.9%; 1964, 2nd Place, 30-5-83.3%; 1965, 6th Place, 28-7-84.0%; 1967, 8th Place, 24-11-79.1%; 1968, 5th Place, 28-7-82.8%; 1972, 12th Place, 21-14-78.1%; 1974, 2nd Place, 30-5-80.5%; 1977, 4th Place, 21-5-83.7%; 1979, 4th Place, 24-7-80.3%; 1980, 3rd Place, 26-5-78.5%. Home: Summer, 44 Ridgecrest Road, Rochester, New York 14626. Winter, 418 Shady Lane Mobile Park, 15400 Roosevelt Blvd., Clearwater, Florida 33520.

STEINHAUSER, MARY. World Tournament record, 9-12-53.9%, in 3 world tournaments. Home: Louisville, Kentucky.

STEINMAN, LEFTY. 1931 Missouri State Champion. 1935 World Tournament, Class B, 10-13-51.5%. 1933 championship division, World Tournament, 16th Place, 9-14-53.9%.

STEPHENS, HUBERTA. 1974, 1975, 1976 South Carolina State Champion, averaging about 35%. H. Willie; children—Rocky, Randy, Sandy, Joe. Garment sorter and packer. S. Imperial; t. reverse three quarter; right handed. Home: Route 3, Box 9, Standing Springs Road, Simpsonville, South Carolina 29681.

STEPHENS, SANDY, b. February 15, 1962. South Carolina Boys State Champion 1974, 4-0-49% and 1975. W. Vicki; child—Christopher. Packer for Stone Mfg., Co. S. Imperial; t. one and a quarter, right handed. Averages 42%. Record in tournaments, 1974–1977, 64-15. Home: Route 3, Box 9, Standing Springs Road, Simpsonville, South Carolina 29681.

STEPHENS RANDY, b. September 15, 1963. 1978 South Carolina Boys Champion, 4-0-34.2%. Box maker for Stone Mfg. Co. S. Imperial; t. one and a quarter, right handed. 44-32 record for three years in junior tournaments. Home: Route 3, Box 9, Standing Springs Road, Simpsonville, South Carolina 29681.

STEPHENS, WILLIE, b. April 8, 1942. Secretary-Treasurer, South Carolina HPA. NHPA Regional Director. W. Huberta; children—Rocky, Randy, Sandy, Joe. Garment packer. S. Imperial; t. one and a quarter, right handed. Class A competitor in regional tournaments. Home: Route 3, Box 9, Standing Spring Road, Simpsonville, South Carolina 29681.

STEVENS, CHARLES. 1960 Florida State Champion, 7-0-60.8%. S. Allen; t. one and three quarters, right handed. Pitched in the 1963 World Tournament. 60% average. Aided in the formation of the Florida Chapter of the NHPA. Home: Bradenton, Florida.

STEVENS, VINCE. 1920 and 1923 Indiana State Champion.

STEVENSON, ROSS. 1965 Junior Boys World Champion, 7-0-65.1%. 1972 Mens Class B World Champion, 73.4%. 1972 Manitoba Provincial Champion. Home: Bader, Ontario, Canada.

STEWART, BARBARA CUNNINGHAM, b. August 5, 1935. Secretary-treasurer, Marion Horseshoe Club 1970–

1973 and Women's Vice-president, Indiana HPA 1974–1976. Presented a service award for service, Marion Club. H. James; first h., deceased, F. Paul Cunningham; Cunningham children—Cathy, Terrie, Mike, Tammi. Owner, BJ's Restaurant, Housewife. S. Allen; t. one and a quarter, right handed. Home: 2303 South Meridian Street, Marion, Indiana 46952.

STILL, CONNIE, b. September 2, 1954. 2nd Place, 1980 Ohio State Tournament, 72.6%. H. Wayne; child—April. Housewife. S. Gordon; t. flip, right handed. High game, 82.2%. Forced World Champion, Ruth Hangen, to go 110 shoes for her longest game, world tournament play. Averages high 60s. Class B World Champion. Class A, 6th Place, World Championship, 5-6-66.8%; 3 World Tournament, Class A performances, composite, 11-18-66%. Home: 4220 West Street, Oxford, Ohio 45056.

STINES, LOU, b. January 14, 1929. Averages 72%; high game, 92%; has hit 30 consecutive ringers. 1974 Heritage Warmup, beat Danny Kuchcinski and Carl Steinfeldt in the Hardwick Open and the New York State Tournament in 1977. W. Rose; children—Thomas, Susan. Maintenance man. S. Allen; t. one and three quarters, right handed. Enjoys pool, archery, ice skating. Pitched for 37 years. Home: 60-31 Cooper Avenue, Glendale, New York 11227.

STINSON, FRANK, JR., b. April 15, 1949. 1961, 1964 Minnesota Boys State Champion.

STINSON, FRANK. b. June 8, 1910. Minnesota State Champion, 1939, 1940, 1941, 1965, 1967, 1969, 1970, 1971. Member Minnesota HPA Hall of Fame. World Champion—Junior Boys, 1924 and Senior Men, 1976. W. Bertha; children—Kenneth, Frank, Jr., Sandra. S. Allen; t. one and a quarter, right handed. Home: 915 East 41 Street, Minneapolis, Minnesota 55407.

STOCKHOLM, ALAN J., b. March 13, 1938. 1972 New York State Champion, 10-1-76.7%. College teacher, State University of New York, Cortland. S. Allen; t. one and a quarter, left handed. 1973, 12th Place, World Tournament, 22-13-74.1%, 1972, 11th place, 22-13-77.7%. Home: 752 Bowling Green, Cortland, New York 13045.

STOKES, ARCHIBALD LAGRAND, deceased 1957. Member Utah Hall of Fame. 1966 Charter Member, National Hall of Fame. W. Mary Lupton Heward; children—Winona, Maurine, Geraldine, Ruth, Tom, John, Annie, Ellen. Postal clerk. S. Gordon; right handed. Organized clubs at Magna and Verreal. President Salt Lake Horseshoe Club, the Utah Horseshoe PA and the NHPA. Brought the 1947 World Tournament to Utah. Namesake of the Stokes Memorial Award, given annually to that person who has done the most to promote the game.

STOKES, MARY LUPTON HEWARD, b. July 11, 1884. Deceased. Member, Utah Hall of Fame. H. Archibald; children—Winona, Maurine, Geraldine, Ruth, Tom, John, Annie, Ellen. Promoted the game from the early 1920s until her death. Established the Archibald Stokes Award.

STOLARIK, ANDREW. b. November 15, 1909. Trustee, Canton Horseshoe Club. Children—Mary Ann, Andrew, Nancy. Electrician. S. American; t. one and a quarter, right handed. Played for 56 years. 1946 Vice-president, NHPA. Past Secretary-treasurer, Rockstroh Club, Canton. President, Secretary-Treasurer Canton Club. 1939 Stark County Title. High state tournament average, 70%; high game, 98%. 1941 Ohio State Runnerup with 850 ringers out of 1200 shoes. 1946 National Championship, 12th Place. Home: 1124 Greenfield Avenue, S.W., Canton, Ohio 44706.

Top, left to right, Floyd Toole, Hall of Fame member; Art Tyson; Bertie Venter of South Africa. *Second row, center,* Carl von der Lancken, Hall of Fame member. *Bottom, left to right,* Jim Weeks; Bob West, Hall of Fame member; Jeffrey Williams, young World Champion.

Top, left, Walter Ray Williams, Jr., World Champion. *Right,* Earl Winston, NHPA Vice President. *Bottom, left,* Vicki Winston, World Champion and Hall of Fame member. *Right,* Al Zadroga, Hall of Fame member.

STONER, MERLE. 1930 California State Champion.

STORY, T. C. 1921 Kentucky State Champion.

STOUT, JACK R., b. March 1, 1929. Recipient, NHPA Achievement Award, 1976. W. Barbara; children—Michael, Kathy, Glenn, Keith. Plant manager, Ace Metal Crafts Company. S. Allen; t. one and a quarter, right handed. Won Northern Illinois Class A league championship, 1967–68; won National AAU doubles title, with Roger Ehlers, 1960–61; won Class B Greenville Ringer Classic, 74.2%, 1967; high tournament, 74.4%, Championship Division, World Tournament, 1969; high game, 87.2%, 1969 World Tournament; helped build scoring devices, equipment, NHPA. Home: 1946 North 18th Avenue, Melrose Park, Illinois 60160.

STOUT, MICHAEL E., b. July 17, 1959. Finished in top seven, Championship Division, Junior World Tournament, 1972–76. Single. Student. S. Allen; t. reverse three quarters, left handed. Won Illinois junior state championship, age 12, 1971, won state titles in 1972–76; finished second, state tournament, 1970; won Class A championships (junior): Midwest Ringer Roundup, 1972, Greenville Ringer Classic, 1974, Heritage Recreation Center, 1974, Eau Claire Open, 1974, Goldendale Open, 1976, Eau Claire Open, 1976; hit 93.7% game, Illinois Boys State Championships; averaged 79.4%, 1975 Junior World Tournaments; voted Most Valuable College Bowler in the nation, 1979, West Texas State College. Home: 1946 North 18th Avenue, Melrose Park, Illinois 60160.

STOWE, BOB, b. January 15, 1919. Alabama State Champion, 1978–79. W. Bernice; children—Robert, Gary. Retired, United States Army. S. Allen; t. one and a quarter, right handed. Won 103 trophies, 59 for first place, Class A, 1969–74; high game, against World Champion Curt Day, Manatee County Fair Open Tournament, 50-shoe cancellation, 22-16-86%; finished second, Missouri state tournament, 1972, 1973; pitched 50 years, 25 in organized play; vice-president, Alabama HPA. Home: 306 Green Park Drive, Mobile, Alabama 36608.

STOWELL, PAMELA, 1965 Massachusetts Women's State Champion, New England States Ladies Champion, 1964. Home: 45 Crosby Road, Dracut, Massachusetts 01826.

STRAITIFF, ROBERT, b. August 3, 1922. Tournament Director, Fayette County Horseshoe Club. W. Nannie; children—Grace, Robert, Jr., Edward, Georgia, Darwin, Robin, David (d.), Roy. Mechanic/miner/steelworker. S. Allen; t. one and three quarters, right handed. Won 1979 Apple Capitol Open, Winchester, 11-0-67.3%; defeated Carl Steinfeldt, 1978 Eastern National, Lockport; high tournament, 69.9%; high game, 85.7%. Home: 57 McArthur Terrace, Uniontown, Pennsylvania 15401.

STRAW, STEWART, 1933 Pennsylvania State Champion.

STRODE, B. E., 1923, 1924 Texas State Champion, first recognized state champion.

STRUTHERS, WILLIAM R., b. October 1, 1911. 1927 Canadian Champion, first recognized champion. W. Dorothy; children—Nadine (d.), Laurel. Retired. S. Diamond; t. one and three quarters, right handed. Teamed with Walter Kane, 1927 doubles tournament champions; with Thomas Buckingham, 1929 doubles crown; won first singles tournament, 1929; won Mueller Trophy, 1925–28; pitched exhibition games with Walter Kane. Home: 840 Trillium Park, Apt. 509, Sarnia, Ontario, Canada N7T 7B9.

STURDEVANT, GUY, Maine State Champion. 1928-30, 1932. Home: South Paris, Maine.

STURGIS, PARKER, State Secretary, Maryland HPA, player, promoter. Home: 522 East Main Street, Fruitland, Maryland 21826.

SUESS, GEORGE, 1948 Minnesota State Champion, 12-2. Pitched one and a quarter turn from stationary position. Home: North Mankato, Minnesota.

SUMMERHILL, SCOTT, 1977 New Mexico Boys State Champion, 30%. U.S. Army, Serial No. 585-13-7119, D Battery—First of the Fifth Field Artillery, Fort Riley, Kansas 66442.

SUMMERS, JENNIE, b. July 3, 1936. 1980 Statesville Autumn Champion. H. Robert; children—Keith, Joey, David, Stella. Sewing machine operator. S. Ohio; t. one full, right handed. Won Parks and Recreation Departments State Championship; won Class A championship, Winston-Salem Workhorse Tournament; Home: 230 Lundsey Street, Statesville, North Carolina 28677.

SUMNER, LISA, 1978 Vermont Girls State Champion, 37.5%. Home: Route 2, Bristol, Vermont 05443.

SUTTON, ROBERT E., b. May 2, 1929. Past Vice-President, New York State HPA. W. Lois; children—Geoff, Scott, Wendy, Holly. Teacher. S. Allen; t. one and a quarter, right handed. Won Northern Open, Canton, N.Y., 70%, 1978; won Class A championships including: 1968 Ottawa Ontario Open, 1969, 1970 Raftsman Opens, Hull, Quebec; high game, 91.6%; most consecutive ringers, 28. Enjoys chess, pool, checkers, ping pong. Home: 94 Skelly Place, Mineola, New York 11501.

SUTTON, SAM, Recipient, Outstanding First Year Entrant award, 1965 World Tournament. W. Lavella Marie. Farmer/shipper/trucker, Brookways Glass Company. S. Allen; t. one and a quarter, right handed. Averaged 80%, ten tournaments, 1965-67;

averaged 83%, 1966 World Tournament; finished second, to Dan Duchcinski, 1966 Pennsylvania State Tournament; high tournament, 88.8%, seven games, Red Mill; high game, 98% against Stan Manker, Greenville Classic; defeated Cracker Williams, 42 consecutive ringers; lost to Curt Day, 50–49, to Elmer Hohl, 52 ringers before Hohl scored winning point. Home: 102 West Hallam Avenue, Washington, Pennsylvania 15201.

SWANDER, HARLEY, b. August 27, 1914. W. Wanga; children—Jay, Lee. Retired. S. Allen; t. one and a quarter. High tournament average, 66.4%; high game, 78%; won two Class A tournaments, 5-0-65.2%, 6-1-66.4%. Home: 305 West 39th Avenue, San Mateo, California 94403.

SWANK, DALE S., b. February 10, 1925. Class B Illinois State Champion, 1971. W. Mary Jane. Machinist, Home Comfort Products. S. Gordon; t. flip, right handed. Played NHPA tournaments since 1969; won more than 60 trophies; right hand injury, 1966; finished fifth, Class A, state tournament, 1979. Home: Route 1, Toulon, Illinois 61483.

SWANSON, DARLENE, 1961 Michigan State Women's Champion, 4-1.

SWANSON, KAREN, 1969 Nevada Girls State Champion.

SWARINGEN, E. C. "VAN," Vice-President, NHPA, 1959. Photographer. Home: Springfield, Illinois.

SWARTHOUT, JEAN, b. December 18, 1926. Michigan State Champion, 1971, 1972, 52.9%, 1974, 58.3%, 1975, 59.2%. H. Stan; children—Linda Shaffer, Donna Thomas. Housewife. S. Reno; t. flip, left handed, Won Curley-Baker Memorial, 1978; won Class B World Championship, 1971, 1973, 1975–77; elected to Wolverine State HPA Hall of Fame, 1975; high game, 78%, 1975 Lake Orion Open; high tournament, 67.5%;

treasurer, WSHPA; member, River Raison Horseshoe League, and Dundee Sportsman's League. Home: 487 West Main Street, Milan, Michigan 48160.

SWARTHOUT, STAN, b. March 2, 1924. Vice-President (two terms) Wolverine State HPA, Assistant District Director, two years. W. Jean. Die setter. S. Allen; t. one and a quarter, right handed. Pitched in Class B,C,D; played in Greenville Ringer Classic, qualifying for Class A, 1977; won Michigan tournaments including Jackson Rose Festival, twice; elected to Michigan HPA Hall of Fame, 1979; defeated Wilbur Kabel, Paul Focht, Jim Knisley, Stan Manker, Glen Riffle, Gary Roberts; finished third, state tournament, 1977, tied for third and fourth, 1978; high tournament, 71.5%, 1978 Sturgis Open; high game, 86% against Floyd Bartley, 1978 state tournament; won Dundee Sportsman's League and River Raison League championships; underwent bypass operation, 1979. Home: 487 West Main Street, Milan, Michigan 48160.

SWARTWOUT, LLOYD, d. 1974. State Champion, 1957, 1959; Member, South Dakota Hall of Fame, 1969. South Dakota State Tournament, 1975 dedicated to his memory; state championship record: 11-0-66.4%, 1957, 11-0-60%, 1959; won Sioux Empire Open, twice; recipient, Achievement Award, 1969; shares state record with Leigh Dunker, 15 four-deads in one game; president, South Dakota HPA.

SWARTZ, ELMER L. "DUTCH," b. November 13, 1919. Fairfax County Champion, 1975–79. W. Grace. Federal government employee. S. Ohio Pro, Deadeye, American, Allen. right handed. High tournament, 65.2%, 1979 Frye Memorial; high game, 84.6%; member, NHPA since 1941. Home: 7406 Englewood Place—#104 Annandale, Virginia 22003.

SWARTZ, PAUL E., b. December 7, 1919.

1961 AAU State Champion. W.; children—Jack, Bill, Cathy, Carol Ann (d.). Employment clerk, Erie Railroad Company. S. Ohio; t. one and a quarter, right handed. Won Marion County title, averaging 60% or better, 1937–61, 1965–69; runnerup to Myron Ferguson, state tournament, 70.2%, 1942; high game, 82%, 29 consecutive ringers, league tournament; averaged 72%, opened one game with 35 straight ringers, 94%; firecracker accident, July 4, 1938, injuring pitching hand; high tournament, 84%; served in U.S. Army (WWII). Home: 274½ South Main Street, Marion, Ohio 43302.

SWEENEY, RUSSELL J., b. September 3, 1919. Massachusetts State Champion, 1970–72. W. Marjorie Edith; children—Catherine, Patricia, Barbara. Quality assurance engineer, Stone and Webster Engineering Company. S. Ohio; t. one and a quarter, right handed. NHPA state secretary, 1970–75; high tournament, 70%; NHPA Achievement Award, 1975; inducted into Massachusetts HPA Hall of Fame (as organizer), 1975, (as Player), 1979, first person to be inducted in two categories. Home: 114 Montclair Avenue, North Quincy, Massachusetts 02171.

SWIGART, GARY, b. November 3, 1964. 1979 Missouri Boys State Champion, 2-1-35.4%. Single. Student. S. Ohio Pro; t. reverse three quarters, right handed. Finished fourth, junior state tournament, 1977, third, 1978; won championships in BCHC club tournament, Missouri state fair, Higginsville club. Enjoys working on 1956 Chevrolet. Home: 2008 Lipper Avenue, Higginsville, Missouri 64037.

SWINEHAMER, ALDEN, 1939 Illinois State Champion. Played in 1948 World Tournament, championship division, qualifying at 520, 12-19-69.3%; high game against Eddie Packham, 82.6%.

T

TAMBOER, MARINES, b. 1904. Kansas State Champion, 1944–46, 1950–54, 1962, 1965, 1980 (11 times); Member, Kansas HPA Hall of Fame, 1975. W. Zella; children— Mary Ann Peninger, Cina Snyder. Farmer. S. Allen or Deadeye; t. one and a quarter, right handed. Won Valley of the Sun tournament five times; won 1959 Florida Open; high tournament, 79.9%, 1964 World Tournament; high game, 92%, 1970 World Tournament, 280-point qualifying round for 100 shoes, Knasas state tournament; finished third, World Tournament, 1951, fourth, 1952; 36 consecutive ringers; World Tournament record (Championship Division): 274-205-74.2%, 505 average points per qualifying round; 1980 state title: 9-2-59.8%, age 75. Home: 3804 South West Street, Wichita, Kansas 67217.

TANNER, L. E., 1933 President, Illinois HPA; NHPA President, 1935–39. Chairman, Tournament committee, 1933 World Tournament at Chicago World Fair. Home: Anchor, Illinois.

TASSEL, GLEN, 1966 New Mexico State Champion, 6-1-64.7%.

TATE, MILTON L., b. August 13, 1906. Illinois State Champion, 1930, 1931, 1933, 1937; Utah State Champion, 1961. W. Frances; child—Patricia S. Grimm. Welder. S. Allen; t. one and three quarters, right handed. Pitched 60 years; set Illinois state record for most shoes in one tournament, 1056, 1937; won 50-42 over Clive Wahlin, 86.6%, 1961 Utah state meet; secretary, Peoria Club, 1950; high tournament, 80%; high game, 87.7%; pitched eight weeks on television station WMAQ Channel 5, Chicago, "Championship Horseshoes."; won numerous tournaments, pitched several perfect games; hit 56 consecutive ringers against Truman Standard, lost to Standard

50-49, Bradley Park, Peoria; won Eastern National twice, 1955–56; qualified for Rocky Mountain Open, 88%, won title, 1956; won Heart of Illinois tournament, 1962, 1965–67; won Moline Open twice, Galesburg twice; pitched in World Tournaments, 1952–59, won Class B, 1953, tied for third with Clive Wahlin, championship division, averaging 80%, 1959; won tournament in Moline to go to Amateur Newspaper Tournament, Chicago; defeated Jimmie Risk, National Championships. Home: 2626 Eugenie Avenue, Peoria, Illinois 61615.

TAYLOR, BURL, b. March 31, 1907. W. Vera E.; children—Bradley, Charlotte, Virgil, Myron, Hallie, Shaaron. Brick, stone mason/farmer/trapper. S. Allen; t. one and three quarters, right handed. Pitched 50 years; high tournament, 75%; runnerup, Class C, World Tournament, 19-79; won Cayuga County Fair Tournament, 1979; Class A pitcher in Indiana. Home: Route 6, Box 308, Greencastle, Indiana 46135.

TAYLOR, HALLIE, b. July 22, 1942. 1958 Indiana Boys State Champion. W. Helen; children—Christine, Mark. Pastor, First Southern Baptist Church of Roselawn. S. Imperial; t. one and three quarters, right handed. Won Class A Men's Championship, Barboursville, Kentucky; won Class B title, Robinson, Illinois; participated in three World Tournaments, 1971, 1975, 1977; graduate, Clear Creek Baptist School, Pineville, Ky. Home: Lot 27, Valley Forge, DeMotte, Indiana 46310.

TAYLOR, VIRGIL B., b. January 25, 1936. 1955 World Class B Champion, 14-0-74.8%. W. Marilyn; children—Bob, Doreen, Sherri, Stacey. IBM employee. S. Allen; t. one and three quarters, right handed. Pitched 30 years, 25 in tournament play; high tournament, 77%; high game, 88%; tied for 10th place, Class A division, World Tournament; won singles and doubles championships, Ft.

Bliss, Texas, U.S. Army; finished third, Midwest Ringer Roundup. Home: Route 4-Box 126, Greencastle, Indiana 46135.

TAYLOR, WELLINGTON, b. April 10, 1911. Past President, Iowa HPA. W. Cloris; children—Randall, Robert, Marla Jean. Farmer/butcher/locker plant operator. S. Allen; t. one and a quarter, right handed. Vice-president, Osceola HPA; qualified in Class A, World Tournament, 5-30-68%, 1964, pitched 70% against Carl Steinfelt, was shut out; responsible for construction of two batteries of playing courts, Decatur County Fairgrounds, and at Osceola; pitched in many tournaments, Class A, won many open tournaments; won Iowa State Fair title several times; won 1962 Iowa Open; hit 1611 ringers out of 2000 shoes, 1963; won 1955 Corn Belt Open, 87% in exhibition match against Jim Wilkinson, defeated ten-time World Champion Ted Allen, 1960 World Tournament; hit 96% game, five-game stint of 215 out of 250, 86%, Birdland Park, Des Moines; was basketball player for several years on team sponsored by Phillips "66", Chicago. Enjoys baseball. Home: Box 234, Grand River, Iowa 50108.

TEMPLETON, L. E., 1962 Virginia State Champion, 15-0-68.3%.

TESSANDORE, HENRY, b. April 8, 1911. W. Gladys; children—Robert, James. Pacific Fruit and Produce employee. S. Sears; t. one and one quarter, right handed. 1928 Washington State Champion, 21-2, age 17; pitched 52 years, one year in tournament play. Was second baseman, high school baseball team. Enjoys golf. Home: 5711 South 129th—Box 36, Seattle, Washington 98178.

THIBEAULT, FERNAND, Quebec Provincial Champion, 1967, 1969–70. Runnerup to Elmer Hohl, 6-1-72.6%, Canadian National Championship Tournament, 1978; hit 80.7%, high tournament, against Roy McLaughlin; qualified for title division,

finished 29th, 16-19-70%, 1976 World Tournament, Philadelphia, Pa. Home: 330 Place Des Trewble—Apt. 2, Sorel, Quebec, Canada.

THIBEAULT, RON, Maine Boys State Champion, 76.7%, 1975, 68%, 1976.

THIBEAULT, SIMONE, Maine Women's State Champion, 1968, 5-0-39.4%, 1969, 10-0-43.3%.

THIELKE, RAYMOND, 1973 Maryland State Champion, 7-0-61.7%.

THOLL, TERRY, b. March 9, 1949. President, Northern Nevada League. H. Paul; children—Randy, Julie. Account manager. S. Gordon; t. flip. First woman to hold office of president in Northern Nevada League; recipient, Sportsmanship Trophy, 1977. Home: 497 Gamble Drive, Sparks, Nevada 89431.

THOMAS, ARTHUR, 1935 Utah State Champion, 10-0-75%.

THOMAS, LORRAINE, 1968, 1974 World Champion. H. Paul; children—Patricia, David. Housewife. S. Reno; t. flip, right handed. Won New York State Championship, nine times, Eastern National five times, Greenville Ringer Classic, twice, Lockport League championship, nine times; runnerup, eight times, World Tournament, finished below fourth only once; first New York player to win world title; first New York women's champion; Charter Member, New York State HPA Hall of Fame; hit 92.2% game against Ruth Hangen, 1970 State Tournament; qualified in Class A in every event she entered except 1980 World Tournament (2nd in Class B); worked as promoter, with husband, ran tournaments, publicity, pitched exhibition games, worked with new members; Class A tournament records: 1964, 7th, 2-5-55.7%; 1965, 3rd, 5-2-68.2%; 1966, 2nd, 6-1-66.4%; 1967 2nd, 6-1-66.5%; 1968, 1st, 7-0-74.9%; 1969, 3rd, 5-2-70.6%;

1970, 2nd, 6-1-67.8%; 1971, 2nd, 6-1-69%; 1972, 2nd, 5-2-70.8%; 1973, 2nd, 6-1-80.9%; 1974, 1st, 7-0-80.2%; 1975, 4th, 3-4-67.9%; 1976, 2nd, 6-1-72.9%; 1977, 4th, 4-3-72.8%; 1978, 2nd, 8-3-72.8%; 1979, 8th, 4-7-62.8%. Home: 456 Pine Street, Lockport, New York 14094.

THOMAS, MICKEY J., b. December 26, 1963. Georgia Boys State Champion, 1974–77. Single. Student. S. Gordon; t. flip, right handed. Enjoys baseball, bowling. Home: Route 5, Box 85, Toccoa, Georgia 30577.

THOMAS, PAUL A., b. November 27, 1934. 1977 Member, New York HPA Hall of Fame. W. Lorraine; children—Pat Kleinhaus, David. Supervisor, Machine and Tool Design. S. Hohl; t. one and three quarters, right handed. Pitched 22 years in leagues and tournaments; past president, vice-president, secretary-treasurer, local club; past president, assistant regional director, New York State HPA, NHPA. Enjoys bridge, bowling, hunting. Home: 456 Pine Street, Lockport, New York 14094.

THOMAS, ROD, d. August 30, 1966. 1963 Washington Sports Writer of the Year. Publicized horseshoes in Maryland, Virginia, and Washington, D.C., 1929–63.

THOMAS, TIM, 1972–73 Georgia Boys State Champion, 4-0, 5-1.

THOMAS, WILLIAM A., b. January 23, 1914. Colorado State Champion, 1969, 1974, W. Betty; children—Jeff, Dean. Cement finisher. S. Ohio Pro; t. one and three quarters, right handed. Won Tri-state Tournament, at Laramie for Colorado-Wyoming-Nebraska, defeating Roger Vogel in playoff; high tournament, 67.2%, 1974 Colorado State Tournament; high game, 89.1%. Home: 16820 Golden Hills Road, Golden, Colorado 80401.

THOMAS, WOODY, 1960 North Carolina State Champion, 9-2-57%. Pitched 25 years.

Home: 601 Abbie Avenue, High Point, North Carolina 27263.

THOMPSON, BILL, b. September 25, 1909. 1980 Oklahoma Senior State Champion, 3-0-38%. W. Marie; six children. Secular work/preacher. S. Allen, Imperial; t. one and three quarters, right handed. Served as manager, president, local club, Mandan, N.D., two years. Home: 116 Enlow, Blackwell, Oklahoma 74631.

THOMPSON, C. R., 1929 Illinois State Champion. Championship Division, World Tournament play: 181-153-50.6%. Home: Tampa, Fla.

THOMPSON, GEORGE C., 1933 Virginia State Champion.

THOMPSON, GIFFORD W., 1962 Arizona State Champion, 9-0-64%. Home: P.O. Box 211, Eureka, Nevada 89316.

THURGOOD, RULON O., Member, Utah HPA Hall of Fame. W. Ordelle W.; children—Blair, Denis. Supervisor of storage, Ogden Army Depot. S. Allen, Gordon, Diamond; t. one and a quarter, right handed. Past president, secretary, Utah HPA. Home: 5227 South 2050 West, Roy, Utah 84067.

TIILIKAINEN, EINO, Colorado State Champion, 1949 (with Jimmie Davis), 1950, 11-1-69.6%, 1953, 11-0-65%. Past state secretary. Home: 314 West Ramona Avenue, Colorado Springs, Colorado 80906.

TITCOMB, DON, b. February 25, 1924. 1960 World Champion; Member, National Hall of Fame, California Hall of Fame. Children—Donna, Judy, William, Marily, Patricia. Head custodian, Leland High School. S. Allen; t. one and a quarter, left handed. Won eight California state championships, 1951–67; won 150 tournament titles; high tournament, 86.1%; high game, 97%; hit 105 ringers out of consecutive 108 shoes; member, National Publicity Committee;

president, San Jose Club; fourth vice-president, Northern California HPA; was first Western States Publicity Director, helped form National Regional Publicity Directors; World Tournament record: 1947, 16th, 18-17-70.1%; 1949, 6th, 28-7-77.9%; 1950, 8th, 24-11-75.1%; 1952, 5th, 28-7-77.4%; 1953, 3rd, 31-4-80.2%; 1955, 2nd, 31-4-80.7%; 1956, 2nd, 34-1-84%; 1957, 2nd, 28-2-86.1%; 1958, 3rd, 26-4-84%; 1959, 4th, 30-5-82.7%; 1960, 1st, 33-2-84.9%; 1963, 6th, 27-8-79.6%; 1979, 13th, 18-13-75.1%; 1980, 11th, 17-14-73.8%. Home: 2855—14 Senter Road, San Jose, California 95111.

TITUS, JIM, b. March 13, 1937. Vice-President, West Virginia State HPA. W. Evelyn; children—Patty, James, Jr. Welder. S. Ohio Pro; t. one and three quarters. Vice-president, Lewis County HPA; organized tournaments since 1974; won Class D state title; won 2nd place, Class B, 1975; ringer percentage, 65%. Home: Route 1, Box 212, Lost Creek, West Virginia 26385.

TOBEY, HENRIETTA A., b. January 13, 1949. 1980 Nevada Women's State Champion, 6-1-35.5%. Child—Allan, T. Legal Secretary. S. Diamond; t. flip, right handed. Won Nevada Women's state championship three times, 33%, 1977, 1979; member, Reno-Sparks Tribal Council (treasurer), serves as Associate Tribal Judge; member, NAIWA (Indian women's group); secretary-treasurer, Nevada state chapter. Enjoys Indian bead work, quilts, pillows. Home: 7360 West Fourth Street—Space 22, Reno, Nevada 89503.

TOBEY, PAUL, 1964, 1972 Maine State Champion (7-0-66.7%). Finished third, New England meet, 1971, hit 70.2% for 15 games; won 1973 Greater Lowell Invitational; won Keene Open; above 60% 26 times, above 66% nine times, 1964–76. Home: Kittery, Maine.

TOLLISON, JOHNNY, b. March 31, 1962. 1976 South Carolina Boys State Champion, 7-0-25.7%. Employee, Winn Dixie Store. Was runnerup twice, state tournament. Home: 115-A, Butler Avenue, Mauldin, South Carolina 29662.

TOLONEN, JAKE, President, Alberta HPA, elected in 1978. Home: Lacombe, Alberta, Canada TOC 1S0.

TOMASEVIC, SAM, b. January 23, 1953. Vice-President, British Columbia HPA. Single. Accountant. S. Allen or Dean; t. one and three quarters, left handed. Treasurer of Greater Vancouver Horseshoe Pitching Club; won Class B British Columbia 1972; Class B Vancouver 1974. High game 62%. Enjoys football. Home: 3658 Rae Street, Vancouver, British Columbia, Canada, V5R 2P5.

TOMAYKO, JOSEPH F., b. May 22, 1898. Pitched 57 years. W. d. Steelmill worker. S. Imperial; t. one and three quarters, right handed. Defeated Pennsylvania State Champion George Curry, 1931. Was duckpin bowler. Home: 1102 Meadow Avenue, Charleroi, Pennsylvania 15022.

TOMKIN, J. ROBERT, Past NHPA Secretary, 1940. Home: Ames, Iowa.

TONEY, ROBERT L., JR., b. July 16, 1917. Virginia State Champion, 1958, 1961, 1964, 1965 (72.7%), 1966. W. Mattie; children—Robert Lee III, Darrell Wayne. City fireman. S. Allen; t. one and a quarter, right handed. Pitched 20 years in NHPA; chairman, tournament committee, local club, past president; won state doubles championship, 1978; won Lynchburg City Championships; won Southeastern Classic title, Winston-Salem, N.C., 1976; high tournament, 79%; hit 95.4% game against Lee Bennett, 1965 World Tournament, N.H.; hit 14 consecutive four-deads, with Carl Steinfeldt, 1965 World Tournament; member, Virginia State

Hall of Fame, 1976. Home: Lakeside Circle—Route 5, Madison Heights, Virginia 24572.

TOOLE, FLOYD C., b. December 30, 1917. 1981 member NHPA Hall of Fame Best Razorback in Arkansas History. W.; two children. Railroad man. S. Allen; t. one and a quarter, right handed. Secretary-treasurer, Arkansas HPA; Arkansas State Champion, 1953; won National AAU championship, 1954, 1957; finished in tie for runnerup, 84.5%, World Tournament, 1965; averaged 92.4%, 66 consecutive ringers, against Jim Solomon, 1964; set record for longest game (178 shoes), with Paul Focht, 1961; hit four consecutive 90% games against Glen Henton, Hugh Rogers, Marvin Craig, Ted Allen, 1965; pitched 21 years with NHPA. Home: 7215 Shetland Drive, Little Rock, Arkansas 72209.

TOOLE, PAUL, b. May 12, 1914. 1968, 1969 Alaska State Champion (7-0-78%). W. Lydia; children—Beverly Strickland, Linda Leftwich, Danial Marie Crites. Electrician. S. Ohio Pro; t. one and three quarters, right handed. NHPA member, 30 members; served as acting director, Alaska, seven years; won 29 of 30 tournaments; high tournament, 84.2%, five games in Cash Creek tournament; high game, 98%, 1930. Home: 300 East Lymaw Road, Topeka, Kansas 66608.

TORBETT, E. A., 1924 Illinois State Champion.

TORBETT, WALTER, 1926–27 Illinois State Champion.

TOTHEROW, SHIRLEY, b. March 20, 1951. 1978–79 Georgia Women's State Champion. H. Joe; children—Bryan, Keith. Quality assurance clerk, Avon Products. S. Imperial; t. flip, right handed. Won 1978 Revus Mountain Doubles, Cherokee Invitational, Ball Ground Open, Ringold Open;

won 2nd place, Alpharetta Open, M.C.C. Singles, Cherokee Invitational Mixed Doubles; pitched 10 years, 3 in NHPA. Enjoys softball. Home: Route 3—Box 140-B, Ball Ground, Georgia 30107.

TOWNE, THOMAS L., b. October 12, 1933. Oklahoma State Champion, 1967, 7-0-62.4%, 1969, 7-0-62.8%; New Mexico State Champion, 1977, 9-0-65.8%. W. Carnella; children—Rick, Tracy. Employee, Sandia Laboratories. S. Allen; t. one and a quarter, right handed. Runnerup, Oklahoma state tournament, 1950; served as first president, New Mexico State HPA. Enjoys square dancing, round dancing, golf. Home: S.S. Box 778, Corrales, New Mexico 87048.

TOWNE, WILLIAM F., b. December 26, 1903. Oklahoma State Champion, 1944–45, 1947. W. Edna; children—Harvey, Tom, Jean, Trina. Retired, Oklahoma Natural Gas Company. S. Diamond; t. one and three quarters, right handed. Enjoys fishing, traveling. Home: Route 9, Box 192, Claremore, Oklahoma 74017.

TOWNSEND, JACK, b. September 3, 1937. President, New York HPA. W. Ann. Clerk. S. Gordon; t. one and three quarters, right handed. Original organizer, president, Northern Horseshoe Club, Canton, 1974–77; produced State Tournament Booklet (84 pages), 1980; won class championship, 45%, 1974 World Tournament; won Class B, Northern Open, 1975, Class C, NE-OS-CO Open, 1975, Class G, New York State, 1974, Class B, NE-OS-CO Doubles, 1976; won Northern Horseshoe Club Men's Handicap League three times since 1976; promoted clinics, exhibitions, publicity; recipient, 1977 Silver Shoe Award, Northern Horseshoe Club, Carl Steinfeldt Award for promotion, 1976; established annual Northern Open. Home: 15 Pine Street, Canton, New York 13617.

TRAQUAIR, ROBERT C., b. May 19,

1933. New Hampshire State Secretary-Treasurer (since 1975); New Hampshire State Champion, 1976, 70.5%, 1977, 73.5% (state record), 1978, 69.6%. W. Deborah; children—Susan, Robert R., Edward, William. Electrician. S. Ohio Pro; t. one and a quarter, right handed. Past State President, 1972; served as delegate, National Convention, 1971, 1974, 1975, 1977, 1978; finished fourth, state tournament, 1971, second, 1972, 1974; set state record, 73.5%, 1977. Home: 18 New Acres Road, Keene, New Hampshire 03431.

TRAQUAIR, ROBERT R. "SKIP," b. January 16, 1963. 1980 New Hampshire State Champion, 3-2-50.3%. Single. Mechanical engineer, Markem Corp. S. Ohio; t. one and a quarter, right handed. Third vice-president, Keene Horseshoe Club. Enjoys hunting, fishing. Home: 18 New Acres Road, Keene, New Hampshire 03431.

TRAQUAIR, SUSAN E., 1976 New Hampshire Girls State Champion. Single. Radiologic technologist. S. Ohio O; t. one and a quarter, right handed. High tournament, 35%; high game, 43%; serves as statistician, New Hampshire tournaments. Home: 96 Main Street, Riverside Terrace, Apt. #4, Suncook, New Hampshire 03275.

TRAQUAIR, WILLIAM COLIN, b. April 3, 1967. 1980 New Hampshire Boys State Champion, 4-0-35.5%. Single. Student/shoe shine boy. S. American; t. flip, right handed. Won New Hampshire Open, Keene Warm-up, Maine Open; high tournament, 39.6%; high game, 59%, inc. five consecutive doubles. Enjoys cycling, painting, basketball, football. Home: 18 New Acres Road, Keene, New Hampshire 03431.

TRAVIS, RALPH, Texas State Champion, 1938–41.

TRENKLE, HERB, Indiana State Champion, 1934, 1936, 1941.

TROLLEN, BEN, Past President, Wisconsin HPA. Elected Vice-president, NHPA, 1961.

TRUMAN, CAROLYN WRIGHT, 1968 Girls World Champion, 48.7%. H. Bryan. Runnerup, 1967 World Tournament; won Indiana Girls State Championship, 5-0; set three world records, 1968 World Tournament: 109 qualifying points, 33 ringers, 12 doubles for 50 shoes (Junior Girls division). Home: Columbia City, Indiana.

TULK, JIM, b. February 9, 1937. Past Vice-President, Colorado HPA. W. Ileen; children—Diane, Laurie, George. Janitor. S. Allen; t. one and a quarter, right handed. Runnerup, Colorado State Tournament, three times; won Laramie, Wyoming Open, 1979, Rawlins Wyoming Open, 1976, 1978, Colorado Springs Open, 1975, Northeast Open, 1964, Class C Valley of the Sun, 1974, Tri-State Open, 1976, 1978, Denver Open, 1958, Ault Highland Open, 1973, 1975, 1976; past president, North Weld Horseshoe Club; high tournament, 69.6%; high game, 86%; finished fourth, Class C, 62%, 1978 World Tournament; won Class B state title, 1952. Home: 248 Ley Drive, P.O. Box 461, LaSalle, Colorado 80645.

TURNER, BRENDA, 1973 Georgia Women's State Champion, 3-0.

TURNER, ELROY, b. May 7, 1936. W. Doris; child—Elroy, Jr. Loader. S. Gordon; t. one and a quarter, right handed. Won AAU title, Columbus City title, Linden Sportsmen tournament, Beattie Park Recreation Tournament; high tournament, 72%; high game, 80% or better; pitched 18 years; member, several championship teams. Home: 408 Morrison, Columbus, Ohio.

TUTTLE, HAROLD, b. February 12, 1904. Senior World Champion, 1964–65, 65%. Single. Head inventory clerk, U.S. Steel. S. Ohio or Allen; t. one and three quarters, right handed. Won Youngstown city championships, 1929–38; runnerup, Intermediate Division, World Tournament, 1968; tied for senior world record, five consecutive four-deads, 1964 World Tournament; won Parkersburg, West Virginia tournament against Al Zadroga, hit seven consecutive four-deads; high tournament, 78.5% high game, 93.5%. Home: 4008 Rush Boulevard, Youngstown, Ohio 44512.

TYSON, ARTHUR, b. August 14, 1939. 1977, 1980 New York State Champion (1977, won two out of three playoff against Carl Steinfeldt; 1980, 11-0-70.2%). W. Regine; children—Arthur, Jr., Arlunga, Antione. Waiter. S. Allen; t. one and three quarters, right handed. Tournament titles: West Rock League, Connecticut Open, 1970; Lewiston, Maine Open, Vermont Open, Massachusetts Open, Rhode Island Open, Carl Von Der Lancken Open, Heritage Club, Joe Zichella Open, 1976 Extravaganza, New Jersey Open, New Haven, AAU, Essex County, Walter Barker Open, Zichella Open, Sharkey Open, Edison County Open, 1970–77; finished eighth, 13-18-69.6%, 1980 World Tournament; played NHPA tournaments, 11 seasons, won 35 Class A titles; served as third vice-president, Connecticut HPA. Home: 363 South Second Avenue, Mt. Vernon, New York 10550.

U

UHLIG, WALLACE W., b. February 2, 1911. 1956, 1957, 1958 Oklahoma State Champion. Divorced; child—Calvin David. Farmer. S. Gordon; t. one and three quarters, right handed. Runnerup, Iowa State Tournament, 1971–72; won Iowa State Farmers Championship, 1969; won Iowa State Seniors Championship, 1974–76, 1978; high tournament, 73%, 1961 St. Joseph, Missouri Open; high game, 91%, Mound City, Mo.; holds state record, with David Baker, seven consecutive four-deads (Mo.); holds Oklahoma state qualifying record, 256 points, 79% ringers. Home: Route 2, Anita, Iowa 50020.

UHLIG, GUY, Nebraska State Champion, 1927–28, 1930.

ULLOM, ARTHUR J., Past Texas State Secretary. W. Barbara; children—Bret, Tracy. Engineering manager, Nucor Corp. S. Allen; t. one and a quarter, right handed. Won Class A Texas Championship, 1974; won Class B runnerup, 1979 Grapeland Open, finished third, Class A, Grapeland, 1977; member, championship team, Colman, S.D., 1970–71, won Madidon Pheasant League; high tournament, 55%. Home: Box 577. Grapeland, Texas 75844.

URBANC, JOHN B., b. December 25, 1922. President Eastern Pennsylvania Chapter. W. Kay; child—Carol. Business machine mechanic. S. Imperial; t. one and a quarter, right handed. Pitched 10 years, eight in NHPA. Home: Route 2, Hemlock Creek, Pennsylvania 18621.

UTLEY, MELVIN H., b. August 12, 1915. Recipient, Hal Libby Trophy for outstanding first year entrant, World Tournament, 1967. W. Margie; children—Melvin Dean, Karen Lea. Retired. S. Allen; t. one and a quarter, left handed. Pitched 35 years, tournament; won LaPorte, Ind. Open, 80%, 1972; set two Illinois state qualifying records: 82%, 261 points, 1968; high game, 84.2% (against Elmer Hohl); finished second, third, Illinois State Tournament; past president, Welles Parl Horseshoe Club, Chicago; qualified for championship division, World Tournament, 1967, posted record: 14-21-70.7%. Home: 571 Huntington Comm. Road, Apt. A-436, Mt. Prospect, Illinois 60056.

V

VALENTINE, ALBERT, 1937 Oklahoma State Champion, 9-0.

VAN DEAR, LINDA, 1977 Wisconsin Girls State Champion, 20%.

VANDEGRIFF, W. C. "BILL," b. December 10, 1916. 1970 Iowa State Champion. W. Ruth; children—Carol, Neil, Gayle. Inspector, quality control, Dexter Company. S. Allen; t. three quarters, right handed. Finished second, seven times, Iowa State Tournament; won Class A titles inc. Monmouth Open, 1975–77, Burlington Corn Belt Open, 1971–72; played in championship division, World Tournament, 1975, 1977–78, best finish, 15th; high tournament, 78.9%; high game, 95.4%; pitched 50 years, 25 in NHPA; regional director; past president, Iowa HPA; graduate, Selma Consolidated Schools, president, school board; chairman, Education Commission, United Methodist Church. Home: 1006 Liberty Drive, Fairfield, Iowa 52556.

VANDERBURG, BILL, Singles Champion, Wellesley Apple Butter and Cheese Festival Tournament, 1979, 62.8%. Class A contender; won several championships. Home: 88 Anaconda Avenue, Scarborough, Ontario, Canada MIL 4M5.

VANDERBURG, GLORIA, 1978 Canadian Women's National Champion, 7-0-66.5%. Won Ontario Provincial Championship, 1977–78; won Scarborough Open, three times, averaging 57.4%; tied for Canadian Women's Championship with Margaret Murray, lost playoff 51-24, 1979. Home: 88 Anaconda Avenue, Scarborough, Ontario, Canada MIL 4M5.

VANDERGRIFF, NEIL, Iowa Boys State Champion, 1959, 7-0, 1962, 9-0, 1963, 11-1.

VAN DEURZEN, LINDA, 1977 Wisconsin Girls State Champion, 20%. Home: 515 Prospect, Combined Locks, Wisconsin 54136.

VAN DINE, ERVINE, Secretary-Treasurer of the Connecticut Horseshoe Pitchers Association from 1959 to 1980. Home: 22 Elliott Street, Apt. 322, Hartford, Conn. 06114.

VAN PELT, EMMETT, West Virginia State Champion, 1931.

VAN SANT, KARL, b. January 23, 1925. Midwest Ringer Roundup winner, 1969, Indiana Indoor State Champion, 1978, member Indiana Hall of Fame. W. Mary Ann; children—Karla, Jennifer. Carpenter. S. Allen; t. one and three quarters, right handed. Shared the longest game in Indiana State tournament play, hitting 147 ringers while losing to Curt Day who hit 150. Averaged 86.2% for an entire tournament, the Vermillion County Open at Cayuga. Hit a 96.2% game in a Bartlesville, Oklahoma tournament. Has been pitching 41 years. Home: P.O. Box 415, Cayuga, Ind 47928.

VECCHITTO, MICHAEL S., b. March 6, 1921. d. June 19, 1977. Member New England Horseshoe Pitchers Hall of Fame, 1975 inducted in promoter category. W. Carmelina; children—Michael, Jeffrey. Postal clerk. S. Allen; t. one and a quarter, left handed. Served as President, Vice-President, Secretary and Treasurer of the Connecticut Horseshoe Pitchers Association. In 1954 organized the Middletown Horseshoe League. Appointed Regional Director of the New England States for 1960 by the N.H.P.A. and became Chairman of Regional Directors, 1961–1963. Pitched numerous exhibitions to promote the game. Designed a postage stamp with a horseshoe pitching motif. Drew the design for the Connecticut H.P.A. patch. Won over 60 trophies including a Massachusetts Open and three Pearson-Sokolowski Memorial, six city championships and six class championships other than A in state tournaments. Hit his high game of

84% in 1941 and in a 1970 Middletown tournament hit 23 consecutive ringers. Home: 25 Howard Avenue, Middletown, Conn 06457

VEESEY, GARY, b. August 8, 1964. Alabama Boys' Champion 1977 and 1978. Student. S. Deadeye or Ohio; t. one and a quarter, right handed. Participated in the 1978 World Tournament at Des Moines, Iowa. Member of NHPA since 1975. Home: 3214 Bayless Drive, SW, Huntsville, Ala 35805.

VEESEY, OSE, b. July 21, 1924. Member of the Alabama Horseshoe Pitchers' Hall of Fame. W. Elaine; children—Gary, Donna, Lynn. Corporate executive. S. Deadeye; t. one and three quarters, right handed. Founded the Huntsville Club. Induced the Huntsville city fathers to build ten courts at Brahan Spring Park, hosting the Alabama State Tournament for three consecutive years. Leader in Huntsville's successful bid for the 1980 World Tournament. Secretary of the Huntsville Club and the Alabama State Association. Home: 3214 Bayless Drive, SW, Huntsville, Ala 35805.

VENTER, ERASMUS ALBERTUS, b. September 26, 1939. First South African Player to qualify for World Tournament. W. Marie; children—Elsa, Stefan, Thomas. Commissioner of Prisons. S. American Professional; t. one and a quarter, right handed. Visited the United States in 1972 to demonstrate Jukskei—a game played in South Africa having much in common with horseshoes. Considered one of the finest players of Jukskei in South Africa. Home: Private Bag 13279, Windhoek, South West Africa 9000.

VERRILL, BOBBY, Maine Girls' State Champion 1972, 1973, 1974, averaging 28.5% in 1973 and 25% in 1974. New England Girls' Champion 1972. Home: Auburn, Maine.

VICE, MAX, b. January 1, 1915. 1970 Washington, D.C. Metro Champion. Won

the 1978 Shasta Seniors Title. W. Audrey. CIA—retired S. Allen; t. one and a quarter, right handed. Secretary-Treasurer of the Sonoma County Horseshoe Club from 1965 to 1969. Has played for 46 years and has been an NHPA member for 20 seasons. His highest tournament average has been 64% and his highest game 90.6%, 29 out of 32. Home: 903 Sequoyah Avenue, Chico, CA 95926.

VIGIE, ANN MARIE, Won the Women's Championship in New Mexico in 1979 by hitting 5-2-32%. Home: 8008 Rio Grande Boulevard Northwest, Albuquerque, New Mexico 87114.

VILES, LLOYD, b. September 2, 1922. Ranks fourth in Texas in ringer percentage. W. Margie; children—Linda, Janet. Rancher-semi-retired.   Former Superintendent of Schools. Formerly with McGraw-Hill Publishing Company. S. Allen; t. one and a quarter, right handed. Posted a high tournament average of 59% and a high game of 74%. Organizer of the Stephenville Horseshoe Club and its current president. Historian for the Arlington Ironbenders Horseshoe Club. Holds an M.H. degree from Colorado State College. Other interests include pottery, woodworking, metalwork, welding and photography. Home: Route 4—Box 211, Stephenville, Texas 76401.

VILES, MARGIE, b. December 18, 1924. Ranks second among women in Texas in ringer percentage. H. Lloyd; children—Linda, Janet. Homemaker, retired elementary school teacher. S. Allen; t. one and a quarter, right handed. Posted a high tournament average of 36.9% and a high game of 53.3%. Historian for the Arlington Ironbenders Horseshoe Club. Began pitching at the age of 55. Other interests include pottery, woodworking, metalwork, welding, photography, raising flowers, and singing in the

First United Methodist Church Choir. Appeared on the NBC-TV program, "Games People Play," during a filming of portions of a two-day tournament in the fall of 1980 which took place at Stephenville courts built by the Viles. Home: Route 4—Box 211, Stephenville, Texas 76401.

VLACHOS, PETER THOMAS, b. April 13, 1925. AA Champion at New Castle in 1977, B titles Beaver County—1968, Fayette County Fall—1976, Fayette County—1976, Uniontown—1976, Dormont—1979, 1977, Eastern National—1977, New Castle—1980, 1978, 1971, Pennsylvania State—1980, 1975, 1970. W. Wanda; children—Colleen, Judy, Peter, Gary. Restaurateur. S. Allen; t. one and a quarter, right handed. Highest game thus far 91.2%, with 31 ringers out of 34 shoes. Won over forty trophies since 1963. Played baseball for the University of New Mexico and the U.S. Navy. Home: 110 Bridge Street, Bridgewater, Penn 15009.

VOGEL, NELSON C. R. "DOC", b. February 9, 1913. d. May 27, 1971. Class A Bureau County Tournament Champion in 1966 and 1968, 1969 Chautauqua Sportsmen Club, Peoria Labor Day Open. W. Margaret; children—Ronald Duane, Roger Nelson, Marilee Ann Isenberg. Farmer. S. Allen; t. one and a quarter, right handed. Pitched for 45 years. In 1954 finished 21st in Class A of the World Tournament and never missed a world tournament through 1970, always playing in Class A or B. Was a Class A contender in tournaments throughout the country, such as the Eastern National, Corn Belt Open, Galesburg National Open, Illinois State. Home: Route 3—Box 359 Manito, Ill 61546.

VOGEL, ROGER N., b. June 18, 1938. 4th Place in the 1973 World Tournament at Eureka, California. 1954 Junior Boys' State Champion of Illinois. 1970 and 1972 Arizona State Champion. 1974 and 1975 Colorado

State Champion. 1978 and 1979 Illinois State Champion. W. Debra; children—Bret, Brock, Nathan, Justin. Senior software analyst for Digital Equipment Corporation. S. Imperial; t. one and a quarter, right handed. Won the 1975 Denver Metro, the 1976 National A.A.U., the 1976 P. D. Riley Spitoon Open, the 1969 Goofy Ridge Sportsmen's Club Open, the 1961 Winston-Salem Open, and many others. Highest tournament average 80.3%. Highest game 96.8%. Holds qualifying percentage record in Arizona with 85%. In championship division of the world tournament has had 170 wins, 140 losses, a 73.8% ringer average and an average qualifying score of 509. Graduated from Illinois State University with major in health and physical education. Head baseball and basketball coach at Rankill High School. Home: 1207 South 18th Street, Pekin, Ill 61554.

VOGEL, RONALD D. b. May 8, 1936. Won Mid-Atlantic Class A championship. W. Janet. Data communication manager. S. Allen; t. one and a quarter, left handed. Secretary Middlesex Horseshoe Pitchers Club. Past President and Secretary of the New Jersey Horseshoe Pitchers Club. Best tournament average is 58.5%. Best game is 73%. Teamed with Dr. Dale Eberhart winning a New Jersey State doubles championship. Home: 8 Orchard Road, Middlesex, NJ 08846.

VON DER LANCKEN, CARL, b. April 22, 1910. 1930–1931 Metro League Champion in Washington, D.C. League. In 1938 won the five borough New York City Championship averaging 72% ringers. Won the 1939 Hudson County Open setting a new Eastern record with nine consecutive four-deads. W. Mary Ellen; children—Carla, Paula. Public Affairs Counsel. S. Imperial; t. one and a quarter, right handed. Listed in Who's Who in American Politics, 1975–1976 (Bowker's) and 1978–1979 (Marquis). Member New York State Hall of

Fame. Member National NHPA Hall of Fame. Editor of the NHPA "How To Do It" Horseshoe Manual. In 1958 won Long Island title at Hempstead Lake State Park. President of New York State Horseshoe Pitchers Association in 1967. President of the Westchester County Club. President of the Tulsa, Oklahoma Club. Third Vice-President of the NHPA in 1941. First State Secretary of the Oklahoma NHPA chapter in 1936. In 1936 gave the first exhibition of horseshoes in England, France, and Spain. Traveled throughout the country to give exhibitions and as roving promoter and trouble-shooter at request of National Secretary R. B. Howard. In 1969 served on NHPA Hall of Fame Committee and as its chairman from 1970–1971. In 1972 received votes for the NHPA Hall of Fame. In 1974 his design of an NHPA lapel pin was accepted by the national executive council. Home: 2100 West Beach Drive, Apt. Y-102, Panama City, Florida 32401.

VOORHIES, MARJORIE, of Asbury Park, New Jersey was first recognized women's champion in 1920.

W

WADE, WILLIAM E. "JOBY", b. April 28, 1917. Class A champion of the city of Fairmont. Played in three world tournaments, 1976, 1979, and 1980. W. Iris; children—Sharon, Barbara, Billy. Alcan Aluminum Employee. S. Allen; t. one and a quarter, right handed. Present president of the Mononghela Valley Horseshoe Pitchers Association. Highest tournament percentage is 56%. Highest game was 94.4% against Jim Johnson in H.H.P.A. sanctioned league play. Has promoted game by building courts in Kiwams Park in Lehigh Acres, Florida, Tice, Florida, Rock Lake, West Virginia, and Consolidated Park, West Virginia. Home: 1713 Lillie Street, Fairmont, West Virginia 26554.

WAGGONER, EARL, b. December 11, 1932. 1979 Class E title in world tournament at Statesville, North Carolina with 5-0-57%. W. Mickey; children—Mike, Debra, Angie. Upholsterer. S. Ohio Pro; t. one and three quarters, right handed. Won Greene County tournament championship eight times in the last ten years, and won many trophies and class championships in open tournament pitching. High game 82%; high tournament, 72.5%. Enjoys coon hunting. Home: 1439 Hoop Road, Xenia, Ohio 45385.

WAGGONER, KENNETH, b. August 26, 1923. Won Greene County championship in 1974, 1976, and 1977. W. Mary; children—Denver, Ronald. U.S. Government employee. S. Ohio; t. one and a quarter, left handed. President of Greene County Horseshoe Club; director of Memorial Day Open at Xenia. High game, 82%, 41 ringers out of 50 shoes; hit nine consecutive doubles in 1980 world tournament; pitched in Class B, 1976 World Tournament. Home: 476 Cottage Grove Ave., Xenia, Ohio 45385.

WAGNER, DOLLY W., 1980 North Carolina Women's State Champion. Children—Teresa, Johnny. Laura Len Corporation and Charlotte Sheraton Center employee. S. Gordon; t. flip, right handed. Winning record, 5-0-31.1%; sister of Doug Walters, a North Carolina Class A contender. Home: Route 1—Box 269, Kannapolis, North Carolina 28081.

WAGNER, FRANK, President, Connecticut Horseshoe Pitchers Association, 1950–80. Served also as assistant secretary, 1935–51; reorganized game with Donald Harrison in Connecticut, 1948; captain of team indoor league, 1936–39, secretary of Tri-County league, 1945–48, state tournament director, 1945–present; helped organize New Canaan Club as tournament director; finished third in state tournament, 1953, won Class B state title in early 1960s; best average: 55%, 1937. Home: 11 Echo Drive, Darien, CT 06820.

WAGONER, LUTHER, 1971 North Carolina State Champion. Best average: 70% ringers. Home: Route 4, Sparta, North Carolina 28675.

WAGONFIELD, KNUTE, b. November 6, 1922. Won 1979 Rose Festival, Richmond, Indiana, 6-1-65.5%. W. Vickie; children—Michael, Dan. Building contractor. S. Allen; t. one and three quarters, left handed. Best average, 65.9%, Kenny Dawes Memorial at Xenia; trustee of local Industrial Horseshoe League, and served as its president and vice-president in past seasons; enjoys baseball. Home: 686 Schwartz Drive, Hamilton, Ohio 45013.

WAHLIN, CLIVE, b. May 24, 1928. Utah State Champion fifteen times. W. Evonne; children—Michael, Peggy, Brian. Technician, Hercules Inc. S. Allen; t. one and a quarter, right handed. Holds about fifty Class A Open tournament titles sanctioned by N. H.P.A.; finished fourth in World Tournament; averaged 80% through a world tournament; has hit 90% in single game; received world Tournament Sportsmanship Award; elected to Utah State Hall of Fame; in championship division, world tournaments, won 156 games, lost 112, averaged 72.8% ringers, and qualified at average of 499 points. Tips: 1. Self-confidence comes first. 2. Relax. 3. Concentrate. 4. Choose comfortable style. 5. Stick to one style. 6. Develop rhythm in your swing. 7. Always pitch the same. Note where you stand and always release shoe the same way. 8. Practice. Home: 4200 South Barker Road, Salt Lake City, Utah 84119.

WAHLIN, ERIC WALTER, d. March 8, 1962. Utah HPA Hall of Fame. W. Mattie Argust (deceased March 4, 1962); child—Clive. Carpenter, Kennecott Copper Corpo-

ration. S. Ohio; t. one and a quarter, right handed. Organizer, first president of Utah chapter of NHPA; formed Magna Club; won many open tournaments, average, 50% ringers; won Class B State Championship many times; coached and played for more than fifty years. Home: Magna, Utah.

WALKER, GLEN, 1973 Washington Boys State Champion, 7-0-64.7%.

WALKER, JACK, Contender for Class A Virginia State Championship, average, 70% ringers. Won doubles championship, was runnerup, and defeated every top Virginia player in tournament competitions. Home: Mineral Springs, Virginia 23117.

WALKER, JOHN MILTON, b. March 17, 1926. California State Champion 1969–71, 1975. W. Hazel; children—Ronald, Laurel, Phyllis, Joyce. Electronics technician. S. Allen; t. one and a quarter, right handed. President of San Diego Horseshoe Club fifteen years; chairman of NHPA Constitution and By-Laws Committee; won Class C World Championship, 1963, 58.9% average; won fifty NHPA CLass A tournament championships, including four California State Championship, average 80% in 1970; high game, 94.4%; highest tournament average, 84.3%; finished fifth in world tournament, 1970, 78.8%, and 1971, Middlesex, New Jersey, finished third, 81.7%; elected to Southern California Horseshoe Pitchers' Association Hall of Fame, 1975; developed arm problems, pitched left handed in 1970s. Tips: 1. Hold shoe comfortably. 2. Keep arm parallel with body to make shoe turn. 3. Open palm and face it upwards on follow through to level shoe. 4. On the swing extend arm straight out and back. 5. Slight pause in back swing just before arm and foot move forward simultaneously. 6. Develop smooth and consistent rhythm. 7. Relax. 8. A beginner should learn fundamentals from book or good pitcher. Home: 570 Parkway, Chula Vista, California 92010.

WALKER, JOHN A., b. February 3, 1913. Tennessee State Champion, 1939, 1943, 1948, 1953. Wife. Beef cattle farmer. S. Allen; t. one and a quarter, right handed. Formed Jefferson City club, 1957, and the East Tennessee League; joined NHPA, 1961; won 160 trophies, twelve other awards; highest tournament, 83%, Jefferson County Championship; high game, 93%; combined with T. R. Little, made fourteen consecutive fourdeads, one short of world record; won 11-0, 78% ringers, in East Tennessee League; president of Jefferson City Club, and served also as secretary and vice-president; tournament director of sectional, East Tennessee League, Jefferson County Fair; record for state titles: 1939: won 6, lost 1, 66.0%; 1943: won 7, lost 0, 69.0%; 1948: won 7, lost 2, 72%; 1953: won 9, lost 0, 74%. Home: Box 323, Jefferson City, Tennessee 37760.

WALKER, RONALD, Virginia Boys State Champion four times. Record: 1971: won 5, lost 0, 50%; 1972: won 3, lost 0, 64.9%; 1973: won 4, lost 0, 60.6%; 1974: won 4, lost 1, 50%; made adjustment to men's forty-foot distance. Home: Mineral Springs, Virginia 23117.

WALL, ED, Missouri State Champion 1926, 1927.

WALLS, ED, Michigan State Champion five times, 1927, 1928, 1930, 1931, 1932. Finished tenth, 1933 World Tournament, Chicago, 13-10-62.1%. Home: Detroit, Michigan.

Walls, J. E., Michigan State Champion, 1927, 1928, 1930, 1931, 1932. Finished thirteenth in 1922 world tournament, 3-12 finals.

WALROD, DONALD W., b. May 14, 1943. Oklahoma State Champion, 1974. W. Janet; children—Donna Lynn, Rose Marie, Denise Ann Lundin. Shop foreman—door

fabricating. S. Imperial; t. one and a quarter, right handed. Served as president, Yukon Horseshoe Club; vice-president, Yukon Club; vice-president, Oklahoma State Association, 1975–76; highest tournament, 58%; high game, 72%; record for state title: 7-0-56.4%. Home: 524 South Third Street, Yukon, Oklahoma 73099.

WALROD, JANET LYNN, b. February 15, 1951. Oklahoma State Champion, 1974–76, 1978–79. H. Donald; children—Denise Ann Lundin, Donna Lynn, Rose Marie. Housewife. S. Imperial; t. one and a quarter, right handed. Won Class D World Championship, 1977, 6-1-52.5%; first husband-wife team to win Oklahoma state championships, 1974. Home: 524 South Third Street, Yukon, Oklahoma 73099.

WALTERS, W. BRUCE, d. January 21, 1981 (age 86). Utah State Champion, 1942, 1947, charter member, Utah Hall of Fame. Pitched in championship division of 1947 world tournament, 9-26-56.6%; was Class A campaigner in Utah; played on Murray City travel team with Arch Stokes, Goff Berger, Garr Lester, Darrell Holfeltz, Bill Adler, Max Pherson.

WALTERS, DOUG, b. June 6, 1945. Won Class A division of Southeastern Classic, 1979, 68%. W. Billie; children—James, Darrell, Mark. Cutter, Laura Len Corporation. S. Ohio; t. one and a quarter, right handed. Won Class B state championship, 1979; won Class B title in 1980 Statesville Dogwood, 72%; finished third in North Carolina state tournament, 1980; high qualifying round, 80%, 40 ringers out of 50 shoes in state tournament; high game in tournament, 79% (against Fred Church in 1979 Statesville Autumn Open); record for 1979 World Tournament: hit 26 consecutive, missed one, hit twelve more consecutive for 39 out of 40; two wins at Snowcamp: 52-49 over Gurney York, 51-33 over Fred Church. Home:

Route 1, Box 267F, Kannapolis, North Carolina 28021.

WALTERS, IRA, Georgia State Champion, 1971. Deceased.

WALWIN GEORGE W., Won men's singles championship of Canada, 1930.

WARD, AL, Officer of New Jersey Horseshoe Pitchers Association. Home: 455 Broad Street, Carlstadt, New Jersey 07072.

WARD, DON, b. June 22, 1939. Tennessee State Champion, 1980. W. Margaret; children—Troy, Mark, Teresa. Vendor. S. Allen; t. one and a quarter, right handed. Won three Bulls Gap Club championships, the 1979 Jefferson City, 1979 Green County Fair; record for state title: 6-1-78.3%; high tournament average, 78.3%; high game, 85%; president, Bulls Gap Horseshoe Club. Home: 1256 Debi Circle, Morristown, Tennessee 37814.

WARD, J. I., First treasurer of National Horseshoe Pitchers Association, 1920. Home: St. Petersburg, Florida.

WARNER, WAYNE, Florida Boys State Champion, 1965. Won five games, no losses, in state championship.

WASH, TONY, Kentucky State Boys Champion, 1972. Record: 7-0-46.7%. Home: Route 3, Frankfort, Kentucky 40601.

WATERS, MELVIN, Past Utah State Secretary of Utah Horseshoe Pitchers Association. Home: 829 East 7525 South, Midvale, Utah 84047.

WATSON, RALPH, Former State Secretary for Vermont Horseshoe Pitchers Association. Home: East Road, Bennington, Vermont 05201.

WATTS, FRANK LEROY, b. February 16, 1945. President, Calhoun County Horseshoe Pitchers Association, and third vice-president, Alabama State Horseshoe Pitchers Association. W. Sue Jones; children—Tina Sue, Thomas Harvey. United States Army. S. Gordon; t. flip, right handed. Heads program at Anniston with future plans for indoor courts; majoring in gerontology. Home: 1111 Johnson Drive, Anniston, Alabama 36201.

WAYMAN, JOHN, First Utah State Champion, 1921. Won same title five consecutive years, lost to George F. Webb, 1926, won it again for last time, 1927. Home: Murray, Utah.

WAYNE, ART, New Hampshire State Champion, 1969. Won 1965 New Hampshire State Championship, 9-0-65.5%; protege of Vic True. Home: 273 Douglas Street, Manchester, New Hampshire 03101.

WEBB, CHARLES HENRY, b. January 19, 1943. Finished third in Illinois state tournament, 1979. Meter reader, Illinois Water Company. S. Allen; t. one and three quarters, right handed. Finished fifth in Class C, 1977, eighth in Class B, 1978, fifteenth in Class B, 1979, twenty-eighth in Class A (8-23-64.5%) in last four World Tournaments; highest tournament, 78%; high game, 83%; hit 25 consecutive ringers in one game. Home: 807 Park Avenue, Cahokia, Illinois 62206.

WEBB, DANIEL R., b. December 23, 1945. Past President, Kentucky Horseshoe Pitchers Association, 1974–75. W. Joyce; children—Tony, Kelley. Truck driver. S. Allen; t. one and a quarter, right handed. Served as state secretary, 1969–73; enjoys bowling, softball; coaches boys Knothole baseball and basketball. Home: 26 Lisa Lane, Alexandria, Kentucky 41001.

WEBB, DANIEL C., b. August 13, 1963. Maryland Boys State Champion, 1978–79. Student, Wicomico Senior High. S. Imperial; t. one and three quarters, right handed. Won 1977 Salisbury Fall Open, 1977 Salisbury

Open, 1978 South Atlantic Open, 1979 Eastern Shore Open, 1978 Elmont, Virginia, Fall Open junior championships; high tournament, 46.5%; high game, 55%; tips to other juniors: 1. Pitch your own style. 2. Beginners pitch a one and three quarters or one and a quarter turn for higher ringer percentages. 3. Don't get discouraged. Home: Route 2, Box 63, Wainwright Avenue, Parsonsburg, Maryland 21849.

WEBB, GEORGE F., Utah State Champion, 1926, 1929.

WEBB, JERRY, Ohio Boys State Champion, 1960, 5-0-50.6%. Home: 105 South Old Mill Road, Union, Ohio 45322.

WEBB, THOMAS, b. November 17, 1932. Won Class A title, Northern California, 1975, 6-2-66.4%. W. Marilyn; child—David. Sawyer in a redwood mill. S. Allen; t. one and a quarter, right handed. Won Class C championship, Northern California, 1973, 7-0-45.7%, again in 1978, 6-2-62.1%; high tournament, 74.9%; high game, 88%; past president, Rio Del-Scotia local club, current vice-president. Home: Box 25—Shively Star, Scotia, California 95565.

WEBER, MIKE, Washington Boys State Champion three times. Hit 67.6%, 1968, 5-0-74.8%, 1969, 6-0-79.1%, 1970 (new state record percentage).

WEDEL, ANN, b. April 10, 1936. 1980 Michigan Women's State Champion. H. Walter; children—Ben, Cindy, Tim, Lori. Housewife. S. Gordon; t. flip, right handed. State tournament record: 5-1-62.6%; won several Michigan weekend tournaments and Michigan Water Wonderland, 1980; second vice-president, Wolverine State Horseshoe Pitchers Association; editor of state's newsletter, "The Ringer Report"; Most Improved Pitcher in Michigan, 1980, 50% in 1979 to 69.1% in 1980; high tournament, 72%; high game, 84%; enjoys bowling, traveling, sewing. Home: 12084 South 44th Street, Fulton, Michigan 49052.

WEEKS, EMILY P., b. July 27, 1921. Past-Secretary-Treasurer, California HPA. 1982 member NHPA Hall of Fame. H. James; children—Jim, Ron, Linda, Sharon; five grandchildren. Housewife. Helped stage multistate and California tournaments, kept records for 25 years; secretary of California Horseshoe Pitchers' Association, 1973; does not pitch. Home: 12133 Graystone Avenue, Norwalk, California 90650.

WEEKS, JIM, b. January 6, 1917. Secretary-Treasurer, Southern California Horseshoe Pitchers' Association. 1982 member NHPA Hall of Fame. W. Emily P.; children—Jim, Ron, Linda, Sharon; five grandchildren. Retired. S. Allen; t. one and three quarters, right handed. Served as president of State Association, 1954; encouraged growth from three a year to fifth-three tournaments in 1979; added classes including Women, Juniors, Handicaps, and does all book work; served on NHPA Land and Buildings Committee, NHPA Hall of Fame Committee, etc.; first pitcher and promoter elected to California Hall of Fame; lifetime ringer average, 70%; won Class A, California State Championship, 1959; placed in top ten, World Tournament, Murray City, Utah, 1959; pitched eighty tournaments, won 48, finished second 21 and third in seven, 1956–65; championship division, world tournament record: won 92, lost 88, 71.9% ringers, 481 qualifying points. Home: 12133 Graystone Avenue, Norwalk, California 90650.

WEIDNER, BILL, 1977, 1979 Alberta Provincial Champion. Won many titles, including 1973 Klondike Days and 1978 Alberta Doubles (title shared with Neil Chrest); zone director, Zone Three, Alberta Horseshoe Players Association. Home: Didsbury.

WEIK, DONALD G., b. April 9, 1926. Connecticut State Champion, 1967, 1969,

1976, 1979. W. Joan; children—Douglas, Guy, Jeffrey. Owner/operator, Donald G. Weik Painting and Decorating. S. Gordon; t. one and three quarters, right handed. Won Keene Open, 1970, 1978, Vermont Open, 1976, Maine Open, Franklin Open, Connecticut Open, 1977, Heritage Club Champion 1976–77, Bobby Clouting Open, 1975–76, Wingdale Open, Tony Osinski Tournament, Turbie Memorial, MacDonnell Memorial, Eastern States Expo Ringerama, Connecticut Warmup, New Haven Fall Classic, etc., high tournament, 78.1%; served as president, Litchfield County Horseshoe Club. Home: Star Route, Lakeside, Connecticut 06758.

WEIS, WILLIAM, 1920 President of the National Horseshoe Pitchers Association. Wrote (with Art Headlough) standard rules for pitching. Home: Akron, Ohio.

WEITZEL, HOWARD, Saskatchewan Provincial Champion. Won men's single championship 1974–77; won doubles championship with Charlie Weitzel, 1973, with Henry Puff, 1974; won mixed doubles with Michelle Douville, 1979.

WELLS, ROBERT L., b. March 19, 1937. Founder of Jackson County Horseshoe Club. W. Trudy; children—Shelley, Alicia. Purchasing manager. S. Reno; t. one and a quarter, right handed. Won thirty-five first-place trophies; won Class A title, Super-Pitch Invitational, Elwood, Ind.; hit twelve consecutive doubles in tournament play; high tournament, 72%; high game, 81%; helped form Johnson County Horseshoe Club, Indiana; served as secretary, president, publicity agent, Jackson County Horseshoe Club, Michigan; served as editor of *Ringer Report* five years; served as president of Wolverine State Horseshoe Pitchers Association; current assistant regional director for Northern Illinois; started mixed doubles league, Lake County. Home: 434 Pintail Lane, Deerfield, Illinois 60015.

WELLS, SHELLEY ANN, b. December 12, 1964. Illinois State Champion, 1980. Daughter of Robert and Trudy Wells. Student, Stevenson High School. S. Allen; t. flip, right handed. Won Michigan State Championship, 1975–77; record for 1980, Illinois: 5-2-34.2%; ranked in top ten girls in U.S.; won Sportsmanship Award, Michigan, 1975; won Most Improved Pitcher, 1976; won Class B World Championship, 1976; high tournament, 43%; high game, 56%. Enjoys volleyball, softball, basketball. Home: 434 Pintail Lane, Deerfield, Illinois 60015.

WELSCH, ED L., b. August 9, 1918. President, Morgan Acres Horseshoe Club, Spokane, since 1971. W. Ruth; children—Joyce, Edith, Glenda. Body shop owner. S. Imperial; t. one and a quarter, right handed. Spokane state and national tournament director; high tournament average, 55%. Enjoys golf, bowling, fishing, woodcraft. Home: North 6821 Smith Street, Spokane, Washington 99207.

WELSCH, RUTH, b. May 22, 1929. 1973 Pacific Northwest Champion. H. Ed; children—Joyce Keen, Edith Sherman, Glenda Echevairia. Secretary. S. Imperial; t. flip, right handed. Helped form Morgan Acres Horseshoe Club; serves as secretary, Spokane Club; served as third vice-president, Washington State Horseshoe Pitchers Association; high tournament, 62.2%, 1980 Lilac City Open; high game, 77.8%, 1979 Northwest. Enjoys fishing, bowling, sewing, cards. Home: North 6821 Smith Street, Spokane, Washington 99207.

WERNER, ED, 1921 Indiana State Champion.

WEST, ROBERT F. "BOB", b. August 19, 1922. Member NHPA Hall of Fame. W. Elinor; children—Mary, Craig. Plywood mill worker and shareholder. S. Allen; t. one and three quarters, right handed. Fifteen times, Oregon State Champion; North Dakota State Champion, 1939–40, 1954; set state record with tournament 84.6%; hit perfect game, 100%, Veronie Oregon tournament; other high games, 97.5%, 97%; serves as state secretary, Oregon State Horseshoe Pitchers Association; played tournaments for forty-four seasons; string of fifty-two consecutive ringers; switched from one and a quarter turn in 1968 to one and three quarters, maintained 80% average with both turns. Won 228, lost 78, averaged 79.2% in world tournament career; finished third twice. Enjoys golf, coin collecting, bowling (inducted in North Dakota Bowling Hall of Fame, c. 1957). Home: 904 Northwest 6th Street, Scappoose, Oregon 97056.

WEST, CARL, 1945 Minnesota State Champion. Antique dealer. t. one and a quarter. Pitches in St. Paul league; record of 8-1-60%, state championship. Home: St. Paul, Minnesota.

WEST, ELLIS, b. October 10, 1913. President, Washington State HPA. W. Dorothy; children—Barry, Roger, Retired freight dispatcher. S. Allen; t. one and a quarter, right handed. Served as president and secretary-treasurer, Seattle City Club; attended University of Washington; high game, 84%. Enjoys golf, cribbage, singing. Home: 3050 N. W. 67th Street, Seattle, Washington 98119.

WEST, STEVE, 1968 Minnesota Boys State Champion. Record: 6-0.

WETHERBEE, DICK, Colorado State Champion, 1966–67, 1970–71, 1977–78. Record: 1966, 13-0-66.3%; 1967, 10-0-67.1%; 1970, 9-0-65.7%; 1971, 7-0-69.5%; 1977, 11-1-59.6%; ringer average, 70%. Home: 695 South Eighth Street, Lot 54, Colorado Springs, Colorado 80905.

WHEELER, GERRY, Won Class D. world championship, 1980. H. Dick; children—

Glenn, Debra, Randy, Rich, David. Merchandiser. S. Gordon; t. flip, right handed. Won Ohio Class B state title 5-0, 1979; won Class C in state tournament, 1980; won Southeast Ohio District Class A, 3-0-53%, 1977; won Class B in state tournament, 7-0-49.6%, 1977; won Class A, Baker-Curley Memorial, 4-0-58.4%; won Northwest Ohio District, 4-0-59%, 1980; serves as secretary-treasurer, Toledo Area Horseshoe Club. Home: 3341 Plainview Drive, Toledo, Ohio 43615.

WHITE, CHRIS, b. June 3, 1967. Won seven Class A titles. Son of Roger and Betty White. Student. S. Deadeye; t. one and a quarter, right handed. Won Class A titles: 1979 July Fourth Preimesberger Open, 7-0-52%; 1979 Northwest Tournament (St. Paul), 5-0-54%; Leyk's 1980 Tri-County Open (Sauk Rapids), 5-1-66%; 1980 Eau Claire Open, 6-1-70%; 1980 Minneapolis Open, 7-0-62%; 1980 Mankato Bend of the River, 6-1-63%; 1980 July Fourth Preimesberger Arena, 10-0-83%; string of ten consecutive four deads, 1980; high game, 90%. Home: 2224 McMenemy Street, Maplewood, Minnesota 55117.

WHITE, CLAUDE E., JR., b. March 8, 1929. Chairman, NHPA Regional Directors. W. Ellen; children—Claude III, Cheryl, Craig. Director of office services. S. Ohio Pro; t. one and a quarter, right handed. Editor and founder, NJSHPA's "Jersey Jargon"; serves as second vice-president, New Jersey State Horseshoe Pitchers Association; served as secretary-treasurer and as executive member-at-large, NJSHPA; won several Class B state titles; high tournament, 60%; high game, 70%; member, NHPA, since 1967; played horseshoes in armed forces. Home: 940 Knollwood Court, Plainfield, New Jersey 07062.

WHITE, HOWARD J., New Hampshire State Champion 1947–59. Shop foreman shipwright, Portsmouth Naval Shipyard. Holds state record for 27 consecutive ringers; state championship average, 60%; won New Hampshire Open, 1956–57; won Jubilee Open, 65%, 1958; averaged 66% for seventeen games, 1956 Eastern National; finished sixth, New England Championships (six tournaments), 1957; chairman, National Regional Directors, 1960–61; served as NHPA regional director for New England, 1956–58, 1962–63, and third vice-president, 1959; ankle injury, 1963; inducted into New England Horseshoe Pitchers Association Hall of Fame, Sutton, Massachusetts, 1974; inducted into New Hampshire Horseshoe Pitchers Hall of Fame, Franklin, New Hampshire; helped organize Portsmouth Horseshoe Club; started pitching, 1937; won first tournament in junior high school; introduced all-white dress with name, city, and state lettered on shirts, scoreboards, ringer percentage charts. Home: 319 Winnicut Road, Greenland, New Hampshire 03840.

WHITE, ROGER O., b. November 12, 1937. Finished fourth, Class C, World Tournament 1980. W. Betty; children—Chris, Dina. Custodian for St. Paul schools. S. Ohio Pro; t. one and a quarter, right handed. Tournament high average, 67%; Eau Claire, Wisconsin, June 1980, six games of 70%, high of 74%; high game, 80%, St. Patrick's Day Open, Preimesberger Arena, March 1979; finished third, Class D, World Tournament 1978; is in top 200 NHPA percentage pitchers. Home: 2224 McMenemy Street, Maplewood, Minnesota 55117.

WHITE, ROLLIE, Served as state secretary, Vermont Horseshoe Pitchers Association. Home: Box 4, Bridgeport, Vermont 05734.

WHITLATCH, George E., b. February 27, 1939. Third Vice-President, Iowa NHPA. W. Linda; child—Heather. Truck driver, Iowa Power and Light. S. Allen; t. one and a quarter, right handed. Past member, Iowa Hawkeye Horseshoe Pitchers Association Hall of Fame committee; played in 1978 world tournament; high tournament average, 62%; high game, 78%, 1975 Southern Iowa Fair; won several local tournaments. Home: 504 7th Avenue Southeast, Altoona, Iowa 50009.

WHITLATCH, HEATHER, b. April 17, 1963. Won 1978 Girls Class B title, world tournament. Daughter of George Whitlatch. Student. S. Allen; t. reverse three quarters, right handed. Runnerup, 1980 Iowa state championship. Home: 504 7th Avenue Southeast, Altoona, Iowa 50009.

WHITMER, DUAINE W., 1978 Florida State Champion. Ringer percentage 59.9%. Home: 1214 West Lake Buckeye Drive, Winter Haven, Florida 33880.

WIEDRICH, BEN, b. December 12, 1925. Vice-President, Oregon City Horseshoe Pitchers Club. W. Irene; children—Duwayne, Geraldine Keller, Lavonne Priester, Eileen, Janet. Cement mason. S. Allen; t. one and a quarter, right handed. Won Lebanon Strawberry Open, 1980, 6-1-75.9%; won Rose Festival, 9-1-74%, Territorial Days, 7-1-73.65%, Greater Portland, 7-1-76.3%, Douglas County-Roseburg, 7-0-69.85%; high tournament average, 73.37%; high game, 88.9%. Home: 18366 South Holly Lane, Oregon City, Oregon 97045.

WIGES, LELAND, Won Iowa Farmers State Championship three times. W. Heather. Coach, science teacher, S. Allen; t. one and a quarter, right handed. Won Iowa Juniors state title three times; won Pacific Championship, Tripler Army Medical Center, Honolulu, Hawaii; reached championship division, World Tournament, 1961, Muncie, Indiana, with record of 12-23-67.5%, finished 24th place; teamed with his father, won state doubles championship, 1976. Home: 410 Fourth Street, Traer, Iowa 50678.

WIGES, EARL, 1957 Iowa State Champion, 14-1. Finished 23rd, championship division, 1961 World Tournament, Muncie, Indiana, 13-22-70%. Home: Route 2, Exira, Iowa 50076.

WILCOX, DONALD W., b. August 22, 1950. 1979 New Mexico State Champion, 8-1-50%. W. Wilma; children—John James and Ann Marie. Electrician—Sound Equipment. S. Allen; t. one and a quarter, right handed. Won Class D Spittoon Open 1976, Most improved pitcher in New Mexico, runnerup in Class A 1977; Won Los Altos Open 1978. Enjoys playing organ and raising rabbits. Home: Star Route 1, Box 182, Estancia, New Mexico. 87016.

WILEY, ENCIL J., b. June 27, 1900. Idaho State Champion thirteen times, 1952–64. W. Edith; children—Hope McFadden, Ralph, Norma Labbe. Union Pacific Railroad employee. S. Allen; t. one and a quarter, right handed. Set state record for highest percentage for single tournament, 1957, with 70%; set state record for single game, 86.6%, 1960; won many Class A tournaments; amputated fingers, stroke, took him out of play. Home: 1020 North Midland, Nampa, Idaho 83651.

WILFON, GAY DONNA, b. September 7, 1939. Nevada State Champion, 1970–71, 1973. H. George. School employee. S. Allen; t. one and a quarter, right handed. Record of championships: 1970, 5-0-21.0%, 1971, 5-0-24.3%, 1973, 4-1-29.0%. Home: Reno, Nevada.

WILFON, GEORGE K., b. June 20, 1924. Past Nevada State Secretary-Treasurer. W. Gay Donna; three children. Toolmaker/postal clerk. S. Detroit Flyer or Deadeyes; t. one and a quarter or one and three quarters, right handed. Played in eight consecutive Nevada state tournaments, finishing second six times, third, and fourth; served as tournament director and as chief judge, 1973 World Tournament; worked with horseshoe program at local Indian colony. Home: Box 7392, Reno, Nevada 89510.

WILHOITE, WALTER, b. December 6, 1918. 1965 Class B World Champion. W. Mildred; children—Betty Jean, Sally (deceased). Lebanon Utilities employee. S. Imperial; t. one and a quarter, right handed. Championship record (Keene, New Hampshire), 62.3%; high tournament average, 70%, 1976 Indiana state tournament; high game (Indiana), 82%; Boone County Champion six times, average above 60%; served as president and vice-president of Indiana Horseshoe Pitchers Association; won Indianapolis Open, 1970, 7-0-66.2%. Home: 120 North Allen Drive, Lebanon, Indiana 46052.

WILKES, LANI, Nevada State Secretary. H. Lee; one child. Elementary school teacher. t. flip, right handed. Home: 5475 Tannerwood Drive, Reno, Nevada 89511.

WILKINSON, JOE, Longest active participation of NHPA. Deceased. Won second place, World Tournament, 1920; won Senior World Championship, 72.6%, 1961, and again in 1962, 61.5%; Home: Clinton, Ohio.

WILKES, LEWIS, 1923 Michigan State Champion, played at Battle Creek.

WILLIAMS, ALLEN WAYNE, b. March 27, 1961. 1978 Texas Boys State Champion. S. Diamond; t. one and a quarter, right handed. Championship record, 8-0-53.5%; high game, 68%; won Matt Bowers Open, 1976, 7-1-40.5%. Home: 2106 Elaine Court, Arlington, Texas 76010.

WILLIAMS, ROBERT D.,, b. May 13, 1934. Finished third in Class A division, Michigan State Tournament, 1966. W. Peggy; children—Bob, Sandy, Randy, Sue, Tom. Repairman for vending company. S. Allen; t. one and a quarter, right handed.

Reached Class A World Tournament, 1967, 4-31-61.1%; high game, 96.9%; NHPA representative, Jackson area; played tournament horseshoes since 1964. Enjoys bowling. Home: 204 Parker Street, Cement City, Michigan 49233.

WILLIAMS, BROWN, 1944 North Dakota State Champion, 1944, won eight of nine games.

WILLIAMS, CAROL GLASS, 1972–73 Kentucky Girls State Champion. H. Steve. Clinical dietitian, University of Kentucky Medical Center. S. Allen; t. flip, right handed. Championship record, 1972, 2-1-27.1%; B.S., 1977, M.S., 1979, University of Kentucky, Home: 106 Fordland Drive, Georgetown, Kentucky 40324.

WILLIAMS, CINDY, b. January 10, 1956. 1973 California Girls State Champion. Student nurse. S. Allen; t. one and a quarter, right handed. Won Girls Class B title, World Tournament, 1970; won Northern California Girls Championship, 1973. Home: 6140 Grant Street, Chino, California 91710.

WILLIAMS, DAVID, 1959 Illinois Boys State Champion, 7-0.

WILLIAMS, ESTHER, 1964 California Women's State Champion. H. Ray; children—Debbi, Barbara, Walter Ray, Jeffrey, Cynthia, Nathan, Jonathan. Housewife. S. Allen; t. one and a quarter, right handed. Finished seventh, Class A division, Eureka, 1973. Home: 6140 Grant Street, Chino, California 91710.

WILLIAMS, JEFFREY ALLEN, b. October 17, 1960. 1973, 1976 Boys World Champion. U.S. Air Force telecommunications operator. S. Allen; t. one and a quarter, left handed. Championship record, 7-0-85.5%, 1973, 8-1-86.2%, 1976; pitched a record high 796 shoes in seven-game tournament, 1975; holds record for highest percentage game for both players (with John Passmore),

1975 tournament; holds world record, junior division, forty-four consecutive ringers; finished sixteenth, 75%, Men's Championship division, 1979; won Class C championship, World Tournament, 1980; won California Boys State Championship, 1974, 80.1%, 1976, 81%; won Northern California title, 1976, 73%. Home: PSC #1—Box 278, Offutt AFB, Nebraska 68113.

WILLIAMS, JOAN, Oregon State Women's Champion, 1965, 13.9%, 1966, 15.1%. Home: 3188 Southwest 27th, Redmond, Oregon 97756.

WILLIAMS, JOHN, JR., b. September 26, 1936. Tournament diector, vice-president of local club. W. Faye; children—Ray Lynn, Roger Lee, Rodney Ray, John Scott. Steelworker, heavy equipment. S. Allen; t. one and a quarter, right handed. Won four first-place trophies, seven second-place trophies in Pennsylvania tournaments; won second place in Apple Festival, Winchester, Virginia; high tournament, 37.5% high game, 50%. Home: Box 37 Ohiopyle, Pennsylvania 15470.

WILLIAMS, JONATHAN, b. August 10, 1965. 1977, 1978 California Boys State Champion. Student. S. Deadeye; t. one and a quarter, right handed. Championship record, 1977, 73%, 1978, 59%; won Boys State Class B Championship, 1974; finished seventh, 5-6, 1980 World Tournament. Home: 6140 Grant Street, Chino, California 91710.

WILLIAMS, NATHAN, b. August 10, 1965. 1980 California Boys State Champion. Student. S. Deadeye; t. one and a quarter, right handed. Championship record, 3-0-65.3%; won California Boys Class B championship, 1972; played in 1980 World Tournament; with twin brother, Jonathan, is youngest of seven pitchers under same roof. Home: 6140 Grant Street, Chino, California 91710.

WILLIAMS, SUE, b. September 4, 1964. 1980 Girls World Champion. Daughter of Bob and Peg Williams. Student. S. Gordon; t. flip, right handed. Championship record, Huntsville, Alabama, 6-1-59.4%, regular round robin, tying with Linda Patenaude; won Michigan Girls state championship, 1979; high tournament, 64.5%, with 19 consecutive ringers; high game, 79%; injured in auto wreck, January 1981. Enjoys swimming, bicycling, softball. Home: 204 Parker Street, Cement City, Michigan 49233.

WILLIAMS, WALTER RAY, SR., b. June 28, 1933. Head of household of nine tournament horseshoe pitchers. W. Esther; children—Deborah, Cynthia, Barbara, Walter, Jr., Jeffrey, Jonathan, Nathan. Salesman. S. Deadeye; t. one and a quarter, right handed. Served as secretary-treasurer, third vice-president, NHPA; serves as secretary-treasurer, Baldwin Park Club; pitched and promoted game since 1959, including organizing clubs in Northern California; worked with Don Titcomb, Los Gatos Club; worked in clubs in Seaside, Hollister, Rio Dell, Eureka, and Auburn. Home: 6140 Grant Street, Chino, California 91710.

WILLIAMS, WALTER RAY, JR., b. October 6, 1959. 1978, 1980 World Champion. College student/horseshoe pitcher. S. Deadeye; t. one and a quarter, right handed. Championship record, Huntsville, Alabama, 85.7%, undefeated thirty-one games; finished second, Western States Indoor Open, 1970, 33.3%; was high qualifier, World Tournament, South Gate, California, 1970, 45 ringers out of 50, 140 points, which earned him nickname "Deadeye" (given by Erma Turner); set world records with 644 shoes, 507 ringers, 78.7%, though lost to Bill Holland, 50-46, 1970; became youngest champion, California State Tournament, 1970, 84.4%; 1971 Western States Indoor Open, 5-0, 85.2% average; became youngest World Champion (age 11), 86.6% average,

set single game record, 96.9%; pitched four perfect sanctioned NHPA games, 1971 state meet against Chris Mohammed and Scott Mohammed, and Northern California Junior Championships against Gary Fontaine and Jeffrey Williams (his brother), 94.3% tournament average; won 1972 World Championship, Greenville, Ohio, 89.2% record average, records of 225 doubles, 40 consecutive ringers, and 87.1% combined game with Alvin Vinsant; injured hand, wore splint in 1973 World Tournament, averaged 78.4%, finished fourth; broke all qualifying records, Keene, New Hampshire, 48 ringers out of 50 shoes (96%), 145 of possible 150 points, 23 doubles out of 25 pitches; won Junior World Championship, 1975, 86.6% (regarded as toughest Junior Division, John Passmore as example, who set world record 89.5%, finished fourth); pitched perfect game against Oregon State Champion Bob West; pitched right handed, 1979 California tournament, Class A, finished second, won Class B left handed; high junior tournament, 94.3%; high, Men's Division, 89.5%, 72 consecutive ringers in three games; won California Men's title 1976, 1977, 1979; won California Boy's title 1970–73, 1975; won Arizona Valley of the Sun, 1977–79; won Northern California, Southern California, and Oregon Open, 1977–79; serves as NHPA statistician; served as president, Auburn and Baldwin Park clubs; served as tournament director, San Bernadino Club; Deadeye pitching shoe named for Williams, sanctioned by NHPA, handled by W. A. Courtwright, 10360 Badgley Drive, St. Louis, Missouri 63126; world tournament record: 1977—finished 8th, won 16, lost 10, 80.6%, 1978-1st, 34, 1, 84.1%, 1979-15th, 16, 15, 73.6%, 1980-1st, 31, 0, 85.7% set state record ringer percentage, 1980 California State, 15-0-87.8%. Home: 6140 Grant Street, Chino, California 91710.

WILLIAMSON, BEVERLEE JOE HOLLIDAY, b. September 10, 1960. 1971 Wyoming Women's State Champion. H. Kenneth; child—J.J. Head bank teller. S. Allen; t. flip, right handed. Won 1973 Wyoming Junior State Championship, 5-1-27.8%; Women's Championship record, 10-0-20.6%. Enjoys softball, bowling, skiing. Home: 930 West Washington, Riverton, Wyoming 82501. (Picture with Herbert Holliday biography.)

WILMORE, EARL, Indiana State Secretary—10 years. Won first NHPA Special Award, 1968, for outstanding local effort.

WILSON, FRANK, 1932, 1933 Colorado State Champion. 20-3-55.6%, 15-0-61.2%, respectively.

WILSON, MARCIA ANN, b. September 25, 1944. Lafayette City-County Championship, 1975-77. H. John; children—Gary, Brenda, Linda. Secretary-bookkeeper. S. Gordon; t. flip, right handed. Won Reynolds Open, 1978; won Flagtown U.S.A., 1978; finished second, Indiana Indoor State tournament, 1976, finished third, 1979; founded first women's league in conjunction with men's Greater Lafayette Horseshoe Club; high tournament, 53.3% (1976 Indoor State); high game, 68.7%. Home: 7286 Rustic Acres Drive, West Lafayette, Indiana 47906.

WILSON, PAUL F., b. April 1, 1938. 1980 Member, New York Hall of Fame. W. Sandra; children—Paul, Pat, Jodi. Boilermaker welder (B.O.C.E.S. Education welding instructor). S. Deadeye; t. one and three quarters, right handed. President, NE-OS-CO Horseshoe Association, 1970–77, 1981–present; served as president, New York State Horseshoe Pitchers Association, 1974–75; won New York State Class B state championship, 1975; finished fifth, championship division, 1980; won several league honors since 1969, including ringer percentage, doubles, singles, team titles. Member, North American Bluebird Society. Home: 7638 Erie Street, Pulaski, New York, 13142.

WILSON, M. W. "WOODY" b. December 9, 1916. Intermediate Class B World Champion, 1978. W. Vira; children—Robert, Ronald, John, Deanne Hughes, James. Retired. S. Ohio Pro; t. one and a quarter, right handed. Finished second, Class B World Tournament, 1980; pitched in championship division, Iowa State tournament, 1979; member, NHPA, fourteen years; pitched fifty-three years; won many Class A tournaments; high tournament, 66.2%; high game, 78.7%; favors elimination of qualifying at major tournaments, shortening games to forty-point cancellation. Home: 1805 West 8th 16A Acorn Acres, Red Oak, Iowa 51566.

WINETROUT, FRANCIS "WINNIE," b. March 26, 1905. Intermediate World Champion 1968–69. W. (married 1974). Gardener (retired). S. Mossman, Ohio, Lee; t. three quarters, one and a quarter. City Champion, 1927, 38%, 1928, 42%, 1929, 45%; finished second, state tournament, 1969; served as State Secretary, 1965–68; helped edit first Washington State Newsletter; was presented first WSHPA life membership, 1967; originated Winter Classic Open Tournament (later re-named Winetrout Winter Open Classic), 1966, and helped direct it every year since its origin; sponsored Washington State Junior Champions to world tournaments; won Intermediate Division Championship, 1968, 72.8%, and 1969; set records in world tournament: (single game, individual) 82.2%, 1968, 76 ringers, 1969, 28 double ringers, 1969, 16 consecutive ringers, 1968; (single game, both players) 74%, 151 total ringers, 56 double ringers, 120 cancelled ringers, 16 "four deads," 6 consecutive "four deads," with Dale Dixon, 1969; served on National Hall of Fame Committee; served as president, Bellingham Horseshoe Club, 1968–70; helped organized Skagit County Horseshoe Club (Mt. Vernon), 1971–72;

named "Mr. Horseshoes 1972," Annual Pacific Northwest Championship Tournament Banquet; elected to Washington State Hall of Fame, 1974. Home: Custer, Washington.

WING, EDWARD, b. April 12, 1909. 1978 Member, Wisconsin Hall of Fame. Grandchildren—Rick Pritzlaff, Brett Pritzlaff. Retired. S. Ohio; t. one and a quarter, right handed. Founder of Goldendale Horseshoe Club, Germantown, Wisconsin; pitched in Milwaukee County League (with shoes once worn by horses), 1934–38; member, Lannon, Wisconsin league, 1967–71; incorporated first Junior Class in the state in Goldendale Open Horseshoe Tournament, 1973; donated horseshoe books to Germantown and Menomonee Falls libraries, distributed "Horseshoe Digest"; served as public relations director, Germantown area club; 60% average; hit 26 consecutive ringers in league game; prefers standard scoring system, either 50-shoe cancellation or 50-shoe count-all. Home: W204 N11912 Goldendale Road, Germantown, Wisconsin 53032.

WINSTON, EARL, b. June 4, 1927. 1955 Missouri State Champion. W. Vicki; children—Keith, Carl. Farmer. S. Ohio or Gordon; t. one and a quarter, one and three quarters, right handed. NHPA third vice-president; served as member of national junior rules committee; serves as voting member, Hall of Fame Committee; won 13th highest qualifier, Murray City, Utah, c. 1950; won many Class A tournaments, including 1950 Des Moines Farmers Fair against John Paxton; high tournament, 82.1%, Springfield, Missouri, 1954; high game, 100%, Gilman City Open, 1978, against Leonard Francis; hit 17 consecutive doubles, seven four-deads; pitched one and a quarter 43 years, switched to one and three quarters, 1980; 1980 World Tournament, 67%, 4-1, Class C-1. Home: Route 2, LaMonte, Missouri 65337.

WINSTON, VICKI CHAPELLE, b. June 10, 1939. Nine-times World Champion. H. Earl; children—Keith, Carl. Housewife. S. Allen; t. one and a quarter, right handed. First woman inducted into National Horseshoe Pitchers Hall of Fame, 1970; won five Missouri State Championships, 1976–80; world titles, 1956, 1958–59, 1961, 1963, 1966–67, 1969, 1973; won Women's Division, 1980 Missouri State Fair; played twenty-eight years in NHPA events; serves as vice-president, Missouri Horseshoe Pitchers Association; served as vice-president, NHPA; pitched in twenty-five World Tournaments; ringer percentages for world titles: 52.2%, 60.9%, 52.8%, 54.9%, 58.6%, 72.5%, 73.6%, 79.6%, 73.5%, respectively; pitched most of career against men. Home: Route 2, LaMonte, Missouri 65337.

WINSTON, WAYNE, b. November 7, 1904. 1967 Intermediate World Champion. W. Leona; children—Earl, Ida Ann, Rosilee, Helen, Clara, Mollie. Farmer. S. Ohio; t. one and three quarters, right handed. Won Class B Missouri State Championship, 63%, 1973; high tournament, 72%, Senior Division, World Tournament, Eureka, California, 1973; finished fifth, Missouri State Tournament, 1923. Home: Route 2, LaMonte, Missouri 65337.

WINTERS, JULE, 1952, 1953 Michigan State Champion.

WINTHER, MARCIA, b. April 9, 1951. Iowa Women's State Champion, 1975, 1976, 1977. H. Walt; children—Clayton, Jason, Walter, Jr. Nurse's aide/cook. S. Allen; t. flip, right handed. Horseshoe Queen, Iowa State Fair, 1968. Home: Bridgewater, Iowa 50837.

WINTHERS, JAMES R., b. April 14, 1945. State tournament director, Chairman of Iowa Hall of Fame Committee, 1979. W. Joann; child—Glenn. Farmer. S. Allen; t. one and a quarter, right handed. Vice-president of local club; judged 1978 World Tournament; served as secretary-treasurer, local club; won Le Mars Open, 1980, 4-1-63.6%; won Fourth of July Open, Primesberger Arena, 1980, 10-1-66% (high tournament); high game: 76%. Home: Route 1, Rolfe, Iowa 50581.

WIPERT, HAROLD, b. March 19, 1927. NHPA member 16 years. W. Virginia; children—Gayla, Kaye, Beverly, Maurice, Dennis, Bruce. Utility systems operator. S. Allen; t. one and a quarter, right handed. High tournament (1974 Ross County Fair), 71.1%; high game (1975 Pike County Summer League), 92%; posted 84% round qualifying for Kingston tournament; won Ross County Fair, 1968, 7-0-64%, 1969, 7-0-64%, 1973, 7-0-69%, 1976, 5-1-63.1%, 1977, 6-1-61%, 1979, 7-0-62%; won Ross County Fall Open, 1976, 5-1-70%; won Greenfield Winter League, 1975–76, 65%; won 1976 Clarksburg Field Day, 7-0-70%. Home: 1064 Camelin Hill Road, Chillicothe, Ohio 45601.

WIPERT, MAURICE, b. October 5, 1954. Won Ross County Championship, 1975, 1976. W. Melanie; child—Christa Maureen. Assistant store manager, F. W. Woolworth. S. Ohio Pro; t. one and three quarters, right handed. Championship record: 1975, 6-2-55.8%, high game, 71.7%; 1976, 4-2-53.2%; high tournament, 64.6%; high game, 76%, 121 points, 50-shoe count-all; best qualifying round, 233 points, 68%, Bainbridge, 1972; longest game, 112 shoes, 1975 Pike County Outdoor League, against Donnie Roberts. Home: 133 North High Street, Apt. 3, Chillicothe, Ohio 45601.

WITTLICH, ROLAND P. "ROLLY," b. June 12, 1920. Class D World Championship, 1977. W. Milla; children—Michael, Barbara, Ann. Banker. S. Allen; t. one and a quarter, right handed. Treasurer, Millstadt Horseshoe Club; finished fourth, Class B World Tournament, 1976; Class A cham-

pionships: 1976, 1977 St. Louis County, 1977 Centralia Labor Day and Hecker Open, 1978 Pinkneyville Threshermen's Pittsfield Pork Day, Millstadt Jaycees, Louisville Yellowstone WAMZ, 1979 St. Augustine Harvest Festival, Jerseyville Open and Mascoutah Homecoming, 1980 Spirit of Vincennes, 61.3%, St. Louis Carondelet, 73%, Red Hill State Park and Oblong Open, 66.7%; high tournament, 73%; high game, 87.7%; won 1937 Illinois High School Horseshoe Tournament. Home: 707 Portland Avenue, Belleville, Illinois 62221.

WOLD, MORRIS, North Dakota State Champion, 1935, 9-3, 1936, 11-0.

WOLF, IRA, 1921 Ohio State Champion.

WOLFE, HAROLD, b. September 6, 1906. 1961 Class C World Champion. Caretaker. S. Allen; t. one and a quarter, right handed. Played in championship division, World Tournament, 1955, 1956, 1957, 1959, 1961 (62.6%), 1962; earned nickname "Giant Killer," 1959 World Tournament, against Floyd Toole, Clive Wahlin, Dean Brown; finished third, Ohio State Tournament, behind Harold Reno, Paul Focht; played fifty-seven years, leg ailments sidelined him, 1976; best finish, World Tournament, 19th; won many Class A tournaments. Home: 5071 Townsley Road, Cedarville, Ohio 45314.

WOLLENBURG, DENISE, b. October 2, 1961. 1977, 1979 Nebraska Women's State Champion. College Student. S. Ohio; t. three quarters, right handed. Record: 1977, 55.9%, 1979, 4-0-47.2%; runnerup, Nebraska Women's State Championship, 1976, 1978. Home: Route 2, Beatrice, Nebraska 68310.

WOLPINK, LORA LEIMBACHER, b. August 27, 1958. 1974, 1975 Indiana Girls State Champion. H. Emie; children—Heather Mae, Jacob Donald. Housewife. S. Gordon; t. flip, right handed. Finished fifth,

1975 World Tournament, Lafayette; joined Westchester Horseshoe League, 1976, posted highest girls qualifying score, 33%; finished second, 1976, first, 1977, second, 1979, Westchester Horseshoe League annual tournaments, Home: 4508 Johnson Road, Michigan City, Indiana 46360.

WOMMACK, W. D., 1951 Missouri State Champion, 6-1-63.3%.

WOOD, IRVING, 1935 Connecticut State Champion, 10-1-49.2%.

WOOD, LUCILLE, New Mexico Women's State Champion, 1974, 5-0-32%, 1975, 5-0-31.2%, 1976. Home: 3730-A Alabama, Los Alamos, New Mexico 87544.

WOODFIELD, HARRY "POP," d. December 6, 1950. Member, NHPA Hall of Fame, 1968. Acrobat/boxer/horseshoe-pitching promoter. NHPA president, 1941–48; edited and published booklet for pitchers; engaged Washington Daily Star, Washington, D.C., to sponsor annual tournament at Monument Park; contacted President Harry Truman, helped install courts at White House, arranged exhibitions featuring Jimmy Risk; (Truman pitched regularly with Admiral Chester Nimitz and others.); presented NHPA membership card to Truman, 1941; served as president, Maryland HPA, Washington, D.C.

WOODMAN, LORRAINE, b. August 4, 1934. Third Vice-President, Washington State Horseshoe Pitchers Association, 1974. H. Daniel; children—Debbie, Daniel, Muffie. Housewife. S. Gordon; t. flip, right handed. Served as secretary, Morgan Acres Horseshoe Club, three years; won Pacific Northwest Women's Championship, 1974, 57.4%. Home: 6415 North Market, Spokane, Washington 99207.

WOODMAN, MUFFIE, b. July 28, 1958. 1974 Washington Girl's State Champion, 5-0-40.9%. Waitress. S. Lee and Gordon; t. flip, right handed. Pitched tournament and league horseshoes for ten years; enjoys sailing, dancing. Home: 6415 North Market, Spokane, Washington 99207.

WOODMAN, SAM. b. June 3, 1957. 1973 Washington Boys State Champion, 7-1-51.6%. W. Sabrina DeMent; children—Samantha, Amanda. Metalworker, Kaiser Aluminum. S. Gordon; t. one and a quarter, right handed. Won Southwest Boys title, 1972; high game as junior, 82%; hit thirteen consecutive doubles against Paul Lishka to win state title; pitched tournament horseshoes for ten years; pitched flip turn as junior, changed to men's forty-foot distance and one and a quarter turn. Enjoys hunting, stock cars. Home: 1312 East Decatur, Spokane, Washington 99207.

WOODS, WILLIAM J., Worked with Sam Goodlander (Secretary, Ohio Buckeye Association) on tournament promotion, 20 years. Nickname, "Woodsie," "Tibby"; does not pitch; photo appears with Goodlander's biography. Home: 2475 Madison Road, Cincinnati, Ohio 45200.

WOODSON, JAMES JOSEPH, b. January 23, 1925. 1968 Texas State Champion. W. Marcella; two children. Accountant. S. Deadeye or Allen; t. one and a quarter, right handed. High tournament, 61%; won many Texas-based tournaments; founder of Independent Horseshoe Pitchers of Texas Association (corporation to promote, improve organized horseshoes, and provide good, privately-owned facilities); won Arch Stokes Award, 1976; contributed articles to *Horseshoe Pitchers' News Digest*; served as regional director, NHPA, three years, as secretary-treasurer, Texas Association, five years, as president or secretary-treasurer, San Antonia Lakeside Club, five years. Home: 235 Rainbow Drive, San Antonio, Texas 78209.

WOODWARD, LLOYD, 1929 Kansas

State Champion, 10-1-60%. Was finalist in 1933 World Tournament, finished fourteenth, 10-13-58.5%. Home: Columbus.

WOOLINGTON, GLEN, 1977 Wyoming State Boys Champion.

WORS, GENE, 1936 Missouri State Champion, 14-1-61.4%.

WORS, JOE, 1941 Missouri State Champion, 14-1-70.9%.

WORSECK, BERNARD, 1977 Member—Minnesota Hall of Fame. Elected for his promotion of horseshoe pitching.

WRIGHT, JOHN, 1979 North Dakota Boys State Champion, 6-1-27.6%.

WROTENBERY, DEBBIE WOODMAN, b. November 23, 1956. Finished ninth, Women's Division, World Tournament, 1973. H. Charles; children—Charlie, Tracy. Waitress. S. Gordon; t. flip, right handed. Enjoys dancing, playing guitar, singing. Home: Mead, Washington 99021.

Y

YAMADA, GENE, 1974 Colorado Boys State Champion. Home: Box 442, Ault, Colorado 80610.

YANNETTI, VINCENT J., SR., b. November 10, 1922. New Jersey HPA Hall of Fame, 1979. W. Irene; children—Vincent, Jr., Mark, Robert, Maryann. Production superintendent. S. Allen; t. one and a quarter, right handed. Class B New Jersey State Champion, 1967, 1973; New Jersey Doubles Champion, with Bob Bishe, 1968, 1969; New Jersey A.A.U. State Champion, 1969, 1973; New Jersey Doubles State Champion, with Bill Kolb, 1970, 1972; Class A Eastern Shore Open Champion, Salisbury, Maryland, 1976; Class A Middlesex Club Spring Tournament Champion, 1976; New Jersey State tournament director, 1969, 1970–71;

1980; president, N.J. HPA, 1974, statistician, 1968–80; first vice-president, Middlesex HPA, 1967–68, second vice-president, 1969–71; received NHPA Achievement Award, 1975. Home: 322 Longwood Avenue, Bound Brook, New Jersey 08805.

YARBOROUGH, CALE, Champion stock car driver enjoys horseshoes. S. any brand; t. flip, right handed. Home: Sardis, South Carolina.

YAUS, RUSSELL, 1948 Ohio State Champion. Two state tournaments held (controversy over count-all or cancellation scoring system), the other won by Ralph Lackey. Qualified with 480 points, finished 32nd in 32-man class, championship division of World Tournament, 1948, 7-24-64.1%. Home: Can, Ohio.

YERNBERG, JOHN, 1958 Minnesota State Champion, 9-2-53%. t. one and a quarter. Home: Duluth in summer, Florida in winter.

YOCKSTICK, MEL L. b. November 9, 1942. Wrote computer program to record all tournaments of Colorado and Wyoming, ranking players by percentage, 1976. W. Bonnie; child—Scott L. Computer management information analyst. S. Ohio Pro; t. one and a quarter, right handed. Held offices in Denver Metro Horseshoe Club: treasurer, 1976–77, vice president, 1978, publicity director, 1979–81; Most Improved Player, 1975 (his team won league championship); won Class F, Denver Speakeasy Open, 1976; won Class D, Pike's Peak Open, Colorado Springs, 1977; played in Class E, World Tournament, Des Moines, Iowa, 1978, high game, 49%, tournament average, 37%. Home: 6625 Pierce Street, Arvada, Colorado 80003.

YOKUM, WILLIAM P., Won 94 games, lost 59, averaged 50.6%, championship division, World Tournament, in the 1920s. Home: Zanesville, Ohio.

YORK, GURNEY, b. May 19, 1929. North Carolina State Champion, 1968, 1970, 1973, 1976. W; three children. Sawmiller. S. All brands; t. one and a quarter or one and three quarters, right handed. 1966 National A.A.U. champion; North Carolina Singles titles, 1968–70; North Carolina A.A.U. Doubles title, with Scotten), 1966–68, 1970, 1973, 1977; Class A titles, 1972 Bethleham, 1976 North Carolina Parks & Recreation, 1971 U.S. Presidents' Open, 1972 Winston-Salem Warmup, 1972–74, Statesville July 4th, 1976 Alexander County Recreation Commission Bicentennial, 1972 Statesville Invitational; served as president, North Carolina HPA, 1979. Home: Route 2, Box 73, Harmony, North Carolina 28634.

YOUNG, CARL R., b. July 4, 1939. Class C World Champion, Keene, New Hampshire, 1974. W. Patricia Ann; children— Mark Allan, Ken Evan. President, Alec Roofing, Inc. S. Ohio Pro; t. one and three quarters, right handed. Averaged 74%, Ohio State Tournament, 1973; high game, 94%, 1975; served as president, New Rome Club; designed and built scoreboards; uses right foot lead; played tournament and league horseshoes 16 years. Home: 640 East Markison Avenue, Columbus, Ohio 43207.

YOUNG, JOY, 1979 Illinois Women's State Champion, 7-0-36.6%.

YOUNG, NELL, Played in ten World Tournaments, 35-48-23.9%. Home: Minneapolis, Minnesota.

Z

ZADROGA, AL, b. November 4, 1915. 1981 member NHPA Hall of Fame. Pennsylvania State Champion, 1962, 1965, 1969, 1972, 1975, 1976, 1980. W. Emma; child— Albert, Jr. River towing. S. Allen; t. one and

a quarter, left handed. Tied in second place, World Tournament, Des Moines, Iowa, 1978; finished third, World Tournament, 1972, 1976, 1977; elected to Pennsylvania Hall of Fame, 1978; won Elizabeth section, Pittsburg Press Tournament, 1931 (age 15); hit highest tournament in Pennsylvania history, 89% for seven games at Spring Fling, New Castle, Pennsylvania, 1976; hit 95% high game, 1976 World Tournament; top qualifier, 1975, 1978 World Tournaments; won four Allegheny County titles: 1963 Perry Sesquicentennial, 1964 Cannonsburg Jaycee, 1964 Northwest Open, 1965 Greenville Ringer Classic, 1965 Northwest Open, 1966 Hill City Open, 1966 Jefferson, 1967 Northwest Open, 1967 Eastern National, 1968 North Hills Open, 1969 Erie Spring Warmup, 1971 VanPort Spring Warmup, 1972 Fall Ringer Roundup, 1972 New Castle Spring Fling, 1973 New Castle Open, 1973 Moundsville Open, 1974 New Castle Spring Fling, 1977 Moundsville Open, 1974 Mingo Junction, 1974 Steelmark, 1975 Kinzua Classic, 1975 Winston-Salem Southeastern Classic, 1975 Elmont Open, 1976 Uniontown, 1976 New Castle Spring Fling, 1977 Moundsville Open, 1977 Shenandoah Apple Blossom Festival, 1977 Elmont Spring Warmup, 1977 Don Virrico, 1977 New Castle Spring Fling, 1977 Kinzua Classic; 54-year career in horseshoes. Home: Route 3, Box 484, Mononghela, Pennsylvania 15063.

ZEIMER, EUGENIA, 1920 Minnesota Women's State Champion. Home: Minneapolis, Minnesota.

ZELLER, RUBEN, Served as state secretary, North Dakota Horseshoe Pitchers Association. Home: Carson, North Dakota 58529.

ZELMAR, VERDAN, b. December 12, 1924. Writes stories for Northern California Horseshoe Pitchers Association, *Horseshoe Pitchers News Digest.* W. Twila; children—

Greg, Michelle, Colleen, Russell, Brian. Publications supervisor. S. Allen; t. one and a quarter, right handed. Served as first vice-president, and 1971–73, as secretary-treasurer, Northern California HPA; introduced 50-shoe competition into Northern California schedule; high game, 80%; high tournament, 69.6%; received 1972 NHPA award for outstanding contributions of increasing membership and tournaments per year. Home: 201 West California Avenue—#1307, Sunnyvale, California 94086.

ZICHELLA, JOSEPH D., b. August 7, 1911. Finished eighth, 1957 World Tournament, 76.7%. Child—Marie. Retired. S. Allen; t. one and a quarter, right handed. Won New York City Employees Tournament and Mayor O'Dwyer trophies, 1947–49; won Mirror and Parks Department Meet, 1950, 1952; won Hartford, Connecticut Open, 1953, Eastern Pennsylvania Open, 1954, Rheingold Invitational, 1955, Pennsylvania Open, 1955, Massachusetts Open, 1955, Connecticut Open, 1963, Atlantic Coast Invitational, 1968. Home: 2883 Randall Avenue, Bronx, New York 10465.

ZIMMERMAN, GUY, b. July 11, 1907. d. March 1, 1960. 1954 World Champion. W. Lenona; children—Eugene, Bob, Joyce, Rosalie. Inducted into National HPA Hall of Fame, 1967; one of "Big Four" (with Fernando Isais, Ted Allen, Casey Jones); world record: 20-0-84.2%; tied Ted Allen for world championship, averaged 86.1%, lost play-off, 1940; finished third, World Tournament, 28-3-86%, 1948 (authored first perfect game in world tournament history against Henry Pergal, 1931 Indiana State Champion, with 44 of 44); won Iowa State Championship, 1934, 1936–37, 1939–40; won California State Championship, 1942–50; averaged 86.7%, 1949, a state record until broken in 1980 by Walter Ray Williams, Jr.; averaged 84.2%, 1950; lost game 50-48 to Ted Allen, World Tournament, 1940, but set world records: 145 ringers, 64 doubles, 88.4%, 50 four-deads in game, Zimmerman opened with eighteen consecutive doubles; son Eugene killed in Korea; daughter Rosalie murdered; complete world tournament record: 1934, 6th, 17-6-67.4%, 1935, 3rd, 18-5-73.3%, 1940, 2nd, 29-2-86.1%, 1947, 6th, 28-3-86%, 1954, 1st, 20-0-84.2%. Home: Iowa and California.

ZINGER, BILLY, 1972 Boys Canadian National Champion, 38%. First recognized boy's champion.

ZOZZARO, PHILLIP, b. August 7, 1922. President, New Jersey HPA, 1969–71, 1977–80. W. Rita. Self-employed paper recycler, S. Reno; t. one and a quarter, right handed. Inducted into New Jersey Hall of Fame, 1974; president, Clifton Inter-City HPA, ten years; member of NHPA Publicity Committee; played in World Tournament five times, twice in Class E, three times in Class D; titles include New Jersey State A.A.U., 1974, New Jersey State Doubles Championship, 1977, A.A.U. Masters, 1978, Middlesex Open, 1978, A.A.U. Championship, 1976. Home: 176 Main Street, Little Falls, New Jersey 07424.

ZUMARAN, PETER S., b. August 21, 1912. Class B State Champion, Oregon, 60.9%, 1980. W. Adeline; child—Yvonne. Retired chiropractor, logger. S. Allen; t. one and a quarter, left handed. High game, 1980, 70.8%, against Ron Miller, with 20 of 22; high tournament, 63.5%, Oregon City Territorial Days Tournament, eight consecutive doubles; won Class B titles at Hermiston, 55.8%, Laurel Hurst Rose Festival, 57.3%; biggest single game win against 1963 World Champion John Monasmith, 1980 Southwest Washington Open; hit 80% game against Ted Miller, Hillsboro Open. Home: 6404 Southeast Schiller, Portland, Oregon 97206.

ZUNIGA, NOLAN, 1975 Nevada State Champion (Boys). Home: 50 Colony Circle, Reno, Nevada 89502.